MOZART AND THE PIANIST

Michael Davidson

MOZART

AND THE PIANIST

A Guide for Performers and Teachers

to Mozart's Major Works for

Solo Piano

Kahn & Averill
London

This second edition first published in 2001 by
Kahn & Averill
9 Harrington Road, London SW7 3ES

First edition published in 1998 by
Go-Bos Press, Leidendorp, The Netherlands

British Library Cataloguing in Publication Data
A catalogue record for this book is available from the British Library

ISBN 1 871082 76 5

Printed in Great Britain by
Halstan & Co Ltd, Amersham, Bucks

Contents

vi

SOME REFLECTIONS AND WORDS OF GRATITUDE

Since I was nine years old, Mozart's music has been a major presence in my life. It has been a joy for me to focus some thoughts on these masterworks, so marvelous, yet, at times, so elusive. I have no illusions that this book will be a "last word" on Mozart interpretation; musical knowledge and opinions never ossify, but evolve, endlessly. Each page has been rewritten innumerable times, and many viewpoints were transformed during the period of writing.

Combining work on this book with public appearances and teaching has not always been easy. But the hours I spent puzzling over the ornaments in the *Adagio* variation of K.284 in the Andalucian heat, or wrestling with tempo choices in K.457 while sailing down the magnificent British Columbian coast, have become fond memories.

Throughout the last eight years many friends and colleagues have contributed to *Mozart and the Pianist* by offering advice and encouragement, or simply by being in my life. I remain extremely grateful to:

Naomi Barlow (Viterbo), Zelma Bodzin (New York City), Wendy Campbell Voullaire (London), Anne Charlotte van Cleef (Blonay), Susan Chinnery (Vancouver), Laura Dobbinga and Michiel Jansen Schoonhoven (St. Robert), Edith Fischer and Jorge Pepi (Tarragona), Bram and Hannie Geerlings (Utrecht), Kenneth Gilbert (Paris), Vana Greissenegger Georgila (Vienna), Inder Hoon (London), Joel Kasow (Lyon), Dores Lignac (De Bilt), Michael and Elaine Massey (Edmonton), Lisa Reese (Redding), Christophe de Voogd (Paris), and in Amsterdam: Lucienne Bouwman, Jacqueline Burgers, Liana Şerbescu, and David Stein.

It has been delightful to work with Jan Willem Bos and Cornelia Golna (assisted by our faithful messenger, Laura) during the editing and other preparations for publication. Jacco Lamfers (The Hague), a fine pianist and musical thinker, helped greatly in the initial editing of the texts. Deirdre O'Donohue (New York City), the well-known pedagogue, gave me support when support was most needed.

Some musicians are "allergic" to books concerning interpretation, for they believe that such an issue cannot be expressed "in mere words." But is one to learn only from imitating recordings, themselves often of dubious value, or from teachers who may also have considerable problems with this music?

So many talented pianists over the entire world yearn to be able to play Mozart's music with more naturalness. During the last years, I have been continually reassured by colleagues that this book will help pianists embark on that voyage to Mozartian delight and depth. Could this book perhaps enhance their playing of other composers too? Working on it has certainly done that for me. I hope that *Mozart and the Pianist* will have a similar effect on those who delve into it.

Michael Davidson,
Amsterdam, November 30, 1997

SOME THOUGHTS ON THE APPEARANCE OF THE SECOND, REVISED EDITION

Some responses to the first edition of *Mozart and the Pianist* have been quite extraordinary. I received touching letters from pianists I had never met. The book has reached thirty countries. After some of my Mozart lectures, people were battling for copies. How Mozart would have enjoyed such scenes!

It is evident that *Mozart and the Pianist* has a future. In this second edition, the text has remained largely unchanged, but there are improvements. Some tempo suggestions and interpretations of ornaments have been modified. There are more references to recent publications. An index has been added.

I would like to express my deep gratitude to Jan Willem Bos and Cornelia Golna (Leiderdorp) for their help in preparing the revised text. I would also like to thank my dear colleagues Carola Grindea (London), Frans van Hoek (Nieuwpoort), and Jeroen Liedorp (Rotterdam) for their support and friendship.

Michael Davidson,
Amsterdam, September 30, 2000

INTRODUCTION

THE NEED FOR THIS GUIDE

How well a pianist recalls the first Mozart sonata he has played, moments that seemed like the beginning of a journey through a magical landscape. But later the player often feels lost in that landscape, which has become misty, foreign, even perilous. Since the composer's death, a flourishing market in dubious concepts regarding Mozart interpretation has created a gulf between these masterpieces and the performer, a gulf that shows few signs of disappearing.

Although Mozart's creations may delight millions, these compositions do not "play themselves." Their perfection places a heavy responsibility on the player. Pianists and their teachers need help in comprehending a musical style which is not only becoming increasingly remote from the spirit of our time, but which has also become clouded by two centuries of misinformation and contradictory performance practices.

The attitude that analysis of interpretation kills spontaneity in performance is not valid. The most subjective aspects of musical experience are enhanced, not diminished, by intensive study and informed dialogue. Musicians have always realized this; in the same year that Mozart completed his C minor Piano Sonata, Christian Friedrich Daniel Schubart wrote:

"What man does not understand cannot touch the heart." [1]

Misconceptions can be dispelled and some quandaries resolved, but Mozart's music requires a detailed approach. This guide takes the reader through all of Mozart's major piano works, with specific suggestions regarding textual interpretation, dynamics, articulation, tempo, rhythm, formal surprises, pedaling, emotion and association. The thorny terrain of ornamentation is thoroughly explored, each ornament being discussed when it first appears in a composition. Some possibilities for improvised ornamentation are also mentioned. Because several fine biographies of Mozart are currently available, historical references have been kept to a minimum.

There are excellent publications in English on the interpretation of the piano works of J.S. Bach, J. Haydn, Beethoven, Chopin and Debussy, among others but, to date, no such work has been available for Mozart's major solo piano compositions. Books dealing with general aspects of this repertoire have been written by Eva and Paul Badura Skoda,[2] Sandra P. Rosenblum,[3] Frederick Neumann,[4] and Siegbert Rampe.[5] Those praiseworthy studies present various facets of Mozart interpretation, illustrated by examples. Unfortunately such an approach cannot address most of the enigmas that confront pianists, professional or amateur. Carl Schachter has also observed that the challenge is not new:

> "The great teaching manuals of the middle and late 18th century ... enunciate general principles ... not always applicable to specific situations ... indeed, no set of precepts, no matter how cleverly conceived, can be adequate to the complexities of musical experience ...The only way to approach these complexities is thorough study of the individual piece..." [6]

The confusion and uncertainty regarding the interpretation of Mozart's piano works remain universal. How amazed Mozart would be to see the agonies suffered by students of his compositions! As recently as 1994, Robert D. Levin warned:

> "At a time when music education is increasingly sketchy, performers are confronted with many decisions – choices of edition, of instruments (historic vs. modern), proper execution of ornaments, use of embellishment or improvisation – for which they are scarcely prepared." [7]

But it is not only professional music students who become noticeably insecure when expected to perform Mozart. Even world famous artists frequently do not dare to include Mozart in their programs.

The inhibitions felt by most players when playing Mozart's piano works can be cured, but the treatment requires patience. Musicians, especially young students, often want quick solutions to complex issues. The reader of this guide will sometimes be confronted with options, not dogmas. For, as Frederick Neumann aptly concluded, mere observation of "correct" stylistic practices will not guarantee a truly communicative performance:

> "Expression and taste are the truly strategic issues of performance; they will not yield their secrets to any rules. Only enlightened insight can be our guide and in the end we have to rely on our own musical sensitivity and intelligence in trying to grasp the spirit of a work prior to communicating it." [8]

In the interpretation of great music, definitive solutions are rare, but clear alternatives are usually evident. Never before has so much of Mozart's music been performed and recorded. Never have there been such diversified biographies of the composer or so many fine editions of Mozart's works. In recent years, the recordings and teaching of fortepianists have contributed much to our comprehension of Mozart's language. However, the attitude that Mozart should be played exclusively on "historic" instruments, or copies thereof, is voiced only by a few. A player's competence and imagination are surely more important than the type of instrument he has chosen. This guide has been written primarily for the pianist playing "modern" instruments, but most of the views expressed are equally applicable to performances on "historic" instruments. There are occasional references to the advantages of using either type of instrument in a particular piece.

For virtually all sections of this book, it is imperative that the reader can follow the text with a copy of the music being discussed. That no musical illustrations have been included, may initially seem a hindrance, but none of the musicians who read this book prior to publication were troubled by their absence. All the *Urtext* editions of Mozart's piano compositions have the measures numbered. This facilitates quick reference to any specific moment in the score. The reader must be aware that older editions of Mozart contain innumerable textual deformations. It is absolutely imperative that a fairly recent *Urtext* edition[9] be used.

Mozart's scores leave most of the interpretative details to the imagination rather than to the eye. Artur Schnabel described this contradiction with his customary wit:

"Children are given Mozart because of the small quantity of notes; grown-ups avoid Mozart because of the great quality of the notes..."[10]

Hopefully this guide will help the player to read better "between the lines" of a Mozart score, and enable him to shape this music with more confidence and freedom. Such insights are rare if an interpretation is based on listening to recordings or using heavily annotated editions. A truly curious musician will learn more from making his own discoveries than copying, robot-like, the attitudes and errors of others.

Virtually everyone who plays the piano owns a copy of the Mozart piano sonatas, which form the focus of this study. All of the sonatas are examined in considerable detail, as are the three Rondos, four of the best known variation sets, and the most significant of the "assorted pieces" (Fantasies, B minor Adagio, etc.). Conspicuously absent are the *Viennese Sonatinas*, awkward transcriptions from Mozart's Divertimenti, which were not made by the composer. Such anachronisms harken back to the nineteenth century, when more arrangements of Mozart's music were in circulation than copies of the original compositions. Also absent is the inauthentic Piano Sonata in F, K.547-a, still found in some older editions.

Three unfinished works have been included because of their unique qualities: the D minor Fantasy, K.397, the G minor Allegro, K.590-a, and the D major Minuet, K.594-a. But then is not everything Mozart wrote unique? Robert Craft perceptively observed:

"The paradox of Mozart is that music history would not be greatly different if he had never existed – though obviously music itself would be immeasurably poorer and classicism more difficult to define ... But if the line of succession leads around, rather than through, Mozart the reason is that his kind of perfection could be neither improved upon nor repeated." [11]

I

USING THIS GUIDE

Hopefully all readers will take the time to read Chapters I and II, which set out much essential information and important theories. Chapters IV-XIX have the same structure and are subdivided under the following headings:

OTHER KÖCHEL LISTINGS
When a piece is known only by its listing in Ludwig von Köchel's 1862 catalogue of Mozart's works (Köchel Verzeichnis, abbreviated in many languages as "K.V.", but in English as "K."), this heading is omitted. Some alternative catalogue listings appeared in Alfred Einstein's 1937 edition of the Köchel Catalogue. Einstein surmised alternative composition dates for many works and gave them new catalogue numberings. Though Einstein's listings are sometimes more accurate than Köchel's, recent analyses of Mozart's manuscripts have made it obvious that yet another listing of Mozart's works would be welcome.

With, for example, four sonatas in C major and three in F, some catalogue identification is necessary. In this book, the original K. numberings, known throughout the world, are used. Einstein's alternative K. entries are given only under the OTHER K. LISTINGS and SUGGESTED LISTENING headings.

COMPOSITION DATE
In 1784, Mozart began his own thematic catalogue, in which he noted the incipit (opening measures) and exact completion date of virtually all compositions from 1784 until his death. Recent research has concluded that the dates of some of Mozart's other major piano works differ considerably from those given in the Köchel Catalogue. For example, the sonatas K.330-333, as well as the variations K.253 and 265, are now presumed to derive from a considerably later period than the composer's Parisian stay in 1778. Arguably such information is not essential to Mozart interpretation, but surely it is useful to have some idea of the chronology of Mozart's piano works within his total oeuvre.

TOTAL DURATION

This factor is determined not only by the tempi chosen, but by how many repetitions are observed. Before the 1970's it was unusual to hear the exposition of a movement in sonata form repeated. In the 1990's sometimes both the expositional and second (development and recapitulation sections) repeats are observed. "To repeat or not to repeat?" is a quandary susceptible to taste and fashion.

Artur Schnabel maintained:

> "The shorter the space between repeat signs the more important the repeat ... In longer sections, however, the repeat is essential only if it is unusual. The first repeat in an opening or closing movement of classical sonatas can often be omitted..." [1]

In the program notes accompanying his splendid recording of the Mozart sonatas, one reads that Malcolm Bilson:

> "takes the repeats of the parts of movements (in most cases of the second half of pieces in sonata form) depending always on the singularities of the movement in question, the naturalness of the embellishments and variations in the repetition, and the balance of the work as a whole." [2]

However, the concept that a player should alter the music when repeating a section is viewed with suspicion by F. Neumann:

> "There remains the problem of literally repeated statements, the alleged site of desirable, if not required, ornamental additions. Before we form the idea that literal repetition is aesthetically objectionable it behooves us to remember that repetition is the most important element of formal design in music." [3]

To complicate the issue further, both J. Haydn and Mozart omitted the second repeat signs in the first movements of their last piano sonatas, Hob.XVI:52 and K.576 respectively. Had both composers concluded that it was becoming unnecessary to demarcate the development and recapitulation sections with repetition signs?

I believe that in sonata form, virtually all expositional repeats are relevant, but that repetition of second sections depends on the composition. This highly subjective matter will be discussed in each INTERPRETATION section.

FORM

Straightforward as this aspect may seem, there are some pieces in which, for example, sonata and rondo elements are so entwined that a one-word definition of the form is insufficient. Such issues are briefly addressed in the subsequent INTERPRETATION sections. Certain motivic relationships and other unusual formal elements will also be discussed in the INTERPRETATION sections, as the blend of logic and surprise in Mozart's music never ceases to astonish us and certainly cannot always be confined to a single noun.

APPROXIMATE TEMPO

Here the adjective is important, as a metronome indication of tempo (for example, $\quarternote$ = 80) can seem dangerously absolute. It is rarely possible to assign a single tempo to any piece of music which suits all its themes, let alone performance situations. Brahms abhorred notating metronomic indications and, during this century, Stravinsky and Bartók frequently contradicted their own highly specific metronome indications in performance.

Entire books[4] and numerous articles have been devoted to tempo choice in Mozart's works. Other elements, in addition to analysis of the work's rhythmic ingredients, play essential roles in the choice of tempo: the instrument (a fortepiano may permit a quicker pace than the heavier sound of a large modern instrument), the character of the performer, the size and acoustics of the performing space, even the time of performance. Therefore a metronome indication listing remains a mere approximation, and to slavishly follow the ticking of a metronome throughout any Mozart piece would be musically repellent.

When a marvelous Mozart conductor like Nikolaus Harnoncourt takes an aria marked *Andante* at a decidedly *Adagio* pace in the opera house, the effect may seem deeply expressive, whereas the same performance on a recording can sound rather sluggish. Similarly a piano piece marked *Allegretto* may be taken leisurely on a large modern piano but sound labored when played at the same pace on a fortepiano.

During each INTERPRETATION section much attention will be given to the choice of basic tempo, as well as to the possibilities for rhythmic flexibility.

DURATION (of individual movements) see TOTAL DURATION above.

SUGGESTED LISTENING

The player's understanding of a piano piece will gain considerable focus from listening to other compositions by Mozart listed under this heading. The listening suggestions for each piece discussed have been motivated by similarity in character, key, form, scoring and chronology. References to the more obscure works have been avoided. Thorough acquaintance with the rest of Mozart's output is essential for all pianists. The operas are particularly important. Jacob Lateiner aptly remarked:

"I feel that the magic key for opening the door to all of Mozart is opera: everything he wrote should be approached from an operatic point of view. Each theme has its own strong physiognomy, just as a character on a stage does"[5]

Listening to pianists' recordings can be misleading. Too many recordings of Mozart's music have been made by artists whose talents are better employed in other repertoire. Of course there are exceptions: Artur Schnabel, Lili Kraus, Clara Haskil, and Malcolm Bilson come to mind. In this guide occasional references to recordings are made to illustrate certain points, not to create some imaginary pecking order of Mozart interpreters. Before listening to recordings of the studied piece, the pianist should have formed a rather clear conception of its content. Ideally the player will have taped his own performance several times before listening to recordings by others.

INTERPRETATION

It is interesting to reflect that the Romans referred not only to translators or arbitrators as "interpreters," but also to those who could decipher dreams. In the twelfth century the French noun *interprétation* had the connotation of "revelation."[6] These ancient usages are significant, for only since 1880[7] has the term been applied to the interpretation of music. We realize that the essence of interpretation is a magical blend of factors, continually evolving and never totally objective. The author of the most significant flute method of the eighteenth century, Johann Joachim Quantz, stated:

"The good effect of a piece of music depends almost as much upon the performer as upon the composer himself. The best composition may be marred by poor execution, just as a mediocre composition may be improved and enhanced by good execution."[8]

During the twentieth century there have been fashions opposed to any "subjective" interpretation, notably the literalism of the 1950-1975 period, and, in recent decades, the literal approach of a few "authenticists." However, most authenticists have greatly enriched our perceptions of baroque and classical repertoire with their performances on "authentic" instruments and their research concerning tempo, articulation, ornamentation, improvisation etc.

Aside from the quandaries and discoveries regarding form, repetition, tempo etc., mentioned above, pianistic aspects like pedaling and technical problems are also discussed in each INTERPRETATION section when these issues seem pertinent or problematic.

Often the guidelines for a Mozart interpretation are evident by their very omission from the written score. Of course such "reading between the lines" applies not only to Mozart's works, but to most music written before the mid-twentieth century. Unfortunately, the training of too many musicians ignores the essential skill to read what is implied, not just what is stated, in the musical text.

Some major pieces by Mozart do not have a single dynamic indication. Mozart's dynamic indications are rarely self-evident; *poco forte* could mean an increase or decrease in sound, depending on the volume of the previous phrase, *piano* could indicate the beginning of a *diminuendo*. In Mozart's piano works *pianissimo* and *fortissimo* are rarely encountered, *mezzopiano* is totally absent and *mezzoforte* found only in the B minor Adagio, K.540. The connotations of *piano* and *forte* in this music are therefore innumerable and the player must be constantly aware of this challenge.

It is unfortunate that even *Urtext* editions give dubious indications that derive from first editions, not from the manuscripts. Other issues are less complex but frequently misunderstood; that *calando* in Mozart's music implies only a diminution of sound, not of tempo, and that the adverb *assai* indicates "very," not, as in Beethoven's scores, "rather."

Much attention is given to phrasing and articulation, two subjects often confused. Phrasing is the shaping and direction of the musical discourse. Articulation concerns the stresses, touches and grouping of notes. Mozart frequently gave the player notated and "unwritten" directions regarding phrasing and articulation, but these are often misconstrued. Confusion is universal regarding the presence or absence of slurs, dots, accents and the interpretation of these signs.

With several excellent *Urtext* editions currently available, actual textual discrepancies are becoming infrequent. Therefore comparisons of *Urtext* editions are made only when contradictions exist, usually in sonata form movements where parallel passages differ in notation. In this study the *Neue Mozart Ausgabe* (usually abbreviated as NMA and published by Bärenreiter-Verlag in Kassel) is generally referred to as the standard edition, but the other *Urtext* editions that have appeared during the last decade are equally reliable (see note 9, Introduction).

Virtually everyone is receptive to thoughts concerning the emotional subtext of a piece. Communicating associative elements of the music is, after all, the essence of a convincing interpretation. Though it may not be difficult to "inspire" a student during a lesson, in a study like this, there is a danger that subjective associations could be taken too literally or accepted without sufficient reflection. Such references are made when the content seems enigmatic, or when, in my experience, most players tend to lose focus. Differentiation between fact and fantasy cannot always be specified, as both contribute to the indefinability that is the essence of truly fine music making.

ORNAMENTATION

What a minefield this subject can be, so inhibiting that some concert artists do not dare to program Mozart! Ornamentation is a very difficult subject for most twentieth-century players. In this guide each ornament is discussed when it first occurs in a composition. This amount of detail may seem dull to a casual reader, but only a thorough approach will benefit the serious pianist or teacher. This aspect of Mozart interpretation should resist misinformed dogma, for, as Frederick Neumann wisely remarked:

"... it is imperative for the enlightened performer to know there are no easy automatic rules; that he has to figure out every case on its merits, realizing the worst thing, then as now, is any sense of rigidity and formulaic stereotype." [9]

Literal illustration of how to render an ornament can severely diminish the subtle effect intended by the composer. Therefore such simplifications are avoided in this book.

Twentieth-century attitudes on ornamentation have arguably been too influenced by Daniel Gottlob Türk's *School of Clavier Playing*,[10] which codified many ornaments in a somewhat rigid fashion, thereby robbing many of their delightful ambiguity. This guide attempts to clarify the function and various expressive possibilities of each ornament. Occasionally the rendition of an ornament is straightforward, but frequently there are alternatives to be considered.

Regarding particularly difficult ornaments, some pianistic advice (touch, hand position, fingering) will be given.

Some general remarks about ornaments in Mozart's piano music:

TRILLS It becomes obvious that these can begin on the principal note, the upper auxiliary or even the lower auxiliary, that the initial note may sound "on the beat," be prolonged and/or stressed, played lightly before the beat, or even stressed before the beat. The trill's rapidity as well as its termination are also discussed when these issues seem relevant. Frequently an ornament indicated as a trill is to be played as a turn, *Pralltriller* (in this study a term applied to four-note trills beginning on the upper auxiliary, obviously without a termination) or *Schneller* (a three-note ornament, with the upper auxiliary note between the principal note and its repetition).

APPOGGIATURE are the most subjective ornaments in Mozart's music. Their interpretation remains a deliciously complex matter. In this guide the confusing terms "accented or unaccented," "short or long" are not applied to *appoggiature*. The functions of the *appoggiatura*, grace note and *acciacciatura*, often confused, are specified in each example. The misconception of an *appoggiatura* assuming an exact geometric rhythmic value ("half the value of the principal note" etc.) is dispelled, for usually the function of an *appoggiatura* is to break the regularity of the metric flow, not to adhere to it.

TURNS are often played too inflexibly. Depending on the context, they can be lively or languid, spritely or yearning.

SLIDES (in German, *Schleifer*) may begin on or before the beat, depending on the effect intended.

ARPEGGI, broken chordal figurations, virtually always end on the beat. On this issue I support the views of Frederick Neumann, whose writings on ornamentation[11] are essential reading for any serious student of Mozart. Admittedly not all scholars agree with Neumann on the subject of *arpeggi*.

IMPROVISED or ADDITIONAL ORNAMENTATION is discussed at the

end of each ORNAMENTATION section. This subject demands from the pianist both unusual imagination and a deep understanding of style. The issue of improvised ornaments is treacherous. Even at international competitions, improvisation of ornaments during a Mozart performance may cost the pianist a prize. Such developments are utterly risible, for the music of the late eighteenth century was greatly enriched by ornamentation, written and improvised. Any changes or additions to the text should be heard as enhancements and not as distractions. In Mozart's time an ornament delighted by providing not only variation, but also by strengthening the expressive effect. R.D. Levin reminds us:

"Ornamentation is most effective when it is fully organic to the expressive and dramatic content of the work; it is not an external process carried out upon a piece." [12]

Conditioning is important; a harpsichordist with extensive experience of baroque ornamentation reacts differently than a listener who, for decades, has heard a Mozart sonata played without a single improvised ornament. Siegbert Rampe states:

"If the player does not want to add ornaments to repeated sections, or is not capable of this, he is advised to ignore repeats as often as possible." [13]

This clearly contradicts Neumann's significant attitude expressed in the third quote of this chapter.

Fascinating as this field is, it is not feasible, nor would it seem desirable, to pinpoint every possibility for improvised ornamentation in these works. One pianist can add numerous ornaments to a Mozart piece that will seem attractive and suitable, whereas another player may add only a few cautious decorations, which are mere schoolish frills and do not enhance the performance. In this guide certain opportunities for improvised ornamentation will be considered, but Mozart's solo piano works need considerably less improvised decoration than his concertos.

TERMINOLOGY AND ABBREVIATIONS USED IN THE GUIDE

Virtually all foreign terms are italicized. It should be noted that *piano* and *fortepiano* refer to dynamic indications; when not italicized these terms refer to types of keyboard instruments. The confusing term "pianoforte" is avoided in this book.

The key of a composition is presumed to be in major mode unless otherwise stated, therefore a "Sonata in C" is a "Sonata in C major." All music in minor key is described as such.

References to the player, student or teacher as "he" is only for the sake of brevity. Worldwide, more women play the piano than men, and women have always been among the most noteworthy Mozart interpreters.

Abbreviations:

m., mm.	measure, measures
ii, iv	second, fourth movements
RH, LH	right hand, left hand
M.M.	tempo measured by Maelzel's Metronome
UC pedal	*una corda* pedal, on both the modern piano and the fortepiano used in very soft phrases
FE	first edition
NMA	*Neue Mozart Ausgabe*, published by Bärenreiter

II

TRADITIONS, MYTHS, FASHIONS,
SOME CONCLUSIONS

Like any long relationship, that of a musician and his repertoire knows its ups and downs. But why do most pianists have periods when they do not feel "at ease with Mozart?" Why do some musicians never find the sufficient empathy and understanding to play these masterpieces convincingly?

In this chapter some causes of these afflictions will be discussed and a few remedies prescribed.

1 MYTHS AND MISCONCEPTIONS

Certain misconceptions of Mozart interpretation have become institutionalized as traditions. Mahler's remark "Traditions are merely bad habits" is still relevant, and such habits die slowly. For the pianist who cannot understand his inhibitions when playing Mozart, and for the teacher who has students who seem allergic to this music, some of the worst traditional misconceptions are described and contradicted below:

a. "Mozart's music may be perfect, but it lacks emotion." To confront this extraordinary supposition, play through two consecutive pages from any piano sonata. A fine example is the slow movement of the B-flat Sonata, K.333. What tenderness, longing, melancholy, even terror are expressed in the first two pages! This emotional landscape may not be painted in dramatic colors, but we hear an astonishing range of primary and secondary tints, which surely affect any sensitive soul; as Charles Gounod noted:

> "Mozart touches and moves us, all of us recognize ourselves in him, and we proclaim that he knows human nature well and truly." [1]

b. "Mozart's music is merely sensual and lightweight." This particular myth, popular with some intellectuals, is not new (after all, even Beethoven had trouble accepting *Così fan tutte*) but in any art, sensual aspects contribute to the aesthetic experience. Regarding Mozart's "lack of weight," William Glock commented:

"In Mozart there is a wonderful and intense levity altogether beyond the reach of any late nineteenth-century composer. And this quality in him (if I am right) is one of the things Amiel must have meant when he said that Mozart 'sets us free'; 'Mozart respects you, reveals to you your strength, gives you freedom and balance'... the recovery of the spiritual attitude that would make possible once more that 'intense levity'... is perhaps one of our greatest needs." [2]

c. "Mozart's music is essentially small scale and predictable." This misconception arose in the nineteenth century; late romantic music thrived on expansive forms and stormy contrasts. Yet listen to the finale of the C minor Sonata, K.457, where each sentence presents a startling surprise, like the camera in a fast film lurching from one situation to another. There is nothing small scale or predictable about such a piece! Nor did Mozart conceive of his music being compressed by a narrow dynamic range. In a much quoted letter to his father[3] he expressed his enthusiasm for the Mannheim orchestra with "ten or eleven violins to a side."

Predictability in Mozart is illusory. If his works seem to evolve with inevitable logic, this "inevitability" is based as much on surprise elements as on logical ones. This can be easily proved by a simple experiment. Listen to a CD recording of a Mozart work you have never heard before. Stop the recording at the end of a phrase and guess how the next phrase will begin. It is highly unlikely that your guess will be totally verified.

d. "Because Mozart was not a revolutionary, like Beethoven, Wagner or Stravinsky, his music is merely conventional." Presumably the meager talents of J.S. Bach and Brahms also belong to the same club of non-revolutionary bores? Mozart usually cast his music in forms that may seem conventional, but that apparent conventionality constantly deceives, and was no doubt meant to do so. Even among the connotations of a tonality there is little conventionality in Mozart's responses. Consider, for example, the diversity seen in the three piano works in the key of A minor; the Sonata, K.310, a wild outburst that embraces the musical styles of three centuries, the finale of the A major Sonata, K.331, a straightforward *scène de ballet*, and the Rondo, K.511, a subtly ordered, extremely emotional monologue. Mozart's contemporaries frequently found his music difficult or complex, far from "conventional."

e. "A composer who is so popular cannot be taken seriously." This peculiar opinion has been voiced more frequently since the 1991 bicentenary. Alex Ross observed:

> "Beethoven's place has been taken by the one beloved of God, the supreme artificer of music, the sublime Mozart, who was also a more reliable worker and a nicer guy ... despite the profound irregularities beneath his comfortable surfaces, Mozart has become a sort of musical Prozac." [4]

Beethoven and Wagner, for example, have each gone through periods of being the Western world's most popular composer. There were not many doubts cast on their profundity, though it is true that one does not hear their music played as often as Mozart's in venues like supermarkets and airports. Popularity cannot be equated automatically with vulgarity, though popularity is, by definition, temporal. Certainly what some felt to be "excessive Mozart exposure" during 1991 does not seem to have damaged Mozart's stature.

f. "Mozart must be played only on 'authentic,' historical instruments." This opinion has become so fashionable in certain countries that some pianists do not dare to perform this music on modern instruments. Frederick Neumann wisely remarked:

> "Such questions as tone color or number of performers should not be subjected to a moral judgement of right and wrong but only to the artistic one of being in rapport with the style and spirit of the work ... Such artistic judgements would be in harmony with the eighteenth-century aesthetic ideas that a desirable performance is one that expresses the 'affections' in the music and moves the listener's emotions accordingly..." [5]

Consider two conductors who, in the past decade, have arguably produced the finest Mozart interpretations, Nikolaus Harnoncourt and John Eliot Gardiner. For Mozart performances, Harnoncourt has generally used modern instruments and Gardiner authentic ones. Both conductors' Mozart is characterized by spontaneity and conviction, yet their interpretations differ considerably.

The unceasing research into the music of Mozart's time and our growing acquaintance with historical instruments (or copies thereof) have contributed to new perceptions of this music. But performers' attitudes are also affected by sociological and aesthetic factors that have nothing to do with musical or methodological texts. Our sense of tempo and dynamics, for example, is naturally affected by such elements as the amount of noise and activity we encounter every day. Harnoncourt commented:

"I have eighteenth-century instruments, but I still don't have an eighteenth-century sound ... a person from the twentieth century is playing sounds of the twentieth century. He is realizing this idea of sound with the experience of a musician who has played Schubert, Brahms, Stravinsky, Stockhausen ... so I know very well that an interpretation of mine, regardless of the instruments I use, is an interpretation of the 1990's."[6]

Charles Rosen seconds this attitude:

"Every performance today is a translation; a reconstruction of the original sound is the most misleading translation because it pretends to be the original, while the significance of the old sounds has irrevocably changed."[7]

and resolutely concludes that:

"A performance is more than a voluptuous noise or a historical echo from the past."[8]

Not many fortepianos from the late seventeenth century provide enjoyable listening. The best copies of such instruments can sound lucid and poetic but seem so different from the originals that their "authenticity" too could be questioned. Is Mozart only to be played on copies of museum instruments? It seems safe to assume that in the future most people will continue to perform Mozart's solo piano music on modern instruments, not on copies of fortepianos, however attractive the latter undeniably can be in intimate surroundings.

Two centuries of misinformed traditions concerning the performing of Mozart's works are not so much the result of the instruments available as they are of changing aesthetic values. The invention of a steel-framed piano as well as the use of larger performing spaces began the trend toward ever-increasing volume. But that single development does not account for innumerable misconceptions of articulation, tempo, *rubato*, pedaling and ornamentation. Such misconceptions undermine the vitality and eloquence of Mozart's music whether it is played on a fortepiano or on a full-size grand piano.

2 THE CHANGING FASHIONS OF MOZART INTERPRETATION

Mozart was not concerned with "authenticity" when he added parts for wind instruments to his arrangements of Handel's oratorios. And during the nineteenth century, respect for all facets of a musical work virtually ceased. New plots were created for operas like *Idomeneo* and *Zauberflöte*. Meyerbeer mutilated the orchestration of *Don Giovanni*. Grieg made heavy-handed arrangements for two pianos of Mozart's solo sonatas.[9]

These excesses are now thoroughly out of favor, but it is important to have some conception of how the various published editions of Mozart's works evolved. From Mozart's death until the more recent *Urtext* editions (the first Mozart edition terming itself an *Urtext* appeared in 1895[10]) there was a gradual transformation of precise indications that misled generations of interpreters. Short articulation slurs, very precisely indicated by the composer, were melted down into longer phrasing slurs, robbing the music of much enlivening detail. *Appoggiature* and chordal notation were frequently and not always logically changed. Pedaling more suitable to Chopin was added. Worst of all, peculiar dynamic indications and bizarre tempo indications were added to "clarify" the text.

In this century not many pianists have been acclaimed for their Mozart interpretations. This was certainly partly due to the lack of accurate editions before the 1960's. And the recent generation of fortepianists have also made many welcome contributions. The republication of methodological works from the late eighteenth century is also valuable, if only to illustrate that even then there was no total unanimity concerning every interpretative matter.

As previously noted, some performances using old instruments are mere recreations of old-fashioned conceptions played on authentic instruments. David Schulenberg stated:

"In practice the expressions 'authentic' and 'historically accurate' have come to mean performance on 'original' instruments, but no reputable performer or scholar today claims that merely using an old instrument (or a supposed copy thereof), or even playing it according to the latest ideas about historical performing practice, assures fidelity to the score or to the composer's intentions."[11]

Prejudices change even more slowly than habits; some harpsichordists confess that they have never been able to tolerate the sound of a modern piano, whereas most pianists remain allergic to the sound of a harpsichord. Yet both types of instrument may suit the same Prelude and Fugue by J.S. Bach. On this subject Charles Rosen made a highly relevant comment:

"Mozart's Symphony in G minor, K.550, exists in two versions, one without clarinets, but it is the same composition ...The clarinet concerto was originally sketched for basset horn ... reconceiving it for clarinet did not entail any process of recomposition. It is clear that for Mozart, as for Bach, composition did not entail fixing all aspects of the sound in advance."[12]

If these issues remain as factious and confusing to professional musicians as they are to the general public, it remains clear that the player, not the instrument, is the key factor in the interpretation of Mozart.

3 SOME CONCLUSIONS

To interpret Mozart's solo piano works convincingly, the player should consider these criteria:

1. Use recent *Urtext* editions of the compositions being studied and develop a perceptive approach to reading, also "between the lines."

2. Listen to the rest of Mozart's oeuvre: the operas, chamber music, symphonies and church music.

3. Perform chamber music and accompany singers in works by Mozart.

4. Study works by the other composers of Mozart's time, to understand how different his music is from, for example, Joseph Haydn's or Muzio Clementi's.

5. Play the music on a fortepiano, to get some idea of how keyboard instruments have changed during the last two centuries.

6. Have some conception of what life was like during the latter half of the eighteenth century. Reading the correspondence of Mozart and his

family is especially recommended and there are some excellent biographies now available in English.

7. Have imagination, wit and passion, as well as a sensitive technique and solid theoretical background. Nikolaus Harnoncourt warned against a purely aesthetic or academic approach:

> "What I find very disturbing is the manner in which historical music is usually performed, not as a direct expression of life itself, but only as decoration ... as a tranquillizer against stress and against the madness of life ... I believe that art is always disturbing and ... represents all the realities of life." [13]

The sounds and after-sounds of great music never cease evolving. Obviously when a player is 20, his relationship with this music is different from what it becomes when he is 40 or 60. And a Brazilian will probably have different reactions on hearing and playing Mozart than a Swede.

But what joy and fulfilment all these experiences provide, as Carl Schachter so wisely concluded:

> "Artur Schnabel said he liked to play music that was better than it could be performed. Mozart's music would certainly fit this description ... performers who try to match the structural richness, emotional depth and easy, unpretentious perfection of Mozart's music in their approach to playing and singing become better performers, and not only of Mozart." [14]

III

MOZART'S FIRST COMPOSITIONS FOR PIANO

1 MOZART'S FIRST 19 YEARS

Both the quality of Mozart's music and his colorful life history attract the attention of many writers. There are several excellent biographies published in English[1] and the serious reader is urged to study the Mozart family's correspondence,[2] which gives a detailed image of life in Europe during the late seventeenth century. Though in his letters many of Mozart's innermost thoughts remain obscure, the correspondence still gives us much valuable information. Wolfgang Hildesheimer astutely observed:

> "The mastery of means which made him the greatest and most mysterious musician of all time also stood him in good stead in his verbal statements. He had at his disposal a tremendous synthetic-emotional range, with which he could assume many shapes or hide himself entirely, and he employed the whole range without hypocrisy, but also without any compunction about objective truth."[3]

The composer's early years were far from normal. The frequent, immense journeys could not have been ideal for the boy's physical development and emotional stability. But all the travels did expose Mozart to a richly divergent range of musical styles and media, an education few musicians of the time could even contemplate. By the age of seventeen, Mozart had already composed extensively in Italian, French, German, and English styles.

This cosmopolitan background contributes to the astounding quality of early works like the piano sonatas K.279-284, music that cannot be dismissed as mere youthful experiment. The composer was already a master, with lauded operas, church works, symphonies, string quartets and other works to his credit. Russell Sherman commented:

> "Mozart was naturally and genetically disposed toward accepting the musical conventions of his time. And what his genes did not determine, the musical training by his father assured ... the shape of future creations depended only upon variables of fate and personality..."[4]

2 MOZART'S KEYBOARD MUSIC BEFORE 1776

Many of the earliest piano pieces were written down by Leopold, who wanted these miniatures preserved for posterity. The role of Leopold in his son's inner life is intriguing and has been discussed by many historians and analysts. It is easy to be critical of the neurotic father of the greatest prodigy Western music has ever known, yet Leopold possessed considerable intellect and was the author of a sound violin method. He was certainly much more than just another court violinist; indeed it is curious how rarely he refers in the family correspondence to his own playing. Leopold's talents were analytical and pedagogical. Initially Wolfgang benefitted greatly from his father's guidance. Later, when the young man should have been building his own life, he had much difficulty breaking free of Leopold's possessiveness.[5]

In his first years, Mozart almost certainly played harpsichords more often than fortepianos. Therefore it is not correct to refer to his earliest keyboard pieces as being specifically "for the piano." However, few of the childhood compositions seem more suited to the harpsichord than to the fortepiano. Many of the pieces listed in Köchel's catalogue as K.1-15 are among the first pieces that every child plays during his studies at the piano. Three of these, the Minuet in G, K.1/1-e, the Minuet in F, K.2, and the Allegro in B-flat, K.3, are considered in the following four sections.

Because it is so difficult to find works by Mozart that are accessible to pianists of modest attainments, it is doubly frustrating to note that so many teachers still assign their students the *Viennese Sonatinas*, which, as already noted in the Introduction, are mere arrangements of various Mozart Divertimento movements by some unidentified hack, not by the composer. Delightful though the original Divertimenti may be, the arrangements create musical and pianistic problems due to the un-Mozartian writing for the instrument.

Few are acquainted with the collection of 38 pieces Mozart wrote in 1764-65, *The London Notebook*. Some of these pieces seem more like sketches than completed structures, whereas others may sound best on the harpsichord, but most of these miniatures offer delight to the young pianist. The variety is astonishing: nos.3 and 9 are certainly Minuets, nos.4 and 9 evoke hunting scenes, no.7 is a preludizing improvisation harkening back to the baroque, whereas the driving frenzy of no.14 predicts the two symphonies in G minor.

3 INTERPRETATION OF K.1-3

When playing K.1 or 2, the pianist should obviously have some sense of the minuet not only as a dance, but also as an atmosphere (see this chapter, section 7). Because even in such short pieces, misunderstandings of text can arise, an *Urtext* edition is essential. With their unauthentic dynamic and articulation indications, annotated editions, so popular among publications for beginners, frequently deform the elegance of these unpretentious miniatures.

The tendency to let every phrase that is not marked *staccato* melt into an amorphous *legato* is regrettable, especially in Mozart's youthful works, where *legato* is more the exception than the rule. No generalized romantic concept of "smooth, singing melodies," but a clear articulation of line, with much sensitivity to the stresses and grouping of the notes brings this music to life. Players of any age can be made aware that less *legato* does not denote less "expression," and that a *non legato* phrase can be shaped with communicative intensity.

4 INTERPRETATION OF K.1

In the G major Minuet, K.1 (1-e), a light-footed *non legato* is the predominate touch. This approach may seem foreign to pianists who drown everything they play with a *legato* sauce that obliterates the finer flavors. Frequently this piece is played *legato* throughout; even the repeated notes can be bound by pedaling. Lazy minds and fingers may unthinkingly join eighth notes to each other, but nowhere in this piece are they slurred. Joining the eighth notes to the subsequent quarter notes is even more regrettable, resulting in a monotonous plodding far removed from any notions of an elegant dance. On a modern instrument or on a fortepiano a *non legato* approach will sound joyful, but the player's wrists must remain free throughout. Though the quarter notes in mm.1,3 or in the bass of mm.5-7 are *non legato*, they obviously should not be played with the same emphasis.

Though the second two-measure phrase is surely less energetic than the first, a conspicuous echo effect would not be typically Mozartian. Due to the sparsity of notes, the shaping of each measure requires considerable sensitivity. The upbeats to mm.1,3,5 are often played too strongly, creating a somewhat rowdy atmosphere hardly suitable in a minuet. Playing all the first beats with the same emphasis also kills any suggestion of a dance. The first beats of mm.1,3,9,11 are surely slightly stronger than those of the subsequent measures.

A whining expression in the suspensions must be avoided. Of course the resolution notes on the second beats must be softer, but the effect is graceful, not melancholic. Most pianists find it natural to play the stressed note of a suspension with a low wrist and to play the resolution note as the wrist rises. Indeed such suspensions are an ideal manner in which to give beginning pianists a feeling of freedom in the wrist.

In mm.7,15 are the first or the second beats stronger? Should mm.6,14 have more weight than mm.7,15? These considerations give this delightful miniature its inner vitality and provide interesting challenges to the musical perception of a fledgling pianist.

Whether mm.17-32 form a second Minuet (K.1-f) or the middle section of the first Minuet is unclear.[6] The abrupt transition to C major and the lurch back to G at the end of the middle section (if one regards this as such) do suggest some childish inexperience. Because of this ambiguity, many editions omit the second Minuet. This is a pity, but in any case, the piece can also be played on its own. Perhaps this second piece/section offers more possibilities for dynamic shading than the first.

Where the second beat is identical with the first, a plodding effect is evaded when the second beat is somewhat lighter. The ascending suspensions in the second and fourth measures are to be slurred even if this is indicated only in the second half of the section. In the eighteenth century all suspensions were to be played *legato*. Care must be taken with the numerous octave leaps. If these are played *legato* and with any accenting of the upper notes, the effect sounds unmistakably like yodeling.

K.1-3 are conceived from a young child's view of the instrument, with the hands playing close to each other in the center of the keyboard. Practicing the RH line an octave higher than written can make the dialogue between the hands clearer to hear and can also give the pianist a sense of more freedom in the arms.

Improvisation of ornamentation requires taste as much as creativity, but students should be encouraged to experiment. For example, when the melody is repeated, on the third beat of m.3, a four-note trill beginning with the upper auxiliary note and without the lower auxiliary could be added. The single notated ornament, the trill in m.7, may be introduced by the upper auxiliary played as a light grace note before the third quarter-note beat. The trill itself should not sound too active and is probably best rendered as a five-note turn. A similar trill can be added to the third quarter-note beat of m.15. In the middle section/second minuet, some sixteenth-note decoration of the third beat of mm.19 and the first beat of m.22 (mm.3 and 6, if one regards this as a separate piece) is certainly possible.

5 INTERPRETATION OF K.2

Though the Minuet in F, K.2, reads more easily than K.1, it suffers even more from insensitive performances. Particular care must be taken that the second beats are not stronger than the first, and that the third beats are even lighter. As in K.1, most eighth notes sound livelier if lightly detached. Especially because the rhythmic variety is minimal, the harmonic movement must be clear. The second measure of each phrase takes on different inflections. Compared to its preceding measure, m.2 seems lighter, m.6 more assertive, m.10 more introspective, and m.14 more optimistic. When it becomes a monotonous alteration of strong and weak measures, this Minuet seems like a boring tennis match.

Though the LH writing seems sparse, the player should be aware that the bass line moves in a very baroque-like way. An imaginary cellist would play the diatonic notes *legato* and the triadic ones *non legato*.

Some possibilities for improvised ornamentation: a trill in the first two beats of m.4, four sixteenth notes, partly diatonic, partly triadic, in the first beats of mm.10, 15, 14-15, 23. The *fermata* indicated in m.20 is perhaps best played like a whispered pause, the young Mozart drawing attention to the "suspenseful" harmony, but a very simple, light *Eingang* (transition to the next measure), even a mere arpeggiated A minor triad, is conceivable.

Minuets are further discussed in section 7 of this chapter.

6 INTERPRETATION OF K.3

The Allegro in B-flat, K.3, is also a frequent victim of careless articulation. Too often the eighth-note upbeats to m.1 and 3 are slurred to the subsequent first beats, creating dull heaviness. Slurring during the repeated note motif, first heard in m.3, is equally inappropriate. The two-note slurs throughout the piece indicate the phrasing, the first note somewhat stronger than the second, but if the second note is played too short, peculiar accenting and syncopation result. Given the lively tempo, the shaping of the bass quarter notes is less varied than in K.2, but the player should avoid a distracting *stac-*

cato or a sticky *legato*. As in the previous pieces, the weight of each beat must be carefully judged. Generally the even-numbered measures are lighter.

The *appoggiature* in m.9 and 27 are to be played delicately and quickly before the first beat. The frequently heard on-beat rendition is more suitable in baroque music. Though there would seem to be little opportunity for added ornamentation in such a lively piece, some changes in the melody are welcome when it is repeated, for example, quick *appoggiature* before both beats in m.5, a quick slide or turn in the upbeats to mm.15 and 19.

These Mozart pieces can stimulate a beginner's sense of orchestral colors, an essential aspect of fine pianism. As soon as a student is acquainted with the sounds of the various orchestral instruments, he should be encouraged to imagine these pieces in terms of a violin playing the upper line, a cello the bass line, a flute answering a motif played on the oboe, etc.

7 MOZART'S MINUETS

Minuets often pose major problems. After all, the world of that subtle dance is very remote from our experience. During the period 1650-1790, the minuet was preferred in the salons above all other dances, but pieces cast in this *genre* tend to make twentieth-century musicians feel very apprehensive, as if they, like so many dancers of the minuet in the eighteenth century, were destined for the guillotine.

M.E. Little gave an excellent impression of how a minuet is danced:

> "... elegant and seemingly effortless performance of complex step patterns ... A number of different step patterns were used, all but a few ornamental ones made up of combinations of *demi-coupés* (rises from previous bends during the transfer of weight from foot to foot), *demi-jetés* (small leaps from one foot to the other) and *pas marchés* (plain steps on to the ball of the foot)." [7]

From this description it is obvious that the physical rendition of a minuet could not have been hasty. The ladies, with their numerous and complicated garments, would have been unable to perform all these steps in a quick tempo. However, it has been maintained that:

> "musicians accompanying dancers or playing stylized minuets should realize that the basic unit of the dance is two bars long (not one or four)." [8]

Therefore the relationship of the original dance movement and the tempo is not always evident. One reads in various texts that a minuet was moderate in pace, somewhat quicker than an *allemande* or a *polonaise*, and considerably faster than the *sarabande* or *pavane*. For Mozart and later composers, a minuet in a symphony or a sonata is a rather short movement, generally not fast but with a marked rhythmic impulse. A distinction can be made between a minuet that is to be danced, like the famous one in the first act of *Don Giovanni*, and minuet movements, like those in Mozart's last three symphonies, which are clearly not intended to accompany actual movement. Concerning the guises assumed by the minuet in Mozart's music and the problem of tempo choice, Jean-Pierre Marty is eloquent:

"from ... the Minuet K.l-d (1761) to Servilia's aria 'S'altro che lagrime' in *La clemenza di Tito*, K.621 (1791), Mozart wrote over three hundred minuets ... only thirty-seven bear any tempo indication besides the denomination *Menuetto* or an unspecified *Tempo di minuetto*. The latter indication is used both in the finale of the Violin Concerto in A K.219 and in Marcellina's aria in *Le nozze di Figaro*, yet it would be inconceivable to perform the two pieces at even remotely similar tempos." [9]

This becomes one of the big quandaries of a modern interpreter confronted by a minuet. Consider the minuets we most frequently hear, those in the symphonies and quartets of Haydn and Mozart. Performances of these movements incline either to pedantry or to haste. Thomas Beecham was one of the very few conductors of the twentieth century who succeeded in shaping symphonic minuets at an utterly natural pace. Is it surprising that young children seem intimidated by Mozart's piano minuets?

In a frequently quoted letter from Mozart to his sister, dated March 24, 1770, national differences in the interpretation of minuets are also discussed:

"I shall soon send you a minuet ... which everyone danced to afterwards at the *feste di ballo* in Milan, solely in order that you may see how slowly people dance here. The minuet itself is very beautiful. It comes, of course, from Vienna ... It has plenty of notes. Why? Because it is a stage minuet which is danced slowly. The minuets in Milan, in fact the Italian minuets generally, have plenty of notes, are played slowly..." [10]

Note values form a relevant factor in determining a minuet's tempo, as in any musical composition. A minuet with figurations in sixteenth notes will probably need a more spacious tempo than a minuet notated only in eighth and quarter notes. Sandra Rosenblum remarked on this:

"Two types of minuets existed during the eighteenth century and through the Classic era. The type more usual in Classic music, a fast piece although often headed *Allegretto*, moves with one pulse per measure; the more moderate minuet ... moves with three beats per measure and sometimes contains subdivisions of eighth-note triplets and sixteenth notes." [11]

Marty observed that:

"in the course of the eighteenth century (which saw the inclusion of minuets in symphonic music) the split between the two sorts of minuets became wider, each variety accentuating its distinctive feature, the faster becoming even faster and the slower slower." [12]

He concludes that most of Mozart's minuets are of the "fast" variety, with a tempo of $\downarrow$ = 126-142, whereas the "slower" minuets assume tempi of $\downarrow$ = 92. Yet even the "authenticists" arrive at strange choices of tempos in minuets; a scholar as serious as Siegbert Rampe draws conclusions that seem bizarre: a M.M. indication of $\downarrow$ = 160 for the first minuet of K.282,[13] or of 144-152 for the minuet in K.331![14]

We have seen in the previous sections how equal stressing of all the first beats in the minuets would create a leaden impression. Such an unimaginative approach petrifies the inner vitality of any minuet movement. The player must also have a clear perception of the minuet's character; is it cheerful with a only few darker moments (Piano Sonata, K.282 ii), basically melancholy (Sonata for Piano and Violin, K.304 ii), or even defiant (Symphony K.550 iii)? Obviously the tempi in all these pieces will differ considerably.

Metric content, first beat stressing, but, most importantly, character determine a suitable tempo for a minuet. No generalities are applicable. Each piece must be carefully considered individually.

8 CHALLENGES AND DELIGHTS
OF THE MUNICH SONATAS, K.279-284

Why do performers and teachers shy away from the sonatas K.279-284? And there has been astonishingly little written about these masterworks. In the first major biography of Mozart (1865), by Otto Jahn, all six are dismissed in a single short paragraph! Dating these pieces was guess work, until Alan Tyson concluded:

"K.279-284 were assigned by Köchel to the year 1777. Plath's *Schriftchronologie* has now suggested 'early 1775,' the time Mozart was in Munich for the production of *La finta giardiniera* K.196, and paperstudies also suggest the sonatas are on paper purchased in Salzburg or Munich around that time." [15]

Therefore Mozart's first six piano sonatas are sometimes described as "the Munich sonatas." Leopold Mozart did try as late as 1784 to sell the manuscripts, but the sonatas were published only in 1799. Few of Mozart's works completed before 1776 were published during his lifetime.

That these sonatas were designed for the composer's own public appearances is evident in the pianistic effervescence of the quicker movements. Mozart played the sonatas frequently during his tours in 1775-78. From Augsburg Mozart wrote his father on October 17, 1777:

"Here and at Munich I have played all my six sonatas by heart several times. I played the fifth, in G, at that grand concert in the Stube. The last one in D sounds exquisite on Stein's pianoforte." [16]

Mozart played these pieces in modest inns as well as in aristocratic salons. During the 1770's harpsichords were more readily found than fortepianos, but this certainly does not mean that this music should be played on the harpsichord. The manifold dynamic markings make it evident that these sonatas were conceived for the fortepiano.

Admittedly this music can readily sound misplaced on large modern instruments, the sparkling articulation in the quick movements easily becoming more laborious than vivacious. Any serious performer of these works will learn much by playing them on a fortepiano. However, as seen in Chapter II, maintaining that this music can only be rendered on historic instruments is an extreme stance. The piano sonatas written in Vienna (K.330-576) may be somewhat more suited to modern instruments than the Munich sonatas, but K.279-284 retain their eloquence on whatever type of instrument, if they are played with stylistic insight and pianistic refinement.

The factors of technical difficulty and choice of instrument are less problematic than certain enigmas in the music itself. Alfred Einstein aptly remarked:

"The six piano sonatas ... do not give a unified or true picture of their composer. They are a microcosm of feeling and of subtlety of form, but a very complicated one..." [17]

Unfortunately, respect for Mozart's later works sometimes inspires teachers to assign these "youthful" compositions to youthful students. This frequently results in musical and pianistic disaster.

Historians and musicologists take delight in tracing elements of Bach's sons, Joseph and Michael Haydn, Ignaz von Beecke, Johann Schobert, etc. in these pieces. Though it is natural that a nineteen-year-old's music is seasoned with influences by other composers, such information is not much help to the interpreter.

The multiple-movement piano sonata was in its infancy and one must marvel at Mozart's mastery, especially his extraordinary sense of structure as well as his pianistic exuberance, which created an atmosphere of spontaneity and surprise.

Before these compositions, Mozart had written surprisingly little of significance for piano. The Piano Concerto in D, K.175, from 1773 and the Variations on a Minuet by J.C. Fischer, K.179, written in the following year, are rarely heard. However, Mozart had already completed two astonishing symphonies, K.183 and 201, and by 1775, Mozart had finished eight theatrical works, which had known much success. There is no better preparation for the student of K.279-284 than acquaintance with *La finta giardiniera*, the opera Mozart wrote during the same period as these sonatas. Nicholas Till observed:

"*La finta* is the earliest opera in which Mozart speaks not only as a miraculously precocious musician, but as an individual giving voice to his own experience, and engaged with the concerns of his generation and class in a language that was unequivocally his own." [18]

The unique blend of seriousness and humor that permeates this opera is very evident in the Munich sonatas.

IV

SONATAS IN C, K.279, IN F, K.280, AND B-FLAT, K.281

SONATA IN C MAJOR, K.279

OTHER K. LISTING   189-d
COMPOSITION DATE   probably 1775
TOTAL DURATION   16 minutes, with expositional repeats

FIRST MOVEMENT   *Allegro*
FORM   sonata
APPROXIMATE TEMPO   ♩ = M.M. 104
DURATION   6½ minutes, with expositional repeat
SUGGESTED LISTENING   Violin Concerto, K.216 i
     Missa brevis, K.220/196-b: *Credo*
     Symphony, K.220/189-k i

1 MOTIVIC SECRETS IN THE FIRST MOVEMENT, K.279

This movement, with its un-Mozartian preponderance of sixteenth notes, can all too readily seem shapeless. Here the pianist needs considerable wit as well as a dexterous technique. An understanding of the motivic construction, so rich in surprises, is also essential.

The first four measures seem like an introduction; even Dennerlein[1] refers to them as "a preambule," but this apparently innocuous opening presents all the motifs that are to populate the busy scene that follows. The first five bass notes are an important figuration, (Motif "A"), or as a three-note Mordent-like figuration (Motif "AA"), lacking the first and last notes of Motif A. In both guises these motifs are evident in the bass line of mm.12-13, 20-21, 25-27. The AA motif makes a comical appearance in the LH thirds in mm.27-28. The A motif becomes the driving force in the bass of mm.33-34. Motif AA ends the *Codetta* with a frivolous flute-like solo at mm.37-38. Motif A returns in mm.39-44, AA in mm.52-55.

Beginning in m.2 is another RH motif that seems inconsequential, the four sixteenth notes of the third quarter-note beat, resolving on the first sixteenth note of the fourth quarter-note measure. This Motif "B" returns in the RH of mm.5-7, is suggested in the following two measures, and forms a conspicuous RH sequence during mm.14-15. To regard the three LH eighth notes of m.2 as a motif may seem far-fetched, but this motif does recur in the RH of mm.13-14 (upper voice, second and third quarter-note beats). This motif "C" is doubled in both hands at mm.25-27, and in mm.31-34 becomes the driving force of the energetic *Codetta*. In mm.48-51 of the development section, the RH's impulses of ascending three-note patterns are reminiscent of Motif C, and at mm.64-65 this motif takes on an operatic intensity.

2 INTERPRETATION OF THE FIRST MOVEMENT, K.279

Perhaps this opening theme has more energy than charm, but with all the motivic molecules swirling about, what joyful energy this is! Hopefully the player has read the previous section; awareness of the motivic relationships will give a performance more vitality and clarity.

Choice of tempo is a delicate matter. The pace must allow the music to surge ahead, without the numerous ornaments and *staccati* becoming garbled. An instrument with a translucent sound certainly helps. A fine modern fortepiano expresses the vivacity of the busy figurations considerably more easily than a heavy modern grand piano.

In the opening measures exactness of note values is essential if the impression is not to become more panicky than festive. Motif C, the three LH eighth notes in m.2, can best be played *non legato*. Fingerpedaling the Alberti bass beginning in m.5 creates a sluggish effect. The *staccati* in m.9 are extremely difficult when the wrist is stiff; it is advisable to begin each four-note group with a low wrist. The LH can play the eighth notes in the lower voice in the second quarter-note beat of m.13. Pedaling is unnecessary throughout the first theme, except perhaps for the first beats of mm.2 and 4.

Many players begin the second thematic group, at m.16, with a coquettish *piano* although *forte* is the last dynamic indication at the third beat of m.14. Surely the *piano* indicated in m.20 would be redundant if the preceding phrase is also soft-toned? In mm.16-19 the RH violin line alternates between a breezy *non legato* and a melting *legato*, whereas the bubbly *non legato* arpeggios in the bass suggest a bassoon. The rapid *staccati* at moments like m.22 need the same wrist freedom as in m.9. The sequence of mm.22-26 remind us of a few moments in the first movement of the next sonata, K.280, where a certain floridity unfortunately wins out over Mozart's usual sense of economy. The pianist should be able to invest the appearance of each motif with a slightly different character.

The *piano* in m.29 may seem illogical but the dynamic contrasts throughout this theme clearly depict a humorous opposition of assertion and playfulness. In the sequence of mm.31-34, the thumbs of both hands must be as relaxed as possible. As a *non legato* approach generally predominates, the *legato* elements of mm.32-34 should be emphasized. In some editions the *staccati* are indicated with wedges, inspiring some players to a nasty and un-Mozartian *staccatissimo*. In Mozart's works, wedges and dots are practically always interchangeable; wedges seldom indicate greater emphasis.

Unlike some other *Urtext* editions, the NMA[2] indicates *piano* in the final quarter-note beat of mm.37, an important detail. Ending the exposition with vigorous tone spoils both the return to the opening and the dramatic minor mode of the development section. Some older editions have an incorrect, hectic *crescendo* in m.37-38. Surely such a hyperactive exposition should be repeated.

The bold sequences in the development should not be thumped out with monotonous heaviness, but colored according to the weight of the changing harmonies. First furious, later playful, much of the section evokes a dialogue between violins (RH) and celli (LH). The climax in mm.45-47 is quite wild. If the eighth notes here are *legato* this operatic phrase becomes more droopy than defiant. The "echo effects" suggested in mm.48-54 inspire some harpsichordists to claim this piece for their instrument, but the numerous dynamic indications throughout the piece clearly necessitate use of a fortepiano, not a harpsichord. Practically all players slur the eighth notes in the second quarter-note beats of mm.49, 51, creating a whining effect. The following six measures are to be played with as little pedaling as possible. All this hyperactivity must not inspire retention of breath, for that would be immediately discernible in the player's timing.

In the recapitulation, mm.62-67 are considerably more expansive than the corresponding measures in the exposition. The fingers should leave the keys at the end of each slur in mm.63-67. Joining up all the slurs totally spoils the agitated sobbing effect of this very inspired line. Measure 84 is easier if the RH plays the first quarter-note beat, the LH the second.

Mozart plays jokes by recapitulating mm.9,11 and 14-15 only in mm.82-85. In its brevity (five quarter-note beats!) the *Coda* is also a good prank. Given the exuberance of thematic material, repetition of the second section surely creates a hectic impression.

Throughout the movement, ability to characterize each phrase without anticipating the next is a challenge. The player should feel excitement, but not frenzy. The constant activity resembles a busy ensemble scene of an opera, with various characters rushing on- and off-stage. Clear differentiation between assertive and charming moments is the essence of the piece.

3 ORNAMENTATION IN THE FIRST MOVEMENT, K.279

m.

1   The arpeggiated notes should be played quickly and held, the uppermost note sounding simultaneously with the bass.

4   The first two notes of the three-note trill must be fitted in as quickly as possible between the sixteenth notes.

5   The *appoggiatura* is better played as a grace note. An onbeat interpretation is rather coarse.

7   At the opening of a sentence a three- or five-note trill, without the lower auxiliary, sounds less lopsided than a frequently heard four- or five-note turn, indicated in some editions.

8   The cheerful slide (*Schleifer*) ends on the first beat.

10   There is a subtle difference between the two onbeat *appoggiature*. The first is gently accented and perhaps slightly prolonged, with the subsequent notes somewhat shortened. The second could be played as a sixteenth note, with the two notes after the resulting suspension slightly detached.

13   With the LH playing the lower line, the trill becomes a three-note *Schneller* or a five-note turn.

14   These three-note trills are not only extremely difficult on modern instruments but cause a spaghetti junction of indecipherable "little notes." This sounds more muddled than playful; perhaps the ornaments are best simplified as light upbeat *appoggiature*.

16   The trill begins on the principal note and consists of five notes, without a termination. If the subsequent *appoggiature* are played before the beat they sound amusing, played on the beat they sound unsuitably cynical.

17   This type of *arpeggio* is clearly different from the arpeggiation in the opening measures. Again the uppermost note sounds on the first beat but the other notes are not held.

20 The *appoggiatura* is played like the first one in m.10.
22 These trills will sound awkward if not played with extreme lightness. Three notes suffice, or four, if one prefers beginning on the upper auxiliary.
25 The phrase is based on Motif B. Therefore the trill is best begun on the principal tone. There should be five notes before the termination.
26 The *appoggiature* become very quick prebeat grace notes.
27 The compound *appoggiatura* could be played around the barline, neither ending nor beginning precisely on the first beat. The following *appoggiatura* is played before the beat.
28 These *appoggiature* sound comically boisterous played as sixteenth notes before the beat.
29 But these *appoggiature* are more amusing played before the beat.
30 The slide *(Schleifer)* is energetic, not soulful, and therefore ends on the beat. The subsequent trill could begin with the upper or lower auxiliary, is as rapid as possible and has a termination.
36 The *appoggiatura* is on the beat, perhaps with the next two notes attached.
45 Due to the melodic line this trill of three or five notes should definitely begin on the main note and has no termination.
49 A quick grace-note upper auxiliary may be charming here. The trill should have five notes, not three, before the termination.
67 Given the relationship with the bass line, this trill can only begin on the principal note.

It is difficult to imagine any additional ornamentation in such a hyperactive piece.

SECOND MOVEMENT	*Andante*
FORM	sonata
APPROXIMATE TEMPO	$\quad \downarrow$ = M.M. 66
DURATION	5½ minutes, with exposition repeated
SUGGESTED LISTENING	Symphony, K.200 ii
	La finta giardiniera: Sandrina's cavatina "Geme la Tortorella," no.11, and Contino's aria " Care pupille belle," no.15

4 INTERPRETATION OF THE SECOND MOVEMENT, K.279

After the bustling world of the *Allegro* we suddenly find ourselves in a very different place. This movement is full of longing, joy and despair. The dynamic contrasts and emphasis shifts create an unstable atmosphere, unmistakably evoking the pains and pleasures of young love. The adjective *amoroso* applied to the slow movement of the Sonata, K.281, would be equally relevant here.

Malcolm Miller has indicated numerous resemblances between K.279 and a piano sonata in the same key by Leopold Mozart, which exists only in fragmented form.[3] But this movement is very much Wolfgang Mozart's, impulsive and never "routine."

Excessive *rubato* is as irrelevant here as a strictly metrical approach. The frequently heard dawdling before the first beats readily becomes more affected than expressive. Conversely, rushing in the middle of the measure makes the listener feel rather seasick.

If the basic tempo is too deliberate, the urgency of the piece evaporates into formless revery. This unrestful atmosphere should not bog down in three heavy emphases in each measure, but from each first beat to the next. The uneasy accompaniment in triplets and the sudden surges to the first beats of mm.4, 6 conjure up youthful ardor. Longing expressed in even more theatrical terms continues in the restless slurred groups of mm.6-10, slightly separated without any overt *staccato* effects.

In the second thematic group, beginning in m.10, the emphatic ornaments on the first beats sound like a girl's firm refusals. Is it too whimsical to imagine in mm.14-17 that she tells our young fellow that she likes him, but that he should calm down before their dialogue continues? The very operatic phrase, mm.17-26, surely belongs to the young man, the frequent suspensions being more like groans of yearning than courtly sighs.

Dynamic contrasts and trills should not break the flow of the expansive phrase in mm.14-17. The LH octaves at mm.18-19 are not *legato*, whereas the RH's suspensions certainly are. The inner voices of mm.20 and 62 are *legato*, even if the manuscript has that indication only at m.60. Mozart was not inclined to give parallel lines different articulations. The rests in the melody at m.22-24 are rarely played accurately; the sobbing effect of the short suspensions will be lost if the resolution notes are prolonged due to careless pedaling.

The expositional repeat may be observed, but one could also continue directly to the following section, where Mozart creates marvels with the principal motivic ideas of the exposition: three repeated notes and yearning suspensions. Too many pianists ignore the *forte* indication at m.29, a sign of optimism more than of volume. However, the following slide into D minor is no passing cloud, but a collapse into real despair. The jolting shift to G minor in m.37 is also startling, taking five more measures to regain the relative stability offered by the tonic key in m.43.

During mm.38-39, the vocal flow again splinters into recitative. The initial triplet notes, not the quarter notes, are gently emphasized. This creates a nervous urgency that makes the *fortepiani* in m.40 more logical. During the short *Eingang* of mm.41-42 to the recapitulation, the *diminuendo* of m.42 can be both *legato* in the suspensions and *leggiero* in the other notes.

Mozart repeats one of his favorite tricks in the recapitulation: mm.6-9 do not return until the beginning of the *Codetta*, at m.68. There we sense that youthful storms have, temporarily at least, been stilled.

Each phrase in this very human confession brings an aria or recitative to mind. The pianist's imagination must conjure up a scene in an opera or *Singspiel*.

5 ORNAMENTATION AND SOME NOTATION PROBLEMS IN THE SECOND MOVEMENT, K.279

m.

1   The sixteenth-note upbeat is best played as such, not as a triplet eighth note. Before mm.29, 31, 33, the upbeats have the same urgent character. The upbeat eighth note before m.3 is notated as an eighth note but is best played as a triplet eighth note; there was no other way to notate this in the eighteenth century (though the methodologists of the time were not unanimous on this subject). The *appoggiatura* and compound *appoggiatura* are probably best played before the beat, as the repeated C's assume such an important role throughout the movement.

11   If the wrist is not supple it is difficult to play all three *appoggiatura* notes before the first beat. Malcolm Bilson[4] begins the *appoggiature* on the first beat with the main note falling together with the first accompanying eighth notes, creating a syncopated effect that is both interesting and debatable. I am inclined to agree with Neumann,[5] who maintains that the orna-

ment should be played before the beat. If a slight delay of the triplets results, this suits such quick nervous impulses and their subsequent *diminuendi*.

15   A three-note trill beginning on the principal note is clearest, but a four-note *Pralltriller* beginning on the upper auxiliary is more piquant. In either case there is no termination. There can be no doubt that the LH upbeat to m.16 becomes a triplet.

16   The trill can best begin with the upper auxiliary on the beat.

21   The *appoggiatura* thirds sound on the beat, but their duration is subjective. The resolutions could sound just before the bass octaves, a rhetoric effect preferred by the Badura Skodas.[6] To play the resolutions of the suspensions simultaneously with the first bass octave of each quarter-note beat (the same rhythm as in the RH of the subsequent two measures) may seem logical but arguably has less character. Playing each resolution together with the second bass octave is also conceivable.

25   The compound *appoggiatura* could begin on or before the second quarter-note beat.

26   This trill sounds awkward if begun on the upper auxiliary note.

27   The approach to this trill is different from that in the previous measure. Yet here too beginning on the upper auxiliary note would sound clumsy.

37   Even some recording artists begin the trill with the upper auxiliary F on the beat, but this spoils the diminished seventh dissonance that results from beginning with the principal note. The subsequent sixteenth notes form the trill's termination.

42   Given the *Eingang* function of this transition, the onbeat *appoggiature* could be somewhat prolonged if desired. The notes after the resulting suspensions have more charm if lightly detached.

With such a wealth of notated decorations, improvised ornamentation hardly seems relevant. When repeating the exposition, the descending octave in the RH in m.4 could be filled in with triadic and/or diatonic notes.

THIRD MOVEMENT	*Allegro*
FORM	sonata
APPROXIMATE TEMPO	♩ = M.M. 116
DURATION	4 minutes, with exposition repeated
SUGGESTED LISTENING	Symphony, K.201/186-b iv
	Entführung aus dem Serail: Chorus "Singt dem grossen Bassa Lieder," no.5; Trio "Marsch, marsch, marsch," no.7; Blondchen's aria "Wonne, welche Lust," no.12

6 INTERPRETATION OF THE THIRD MOVEMENT, K.279

This finale may be lighthearted, but it is a masterpiece of motivic cunning. Though the scoring looks like that of a string quartet, the piece has the vigor of a piano concerto or an opera finale. The pianist needs considerable technique and a well developed sense of humor.

Though the piece is not complicated, it is fascinating to examine briefly the structure of the principal themes. The entire movement evolves from two tiny cells heard in the incipit; "Motif A" being the RH leap of a fourth, and "Motif B" a LH diatonic descent of three notes. The beginning of the second thematic group (from the upbeat to m.23) sounds so familiar because the upper voice is obviously based on Motif A and the middle line on an inversion of B. The manuscript has slurs over Motif B at mm.77-78 and subsequent appearances, therefore it can be presumed that this motif is to be played *legato* from the beginning. However, the LH eighth notes in m.3 and 7-10 are not derived from this motif and sound more lively if played *non legato*.

The frequently heard slowing at the cadences in m.10 and 18 causes regrettable loss of momentum. The RH must be able to make very supple horizontal movements to accommodate all the details of articulation in mm.10-21, a difficult passage where the fourth finger should be used as infrequently as possible.

That the upbeat to the second theme, before m.23, is not marked *staccato* does not mean that it is slurred or played longer than the subsequent notes.[7] The middle line in mm.24, 26, 28 is more easily played by the RH. The RH must also play the upper line of the octaves in mm.32-33 if they are to sound *legato*. Because the whole piece is full of quick leaps the player should not sit too rigidly "centered" or too close to the keyboard. The high spirits in this frothy piece build to a climax in the last measures of the exposition. Given the brevity and swiftness of all this activity the exposition is best repeated.

During the development section some redistribution of the material is necessary; the second and third eighth notes of the middle voice at m.58 etc. can be played by the RH, and the LH can play one of two notes of the middle line of m.64 etc. In mm.73-75 the tone should be vigorous but not noisy. Throughout the entire movement the player should give much thought to which stringed or woodwind instruments are evoked in this delightfully orchestral writing.

The gravity of the "false recapitulation" in mm.77-86 is tongue-in-cheek, and the actual recapitulation at m.87 slips in almost unnoticed. It should be played *piano subito*; the element of surprise would be lost if preceded by a *diminuendo*.

The recapitulation is full of youthful exuberance, with unexpected juxtapositions of themes and flirtations with minor mode. The *forte* phrases should sound energetic, not pompous. Especially on modern instruments, the bass octaves in m.139-146 have more character if the upper and lower notes are not equally strong.

As in the opening *Allegro*, the music's immediate charm and energy makes the listener unaware of astonishing structural ingenuity.

7 ORNAMENTATION IN THE THIRD MOVEMENT, K.279

m.

10   A five-note trill is not only difficult in this tempo, but sounds unclear. Because a four-note turn gives the beginning of the sentence a lopsided twist, a three-note trill is recommended.

20   Though some editions suggest turns as alternatives, these would obscure the line, and again three-note trills are preferable.

38   These *appoggiature*, and those in mm.43-44, lose their vivacity when played on the beat.

75   Given the high spirits of this symphonic outburst, playing the *appoggiature* quickly on the beat could create an exuberant, comic effect. However, they are usually played before the beat.

87   The *appoggiatura* should be slipped in just before the first beat.

157 The RH chords are to be arpeggiated as quickly as possible, the uppermost note sounding with the bass octave.

SONATA IN F MAJOR, K.280

OTHER K. LISTING	189 - e
COMPOSITION DATE	probably 1775
TOTAL DURATION	12½ minutes, with expositional repeats in i and iii

FIRST MOVEMENT	*Allegro assai*
FORM	sonata
APPROXIMATE TEMPO	♩ = M.M. 122
DURATION	5 minutes, with exposition repeated
SUGGESTED LISTENING	Symphony, K.162 i
	Symphony, K.199/161-b i
	Exsultate jubilate, K.216, both *Allegro* sections

8 INTERPRETATION OF THE FIRST MOVEMENT, K.280

Why is this sonata so rarely heard, even in conservatories? The eminent musicologist László Somfai commented:

"The F major Sonata is one of the Mozart sonatas to have been rendered dull ... mainly because of bad choices of tempo and character."[8]

There are many unifying elements in what first seems a very diverse sonata. All three movements are in a triple meter (an *Adagio* in 6/8 can also be perceived as being in triple meter) and even share motivic material. The initial themes of all three movements are made of the same ingredients; repeated notes, followed by a leap of an ascending fourth and a diatonic descent of four notes.

The first movement frequently baffles players. Yet the structure is subtle and the "scoring" rich in contrasts. The constantly changing textures of the piece, very like a piano concerto, must be clearly projected. Whereas the opening measures are clearly "orchestral," the flourishes in mm.7-8, 10-11 are definitely pianistic.

The tempo is brisk. From comparison of Mozart's works we can conclude he added the adverb *assai* to denote an increase in the *Allegro* pace, not, as Beethoven did, to moderate it.[9]

In the confident opening statement one could imagine a large group of stringed instruments, even trumpets. On big modern pianos the bass sound should be moderated. The two RH suspensions in mm.5-6 are interrogatory, not soulful. Throughout the jovial transitional theme beginning at m.13, pedaling is possible if the *forte* is not heavy and the pedal changed on each quarter-note beat. This long sequence of descending triads, elaborately disguised by other writhing figures, rambles somewhat and is more convincing at its more economical appearance in the recapitulation. Surely the darker harmonies of mm.18-22 are more a search for harmonic stability than an apocalyptic struggle. The second LH octave of each measure should be considerably softer than the first.

At m.27 the low instruments of our imaginary orchestra play three octaves, with clearly separated pedal strokes. The "soloist" replies with sixteenth notes that must sparkle, the slurs denoting three *leggiero* note-groups, the first note of each slightly emphasized. Neither a generalized *legato* approach nor separation of groups is desirable here. At m.35 another sequence begins, somewhat Haydnesque in its unpredictability. The *forte* measures should be played with a sense of surprise, not mere heaviness. Throughout, one could imagine an alternation of stringed and woodwind instruments. Here too, the slurs indicate slight emphases on the first note of each group rather than separations. Any tension in the RH wrist will make the cheerful *staccati* sound like nails dropping on a wooden floor.

In the new theme beginning at m.43, the writing is more pianistic but there should be no pedaling. It is interesting to note that the slurs here seem to indicate which quarter-note beat is strongest: in mm.43-45 the second, in m.52 the third. The climax at mm.51-56 should be exuberant; unaccountably, many players play delicately here. During the effervescent *Codetta* theme, lasting only three measures, any finger-pedaling of the Alberti bass reduces the momentum. The final chord should be light. Because this exposition is not easy to comprehend on a first hearing, repetition is strongly recommended.

The development section is full of rhetoric, though not of a thundering romantic kind. The constant shifts of harmony and scoring again remind us of Haydn, but the entire section has a specifically Mozartian operatic confidence, quite remarkable for such a young composer. Russell Sherman wrote perceptively on this subject:

"The rhetoric of Haydn goes across the board and, relatively speaking, unites all layers in common purpose for uncommon deed. More precisely, rhetoric and structure coincide. Mozart is far more surreptitious. The friendly exterior veils active strains of disturbance and detour, doubt and defiance." [10]

This section begins with two "oboe" lines in the RH and a "bassoon" line, definitely not pedaled, in the bass. There is an intriguing evocation of mm.3-4 in the lower RH line of m.63-66. All the sixteenth notes of the two-note slurs should be played very lightly, but not *staccato*. The last eight measures of the development stride with extrovert orchestral gestures. There pedaling on every quarter-note beat is welcome. Measures 78-80 form the conclusion to the climax of the entire movement. The droopy *diminuendo* frequently heard here is unsuitable and renders the delightful *piano* indication at m.81 redundant.

In the recapitulation the texture of the transitional theme is changed. Avoid the tendency to play mm.101 and 103 artificially softer than the preceding measures. If the player leans more towards the right side of the keyboard during this sequence, the crossing of hands is not difficult. Throughout the entire movement there is much leaping from one register to another. The player's upper body must remain utterly free to make these transitions without physical jerkiness.

The writing in mm.117-122 gives many players trouble. Haste in the middle of each measure or dawdling before the first beats should be avoided.

The sequences in this movement can lose their effect if the player does not have the ability to present each motif as if it were a surprise and not a mathematical certainty.

9 ORNAMENTATION IN THE FIRST MOVEMENT, K.280

m.

1   The initial arpeggiation is played as briskly as possible, with pedaling, the uppermost note sounding with the bass octave.

2   In this tempo, the trill can only be a three-note *Schneller* squeezed between C and A. On a heavy modern instrument even this may sound cumbersome, and a quick grace note C is a suitable alternative.

42 After the resolution of the onbeat slightly accented *appoggiatura*, the two subsequent sixteenth notes can be slightly detached. As the trill is on the leading-note, the principal note sounds on the beat, but the upper auxiliary note could be played as a quick upbeat.

43 The onbeat *appoggiatura* is not accented.

47 The compound *appoggiatura* begins on the second quarter-note beat and the trill should have a termination.

48   Exceptionally, the *arpeggio* must begin on the beat. Otherwise
      the first beat will be slightly delayed, an unnatural effect. The
      final D of m.47 should be held until the uppermost note of the
      arpeggiated chord sounds.
54   This trill is like that in m.42.
56   The final chord may be too conspicuous if arpeggiated.
69   The dramatic *arpeggi* beginning in this measure sound mud-
      dled if ending on the first beat. But I do not agree with Siegbert
      Rampe that this also applies to the *arpeggi* in mm.1 and 10. [11]

SECOND MOVEMENT	*Adagio*
FORM	sonata
APPROXIMATE TEMPO	♪ = M.M. 92-94
DURATION	4 minutes, with no repeats
SUGGESTED LISTENING	String Quartet, K.168 ii
	String Quartet, K.156 ii
	Piano Concerto, K.488 ii
	Das Lied der Trennung, K.519

10 INTERPRETATION OF THE SECOND MOVEMENT, K.280

It is difficult to imagine a starker contrast to the opening movement than this tragic statement, another of Mozart's timeless compositions, blending elements of the baroque, classical and romantic periods. Though there are frequent parallels made to the slow movement
of Haydn's F major Sonata, Hob.XVI:23, this movement has a sobriety that also reminds us of the serious sonatas by Domenico Scarlatti
or Antonio Soler. Mozart rarely wrote in this key and it is interesting
to note that especially in his early operas, F minor denoted grief for a
deceased loved one.
      Surely the beginning sounds like a dramatic soprano proclaiming
her sorrow. The unusually placed dynamic markings should not be
softened by noticeable *diminuendi* in the second half of mm.2,4,6.
Crescendi in the second half of mm.3,5 should also be avoided. The
forte at the end of m.7 suggests fatalistic heaviness more than volume.
It is fascinating to note that in this despondent theme the only notes
which are marked *legato* are in the second half of the first measure.
Therefore all the eighth notes and even perhaps the sixteenth notes in
this theme can be played *non legato*, but pedaled, of course, and

phrased with a *legato* sense of line. Such a pedaled, *non-legato* touch expresses the stark emotions much more strongly than a generalized romantic *legato*.

Mozart condenses the sonata form by omitting a transitional theme. In the recitative-like sentence beginning in m.9, it is easy to imagine words to these two- and three-note gasps: "How, oh how, can this be? My life, my hope, has perished." The LH should finger-pedal the lower notes but if the pianist is not alert, the thumb too will automatically play its notes *tenuto*, creating an impression more sticky than expressive. Throughout this theme, the pedal must be changed on each eighth-note beat; the gasping rests are too often obliterated by careless pedaling or prolongation of the preceding eighth notes. Slurred and unslurred pairs of notes must be clearly differentiated. In mm.17-18 the second RH note of each pair must be very soft. The RH sound at the climax of mm.19-20 should not be too strong. In the sober Gluckian *Codetta* (mm.21-24) the pedal can be changed with each harmony, but only the slurred notes are played *legato*.

The development section is searing in its desolation, like someone keening with grief, high up in some awful rocky place. The slowly writhing theme at m.29 is startling because it is in B-flat minor, a key hardly ever heard in Mozart's music. The motivic idea is not new, however, but has already been suggested in the agonized thirds of mm.4-7. Avoid any hysterical *rubato* or wilful dynamic changes; exhaustion and futility are more evident here than dramatic strife.

Repetition of the development and recapitulation sections certainly does not seem relevant. In this movement, it is debatable if even the expositional repeat should observed.

11 ORNAMENTATION IN THE SECOND MOVEMENT, K.280

m.

1   The ornament must begin on the principal note. Given the line, there should be no termination. On a modern instrument a five-note trill is sufficient, whereas on a light instrument seven notes can sound beautiful.

19   This onbeat *appoggiatura* is very soulful, with the resolution sounding after the eighth LH sixteenth note.

20   The onbeat *appoggiatura* is like that in m.19. The trill could begin with either the upper or lower auxiliary.

28   The *arpeggio* can be played quickly or broadly, but it is *tenuto* and the uppermost note sounds with the bass.

45   The dissonances of the sobbing *appoggiature* here and in m.49
      sound on the fourth eighth-note beats, the subsequent resolu-
      tion notes whispered.
54   The *appoggiatura* is like that in m.19. It would be harmonically
      incorrect to begin the startling trill on the upper auxiliary. The
      trill should not be too rapid and is probably more expressive
      without a termination.
56   This type of compound *appoggiatura* before the trill is an un-
      usual ornament. The appoggiatura could sound with the LH on
      the second main beat, or there could be an agogic moment of
      hesitation, with the trill beginning on the delayed second beat."

The starkness of this movement certainly does not lend itself to
further ornamentation.

THIRD MOVEMENT	*Presto*
FORM	sonata
APPROXIMATE TEMPO	♩. = M.M. 88
DURATION	3½ minutes, with exposition repeated
SUGGESTED LISTENING	Violin Concerto, K.207 iii
	Symphony, K.200 iv
	Symphony, K.182/173-d-a iii
	Piano Concerto, K.175 iii

12 INTERPRETATION OF THE THIRD MOVEMENT, K.280

Musically this is a straightforward romp, and as in most pianistic
romps, considerable technical resources are required. This is one of
the rare instances in any of the piano sonatas when Mozart indicated
Presto, so the player must throw caution to the winds. Inexplicably,
many recording artists assume a cautious pace in this movement.
     The dynamic contrasts of this joyful piece sound wittier on a forte-
piano than on most modern instruments. Because of the speed and
lightness, pedaling is not relevant, though it could perhaps be used to
bind the repeated notes of the second theme, beginning in m.38, and
to give body to the *forte* chords at mm.102-105.
     As noted at the beginning of section 8 of this chapter, the opening
themes of the preceding movements are evoked here in a bucolic way.
In the first and transitional themes we can imagine dialogues between

woodwinds and stringed instruments. Throughout the movement, humor and vivacity are immediately lost if any rests are smothered by careless pedaling or note values. Although the "first violin" line is slurred at m.132 in the recapitulation, surely in mm.25-28 and 132-135 the slurs do not imply *legato* touch, but that the first RH tone of each measure is the strongest. The suspension in mm.34-35 is much easier if played with the RH. The entire theme flies past in four-measure units.

In the second theme the pace is more in two-measure units. The RH note repetitions, as in m.38, are not difficult as long as the thumb and wrist remain relaxed. The buoyancy of the writing would be spoiled by any pedaling or finger-pedaling. The dynamic inflections during mm.59-64 should not be rough. In mm.66-71, surely there is no difference in touch between RH and LH. First-beat accents here sound ridiculous, not amusing.

In the development section, the dynamic contrasts are more theatrical but should still be conceived in terms of orchestration. Obviously broken octaves in the bass will automatically sound stronger than in a higher register. On a modern instrument, the sound can easily become too thick at these moments. Many students have trouble with LH broken octaves; the *Trio*, in the third movement of Beethoven's Sonata Opus 28, is another notorious case. The player should avoid any tension in the middle fingers and minimalize jerky movements between white and black keys.

Note that the upper RH line in mm.82-85 derives from mm.2-5. If this is not played with a full tone, it will be submerged by the bass octaves. Swirling energy marks the climax of mm.102-105. Again the player is reminded that all the abrupt shifts of register will sound more organic if his back is free and if he avoids sitting too close to the keyboard. Humor and charm have little to do with a Buddha-like manner of sitting at the piano.

13 ORNAMENTATION IN THE THIRD MOVEMENT, K.280

m.

2   Neumann[12] too maintains that the *appoggiature* must be played before the beat, as this clearly emphasizes the motivic line of the eighth notes.

39   Given the tempo, it is difficult to begin the slide before the first beat, but beginning it on the beat makes for a lopsided effect. As noted above, if the thumb can play the preceding notes and

49   the first note of the slide without tensing, the prebeat rendition
     sounds clear.
49   A three-note *Schneller* beginning on the beat suffices. On a
     light-toned instrument a five-note turn is possible.
102 Best begun on the beat, this *arpeggio* is to increase the empha-
     sis of this chord. Obviously it must be extremely quick. For
     more tone, pedal strokes are possible, but the rests must not be
     erased by careless footwork.

SONATA IN B-FLAT MAJOR, K.281

OTHER K. LISTING	189-f
COMPOSITION DATE	early 1775
TOTAL DURATION	13 minutes (with expositional repeat in i and all repeats in iii)

FIRST MOVEMENT	*Allegro*
FORM	sonata
APPROXIMATE TEMPO	♩ = M.M. 63
DURATION	5 minutes (with expositional repeat)
SUGGESTED LISTENING	Symphony, K.182/173-d-a i
	String Quintet, K.174 i
	La finta giardiniera: Podestà's aria "Mie Padrone," no.25

14 INTERPRETATION OF THE FIRST MOVEMENT, K.281

There is a certain blend of styles in this sonata that suggests the
composer's youth. Einstein[13] commented that "the first two movements seem more like Haydn than Haydn himself." Mozart played
this sonata and the D major, K.284, for the famous pianist Ignaz von
Beecke in 1777.[14] The older artist, an exponent of the "*galant* style"
praised both pieces.

As in the previous sonatas there is much pianistic writing, but the
textures here are less extrovert than in K.279 or K.280. Of all Mozart's piano sonatas, this is perhaps the least suitable on modern
instruments; especially the first movement becomes unwieldy or
artificial on large, modern pianos, whereas its wit is easier to achieve
on a fortepiano. The contrast of registers, so effective in all the move-

ments of this sonata, is diminished on modern instruments. The frothy humor of the *Rondeau* is also difficult to portray on a big modern instrument.

In this fine, string quartet-like piece, the pianist must be careful to avoid a monotonous weighting of first beats. Slurs over sixteenth and thirty-second notes here indicate emphasis on the initial note of each group more than *legato* binding. In mm.9,11, for example, the slurs suggest *diminuendi*, not a *legato* touch. In m.12 we realize the perils of a hasty tempo. The atmosphere is surely more festive than hectic. All the rests should be accurately observed; many players, often distracted by the demanding traffic in this movement, too often shorten longer notes. Such miscalculations create an unwelcome breathlessness.

As in the two previous sonatas, *staccati*, like those in mm.12-16 are undeniably difficult on a modern instrument, but if the wrist remains free and the fingers stay close to the keys, these passages can sound as joyous as they should.

The second theme, beginning in m.17, should smile and have no sense of haste. During the subsequent sequence of thirty-second notes, the inherent difficulties will be minimalized if the pianist avoids rushing. In the LH passages of mm.23, 25, the fourth finger should be used as infrequently as possible. The climax at mm.34-38 is more playful than loud. Pedaling should be avoided in the brief, joking *Codetta*; indeed, pedaling is unnecessary throughout the entire exposition.

The development begins with rather anxious figurations that fade at m.45 into the initial motif, now in F major. The subsequent lurch to G minor is most unexpected in this genteel atmosphere. Though the six *forte* measures should be played *non legato*, unpedaled, and with very active fingers, there can be considerable variation of tone during this theatrical eruption. After one measure of writhing uncertainty the defiant G minor returns. In mm.57,59 the RH should suggest two lines; if the higher notes are considerably softer than the lower, these moments are less confusing for the ear. The climax reached at mm.63-66 is a joyous affirmation of the major mode.

After such a turbulent development it is not too surprising that the recapitulation is virtually the same as the exposition. It is doubtful that the second repetition is justified. Throughout the movement the player must not seek theatricality in the dynamic contrasts. Drama is found only in the development section.

15 ORNAMENTATION IN THE FIRST MOVEMENT, K.281

m.

1   A trill at the opening of a piece virtually always begins on the principal note. The two subsequent notated thirty-second notes form the termination; therefore there is no lower auxiliary note.

3   Each arpeggiated chord should be played very briskly, the uppermost note sounding simultaneously with the bass.

4   The onbeat *appoggiatura* is energetic, probably somewhat shorter than a sixteenth note.

7   These *appoggiature* become accented thirty-second notes on the last eighth-note beats.

23   One frequently hears these trills begun on the upper auxiliary. Though that is easier to play, Mozart presumably wanted the vigorous repetition of the upbeat note and the first note of the trill (as in the opening of the C minor Sonata, K.457). In any case, beginning with the upper auxiliary would result in octave formation with the bass. A three-note trill plus the indicated termination is sufficiently lively.

31   Because of the abrupt drop in tone, a slight *caesura* is caused by this ornament, the uppermost note of the arpeggio sounding with the first bass note.

33   The suspension resulting from the first onbeat *appoggiatura* can be slightly detached from the subsequent two notes. The second *appoggiatura* is often played too quickly. It sounds charming and clearer played as an approximate dotted sixteenth note.

41   The placing of the compound *appoggiatura* is a subjective matter. Perhaps it is has a more nervous character if begun on the beat.

42   These onbeat trills become three-note *Schneller*. Neumann[15] suggests that the upper auxiliary could precede each trill as a grace note, but this surely complicates the line.

58   In a single measure we get a fascinating example of how subjective trills can be. Given the bass F-sharps, the first trill would sound bizarre if begun on F. It is best begun on the principal note, with the subsequent thirty-second notes forming the termination. The second trill is quite different and has more character if begun on the upper auxiliary. It has the usual termination.

63   The bass *arpeggio* is quick, the highest note on the beat.

SECOND MOVEMENT	*Andante amoroso*
FORM	sonata
APPROXIMATE TEMPO	♪ = M.M. 103
DURATION	3 minutes (no repeats)
SUGGESTED LISTENING	Piano Concerto, K.238 ii

SUGGESTED LISTENING: *La finta giardiniera*: Sandrina's aria "Noi donne poverine,, no.4, Ramiro's aria "Dolce d'amor" no.18

16 INTERPRETATION OF THE SECOND MOVEMENT, K.281

The beginning of the piece seems to emerge from a dream state, the first sixteen measures more an atmosphere than a clear statement. Dreamlike or not, throughout this very human movement, the UC pedal on modern instruments is best left untouched if an effect of over refinement is to be avoided. Puritans will not be the most convincing interpreters of this sensual piece; some old editions even amended the *amoroso* indication to *espressivo*!

In the first measure the LH octave has an upbeat function even if it is on the first beat. The responding thirds can be pedaled and sound more fluent when the LH takes the lower line. A slur extending over three measures was unusual in Mozart's oeuvre from this period; it evokes two voices or violins, answered in m.3 by the lower stringed instruments. This arching phrase should sound as if it is played in one breath, coming to rest only at the first beat of m.8. In mm.8-9 we hear two yearning sighs and in mm.10-11 two regretful diatonic figures. These are swept away by a somewhat perfunctory return to the tonic key, a brusque call to order.

There is no transitional theme. In the second thematic group, beginning at m.16, there seems to be a dialogue, a youth declaring his love and a girl's feeble protests against his attentions. The pedal must be changed on each eighth-note beat and the lowest bass notes finger-pedaled. The melody notes on the first beats of mm.21,23 should be light. At mm.24-25 the polyrhythmic unease of C minor predicts danger, but this is rapidly dispelled in a quiet cadence.

A new theme is announced by LH octaves at m.27. These should sound positive, not heavy. On a modern instrument, the lower notes of the octaves are best played very lightly. Some editions place wedges on the RH eighth notes in the last beats of m.29,31 and 32. These tones are not to be accented, but clearly separated from the surrounding notes. The RH sixteenth notes of mm.33, 37 are usually played *legato*, which diminishes the heartrending effect of nervous longing. A pedaled *non legato* touch is preferable. The *forti* indicated in mm.39 and 41 are quite dramatic (our imaginary young man is becoming quite distraught?) and are stronger than the *forti* of the affirmative cadential figure in mm.12-14, 43-45.

The development section is so brief that it seems advisable not to repeat the exposition. The prelude-like opening of the piece would arguably be dulled by repetition and, given the lack of harmonic evolution in the development, playing all sections only once seems logical. The tentative RH triplets in m.47 are under one slur, whereas the LH triplets of the following measure are under three slurs, indicating a more agitated emphasis of each beat. The numerous *forti* suggest here violinistic warmth of tone, not heavy volume. The entire section is a disguised pedalpoint on the dominant.

That both hands share the descending lines of mm.59-61 is even more desirable than in the corresponding measures of the exposition. The NMA[16] has an interesting suggestion for m.68; the first four RH sixteenth notes are *non legato*, and the C is tied over until m.69's B-flat sounds. Another textual puzzle is the last bass note of m.95, usually printed as F, but in the manuscript is E-flat.[17] The scene ends peacefully; for our imaginary lovers, things seem to have turned out fine.

This movement is one of the least complicated Mozart wrote for solo piano. It holds few mysteries, although the opening can be puzzling for younger students. Players with a more impulsive character should avoid romantic *rubato* in the bass line; persistent lingering before first beats sounds affected. Players of an overly intellectual cast, however, may be rather ill at ease here; Glenn Gould produced some of his most perverse, textually indefensible playing in a recording of this movement.[18]

17 ORNAMENTATION IN THE SECOND MOVEMENT, K.281

m.

7   The upper auxiliary could be played as an upbeat to the trill, but, given the close part-writing here, beginning the trill with the auxiliary on the beat sounds muddled. The "second violin's" F is best played by the LH.

10 In the arpeggiated chords the uppermost notes sound on the beat.

17 It is a very subjective matter if these *appoggiature* are before or

on the beat. They seem somewhat sarcastic if played on the beat. Neumann[19] too prefers a prebeat rendition.

24   In this more dramatic context, the *appoggiature* are best played on the beat.

33   The onbeat *appoggiatura* is accented and lasts somewhat longer than a sixteenth note.

34   The trill is best begun on the principal note, which should not be accented. Beginning on the auxiliary note would form an unattractive fifth with the bass.

48   This slurred trill must begin on the principal note. Five notes and a termination seem suitable at this ecstatic moment.

THIRD MOVEMENT	*Rondeau: Allegro*
FORM	rondo
APPROXIMATE TEMPO	♩= M.M. 84
DURATION	5 minutes, with repeats
SUGGESTED LISTENING	*La finta giardiniera*: both finales
	Piano Concerto, K.238 iii

18 INTERPRETATION OF THE THIRD MOVEMENT, K.281

Einstein redeemed his questionable remark about the first two movements being "more like Haydn than Haydn himself" by continuing:

"the finale ... is Mozart at his most characteristic and individual. If the date of this rondo, with its air of a modest concerto and its melodic grace, were not so definitely fixed, we should certainly place it ten years later in the Vienna Period." [20]

The form of this sonata finale is delightfully ambiguous. Sonata elements melt into the French *rondeau* style, with its succession of contrasted couplets, of Couperin and Rameau. The theme in mm.28-43, usually regarded as the first episode, takes on the significance of a second theme in sonata form, especially when it is recapitulated in the tonic at mm.124-140. The initial theme adds to the playful unpredictability by not always returning in its entirety; some of its motifs appear later at unexpected moments. The young composer had already become a master of this form:

"Mozart, in the String Quartet K.157 (1772-73), composed the first known sonata-rondo; during the remainder of his career he refined the form, experimenting with a wide range of structural possibilities."[21]

Later Beethoven often chose this form, but his use of it was more conventional than Mozart's.[22]

A concerto-like atmosphere is evoked by the brilliance of the piano writing, by the *Eingang* in m.43 and the rest in m.70 where another *Eingang* would be welcome. But the cheerful bustle of this movement is also close to the spirit of a comic opera.

The theme has an obvious dancelike character. The lightness of the graceful tune is ruined by pedaling or by leaden accentuation of strong beats. Few pianists notice that the second quarter-note beats in the first two measures are not slurred and that these eighth notes have much more character when played lightly *non legato*.

Levity of touch and accurate stressing are supremely important throughout this movement. During mm.8-16, the second beat is consistently stronger than the first and the unslurred bass notes of mm.8-16, 22-25 are best played *non legato*. The cheerful cadential flourish in mm.16-17 recurs twice later, creating uncertainty at mm.87-89 and becoming a very frivolous *Coda* beginning in m.158.

The unbridled humor of mm.18-19 brings a figure like Falstaff to mind; first we hear a belly laugh, then two giggles! In m.28, the line will be clearer if each melodic note is slightly separated, with the bass, especially on modern instruments, played very lightly. During mm.22-33, the themes played by both hands frequently change register. On a fortepiano this is amusing, but the player of a modern instrument will have to work harder to project similar effects. The *fortepiani* at mm.39-42 should be interpreted literally, the first note of each trill vigorously accented, followed by a *piano subito* (a *diminuendo* sounds peculiarly romantic here). Such an accent is more humorous than dramatic, the climax of the section having already been reached in mm.37-38.

In the first episode mm.52-70, there is an interplay of wind instruments, which anticipates the slow movement of the C minor Concerto, K.491. The articulation and dynamics are so clearly indicated, there are no ambiguities. Though a slightly slower tempo could be assumed, romantic *rubato* would be disturbing. Decoration of the *fermata* in m.65 seems highly inappropriate, but at m.70, an *Eingang* seems justified even if there is no *fermata* indicated there.

The central "C" section, the second episode of mm.90-113, begins

with the most gentle measures of the movement, but these must not
sound cloying. The *fortepiani* in mm.91,93 should not be exaggerated
and the *forte* of the subsequent measures is not as vigorous as in
mm.102, 104-112. Theatrical unrest returns in m.102, where the
slurred chordal movement can be played with the pedal changed on
each quarter-note beat. The unslurred *arpeggi* in mm.109-112 should
not be pedaled. The climax of this extended movement is suitably
generous in scale, extending from m.105 to m.112.

When the initial theme returns in the bass at m.114 there are no
slurs over the first two quarter notes, but naturally, these should be
played as at the beginning. The long trills must not sound fuller than
the theme.

The entire finale exudes a tremendous *joie de vivre* and is such a
strong piece that it has much impact even when played on its own.
This is arguably the richest single movement to be found in the first
five sonatas.

19 ORNAMENTATION IN THE THIRD MOVEMENT, K.281

m.

1   The onbeat *appoggiature* are usually played as eighth notes.
The theme's vivacity is damaged if the eighth notes in the second quarter-note beat are slurred.

7   The compound *appoggiatura* is best begun on the beat. The
trill should be rapid and have a termination.

17   Neumann[23] is of the opinion that the *appoggiature* should be
played before the beat. Playing them on the beat creates a
burping effect.

18   At the opening of a theme a trill should begin with the principal
note, here creating a comical effect of "primitive" octave formation with the bass.

28   The RH's A becomes a triplet eighth note. The subsequent *appoggiatura* is played on the beat, but its duration is a very subjective matter.

29   Suiting the cheerful context, this slide *(Schleifer)* is best played
ending on the beat.

30   The first beat ornament is unclear in the manuscript. Perhaps a
three-note trill or a mordent is preferable to the usually heard
turn.

34   These onbeat trills become three-note *Schneller.*

39   These trills must begin on the principal note, causing theatrical
dissonance with the bass.[24]

59   Beginning on the principal note, this rhetorical trill is arguably more effective with five notes, the last somewhat longer than the rest, and no termination.

65   This *arpeggio* should be startling but not thunderous. Certainly the subsequent rest, not this chord, is to be prolonged, but in some editions this is not clearly notated.

97   Given the line, this trill begins with the principal note. A five-note trill without a termination (as in m.59) has more energy than a five-note turn.

114   The trill begins on the principal note and continues, without a termination, until the first beat of m.118.

119   This trill must cease, without a termination, on the fourth quarter-note beat of m.122. Players of modern instruments must take care that these trills do not become noisy or mechanical.

Additional ornamentation seems irrelevant in most of this well notated movement. In his recording,[25] Malcolm Bilson improvises very inspired ornaments at mm.52-70. In the NMA[26] an *Eingang* is suggested at mm.70-71.

V

SONATAS IN E-FLAT, K.282, AND G, K.283

SONATA IN E-FLAT, K.282

OTHER K. LISTING   K.189-g
COMPOSITION DATE   probably early 1775
TOTAL DURATION   14 minutes (with most repeats)

1 A HYBRID COMPOSITION; E-FLAT MAJOR IN MOZART'S EARLIER WORKS; UNIFYING ELEMENTS IN K.282

Among the Munich sonatas one of the most appealing is K.282, a short masterpiece, which ranges from perplexing ambiguity to ribald humor. The E-flat Sonata is a hybrid, combining elements of the older Italian sonata style, which begins with a slow movement, and the more "modern" Viennese style of the last two movements. The second movement, given the old-fashioned title *Minuets One and Two* (rather than *Minuet and Trio*), may seem innocuous, but it is more than merely gracious. The finale has been often seen as Haydnesque and therefore somehow less "worthy." Einstein seems to be condescending about the entire sonata:

> "Not only is the finale quite Haydnish, but the irregularity and the subjectivity shown in the sequence of the movements reflect Haydn's influence. Mozart is not entirely himself; he needs to find himself again." [1]

Though various stylistic influences are evident in K.282, every measure of the piece is indisputably Mozartian. Far from being the most derivative of the Munich sonatas, the E-flat is arguably the most original.

Many players are puzzled by the first movement. It may seem to lack emotional consistency; solemn phrases suitable in a mass are heard next to jaunty dancelike tunes. As the movement is conspicuously vocal in style it is relevant to consider how Mozart employed E-flat in his early operas; in *Mitridate* (the Aspasia-Sifare duet), and

Lucio Silla (in two of Giunia's arias and Cecilio's "Ah se a morir") the dead are invoked. In *La finta giardiniera*, dating from the same period as this sonata, the most serious ensemble, the septet ending the second act, is also in E-flat. In the same opera the key is also associated with Contino Belfiore; two of his arias (nos.6 and 19) are in E-flat and express the perils of love. Nicholas Till wrote eloquently about Belfiore, a caricature:

> "... illustrating all that is wrong in those for whom social display has overtaken the expression of true feelings ... Later in the opera Belfiore ... goes mad ... (believing) himself to be in a classical dreamland constructed entirely of the inflatedly poetic language of *opera seria*. Social artifice is exposed as its own sort of madness, destroying the personal integrity of the individual as cruelly as insanity." [2]

In his first aria Belfiore's music is soulful but somewhat formal, the colors expressing both sincere and assumed emotions. Several melodic figures that appear in the *Adagio* of K.282 can be heard in this aria. Is it not possible that the first movement of K.282 also inhabits that nebulous world where feelings are not always what they seem?

There is a veritable web of melodic and rhythmic motifs uniting this sonata. Here are some of the more conspicuous threads:

1. The rhythm of the *Adagio*'s initial three notes is recurrent in *Minuet One*, either as in mm.10-12, or, modified, as in the beginning of the *Minuet*.
2. The opening phrase of the second *Minuet* is an ornamented version of the *Adagio*'s initial.
3. The melodic motif of mm.4-5 in the *Adagio* recurs in a different guise in the *Allegro* (mm.16-17, etc.).
4. The bass line of mm.1-4 in the *Adagio*, descending an octave, is reversed later. Variants of this motif also recur at mm.5-7, 16-20,29-31 of the second *Minuet*, and there are several running passages ranging over an octave in the *Allegro*.
5. The development section variant of the *Adagio*'s opening (m.16) with its conspicuous octave leap becomes the opening motif in the *Allegro*'s first theme.
6. There is considerable similarity in the chromatic outline of the development sections of *Minuet I* (mm.12-14) and the *Allegro* (mm.48-55).

Superficially this sonata may seem more like a suite, but instead of being the most disjunct of the Munich Sonatas, K.282 is perhaps the most unified.

FIRST MOVEMENT	*Adagio*
FORM	sonata or binary
APPROXIMATE TEMPO	$\flat$ = M.M. 82
DURATION	6½ minutes, with both repeats
SUGGESTED LISTENING	all the music mentioned above in section 1 of this chapter, particularly Belfiore's aria (no.4) from *La finta giardiniera*
	String Quintet, K.174 ii
	String Quartet, K.160/159-a ii

2 INTERPRETATION OF THE FIRST MOVEMENT, K.282

This *Adagio*'s emotional ambiguity, discussed in section 1 of this chapter, makes it unsuitable material for any player who lacks feeling for rhetorical detail. Devotional or loving, deeply serious or slightly tongue-in-cheek, the opening phrase does not support a ponderous *Largo* tread or an overly gracious *Andante* flow. Almost as if he too were surprised by this fascinating inspiration, Mozart did not repeat this phrase. Only the opening is suggested in the first beats of the development, and there is a variant beginning at m.34 of the *Coda*.

The line of the initial sentence is very operatic, the words for an aria or a recitative easy to imagine. In the first quarter-note beats of mm.1-2, the melodic C and the subsequent B-flat are not slurred. Detaching these notes slightly makes the *legato* slurs in the rest of the theme even more affecting. Similarly, the fingers should not join the two-note suspensions in the first three measures to the subsequent notes. All these finesses may have discreet dabs of pedaling if desired, but an unvaried *legato* approach to this richly inflected phrase would be stultifying. The intensity of the line is seriously undermined if all the suspensions are given the same weight.

In the following sentence we seem to hear a soprano, expressing yearning in *forte* and apprehension in *piano*. The highly expressive notation, as given in the best editions, should be observed, the hands sometimes playing at considerably different levels of volume. Anticipating these strong emotional shifts with *crescendi* and *diminuendi* reduces a classical severity to mere lyricism. During mm.4-7 the pedal can be changed with every eighth-note beat and the lowest bass notes finger-pedaled. In the eerie cadence at m.8, the distribution of *legato* tone among the four voices is easier if the two E's in the "second violin part" are played by the LH thumb. A large *ritenuto* sounds soporific but the final rest could be somewhat prolonged.

The RH theme of mm.9-11 can sound startlingly banal unless the player can identify with an immediate and total change of character. As if to underline the element of surprise here, Mozart clearly marked the first bass note of m.9 *forte*. As in Belfiore's arias from *La finta giardiniera* (see previous section), serious emotions are mixed with gentle parody. The vocal or violinistic phrasing is not complicated if the player remembers that generally the first note under a slur is the strongest of that group. Obviously in this graceful context the RH wedged descents of a third imply gentle separation of the notes, not accents. Pedaling is absolutely unnecessary throughout the entire theme, though some finger-pedaling of the bass in mm.11-12 may be welcome.

At the broader phrase beginning in the second beat of m.11 the warmth of the beginning blends with the light tone of the previous two measures. The articulation of the RH is somewhat unclear. The manuscript's notation of this phrase and the parallel passage in the recapitulation is not consistent; the thirty-second-note patterns of a descending third in mm.11-12 have two slurs in the exposition but only one in the recapitulation. It is not being fussy to ponder this detail, as the two effects are considerably different. The version stated in the exposition seems nervous and filled with longing, the first note of each slurred group gently stressed. A slur over four thirty-second notes seems less expressive and readily brings yodeling to mind. The pianist must take care to avoid hyperactive hand movements here, which can create a choppy effect. Similarly the long slur extending from the beginning of m.13 to the third beat B-flat is lacking at the parallel moment of the recapitulation, where only the first four thirty-second notes are slurred. Here the recapitulation version is perhaps more lively and less generalized.

The dynamic notation of mm.13-15 can be regarded as indications of activity and relaxation. A considerable *diminuendo* in m.15 is inappropriate as there should be a surge of energy before the expositional repeat or beginning of the development section.

The theatrical diminished seventh harmony of m.16 is chilling, reminding us of the accompanied recitative to Belfiore's "Ah non partir..." mentioned above. Because there are so few notes, the player must make conscious decisions and be able to project them clearly; for example, does the *crescendo* in m.17 begin with the LH in the second quarter-note beat or with the RH's subsequent A-flat? Throughout the entire section there are dynamic contrasts indicated in each measure, swinging from wrenching pain to gentle longing.

The recapitulation maintains this highly emotional intensity. Omitting the entire initial phrase, Mozart lurches in m.22 to an intense variant of mm.4-8. To balance these surprises, the second theme returns virtually unchanged. Slowing down and whispering at the cadence in m.33 should be avoided. Even if the player chooses to proceed to the *Coda* at this moment, some energy in the tone must remain until the relaxation of the two final measures.

Interpretation of the repeats in this movement is a very subjective matter. After much experimentation during concerts and listening to other performances, I have become convinced that both repetitions should be made.[3]

3 WRITTEN AND IMPROVISED ORNAMENTATION IN THE FIRST MOVEMENT, K.282

m.

2   This onbeat *appoggiatura* is even more expressive if slightly prolonged. The two sixteenth notes after the resulting suspension are not *legato*.

3   Conceivably the trill could be played only in the expositional repeat. If the upper auxiliary sounds at the beginning of the trill, it is best played as a fairly slow grace note, not on the beat.

4   The slide *(Schleifer)* is an energetic impulse, not a melancholy one, and therefore ends on the beat.

5   Because the principal note functions as a suspension, it would be incorrect to begin the trill with the upper auxiliary.

6   Because of its mournful expression, the compound *appoggiatura* is best begun on the beat.

13   The *appoggiature* are probably best played on the sixteenth-note beats but unlike the same written-out pattern in m.15, the upper line is more prominent here (see Neumann[4]) and should be emphasized.

14   This trill can begin with the upper auxiliary.

15   The little *arpeggio* should definitely end on the second quarter-note beat.

17   At such a subjective moment one cannot be dogmatic about the placing of the *appoggiature*. They should, in any case, not have the same timing. Here the rigid concept that an *appoggiatura* always takes half the value of the principal note would be especially dull.

21   The trill must begin on the dissonant principal note and has a termination.

22   If played on the beat, the *appoggiatura* would sound lopsided.

35   This *appoggiatura* is something of a *cause célèbre*. Viewed as a vocal inflection it would normally fall on the beat. But this creates an unpleasant open fifth with the bass octave, whereas the E-flat itself forms an expressive *appoggiatura* with the bass. Therefore the *appoggiatura* is best played very lightly before the beat, without the fingers joining it to the previous E-flat.

36   The onbeat *appoggiatura* is more poignant if it becomes somewhat longer than a sixteenth note.

IMPROVISED ORNAMENTATION

It is unlikely Mozart would have played repeats in such a vocal piece without improvising some ornaments, but literal repetition of his text is better than adding any distracting or unnatural frills. A few possible added ornaments are listed below, but the reader must remember that these apply only to the repetitions of the measure in question:

m.

2   A turn before the RH F.

3   A diatonic descent from the RH E-flat to B-flat. The notated trill is perhaps more effective if played only in the repeat.

10   Some diatonic thirty-second notes in the RH third quarter-note beat and in the first quarter-note beat of the following measure are conceivable.

16   The RH's dramatic octave descent from the high B-flat can be emphasized in various ways. Even a mere scale can sound rhetorical here if shaped with suitable intensity.

21   The last three quarter-note beats could be played as a "free" *Eingang*, with some additional decoration in the second quarter-note beat.

24   The RH upbeat notes to the third quarter-note beat, and the first and third quarter-note beats of the following measure, could be enhanced by ornamentation (turns, repetitions, slides, or

changing-note flourishes) but if each ornament is not different, the changes seem more academic than spontaneous.

26   A slow trill between the last two melody notes is conceivable.

28   In the RH the third quarter-note beat and the first of the following measure could be decorated but not in the same manner as in parallel mm.10-11.

The subject of added ornamentation remains highly personal in this fascinating movement. On weaker toned instruments or in halls with dry acoustics, it would be possible to play even more ornaments than those mentioned above. Spontaneity is essential; if any "improvised" ornaments do not sound as such, their effect is lost, and the player can best omit them.

SECOND MOVEMENT	*Minuets One and Two*
FORM	ternary
APPROXIMATE TEMPO	♩ = M.M. 126 (One), 120 (Two)
DURATION	4¼ minutes, with most repeats
SUGGESTED LISTENING	Symphony, K.201/186-a iii
	Symphony, K.202/186-b iii
	String Quartet, K.168 iii

4 INTERPRETATION OF THE SECOND MOVEMENT, K.282

After the *Adagio*'s curious blend of the spiritual conflict and operatic expression we find ourselves here in a playful and sensual atmosphere. Any darkness is fleeting. If the first movement suggested vocal or violin lines with orchestral accompaniment, the second is definitely conceived in the textures of a string quartet or a small ensemble of wind instruments. Anyone attempting this piece must be very aware of this, for pianistic figurations are utterly lacking. The minuet section of Chapter III is also essential reading for any player attempting this piece.

The "A" section of this triptych alternates with a jaunty *Ländler*-like *Trio*, the "B" section, titled "*Minuet Two*." In *Minuet One*, the activity is extrovert and public, whereas *Minuet Two* is on a more intimate scale. Though *Minuet One* could be marginally faster than the tempo indicated above, *Minuet Two* would sound rushed at a faster pace. There is no law dictating that both sections must be played at precisely the same tempo, but any divergence should not be conspicuous. Lively articulation and avoidance of misplaced accents are of paramount importance here. In mm.2, 4, 7-12 the first beats should be very light. Atypically the third beat is often the strongest, contributing to the humor of the piece. Slurs written before and after the barlines should not be joined by the fingers or the pedal. This gives a welcome lift to the first beats, which otherwise could sound heavy. Throughout the entire movement repeated notes and chords must not be emphasized. Pedaling is unnecessary during the first twelve measures.

Only during *Minuet One's* miniature middle section (from the third beat of m.12 to the second beat of m.18) are separated strokes of pedal recommended with the dramatic or mock-dramatic chords in mm.12-14.

Minuet One's elegance, intended or parodied, gives way to flirtatiousness in *Minuet Two*. Again very little pedaling is needed. In the context of these amiable lines, the player must not exaggerate the *forti*; the tone is conversational, not dramatic. In phrases like mm.5-7 most of the slurs merely mark the triplet rhythm and do not imply separation of slurs. The wedged quarter notes in the RH at mm.9, 11 are to be clearly separated, not accented but with the second lighter than the first. The repetitions in mm.13-14 should not be joined by pedaling and the third beats are lighter than the second beats. Though the brief middle section (mm.16-24) suggests drama, with the nervous upward suspensions and rests gasping for air, the *forti* are mere accents and do not justify a blood-and-thunder heaviness. Surely the rest in m.24 should be prolonged?

Note that in the NMA[5] there are four *fermata* signs in m.32; these refer to the possibilities of conclusion or repetition. It seems preferable that the second LH B-flat should be omitted when proceeding to *Minuet Two*. Omission of that note at the conclusion of the movement is another possibility. But should one play all the repetitions? As usual this is no straightforward matter. Rules and traditions apart, the material here is simply too delicious to be rushed through. As in the first movement there are some splendid opportunities to add some ornaments during repeats if the player feels confident about this. Unfortunately there is a mistaken tradition, handed down from the nineteenth century, that one could simply play through such a movement, ignoring all repeats, or at least omitting repetition of any second sections. Observing all the repetitions will not seem dull if the player's approach has enough humor and flexibility.

5 WRITTEN AND IMPROVISED ORNAMENTATION
IN THE SECOND MOVEMENT, K.282

MINUET ONE:

m.

12 The *arpeggi* should be played very energetically, the uppermost notes sounding with the bass octaves.

16 The onbeat *appoggiatura* is more expressive when it lasts slightly longer than an eighth note. The notes of the second quarter-note beat are not *legato*.

MINUET TWO:

m.

12 This onbeat *appoggiatura* is very light.

13 The first onbeat *appoggiatura* is usually played as an eighth note, but given the sunny character of the phrase, should be much quicker. The subsequent sixteenth notes are not *legato*.

In the entire movement, choices regarding IMPROVISED ORNAMENTATION are obviously bound up with the highly subjective terrain of repetition. Two American fortepianists, for example, made very different decisions when recording this movement in recent years. Anthony Newman[6] played the repetitions of *Minuet One* only during its first appearance. He did not play any repetitions in *Minuet Two* or in the final statement of *Minuet One*. Only a year later Malcolm Bilson's fine recording, referred to above, appeared with all repetitions observed excepting the final repeat of *Minuet One*'s second section.

I have at times played all the repetitions, adding as many as thirty ornaments during the movement. But too much decoration tends to submerge the lean lines. Perhaps it is best to observe all the repetitions and to add a few decorations to the repeated sections of *Minuet Two* and the final statement of *Minuet One*.

In *Minuet Two* the ascending RH line of mm.17-20 could be enhanced by the addition of a turn on the second D of m.17 and a flourish (A, C, then two B-flats) during the first quarter-note beat of m.20. In m.26 F and another E-flat could be added between the first two melody notes. During the final quarter-note beat of m.35 and the first of m.36 there are many possibilities for decorating. A grace-note high C could be added before the third quarter-note beat of m.39.

After *Minuet Two*, the first section of *Minuet One* is probably best played without any added decoration. When restated for the final time it would be possible to change the first quarter-note beat of m.3 to a five-note turn on D and to add a three-note trill to the last eighth note of m.6. In the first quarter-note beat of m.9 one could omit the C and play a G minor triad descending from D. An escape note G could be added between the two notes of the uppermost voice, third quarter-note beat, of m.11. When repeating the second section for the last time, one could play some grinding suspensions in the uppermost voice of some chords during mm.13-14. A turn could be interpolated between the two RH notes of m.15. A turn in the bass line at the third quarter-note beat of m.20 is a cheerful touch. Humorous, light *appoggiatura* A's could be added before the bass B-flats of mm.29-30.

These are only a few of the possibilities of enhancing the repeated sections of this delightful piece, one of the few in Mozart's oeuvre for piano solo that lends itself to considerable improvised ornamentation.

THIRD MOVEMENT	*Allegro*
FORM	sonata
APPROXIMATE TEMPO	♩ = M.M. 126
DURATION	4½ minutes (with both repeats)
SUGGESTED LISTENING	Symphony, K.200/189-k iv
	Piano Concerto, K.271 i & iii
	Die Entführung aus dem Serail: Blondchen's aria "Welche Wonne"

6 INTERPRETATION OF THE THIRD MOVEMENT, K.282

Modest as K.282 may seem on paper, this short sonata embraces three very different worlds of expression. Whereas the first movement seemed predominantly vocal and the second suggested chamber music, the third, so full of orchestral colors and pianistic exuberance, unmistakably evokes the finale of a piano concert. The difference between the *tutti* and the more intimate phrases must be evident. Vitality of spirit and an agile technique are priorities here.

Despite all the bustling activity, to ignore numerous fine points of articulation would seriously diminish the vivacity of this piece. The first B-flat in m.1 should not be joined to the second, an octave higher. This becomes obvious when one sees that in the following measure, the first beat is slurred and clearly emphasized. First beat *appoggiature*, as in m.3, are also slight accents.

The difference between slurred and unslurred sixteenth notes is not always observed. Given the slurring in the development it is probable that the sixteenth-note groups of mm.3-4 should not be separated at the bar-line. However, in mm.13, 23 or 36 a slight break, a quick lifting of the hand between the two groups of sixteenth notes, adds character and makes it easier for the ear to comprehend these quick passages. Unslurred sixteenth-note figurations as in mm.31 and 35 have a more propulsive function and should be played with a peppery *non legato* touch. The wedges above the quarter notes in the second beats of mm.32-33 indicate a lively separation from the surrounding notes, not rough accenting.

The bass must be alertly played; if the quarter notes in mm.1-2, 16-19, 24-27 are not given full value, the rhythmic interplay with the RH line is spoiled. Though the bass eighth notes of mm.3-4 are not *legato* they are less detached than those in mm.36-38. The subsequent Alberti bass patterns lose energy if finger-pedaled.

The energy of the piece can be clearly directed without reducing the surprise effect of dynamic contrasts. *Crescendi* in mm.9 and 27 or *diminuendi* in mm.14 and 22 are not desirable. The tone of the climax at mm.32-35 should be exuberant. Some players incline to play phrases like mm.16-19 with misplaced pathos and drooping tempo, foreign to the high spirits of the piece.

In the development section the colors immediately darken. The minor mode prevails. During mm.42-43 the RH slurs (obviously a single impulse that should not be separated at the bar-line) do not indicate *legato* as much as a surge to the high A-flat. The dramatic contrasts of the suspenseful sequence at mm.48-55 have orchestral impact, but on a large modern piano, if the *piani* are not more emphasized than the *forti*, the result can seem pompous. The contrast of *legato* and *non legato* in mm.56-59 heightens the rhetorical tension of this short, churning phrase. The rest in m.59 could be prolonged, but the two subsequent measures should be in tempo. A *ritenuto* effect is droopy, whereas a *diminuendo*, slithering into the recapitulation, provides a delightful surprise.

Though not easy to play, the lively articulation of the RH slurs in the final four measures must be observed. The final chord sounds foolish if shortened, yet prolonging it makes the conclusion sound pompous. Given the extreme brevity of the material and the length of the first two movements, it seems advisable to observe both repetitions in this finale.

7 ORNAMENTATION IN THE THIRD MOVEMENT, K.282

m.

3   Obviously this onbeat *appoggiatura* should not be accented. Here and elsewhere in the movement the two notes after the suspension could be played less *legato*.

9   Here and in m.12, the trill consists of three notes.

20 The arpeggiation is very energetic, the uppermost note falling on the first beat. The other *arpeggio* notes are held.

22 In this context the onbeat *appoggiature* are slightly accented.

31 This onbeat *appoggiatura* presents a comically abrupt change of direction in the line and could be slightly prolonged.

57 Probably the best interpretation of the trill is to play a four-note *Pralltriller*, beginning on the upper auxiliary and without a termination.

93 The trill can begin on the upper auxiliary and have six notes. A termination would sound muddled here.

In such an exuberant movement additional ornamentation would be distracting. When repeating the development section it is possible to add a descending figuration during the rest of m.59. When repeating mm.89-90, one could conceivably add a mixture of RH diatonic and triadic sixteenth notes.

SONATA IN G MAJOR, K.283

OTHER K. LISTING	189-h
DATE OF COMPOSITION	probably early 1775
TOTAL DURATION	12½ minutes (expositional repeats in i and ii)

That the G major Sonata is so popular among young players and those who are "young at heart" is hardly surprising. It is an unusually sunny, engaging piece with few formal puzzles, yet all the movements offer a wealth of subtleties that lie beyond the comprehension of an average child. Every reasonably competent pianist attempts the opening *Allegro*, the most frequently heard single movement from the Munich sonatas. However, only players with a nimble technique can cope with the demands of the finale.

FIRST MOVEMENT   *Allegro*
FORM   sonata
APPROXIMATE TEMPO   ♩ = M.M. 126
DURATION   4½ minutes (with expositional repeat)
SUGGESTED LISTENING   Symphony, K.199/161-b i
                      Piano Concerto, K.453 i

8 INTERPRETATION OF THE FIRST MOVEMENT, K.283

Any piece that sounds as naively cheerful as this *Allegro* may seem simple, but Mozart's structural ingenuity here is a superb example of unobtrusive craftsmanship. The entire composition is based on two motifs, and every player attempting the piece should be aware of this. The first five RH notes span the interval of a sixth. The second statement of this motif follows immediately, expanded to the interval of a seventh. The sixth, filled in by descending diatonic notes, becomes the basis of the second theme group at mm.23-24 and mm.45-46. The development section begins with another variant of this diatonic motif, answered by the motif extending over a seventh, which dominates mm.56-68. The second motivic idea derives from the RH line of mm.4-5 and consists of four diatonically descending tones (G to D). This motif is inverted at mm.16-17, where we hear the first of several patterns of four diatonically ascending tones. Stated in both hands, this motif is heard six times, forming an energetic conclusion to the first theme group. The four-note motif, in the version heard at m.16, makes a canonic appearance at mm.43-44.

If the player is aware of these motivic relationships, his interpretation will gain in projection as well as in profile; both the logic and the surprise elements will become clearer.

The opening theme is a playful blend of energetic and sighing figurations. Melancholy souls will be distracted by all the suspensions and choose a droopy tempo, with three impulses, rather than one, to each measure. Many commentators, among them Landowska,[7] have remarked on the minuet-like quality of the opening. As Mozart occasionally wrote minuets marked *Allegro*, the contradiction is not as unlikely as it may seem.

Given the high degree of motivic organization, it is obvious that any noticeable deviation of tempo in this piece would be capricious. But in such a dance-inspired work, a metronomic approach would be even more disastrous. The phrases must breathe easily and not sound driven. Agogic effects are sometimes necessary (for example, before the third beat of m.10 or the sixteenth notes in m.16 and during the rest of m.22).

The opening measures show how expressively slurs can function when they do not extend over bar-lines. The hand should leave the keys after the RH's initial sixteenth note, the articulation indicating that the upbeat is stronger than the first beat. In the following sighing figure the upbeat is also stronger, but this suspension has a totally different character. With only five notes Mozart has created a dialogue. The lower notes of the bass could be finger-pedaled but pedaling is unnecessary.

The *fortepiani* of mm.5-6 merely indicate that those first beats are stronger than the upbeats. The *forte* in the third beat of m.6 makes it clear that in response to the previous *galanterie*, the tone remains energetic until the first beat of m.10.

Though many pianists play a *piano subito* in m.16, this is hardly suitable to the explosion of energy implied. In this tempo, low octaves on any fortepiano from the composer's time would certainly have sounded crunchy. On a modern instrument the sound may thicken if the LH fifth finger does not play quite lightly. The entire transitional sentence in mm.16-22 is vigorous, without any coy, whispered effects. Conspicuous accenting of first beats must be avoided; generally the third beats are stronger here. Pedaling is irrelevant during this exuberantly orchestral sentence.

In m.23 there is an abrupt change of character, the first and second violins of our imaginary orchestra in a tender dialogue. Because of this theme's motivic background, noted above, it may be more logical to shape the RH line of the first two measures as a line of six notes (as in the bass), not two groups of three, as in the bass line of mm.45-46. An embellished version of mm.23-26 follows. In the RH of mm.25-26, the first note of each slurred pair of notes receives a humorous emphasis.

The abrupt upbeat in m.30 to the following measure is a comical cello solo. According to most editions, these sixteenth notes are to be played by the RH, a crossing-of-hands effect that Mozart liked, with the LH thumb playing with the first note in m.31. Again the third beats become the strongest. The subsequent comical suspensions of mm.33-34 are more like belches than sighs. From m.35 until the end of the exposition the writing looks pianistic but the colors are orchestral. If the player's RH does not make very supple horizontal movements for each group of sixteenth notes, these joyous phrases will sound laborious. Not all the first notes of the slurred groups should receive the same emphasis.

The quarter notes in mm.48-49 can be played to seem *legato*, requiring tricky pedaling but more consequent with mm.45-46. At the end of the exposition pedaling should be avoided; the RH chords in mm.51-53 should sound cheerful and *non legato*, not weighty.

Though some writers describe the development section as being an episode, it has been noted above that some of the initial motifs return here. The RH thirds of mm.63-67 should not be pedaled and all the bass notes are *staccato*. Throughout the section the *forti* are more humorous than dramatic. At mm.68-71, the *Eingang* to the recapitulation is smiling, not sentimental, and should be played without pedaling or slowing down.

In the recapitulation there is a recurrence, in a startling A minor, of the opening measures at mm.75-79. Some agogic freedom is suitable in this rhetorical moment, and the bass thirds could be played *legato* or *non legato*. The movement ends in such a perfunctory manner, that this too sounds like a prank.

9 ORNAMENTATION IN THE FIRST MOVEMENT, K.283

m.

22   Though a trill is marked, an ornament with the lower, not the upper auxiliary, seems more relevant. Three or five notes are possible.

37   These onbeat *appoggiature* are accented.

43   Each trill certainly begins on the principal note, which must not be roughly accented. Five or seven notes, without a termination, suffice.

54   The *appoggiatura* sounds almost inconsequential if played before the beat. Played on the beat it has more character.

56   The *appoggiatura* is to be played quickly before the beat.

57   The onbeat *appoggiatura* becomes an approximate sixteenth note.

58   The duration of the onbeat *appoggiatura* is a matter of taste. A sixteenth note is certainly humorous.

59   This resembles the *appoggiatura* in m.57, but here some separation between the suspension and the subsequent sixteenth notes (to be played *leggiero*, not *legato*) is more relevant.

61   The first *appoggiatura* must be played before the beat, as an on-beat rendition suggests the braying of a donkey. The second

appoggiatura is like that in m.57.
80 This *appoggiatura* is played on the beat and, given the cheerful character of the phrase, must be shorter than an eighth note.
83 The spicy onbeat *appoggiatura* should be played as quickly as possible.

Additional ornamentation seems unnecessary in this highly organized movement. In his fine recording, Malcolm Bilson[8] adds some delightfully expressive variants to the first eight measures of the development section when he makes the second repeat.

SECOND MOVEMENT	*Andante*
FORM	sonata
APPROXIMATE TEMPO	♪ = M.M. 108
DURATION	5 minutes (with expositional repeat)
SUGGESTED LISTENING	String Quartet, K.170 ii
	Symphony, K.201/186-a ii

10 INTERPRETATION OF THE SECOND MOVEMENT, K.283

Most editions create a visual illusion of expansiveness in their printing of this movement, but the piece is actually exceptionally compact, the exposition lasting only twelve measures. Though Mozart wrote four different endings to the two sections, most recording artists choose to ignore both repetitions. Certainly in this case the issue of repetition is not straightforward.

A tempo must be chosen that also suits the second theme, beginning in m.9. Even if the metronomic indication suggested above is measured in eighth notes, the music must seem to flow in half-note beats; otherwise the pace becomes ponderous.

The instrumental style of the *Allegro* is continued here, but the scale is now more that of a string quartet than of an orchestra. It is easy to imagine two violins and a viola at the beginning, with the cello joining in at m.3. The repeated notes of the opening theme are best not played with the same intensity. Pedaling, changed on each eighth beat, is welcome. The gently urgent phrase seems to be asking something like "Do you love me? I must KNOW!", the unusual emphasis on the last beat indicated by the wedge over the quarter note.

An all-purpose *legato* approach deadens the RH's tender, graceful phrases. The melody notes in the fourth eighth-note beat of m.2, the second of m.4 and the last two eighth notes of m.11 are not slurred. It is curious how most pianists choose to begin m.5 softly, thereby ignoring the *piano* indicated in the third quarter-note beat. Such a misreading dulls the delicate *staccati* in mm.5-6, each pair of notes being like a tentative question, with both the notes and rests clearly separated. The wedged RH notes of m.9 should be clearly detached, without pedaling, though some LH finger-pedaling of the bass is welcome here. The wedged notes in m.10 should not sound accented. If the tone in the brief climax at mm.11-12 expires too soon, an ecstatic moment becomes mere wheezing. Playing slight separations between the RH eighth-note beats of mm.13-14 and gently emphasizing the first note of each group create the slightly restless quality suggested. Given the brevity of the exposition, the repeat must surely be observed.

The development section is full of ingenious and startling surprises. A statement of the opening theme in D minor, a shadow more than a drama, slides back to the C major in m.18 suggesting a "false recapitulation." This is abruptly broken off in the next measure by a jarring diminished seventh chord. In the four subsequent measures Mozart delays a return to the tonic harmony and combines both elements of the theme's first measure (repeated notes, now transformed into slow-motion *tremoli*, and the ascending fifth, which is then inverted, and in m.21, stretches to an octave). Even in a movement of what seems total simplicity Mozart could not resist showing off his ingenuity.

The three-measure *Coda* is so wistful yet musically fulfilling, it seems to predict similar moments in operas Mozart was to write ten years later. We almost feel like intruders on an intimate scene.

11 ORNAMENTATION IN THE SECOND MOVEMENT, K.283
m.

2   The onbeat *appoggiatura* is gently accented. Unlike the *appoggiature* in mm.12-13 there are no slurs indicating that the two notes after the suspension are to be connected to it. The trill will sound muddled on a modern instrument if not played with three notes, ending on the fourth quarter-note beat.

6   Because this trill is slurred it must begin with the principal note; five notes and no termination seem the best choice.

12   This trill may resemble that in m.6 but is not slurred and has a somewhat more nervous character. Therefore it could be pre-

13 ceded by the upper auxiliary note played as a grace note.
These onbeat *appoggiature* are more emphasized than the first notes of the fifth and seventh eighth-note beats.
21 This trill is the most startling moment in the entire movement. To begin with the upper auxiliary note would spoil the rhetorical dissonance with the bass.
27 This trill could be introduced by a prebeat upper auxiliary note and has three or five notes plus termination.

Mozart has already included considerable ornamentation, and this short piece has an inherent placidity that resists much change. Perhaps mm.4-6,27-29, when repeated, offer some opportunities for IMPROVISED ORNAMENTATION.

THIRD MOVEMENT	*Presto*
FORM	sonata
APPROXIMATE TEMPO	$\downarrow$. = M.M. 88
DURATION	3 minutes with no repeats
SUGGESTED LISTENING	Symphony in G, K.124 iv
	Symphony in C, K.162 iii
	La finta giardiniera: Serpetta's aria "Appena mi vedon" (no.10) and the aria of the Podestà "Una damina" (no.17)

12 INTERPRETATION OF THE THIRD MOVEMENT, K.283

This finale unmistakably inhabits an orchestral world, with flashing contrasts between stringed and woodwind instruments, exuberant *tutti* and delicate *soli*. Dennerlein remarks:

"[In] this most Italianate of the early sonatas ... the light clarity and vigor of the themes bring to mind an *opera buffa*." [9]

Landowska found other Italianate elements in this whirling finale:

"A new rhythm which has nothing of a minuet or of a waltz. It is a *ronde*, like one of those danced at the end of fairs. This type of 3/8 meter derives from the Neapolitan *forlana*. Inspiration of the same nature can be found in the chorus from *Don Giovanni*, 'Giovanetta che fate all'amore.'" [10]

Though a certain rushed quality is welcome here, mere speed will render passages in sixteenth notes unintelligible. The rhythmic thrust should be felt in impulses of four measures, not of two. The energy of the piece speaks more freely when there are as few first beat accents as possible.

The opening has a peasant-like breeziness; Dennerlein[11] was reminded of tambourines and bagpipes. It would be unnatural to play the first phrases delicately; the *piano* indicated in m.18 confirms that the preceding phrases should be played exuberantly. The RH's first thirds are not slurred, but practically all pianists try to play them in a *legato* line, which not only is incorrect, but also virtually impossible (see next section). The harmonies and the RH slurs of mm.13-16 indicate that the upbeats are stronger than the first beats. The triadic figures of mm.26, 28 should sound like violin lines, not pianistic blocks of sound. Nowhere in the first thematic group, ending at m.40, is pedaling necessary.

Mozart's slurring of the first four measures of the second theme (mm.41-44) is not consistent. In the exposition there is a two measure slur at mm.41-42, but not in the "viola" imitation in the two subsequent measures, nor in the "first violin" line of mm.49-50, whereas during the recapitulation, two measure slurs are marked at the two latter moments. As this figuration is halved at mm.57, 228, etc., it is arguable that one measure slurring is logical. Yet two-measure articulation may seem preferable to the somewhat pedantic, segmenting effect of a consistent one measure articulation. This remains a very subjective issue, depending on the player, instrument and tempo.

To separate the sixteenth notes in mm.46-49 from the subsequent eighth notes is not only correct, but also delightfully flippant. Pedaling would blur the humor of mm.57-63, but this delightful passage can only sound *legato* if the first of each group of four octaves is played as indicated and the rest are divided between the hands. This is not difficult, sounds wonderfully fresh, and is a theatrically visual effect that Mozart himself probably employed. The bustling activity builds to an assertive cadence at mm.71-73. An amusing woodwind interplay follows, the opening melodic motif of three ascending notes now inverted, the answering motif, the ascending fourth leap of mm.2-3, now cunningly disguised as a fifth at mm.75-76. The excitement builds to an unmistakably orchestral climax in mm.93-97.

There is much trapeze-work in this finale, which requires quick body reactions. The player should not sit too close to the keyboard, and he must be able to make quick sidewise movements, not only with his arms, but with his upper body.

In all the frothy counterpoint, pedaling should be minimal. The final chord of the exposition should not be prolonged, as the development section should be launched without any hesitation. I believe that the terrific energy of this movement is diminished by any repetition.

This development section is a wild explosion of energy, which few pianists play with total commitment, Lili Kraus[12] being a notable exception. In such turbulent music, rests are supremely important. If pedaling is used on the first-beat chords in mm.143,145,147, the subsequent rests must not be shortened. Pedaling during the operatic sequence of diminished-seventh passages at mm.107-121 is subjective; on a fortepiano longer pedal effects are possible, but on a modern instrument "half" or "*tremolo*" pedaling is desirable. The beautiful part-writing in mm.159-160 sounds more fluent if the three notes of the middle line are played by the LH.

At the end of the recapitulation in mm.264-267, pedaling, changed on the first and third beats, is welcome. The breathless surge of the piece is stronger when the pianist himself does not run out of breath, a danger particularly evident during the recapitulation.

After all the fun and genius, Mozart's mini-*Coda* of two chords is so grotesquely abrupt its very sparsity sounds witty. R.D. Levin too sees this as a "practical joke."[13]

13 ORNAMENTATION IN THE THIRD MOVEMENT, K.283

m.

1   When the theme is played *non legato*, it is not difficult to squeeze in a three-note trill, beginning on the third beat, and with the fingering 2-3-2.

4   Because the theme moves in thirds, the *appoggiatura* should be played lightly before the beat.

72   Here and in m.80 the trill has more bite when it begins on the upper auxiliary. Six notes and a termination suffice.

107   All the bass chords in mm.107-119 could be vigorously arpeggiated, with the uppermost notes falling on the beat.

In this delightfully symphonic whirlwind of activity, there is little place for improvised ornamentation. What a festive conclusion this is to one of the most joyous, untroubled sonatas Mozart wrote!

VI

SONATA IN D MAJOR, K.284

OTHER K. NUMBER | K.205-b
DATE OF COMPOSITION | early 1775
TOTAL DURATION | approximately 25 minutes (with some repeats)

1 UNIQUE ASPECTS OF THE DÜRNITZ SONATA

This sonata inhabits a different world from the previous five. K.284 was written for Baron Thaddäus von Dürnitz, a Munich musical amateur who was not only titled but also wealthy. In a letter to his father dated October 23, 1777,[1] Mozart referred to "my last sonata in D, written for Baron Dürnitz" with whom the composer socialized during his Munich stay in the winter of 1774-75. Three years later,[2] Leopold was still asking if his son had ever received any recompense for K.284.

This D major sonata is often labeled the *Dürnitz* Sonata to differentiate it from two later sonatas in the same key, K.311 and 576. Unlike the other five piano sonatas from the Munich period, the *Dürnitz* sonata was published in Mozart's lifetime, appearing in 1784 together with the B-flat Sonata, K.333, and the Piano and Violin Sonata, K.454.

Until quite recently scholars maintained that K.284 was written later than the first five sonatas. Opinions that K.284 did not belong to the same period as K.279-283 are understandable. Abert[3] commented that the D major Sonata "is the first to completely exploit the expressive possibilities of the new *Hammerklavier* while the other five sonatas do not really reach beyond the technical resources of the clavichord." On October 17, 1777, this observation was reinforced by Mozart's own comment in another letter to his father:

"Really I cannot describe the amazement of the *Kapellmeister* and the organist, who kept crossing themselves. Here and at Munich I have played all my six sonatas by heart several times ... The last one in D, sounds exquisite on Stein's pianoforte."[4]

When Mozart wrote this letter, he was full of enthusiasm for the technical and expressive range of the Stein piano, which he had just encountered.

A dance becoming the slow movement, and a set of variations the finale of a sonata are also to be found in various sonatas by J. Haydn and J.C. Bach, but K.284 certainly seems more like an exuberantly contrasted suite than a sonata.

If the sonata is so original, why is it so rarely performed? This is an intriguing paradox. The piece was definitely for public performance, as Girdlestone commented:

> "The key of D major ... is the concerto key par excellence and in those which Mozart has written in D virtuosity plays a great part. Of his violin concertos, the most difficult are in this key, his D major flute concerto is more virtuoso than that in G ... also true of his only violin sonata in this key." [5]

Certainly the pianistic challenges of the outer movements place this music beyond the reach of most amateurs. The expression and ornamentation in the *Rondeau* form is a different type of stumbling-block for many others. There is too the problem of holding the attention through what is, by Mozartian standards, a long sonata, even if only some repeats are observed. But surely all these problems are banished by the enormous vitality and variety evident in this sonata.

FIRST MOVEMENT	*Allegro*
FORM	sonata
APPROXIMATE TEMPO	$\downarrow$ = M.M. 129
DURATION	5½ minutes (with expositional repeat)
SUGGESTED LISTENING	*La finta giardiniera*: Overture, also finale (no.28)
	Piano Concerto, K.175 i
	Haffner Serenade, K.250 i
	Violin Concerto, K.216 i
	Violin Concerto, K.218 i

2 INTERPRETATION OF THE FIRST MOVEMENT, K.284

Only players with exceptionally fleet fingers emerge victorious from this hurdle race. It is doubtful if there is another movement among Mozart's piano sonatas that seems so intent on impressing an audience. But this does not mean that there is only superficial appeal;

although there is less motivic development than in many other sonata movements, the succession of energetic themes is irresistible in its drive and diversity. Unfortunately the *Allegro* is too often rattled off in a thoughtless way, with the player preoccupied only with display. Unusually, two drafts exist of the *Allegro*, and for any serious student of Mozart it is interesting to compare them. In an appendix, the NMA[6] includes this first version, which gives fascinating insights into Mozart's thought processes. Except for the initial measure, the first theme group is completely different in the second draft, considerably richer, less dependent on repetition and sequential patterns. The second theme group is mainly unchanged in both drafts, but takes a different course from m.47 (in the first draft, m.44 in the second) until the end of the exposition, where again the second draft is a considerable enrichment of the first's somewhat perfunctory material. In the original draft, the development section was based on a two-measure motif from the exposition's conclusion, but soon became bogged down in dull sequences. It is hardly surprising that Mozart scrapped this, replacing it with one of his most dramatic development sections. The revised section has such explosive force that it can seem unrelated to the rest of the movement and has been erroneously described in some formal analyses as the middle section of a ternary form.

Richard Rosenberg[7] observed that the development section's first two motifs in eighth notes have already been heard at mm.9-10 and mm.17-19 respectively. Though the rest of the development seems to consist of new material, the resemblance of mm.66-69 to mm.30-33 is obvious. The motivic activity is extreme, as L.G. Ratner remarked:

"There are many shifts of topic, more than twenty. No topic is given more than a few bars; each is sharply etched, set in high relief by juxtapositions and by contrasts in texture and melody."[8]

Only players who can cope with the technical demands of such sonatas as Beethoven's Opus 2 nos.2 and 3, Opus 10 no.3, or Opus 31 no.3 should attempt this piece. A refined technique is required to project the array of brilliant orchestral effects; double thirds imitating woodwinds, *tremoli* evoking violins, LH octaves that reproduce the vigorous bowing of celli and double-basses.

To evoke suitably orchestral weight, the wedged quarter notes in m.2 should not be played too *staccato*. Similarly the following unslurred eighth notes are best played slightly detached, the fingers close to the keys. Though the *forte* indications in mm.5-6 refer to the first half of each measure, the result should not be gross accenting of the second quarter-note beats. The brilliant passage in mm.7-8 should not seem like an avalanche of sixteenth notes, but be clearly heard as four groups of eight sparkling tones. During the polyphony in mm.9-12, woodwinds join the stringed instruments. The RH writing lies awkwardly under the hand. The situation is much easier and sounds clearer when the LH thumb plays the first beat B in m.10. It should be noted that there is no slurring in m.10, where Christian Zacharias[9] is one of the few recording artists who does not play the second quarter-note beat *legato*, a delightfully vivacious touch.

At m.13 there is an eruption of sound, but it is astonishing how many pianists, students and concert artists alike, shy away from the *forte* indicated and begin this manly sequence *piano*, followed by a very inappropriate Rossinian *crescendo*. In this exuberant passage pedaling is relevant (how *legato* it should be is subjective) with clear changes on each quarter beat. The end of the first theme group should drive to m.21. A coy *diminuendo*, or worse, an "echo effect" in mm.19-21, would drain the cadence of its vigor and spoil the contrast offered by the opening of the second theme.

The articulation of m.22 is problematic, as Mozart used three different notations (m.93 as well as the two versions of m.22) of this upbeat motif. The choice remains personal but I am not alone[10] in preferring the first version's separate slur over the second half of the measure. In any case the second quarter-note beat is stronger than the first.

Though there are many suspensions stated or implied in the opening of the second theme group, this should not inspire a melancholy approach; the atmosphere is still joyful, only, at times, gentler. The subsequent LH thirds sound mechanical if the fingers do not remain close to the keys. The melodic contour of mm.23-29 becomes clear when the first note under each slur is the strongest of each slurred group. The *crescendo* in the first half of m.26 (in the first edition, not in the manuscript) may seem peculiar but does make for an amusing *opera buffa* effect when the second half of the measure is played *subito piano*. Not all editions give the wedge, here obviously an accent, on the last RH eighth note in m.27. In the next measures two-part RH writing is implied though not marked, with the upper line sounding stronger than the "second violin" line.

The last beat of m.29 could be played as an assertive *crescendo*, but in m.30 too many players play softly and make another un-Mozartian *crescendo* during the next measures. Worst of all is the *subito piano* which many pianists make at the climax of this sentence, m.33. Lili Kraus,[11] with her marvelously earthy approach to this sonata, is one of the few recording artists to avoid such unsuitable romantic effects. The composer clearly indicated that the sound ebbs only during the second beat of m.34. The shaping of the hidden melody in mm.34-37 is a fascinating example of how Mozart could disguise a simple pattern of four descending tones. In mm.34-35 there is another patch of two-part writing which is difficult to play smoothly. This sounds better if the LH thumb takes at least some of the notes of the lower line written in the treble clef.

The rest of the exposition is festive, but all too often the exuberance is dampened by the player's technical limitations or ill-chosen fingering; for example, it is advisable to begin m.38 with the thumb, not the index finger, on C-sharp. The first five sixteenth notes of the following measure are best played with the fingering 2-3-5-3-5. In m.40 the extremely rapid RH double-thirds are not difficult if played *non legato* as marked; it is essential to detach the thirty-second and eighth notes here. The dynamics too should be sharply profiled, with a *subito piano*, no droopy *diminuendo*, in the second half of that measure. Hesitations before mm.40, 43 would disturb the surge of this effusive sentence. In mm.48-51 pedaling can enhance the volume, but the pedal must be clearly changed on each quarter-note beat to avoid any vacuum-cleaner effects.

The beginning of the development section lacks a dynamic indication in both manuscript and first edition. Most modern editions suggest *forte* here, which certainly seems appropriate, but the choice of too many pianists here for mystery over drama evokes a nineteenth century atmosphere more than Mozart's vigor. Surely the *forte* in m.60 does not necessarily imply that the preceding measures are to be played *piano?* The crossing of hands in these measures is not difficult if the player's spine is not stiffened. The sound here, certainly on a modern instrument, can be enhanced if the pedal is half-depressed and changed with each quarter-note beat. In the final sequence of this stormy section (mm.66-69), playing the LH thirds *legato* would be incorrect. What a glorious explosion of energy this is, evoking both the virtuosity of a piano concerto and the joyous fireworks of Vivaldi or Corelli.

In the recapitulation the RH octaves in mm.122-23 will sound *legato* only when the lower voice, except in the first octave, is played by the LH. In m.126 many editions give the sixteenth notes in the second quarter-note beat as A and F-sharp. This reading, taken from the first edition, contradicts the manuscript and the similar measure of the exposition; F-sharp and D are more logical.

There may be many opportunities throughout this movement to display instrumental prowess, and the joyful thrust of this music can easily be drowned in a flood of "passage-work," a depressing term that well describes the fleeting effect of such an approach.

3 ORNAMENTATION IN THE FIRST MOVEMENT, K.284

m.

1   The *arpeggio* can better end, not begin, on the beat, with all the chordal tones held. A pedal stroke that does not obscure the subsequent rest adds body to the tone. The onbeat *appoggiatura* are accented and, in this context, the two sixteenth notes after the suspension can be clearly *non legato*.

19   The *arpeggio* is best played with the highest note sounding on the beat, but this requires a very quick hand movement, easy if the wrist is low when beginning the *arpeggio*.

23   The first trill, in itself a suspension, should not begin with the auxiliary note. Both Neumann[12] and Rosenblum[13] maintain that the best rendition is to play the upper auxiliary as a grace note. The second trill is usually played as a grace note F-sharp; a three-note trill at this moment sounds very complicated.

29   As in m.1 this onbeat *appoggiatura* becomes an accented sixteenth note, but the resulting suspension is slurred to the subsequent sixteenth notes, creating a strong impulse to the following measure.

37   The onbeat *appoggiatura* is not accented and there should be no suggestion of a *crescendo* in the final quarter-note beat, where a *forte subito* is surely the desired effect.

45   The chords are best arpeggiated as in m.1.

49   The trill should sound brilliant, played as rapidly as possible. It begins with an onbeat upper auxiliary note, not too roughly accented and perhaps slightly prolonged.

ADDITIONAL ORNAMENTATION

The hyperactivity of this movement allows virtually no opportunities for improvised ornaments. During the repeats, Christian Zacharias, in his recording, added a piquant trill to the second beat of m.73, and Alexey Lubimov,[14] a RH trill to the third beat of m.90.

SECOND MOVEMENT	*Rondeau en Polonaise*
FORM	rondo
APPROXIMATE TEMPO	♩ = M.M. 72
DURATION	4½ minutes
SUGGESTED LISTENING	String Quartet, K.158 iii
	Piano Concerto, K.175 ii
	La finta giardiniera: Sandrina's aria "Una voce sento," no.16
	Divertimento, winds, K.439-b v

4 INTERPRETATION OF THE SECOND MOVEMENT, K.284

In the titling of this movement, Mozart may perhaps be referring to the older *Rondeau* style of the French masters, in which a fairly short theme, always in the tonic key, alternates with episodes (couplets) of approximately the same length. Even if this experiment with *rondo* form is less adventurous than the last movement of the Sonata, K.281, here too is Mozart's individuality manifest.

The *Polonaise* of Mozart's time did not yet have the fiery character we know from pieces by Beethoven, Schubert or Chopin in this genre. The *Polonaise* has been described by various historians as resembling a stately procession more than a dance. It became popular at the court of Louis XV, whose wife, Marie Leszczynska, was Polish. Baron von Dürnitz, to whom K.284 is dedicated, was also of Polish origin, which could account for the presence of this unusual movement in the D major Sonata.

Compared to the *Allegro*, there are few technical challenges but stylistic and textual problems abound. Modern editions include numerous dynamic indications added when K.284 was published nine years after its composition. Unfortunately some editions do not clearly differentiate between the indications that derive from the manuscript and those added in the first edition. The natural shaping of phrases in this forest of dynamic details and unusual ornaments requires much insight.

The tempo should be fluid but without a trace of rushing. As in all moderately paced dances in triple meter, the player must try to project the music with a single impulse, not three, in each measure (the player of this piece is advised to also read the minuet section of Chapter III). The numerous dynamic inflections, sudden changes of register, and almost programmatic shifts of emotion may suggest that this piece can sustain more *rubato* than most of Mozart's piano music, but excessive lingering, especially before first beats, will evoke a nineteenth-century atmosphere far removed from eighteenth-century sensibility. If the player's tone is too dainty, this movement loses its character. Konrad Wolff commented on Mozart's piano works:

> "Even though the textures ... are more transparent and less thick, on the whole, than Haydn's and Beethoven's, they should not sound less full; it is just that Mozart was raised in a different Italian-style tradition ... in which clustery writing was excluded for the sake of better-sounding top voices." [15]

The contrasts between *forte* and *piano* in the first 16-measure theme do not have to be extreme but merely indicate changes of scoring, like civilized exchanges among the members of a string quartet. In this expressive piece the amount of slurring is conspicuous. But joining all the slurs in an oily *legato* ruins the dance elements present throughout. The music breathes better if slurs are generally not extended over bar-lines. Rarely heard is the clearly indicated *non legato* in the LH of mm.7-8 and the first beat in the RH of m.8. This delicate theme's only expansive moment is the surge to the cadence during mm.15-16.

The ornamented suspensions of mm.17-30 may be joined to each other by pedaling but become dull if the hand plays these *legato*. Some finger-pedaling is welcome in the bass of mm.17-20 but would have a braking effect in mm.25-28. The *forti* in m.29 suggest an unexpected, rather nervous phrasing and should be moderate.

The restatement of the first theme (mm.31-46) poses some textual questions. The unusual reversal of dynamics in mm.31-36, compared to the movement's opening phrase, is in the manuscript, and supported by the octave doubling in mm.32 and 34. However, this evokes a change of dance gesture more than a change in emotion and should not be too heavy handed. Whether one plays the first RH G-sharp in m.37 as a sixteenth note (manuscript version) or as a thirty-second note (first edition) is a matter of choice, but on a modern instrument, the first edition's octave doubling of the bass in the following measure is not attractive. In the charming variants of mm.40 and 42 (which may sound better if the hands are not crossed), Mitsuko Uchida[16] emphasizes the lower line, a lovely and interesting effect. The NMA[17] editors point out that the last notes in mm.43-44 were marked as thirty-second notes in the manuscript; certainly the usually heard six-teenth notes sound dull. The RH slurs in mm.45-46, in which the first note of each group is the strongest, may be joined to each other by pedaling but become lifeless if joined by the fingers. With all these variants and textual details, the player must not allow the phrases to become segmented.

A very brief second episode (mm.47-52) is the shadow at the core of this gracious scene. A modulation to F-sharp minor may not seem surprising in an A major piece, but Mozart's music rarely gravitated towards this dangerously black key. A *diminuendo* in the first beats of mm.47-50 would reduce spiritual pain to trivial dissatisfaction. Theatrical contrasts in the *piano subito* beats are necessary. The panting suspensions and rhetorical rests in mm.66-69 resemble a concerto *cadenza*. After a brief detour to A minor in m.68 the music finally comes to rest on the dominant of A major.

The richly ornamented return of the first theme seems improvised, as if Mozart were letting his fingers wander over the keyboard during this tender dance memory. The upbeat thirty-second notes in mm.79, 81,84 are not slurred. The *legato* octaves of mm.82-83 sound smoother when the LH plays the lower note of the second octave in each group.

Where the music begins to fade, dreamlike, in m.85 a *diminuendo* in mm.88-89 is much more expressive than a weary *ritenuto*. The movement ends with a surprising recall of mm.15-16. The double thirds in the last measure will sound more *legato* if the LH thumb plays the first beat A. It is no surprise that this civilized dialogue, so laden with emotion and unexpected change, ends with a whisper.

5 ORNAMENTATION IN THE SECOND MOVEMENT, K.284

m.

12   The *appoggiatura* would sound banal played before the beat, yet a quick onbeat interpretation seems very brusque. Perhaps it is best to play it as an eighth note, the resolution note sounding as an octave doubling of the "second violin line." This effect is also suggested at mm.32, 34.

13   This *appoggiatura* sounds more natural as a grace note before the third quarter-note beat.

17   The maze of indications here (turns, trills, mordents) implies that different ornaments can be played here, but Neumann[18] maintains that none of these should begin on the upper auxil-

iary. As noted above, these ornaments should not be joined to each other, but form a series of tense suspension figurations.

18   The *appoggiatura* is probably best played very quickly and before the beat. The resolution note D is not to be joined to the following C-sharp.

31   This unusual type of prebeat *appoggiatura* would sound like yodeling if played too emphatically.

35   The compound *appoggiatura* at the beginning of the measure is another unusual ornament. Neumann[19] thought that the *forte* refers only to the trill, in which case, the compound *appoggiatura* is best played before the beat. The subsequent prebeat escape-note *appoggiatura* could form the termination of the trill, if there is a slight pause on the previous tone. A normal termination here seems clumsy.

38   Obviously the *appoggiatura* in thirds falls on the beat, but here the two thirds after the suspension are neither *legato* nor noticeably *staccato*.

48   This very dramatic trill should begin on C-sharp. Beginning on the upper auxiliary would weaken the desired dissonant effect. Few recording artists play this trill with a termination and most trill only until the second eighth-note beat, creating a shuddering effect that seems appropriate here. Lili Kraus trills from the second to the third eighth-note beat, which is also effective.

70   At the beginning of a phrase, this trill should begin on the principal note, which may be slightly prolonged. The trill will sound misplaced if played too quickly and, given the subsequent quick notes, a termination is not desirable.

74   The turn begins on the second quarter-note beat with the upper auxiliary.

84   Each trill begins on the principal note and consists of three notes plus the termination.

In a movement so rich in *galant* sentiments, it is not easy, or even desirable, to suggest that there are definitive renderings for many of the ornaments. Certainly Mozart's indicated ornamentation is so generous and inventive that added decorations rarely seem appropriate. A very short decoration of the *fermata* in m.89 is conceivable.

THIRD MOVEMENT	*Theme with Variations*
FORM	variation
APPROXIMATE TEMPO	♩ = M.M. 63
DURATION	15 minutes (with first repeat of each variation)
SUGGESTED LISTENING	Sonata for Piano & Violin, K.305/ 293-d ii
	Variations for Piano on a Minuet by J.C. Fischer, K.179

6 INTERPRETATION OF THE THIRD MOVEMENT, K.284

Because K.284 is more a suite than a sonata, there are few convincing reasons why the finale could not be played on its own. Yet it is rarely heard and this neglect is especially regrettable as these variations rank among Mozart's best compositions in the genre. Certainly none of the independent variation sets for piano written before K.398 display the originality evinced here. Some commentators find the piece as fine as the famous first movement of the A major Sonata, K.331, or the *Gluck* and *Duport* sets, K.455 and 573.

Perhaps length is the most intimidating factor. Since the last two variations are through-composed, it seems willful to omit any repetitions in the other ten variations, yet this does result in a piece that by Mozartian standards seems rather long-winded. I believe that here it is best to repeat the first section of each variation, but since there is a return of the opening measures within the second section, repetition of these latter sections does not seem essential.

Tempo is a murky issue here. The manuscript and some modern editions do not indicate a tempo. Other publications opt for the first edition's *Andante*, while others state *Allegretto*. Some recording artists, like Glenn Gould[20] and Desko Ránki,[21] assume a pace for the theme that would suggest an *Allegro*. Surprisingly, this approach also seems valid, though it would no doubt appall writers like Dennerlein,[22] who hear elements of a *Gavotte* in this theme. Perhaps Mozart or an editor added the *Andante* indication to the 1784 first edition to caution against beginning too hastily. Since the theme lies easily "under the fingers," if the player is not attentive, the pace can easily become hectic. Conversely, an *alla breve Andante* certainly does not indicate a solemn tread; the music flows with one impulse, not two, in each measure.

The THEME's structure is unconventional. Due to a humorous silence in mm.12-13, it has seventeen measures, instead of the usual sixteen. Like most themes on which variation works are based, the tune is not harmonically and melodically complicated. With such a violinistic theme, the player will find it easy to get the right inflections if he imagines bowing it. The difference, more in emphasis than in separation, between slurred groups of two or four eighth notes should be audible. The pedal should be changed on every quarter-note beat, with the lowest slurred bass notes sometimes finger-pedaled. It is a pity that too many players shy away from the clearly indicated contrast in the fourth measure, where the writing takes on a vigor that is more orchestral. Given the preponderance of eighth notes, the bass gains character if its quarter notes are played *non legato*.

VARIATION 1 is a study in the subtlety of Mozart's slurring. To reduce all the RH figurations to a long *legato* flow would be mechanical and boring. As in the theme, separations of slurred groups are not as important here as the gentle emphasis given to the first note of each. Therefore mm.1-2, for example, are smoother than m.3 or 7. The suspensions in the bass of m.9 could be played *legato*, but the eighth notes in the following measure become sticky if played *legato*. Throughout this variation, humor and melodic flow are more important than dynamic contrasts.

In VARIATION 2 a busy street scene is conjured up, the chatter sometimes robust, at other times, genteel. Detaching the unslurred triplets contributes to the humor.

VARIATION 3 is a pianistic romp but some caution is advised. If the tempo is too fast, this piece becomes not only a marathon for the fingers, but also for the right foot; the LH octaves can only sound *legato* if the pedal is changed on each eighth note. The half-measure slurs are articulated with clear separations. The syncopated effect of the upper line in m.6 is another delightful surprise.

VARIATION 4 begins with a comically low A that sounds more like a conclusion than an upbeat. There is no *piano* indication at the beginning and certainly the exuberant writing here suggests full tone until the *piano* indicated in the upbeat to m.9. The rapid LH writing is difficult; very quick horizontal wrist movements are necessary here and some of the leaps require the dexterity of a fine jazz pianist. Contrasting with the prevailing earthiness is the unexpected, quasi-polyphonic style of mm.9-12, which recalls the baroque. A slight pause after Variation 4 is recommended.

VARIATION 5 suggests a divertimento for wind instruments, and any rushing would spoil its calm atmosphere. A slower tempo than in the previous variations is certainly relevant. Pedaling can be used throughout, but if the slurs and the rests are not audible, the lines lack character. For the *legato* thirds in the LH a fingering must be chosen that makes the upper line sound as smooth as possible. The *forte* sound in this variation does not need to be very emphatic.

VARIATION 6 is strongly reminiscent of the first movement's thrusting energy. The absence of dynamic indications would suggest that the *forte* in the conclusion of the previous variation applies throughout. The LH's rapid leaps over the RH, a familiar Mozartian effect, suit the exuberant music, though from the second half of m.8 to m.11, the normal alignment of hands is perhaps preferable.

VARIATION 7 may seem innocuous on the page but it is something of a milestone in the composer's total *oeuvre*. For the first time, Mozart included a piece in minor mode in a set of variations. Often pianists take such minor-mode variations considerably slower than the rest of the piece. However, unlike the tempo changes marked in the final two variations, there is no change of pace indicated here. The bustling pace of the previous variations, however, is perhaps too brusque. The moderated tempo of Variation 5 is best. The key of D minor in Mozart's music generally signifies unrest more than melancholy. When not played in a morbid *Adagio* pace, the piece becomes a menacing mini-drama. The pianist must not soften the dynamic contrasts, which are more numerous here than in most other variations. The notation is full of rhetorical subtleties; the writhing half-measure slurs in mm.9-10, for example, should sound different from the fatalistic whole-measure slurs. This variation is a sudden glimpse into an abyss. The silence at the end should be longer than a mere quarter beat, giving us time to absorb this troubling interlude.

VARIATION 8 sounds like various woodwind instruments playing boisterous jokes. Tension in the hands and arms when playing *forte* renders the sound here particularly unpleasant and dull. Pedaling is needed only in mm.10-12. The lower voice of the octaves in m.12 can best be played by the LH.

VARIATION 9 continues the optimistic tone. If the fingers stay close to the keys and play the unslurred octaves *staccato*, these figurations will not sound dry. Unfortunately, players of modern instruments must reduce the tone in the low register. The quarter notes in the cadential measures 7-8, 16-17 lose their humor if played *legato*. The interaction of rhythm and touch here is not easy.

VARIATION 10 conjures up the colors of a full orchestra, the violins playing a *tremolo* in the opening bars, two horns sounding in the bass. Many pianists, especially younger ones, find the broken octaves (in m.7, for example) difficult because the thumb is too tense when changing position. The player must choose between emphasizing the lower notes of such *tremoli*, making for a thicker, more pompous sound, or the upper notes, giving more vitality and brilliance. The balance between the hands demands alertness. The pianist must focus his attention on the bustling good spirits of the piece; concentration on the technical demands belongs in the studio.

VARIATION 11, like the penultimate variations of Mozart's other works in this genre, assumes a slower tempo. Einstein remarked:

"Not even the somewhat old-fashioned and lengthy adagio variation interrupts the flow of the creative imagination." [23]

This may be true of the composition, but not of most performances. This piece poses considerable challenges to the player, but the choice between the two versions of the melody should be seen as a pleasure, not a problem. This issue is thoroughly discussed in the following section.

In the heading, *cantabile* is perhaps more relevant than *Adagio*. The metrical indication remains *alla breve*, therefore the pace is not conspicuously slow. A dirge-like progression through this elegant landscape would be deadly. A tempo of $\flat$ = 96 is suitable for most of the piece, with some freedom during the busiest figurations. Every note must be conceived vocally, though the actual touch during the most rapid ornamentation is more *leggiero* than *legato*. The lowest bass notes can be finger-pedaled throughout as the pedal must be changed very quickly to avoid any smearing of the vocal line.

VARIATION 12 was indicated *Allegro* only in the first edition. Mozart usually liked to end his variation works with a quick finale, but as in the previous variation, the tempo indication is more connotative than literal. If the initial tempo is too quick, the subsequent sixteenth notes will become jumbled. An approximate tempo of $\downarrow$ = 120 does not suffocate the humor of the piece. The gentle character of the theme is transformed here into jocular carousing, the dactyls of mm.9-16 bringing drunken revels to mind. Perhaps the dynamic contrasts are strongest in this unbuckled variation. In m.9, the RH eighth notes should not be joined to the subsequent sixteenth notes. If the player's forearms or thumbs are tense when playing the rapid broken octaves, this irreverent finale becomes more a battle than a comedy.

7 WRITTEN AND ADDED ORNAMENTATION IN THE THIRD MOVEMENT, K.284; COMPARISONS OF TWO VERSIONS IN VARIATION 11

VARIATION 2
m.
1   During all its recurrences in this variation, the *Schleifer* sounds rather lumpy begun on the beat and is better begun before the beat.

VARIATION 3
11   The onbeat *appoggiature* could be slightly accented and prolonged.
12   A turn could be added after the uppermost note on the first beat.

VARIATION 4
1   The *arpeggio* is played energetically, all the notes held, the uppermost sounding on the first beat.
11   The trill has more bite if played with five or seven notes and no termination.

VARIATION 5
8   To play the onbeat *appoggiature* as eighth notes is a dull choice. As sixteenth notes they have a suitably crunchy effect and in this *forte* context are quite strongly accented.

VARIATION 7
1   Some artists prefer to begin this trill on the upper auxiliary, a rather hysterical effect, which can sound unclear at the beginning of a slurred group. The speed of the trill should be more vocal than pianistic. The subsequent sixteenth notes function as a termination.

VARIATION 11

Here arises the intriguing possibility of choice offered by two versions of the text, which are given in all reliable editions of this sonata. Hereafter the manuscript version (*Autograph* in German editions) will be referred to as "A," and the version from the first edition (*Erstdruck* in German) as "FE."

m.

1   Though the initial *appoggiatura* in A is marked as an eighth note in FE, it is more expressive if it lasts somewhat longer. Arguably the subsequent turn is better placed in A, beginning on the sixth eighth-note beat, and not after it.

2   The FE *appoggiatura* and the slight accent seem fussy. Like Lili Kraus, I would omit this ornament. It is interesting to note that, unlike most other recording artists, Kraus chose the less decorated A version of the first eight measures, and this seems satisfying.

3   The FE's more vivid sighs are welcome. The melody does not have to be played here with metric strictness, but the bass line should remain absolutely steady, a fine instance of Mozartian *rubato*.

4   If one chooses to play the FE turn, it should end on the second eighth-note beat. Perhaps it is best reserved for m.12.

5   The FE version of the first half of this measure seems welcome, but I find the trill in the fourth quarter-note beat too fussy. It is perhaps more appropriate on a fortepiano, though on his recording the fortepianist Malcolm Bilson[23] also chooses to omit it.

6   Does not the FE ornamentation in the second quarter-note beat suggest yodeling?

7   The shifting of emphasis in FE seems pedantic and the notation of the fourth quarter-note beat in A seems more expressive, with another sighing *appoggiatura* and the two subsequent sixteenth notes *non legato*, a different articulation than in the following measure.

9   In FE the first beat *appoggiatura* and the shaping of the second half of the measure are desirable.

10   Perhaps the FE version of the first half of the measure is more interesting than A's but the *forte* should not be exaggerated. The fourth quarter-note beat trill begins on the principal note and does not need a termination.

11   A gives the rendition of the first beat *appoggiatura*, which in this placid context does sound better played on the beat. The trills become three-note *Schneller*. The FE states the rendition of the final quarter-note beat.

12   The turn ends on the second eighth-note beat.

13   A's trill on the fourth eighth-note beat is rarely played, as it obscures the line.

14   Both versions can readily evoke a beehive. Whichever version he chooses, the performer should not play the trills too rapidly, and he should avoid any lumpy accenting during the chain of trills. The FE compound *appoggiature* begin on the principal beats.

15   In the FE the line seems fussy. The dynamic indications in the subsequent four measures are either obvious, as in mm.17-18, or questionable, as in m.19. The FE ornaments in m.19 are another very subjective choice.

21   The FE version gives a clear rendition of A's line.

22   The *appoggiatura* of A is preferably long, as given in FE. The trill in FE, beginning on the principal note and with the indicated termination, adds more character to the line than the compound *appoggiatura* of A.

23   Arguably the second FE turn is sufficient decoration here.

24   Obviously the octaves sound more *legato* if, where possible, the LH plays the lower line. The FE's syncopation seems academic, but the FE version of the cadential trill, not to be played too rapidly, is suitable.

25   Many pianists omit the FE ornament before the third quarter-note beat.

26   The FE version is fine, but the rapid ascending chromatic scale becomes vulgar if played *crescendo*.

27   The onbeat *appoggiature* sound better if played as approximate thirty-second notes, each suspension slightly separated from the next. A's more characterful notation seems more relevant than the generalized *legato* in FE.

30   In A the separation of the trills is welcome. Each trill consists of three or five notes, without a termination.

31   Perhaps the best solution for the first beat is the FE version. Playing all these trills can create a mechanical effect if they are not given different inflections. The trills become three-note *Schneller* (see Neumann[25]).

32   Clearly the uppermost note of each *arpeggio* is emphasized.

33   The FE trill seems preferable and, in a lovely *rubato* effect, could sound slightly after the beat.

VARIATION 12

1   The NMA[26] editors state that the *appoggiatura* is indicated as two eighth notes in FE. An onbeat sixteenth note is much fresher.

6   Perhaps the LH should also be arpeggiated here, making for an even more dramatic effect. All the other arpeggiated chords in this variation are to be played with all the notes held, the uppermost sounding on the beat.

VII

THE SONATAS IN C, K.309, AND IN D, K.311

1 MOZART IN MUNICH, AUGSBURG AND MANNHEIM

After the success of *La finta giardiniera* in March 1775, Mozart returned to Salzburg and remained there for two and a half years. During this tranquil period he created such masterpieces as the five violin concerti and the *Jeunehomme* Piano Concerto, K.271. For Archbishop Colloredo's court he completed *Il rè pastore* and much delightful chamber music; for the church numerous masses were completed, and for the burghers of Salzburg Mozart created unique works like the *Haffner* Serenade, K.250/248-b, and the *Lodron* Concerto, K.242, for three pianos. The gentle B-flat Concerto, K.238, also dates from these years.

In August 1777, the Archbishop finally granted Wolfgang some time off from his duties. Presumably the young man yearned to escape the domination of his father as much as the confines of the Salzburg court. Leopold, forced to remain in the stifling atmosphere of Colloredo's employ, was despondent when Wolfgang, accompanied by his mother, left for Munich. The young man had no intention of returning to Salzburg.

At the Munich court, however, it soon became evident that Mozart had no chance of gaining a position, and on October 11, Wolfgang arrived in Augsburg, where he first encountered the new fortepianos built by Johann Andreas Stein. For pianists, this was an important development in Mozart's life. Nathan Broder reminds us:

"... though pianos were by no means plentiful before the last quarter of the century, Mozart had heard about them, seen them, and even occasionally played upon them since his early childhood."[1]

Mozart wrote Leopold several times praising the responsiveness of these instruments. About the piano playing of Stein's daughter, Wolfgang was less positive:

"... she has great talent for music. But she will not make progress by this method — for she will never acquire great rapidity, since she definitely does all she can to make her hands heavy. Further, she will never ac-

quire the most essential ... requisite in music ... because from her earliest years she has done her utmost not to play in time."[2]

In late October 1777, Mozart and his mother traveled to Mannheim. There he wrote a piano sonata in C, which he had already improvised in Augsburg. In Mannheim Wolfgang had been impressed by
the piano playing and beauty of the 14-year-old Rosa Cannabich:

> "As soon as I can, I shall have the sonata which I have written for Mlle.
> Cannabich copied out on small paper and send it to my sister. I began to
> teach it to Mlle. Rosa three days ago. We finished the opening Allegro
> today. The Andante will give us most trouble, for it is full of expression
> and must be played accurately and with the exact shades of forte and
> piano, precisely as they are marked."[3]

None of Mozart's other compositions for piano is mentioned so
often in the family correspondence. When the young man announced
to the Cannabichs that he would soon be leaving Mannheim, Rosa
"played my sonata very seriously. I assure you, I couldn't keep from
weeping."[4]

Mozart and his mother were chronically short of money and largely
dependent on being invited out for meals. Yet despite all the difficulties, their days were far from unpleasant. Mozart was thoroughly enjoying his freedom from his father, and he had fallen very seriously in
love with the talented singer Aloysia Weber.

Leopold totally rejected the idea of Wolfgang marrying. The
correspondence between father and son became tortuous, with as
much deception as affection. Joseph Kerman observed:

> "Once taught the art and artifice of letter writing by his father, Wolfgang
> used it against him in the long... war of independence from Leopold's
> overbearing domination. All of Mozart's statements of fact must be scru-
> tinized as possible disinformation, all his declarations of piety and vir-
> tue as possible camouflage."[5]

After much nagging and emotional blackmail from Salzburg,
Wolfgang and his mother set out in March 1778, for the French capital. The stay in Mannheim had been hectic but, fortunately for pianists, did produce two very delightful sonatas.

SONATA IN C MAJOR, K.309

OTHER K. LISTING	284-b
COMPOSITION DATE	October-November 1777
TOTAL DURATION	20 minutes (with first repeat in i)
FIRST MOVEMENT	*Allegro con spirito*
FORM	sonata
APPROXIMATE TEMPO	♩ = M.M. 134
DURATION	6½ minutes (with first repeat)
SUGGESTED LISTENING	Violin Concerto, K.219 i
	Piano Concerto, K.246 i
	Piano Concerto, K.271 i

2 INTERPRETATION OF THE FIRST MOVEMENT, K.309

How can any pianist not revel in this mini-symphony, so full of surprises yet so radiantly clear in outline? The composer's manuscript has been lost, but there is a copy by Leopold, which in the following sections will be referred to as "L. Copy." The C major Sonata, together with the piano sonatas K.310 and 311, was first published in Paris in 1781 or 1782.

The opening motif, anticipating Beethoven in its compactness and orchestral tone, is later echoed in a very different context: the opening to the minuet of the A major Sonata, K.331. In this C major Sonata, the trumpetlike energy of the initial six-note motif can be supported by pedaling, but without the fingers binding any of the notes. The more recent *Urtext* editions give only the upper C in the bass, making for logical and pleasing part-writing. Elsewhere in the movement, volume seems to have been more important, as the initial bass note is always doubled to form an octave.

Pedaling would ruin the phrase in mm.3-7, so finely "scored" for first and second violins. Frivolity is surely more relevant here than pathos. In mm.6-7 the slurs should be audibly separated, but without lumpy accents. A romantic *ritenuto* in mm.12-14 would be an artificial effect; slight elongation of the rests and a theatrical fading of tone are much more eloquent.

Beginning at m.15, the next theme has a festive character. Wind instruments are evoked, also in the bass. Any pedaling, therefore, would be regrettable. The sequence at mm.21-26, however, has an unmistakably "string sound," woodwinds joining in only on the first-beat chords. The *fortepiani* and *crescendi* stated in some editions during this sentence are lacking in L. Copy and in the NMA.[6] Obviously it would be unnatural to play all the phrases between the *forte* of m.15 and the *piano* at m.33 with the same strength of tone. But the sequence can dissolve into silent-movie effects if there are exaggerated contrasts in volume. Note that the bass is *non legato* throughout, even in mm.15-20 and 27-28. The baroque dotted rhythm heard in m.31 is very lively, but the doubling of the two lines can sound crude if played too *legato*. Any suggestion of a *diminuendo* in the last four measures of this theme spoils the charming contrast heard at the beginning of the second theme group in m.33.

At m.35 we hear a cheerful motif, like someone whistling out of doors; even the serious Dennerlein[7] referred to this as a "farmer's tune." To prevent a choppy sound, the RH fingers can best remain close to the keys. The written-out *appoggiature* in mm.37-38 should be played with audible rests, clearly different from the variant heard three measures later. In mm.43-44 the LH accented initial sixteenth notes are not joined to the following notes; this is quite difficult to play if the wrist is not low when the thumb plays its notes. The bass of mm.45 is *non legato*. The accenting of weaker beats in mm.48-49 is playful, not dramatic, the eighth notes clearly separated from the quarter notes.

The conclusion of the exposition is rich in exuberant figures. Articulation should be very precise if a blurred rush of notes is to be avoided. The exposition's climax in mm.52-53 is accompanied by rapid Alberti bass writing, which gives many students trouble. When Mozart referred to limitations in Rosa Cannabich's LH technique, this was surely one of the places where she faltered:

> "Her right hand is very good, but her left, unfortunately, is completely ruined ... I have told her that if I were her regular teacher, I would lock up all her music, cover the keys with a handkerchief and make her practice first with the right hand and then with the left ... until each hand is thoroughly trained."[8]

It must also be observed that in such LH figurations, any unnecessary tension in the thumb causes excessive lifting and reduced mobility in the fingers.

The tongue-in-cheek dialogue that opens the *Codetta* at m.54 should be played with a warm touch, close to the keys. If conceived as a single line, the final *forte* RH flourish in sixteenth notes is technically impossible to play metrically. But the leaps can be heard as demarcations between the first and second violin parts. When the RH line twice leaps upwards a sixth, 1-2 is the most secure fingering. Panicky resource to the pedal here only makes the difficulties more evident.

Though the development is of customary length, approximately half that of the exposition, it seems longer because so much happens. The strong contrasts and surprises of the Mannheim symphonists are very apparent. The initial motif strides confidently through a turbulent landscape, sudden modulations causing abrupt changes of emotion and color. Major technical problems can arise if the player thinks that the first motif's sixteenth notes should be *legato*. In m.61 the LH's first sixteenth note should be played almost *staccato* because it is immediately repeated by the RH.

Mozart did not often indicate *pianissimo* (*piano* given incorrectly in some editions) as in m.62, a dramatic whisper. The UC pedal may be welcome here, but not in the grief-stricken measures 63-66, which should have a vocal immediacy. If the plaintive slurs in the melody are joined to each other, a tragic statement is reduced to whining. Similarly, in mm.74-78, the RH is inclined to bind the sixteenth notes to the subsequent quarter notes, but this is not indicated and a tiny break at these moments gives the line more urgency. Too many pianists shy away from the orchestral fury of this sequence and play a *diminuendo* in mm.79-82, spoiling the contrast of the ghostly *piano subito* in m.82. The following *forte* outburst should not be pedaled. The lurch to G major in m.90 is startling after such a long stay in minor mode.

It is a relief to hear the initial motif back in the tonic key at m.94, but Mozart has still more surprises for us. The expansive transformation of the initial measures *in minore* during mm.101-107, as well as other changes in the first theme group, give the recapitulation more weight than the exposition. At m.127 the music is literally turned upside down, a touch which must have delighted the young Rosa Cannabich. After all the harmonic and motivic adventures experienced in this movement, the *Coda* beginning at m.152 takes a reassuringly predictable course, with a repetition of the initial motif and a conventional cadential figuration.

3 ORNAMENTATION IN THE FIRST MOVEMENT, K.309

m.

1   Beginning the energetic *arpeggio* on the beat would obscure the doubling of the initial motif by both hands. The three initial triadic notes are not bound by the hand or pedaling.

4   The *appoggiatura* is probably best played as a lightly accented onbeat sixteenth note. A droopy eighth note, though frequently heard, is definitely not suitable in such a cheerful phrase. Some artists, among them Lubimov[9] and Kocsis,[10] play a prebeat grace note.

17 The onbeat *appoggiatura* is a sixteenth note and, if possible, the two notes after the suspension should be played less *legato*. Given the tempo, the trill is best played as a five-note turn beginning on the principal note, but preferably preceded by the upper auxiliary as a grace note.

21 Though it is often played on the beat, this *appoggiatura* has more character if played as a very quick grace note.

23 The *arpeggio* is apparently[11] to be found only in m.118 of the L. Copy, but obviously these chords gain vitality if vigorously arpeggiated and all the notes are held.

27 The *appoggiature* are like that in m.17. The *arpeggio*'s notes must not be held.

51 To maintain clarity of the line at this tempo, these trills become three-note *Schneller*. Naturally, each trill is bound to the subsequent eighth note, as in m.145.

53 The upper or lower auxiliary begins the trill on the beat. It should be played as quickly as possible, with bright tone in the upper notes. The termination should be clear and not end with the frequently heard thud.

65 I prefer beginning on the principal note, but beginning on the upper auxiliary is also possible.

72 If the compound *appoggiatura* was to sound as two sixteenth notes it could have been marked as such. It seems best to begin this unusual ornament just after the second quarter-note beat.

In such a spirited "orchestral" piece there is little place for improvised ornaments. Malcolm Bilson[12] adds very effective variants when repeating more vocal phrases like mm.66, 71-72, 104, 106-107. However, it remains a subjective choice whether this repetition should be played. Though the development and recapitulation are rich in surprises, repetition of both sections may weaken the total impression.

SECOND MOVEMENT	*Andante un poco adagio*
FORM	blend of sonata, rondo and variation forms
APPROXIMATE TEMPO	♪ = M.M. 90
DURATION	6 minutes
SUGGESTED LISTENING	Sonata for Piano and Violin, K.305/293-d ii
	Ariette *Oiseaux, si tous les ans*, K.307
	Piano Concerto, K.246 ii
	Flute Concerto, K.313 ii

4 INTERPRETATION OF THE SECOND MOVEMENT, K.309

The hypothetical biographical origins of this movement have attracted so much commentary that other facets, such as the unusual form, are forgotten. Is the player helped by the knowledge that this *Andante* could have been a "portrait of young Rosa Cannabich"? Essentially this movement is not difficult for players with a fine *legato* touch and a sense of vocal or violinistic phrasing. But the form, the dense forest of ornamentation, and certain puzzles in the text daunt many performers.

To play this tender movement well, the pianist must be able to suggest a combination of serenity and refined vitality far removed from twentieth century life. Mozart's tempo indication is unusually specific, but ironically it seems all too often to inspire dull gravity more than *Andante* tenderness. S.P. Rosenblum observed:

"The use of *Andante un poco adagio* in the sonata K.309 is among the indications that for Mozart, too, *adagio* was closer to *andante* ..." [13]

In any case the flow of the music is with three impulses, not six, in each measure. Though some rhythmic plasticity seems desirable, overly frequent *caesurae*, lingerings, or surges easily lapse into cosmetic expressivity.

The form is very original. Was this one aspect of K.309 that inspired Leopold's ambivalent reaction after receiving his son's copy? The first "A" theme consists of eight-measure phrases, which are repeated and varied in mm.17-32. At m.33 a second "B" theme is heard. Because it is in the dominant, this theme lends a sonata-like shape to the movement, but it is interrupted at m.45 for another, shorter variation of "A". At m.53 "B" unexpectedly returns. During mm.65-72 "A" is given a last variation, followed by a short *Coda* (mm.76-79). The structure is a hybrid blend of rondo, sonata and variation elements.

To an alert listener the opening sounds are familiar. Richard Rosenberg[14] noted that if the thirty-second notes are omitted, the initial motif recalls the cheerful second theme (m.35) of the first movement. If one regards this *Andante* as being a portrait, the slurring could be compared to brush strokes, the dynamics to a color scheme. All the thirty-second notes of the first theme are to be played extremely lightly on a modern instrument. However, the initial *forte-piani* are mere enhancements of light and shade. The player must give much thought to the numerous indications. Does the *piano* in the second measure have the same sound as in the first? Does not the *forte* in m.3 indicate the high point of the phrase more than strong volume?

Sometimes Mozart makes minute variations in the articulation, slightly altering the character of a phrase. In the third beat of m.5, for example, the RH sixteenth notes are under one slur, whereas in the next measure, the same figuration has two slurs. It is not pedantic to observe these details; subtlety of articulation is the essence of these tender, sometimes impulsive musings.

The theme introduced at m.33 opens new perspectives. Whereas the previous sentences were introvert reflections, constantly interrupted by rests (a girl's hesitant reactions?), this C major theme strides in long triadic outlines (Mozart's feelings about Miss Cannabich?). Metaphors aside, the tone should remain full until m.35, where the indicated *piano* can be seen as a *diminuendo* or a *subito piano*. Throughout this theme the pedal must be changed on each eighth-note beat to preserve the orchestral impulses in the LH. The RH's first two sixteenth notes in mm.37-38 are not slurred, though many editions give slurs here, creating a vulgar *portamento* effect at the first climax of the piece. The LH eighth notes in mm.40-43 are also not *legato* but must be sensitively phrased.

Presumably the articulation of the upbeat octaves in mm.48-50 is the same as in mm.4-6. When the LH takes the lower notes of m.49's octaves, it is not difficult to achieve smoothness of line. The RH's ecstatic ascending scales in mm.57-58 will sound lumpy if the wrist is not supple, for the thumb must hold the initial note. The bass line of mm.60-64 must not dominate and the longer RH notes should sound full. Pedaling is not desirable in all thirty-second-note passages and the rapid broken octaves in mm.72-74. This *non legato* phrase also requires no pedaling. In the two final measures of this extraordinary movement the *una corda* pedal may be relevant, but elsewhere players must be wary of too much UC pedaling, which reduces a lovely portrait in watercolors to a bland charcoal sketch.

There are numerous minor textual puzzles in this *Andante*. In the absence of a manuscript, modern editions are based on the L. Copy and the first Paris edition; this inevitably leads to discrepancies. The NMA[15] prints the preferable alternative B-flat for the LH upper line (second beat, mm.13 and 29). The two versions of the melodic line in m.19 make for a more difficult choice. The second and third *appoggiatura* notes would usually be C and E, though most pianists play the first edition's version E and F. Even more subjective are the choices in m.55, where the first RH thirty-second note could be G or F and the third sixteenth note in m.56 F or D-sharp. The NMA's preferred version[16] for the bass line in m.64 is definitely more lively than the first edition's version. In the penultimate measure, the third A-C is preferable to the bare C usually played on the second eighth-note beat.

Mozart's remark to his father that this movement had to be played with much attention to detail was certainly an understatement! Yet what a human scene we experience here, full of expectation and resignation.

5 ORNAMENTATION IN THE SECOND MOVEMENT, K.309

m.

4   This trill, and that in m.12, can best begin with the principal note on the beat, thereby avoiding octave formation with the bass. Five notes and a termination are suitable.

7   The duration of these onbeat *appoggiature* is subjective. If lasting longer than sixteenth notes, they seem melancholy; if shorter, they become playful.

14 Surely the turns here and in m.31 are graceful, not rushed.

15 This onbeat *appoggiatura*, and that in m.31, become sixteenth notes or somewhat longer. The two sixteenth notes after the *appoggiatura* are not *legato*.

17 These *appoggiature* should definitely become quick grace notes. Rosenblum[17] observed that another rendition "will result in rhythmic and melodic chaos."

39 The onbeat *appoggiatura* can be played very lightly and quickly, or as a wistful (approximate) eighth note.

43 The trill here and in m.63, in the RH's lower voice, are best played with three notes, very softly, the thumb totally relaxed. The subsequent *appoggiatura* in thirds is better played on the final eighth-note beat.

57 The LH trill could be rendered as a three-note *Schneller* or a four-note *Pralltriller*.

73 Given the preceding figuration in broken octaves, some might

presume that the *appoggiatura* should sound on the beat. But the *fortepiano* clearly indicates emphasis on the upper note of the octave leap. A grace-note interpretation is definitely preferable, resulting in a charming *rubato* effect.

Dennerlein remarked that here "the technique of ornamentation stretches the limits of what is possible."[18] There certainly seems to be little place for more decoration.

THIRD MOVEMENT	*Rondeau: Allegretto grazioso*
FORM	rondo
APPROXIMATE TEMPO	$\downarrow$ = M.M. 80
DURATION	7 minutes
SUGGESTED LISTENING	Concerto for Flute & Harp, K.299/297-c iii
	Piano Concerto in C, K.246 iii
	Il Rè pastore, K.208, Overture

6 INTERPRETATION OF THE THIRD MOVEMENT, K.309

After the ruminative *Andante* we find ourselves in a maelstrom of activity. If the first movement was unmistakably symphonic and the second suggested a string quartet, this finale evokes the atmosphere of a piano concerto. As in the previous movement, the form is unorthodox and must have startled Leopold when he first read through the manuscript. In this finale Mozart indulged to the fullest the sharp contrasts and abrupt modulations of the Mannheim School.

Though it seems to "roll out of the hand," as if improvised, the opening theme needs careful shaping. Note that the upbeat eighth notes, the RH sixteenth notes that function as passing notes, and none of the LH sixteenth notes are to be played with a *legato* touch or finger-pedaling. Indeed, given the effervescent quality of the theme, pedaling should be avoided throughout. Unfortunately one usually hears not only excessive pedaling here, but the use of the UC pedal as well, making the theme superficially delicate. Are high spirits and humor delicate? The *gracioso* quality has more to do with flow and inflection than with daintiness.

In such a festive piece the *Allegretto* indication certainly does not designate a cautious pace, but warns against haste. The apparent simplicity of the theme should not result in all the first beats being played with the same emphasis. There are moments when harmonic inflections in the bass, as at mm.13-15, can be underlined, though preferably not finger-pedaled.

At m.19 the imaginary orchestra takes over, the initial fanfares "scored" for wind instruments. None of the sixteenth notes here, excepting the *appoggiature*, are slurred and, in such a lively context, they should be played *non legato*, with absolutely no pedaling. The blend of string and wind textures in mm.31-39 is a delight, but the repeated C's heard in the inner voices of mm.34-35 should not be too evident. The humorous thirds "for woodwinds" in the bass of m.39 are best clearly detached and unpedaled, though many editions have slurs here.

At m.40 the imaginary solo pianist bursts back on the scene, playing a completely new theme ("B") of concerto-like brilliance, which poses no problems when the RH thumb is not tense. *Decrescendi* would dissipate the music's surge in mm.41-42 or 45-46, where the indicated reductions in tone should be abrupt. Rosenblum[19] refers to this phrase as a fine example of "echo effect," rare in Mozart's music.

Virtually everyone plays a *diminuendo* in mm.51-52, thereby erasing the surprise *piano* of m.53. Another lamentable "tradition" is slurring the first two RH notes of m.53, which clearly are very different from m.55. If changed with each eighth-note beat, pedaling is possible during the restless mm.53-57.

In m.58 Mozart plays a splendid joke. After all the turbulence, we expect some dramatic statement, but instead we hear something like robust laughter! The RH's "violins" play an energetic *tremolo* while the LH's "wind instruments" blow jaunty retorts. Depending on the instrument, this passage needs little or no pedaling. On fortepianos the *tremoli* make a splendid racket, but on modern instruments the effect can easily become coarse. In these *tremoli*, players with small or tense hands often experience cramp, which can be avoided if the middle fingers remain as relaxed as possible. Too many pianists introduce echo effects here, which sound precious and spoil the teasing humor of the pianist's brief appearance at m.66. Three measures later Mozart plays yet another prank; the buoyant orchestral phrase of mm.58-62 returns, now cast in minor mode, mockingly dangerous. After lurching through some startling modulations the music comes to rest in G major at m.77. Given m.74's *fortepiano* and the *piano* in m.77, it may be presumed that the latter half of m.75 forms a *crescendo* leading to the cadence.

The "scoring" of the comical measures 77-85 is for both soloist and orchestra. The *staccati* are witty, not to be played with dry "even" tone. Orchestral weight is evident in mm.85-89, with pedaling preferably only on the first eighth-note beat of each measure. In m.89 the orchestral activity fades for four measures of a delicate piano solo before the initial theme returns at m.93. The extensive dominant preparation of the second "A" section has a Beethovenian insistence. This time theme A is given some frisky decorations. In m.110 there is a delightfully mischievous transition, a giggling *decrescendo*, which is rarely articulated correctly; the RH has slurs over each quarter-note beat, whereas in the LH each eighth-note beat is clearly separated. This leads to the wild orchestral outbursts heard already at mm.58-62 and 69-75, but now with a different bass line.

Measure 115 is another short transition that must be exactly formed, the tone full until the second half of the measure. Too many players seek tinkling melancholy in the next section, where the new "C" theme is introduced. Any diminution of energy here seriously deflates the momentum of the entire finale though. The second quarter-note beats should be light. Pedaling is best avoided if this F major tune is to remain cheerful and not become a dreamy monologue. There is very little *legato* indicated here. Virtually all of the RH sixteenth notes are *non legato*. In the second half of mm.117 and 121 too, if the RH's two eighth notes are played *legato*, the effect is soporific. The bass should be very light and not finger-pedaled.

The transition in mm.131-136 provides the piece's first darker moments, but these are transient. If the tempo slackens there will be a clumsy change of gear when the "B" theme returns at m.137. The *fortepiani* of mm.132 and 134 are melodic emphases, not dramatic accents.

The succession of themes in the rest of the movement defies usual concepts of what constitutes a rondo form. Especially on modern instruments, the octaves of m.217 will sound more joyful, and less heavy, when the RH plays the upper line. Though the uppermost note in mm.230-31 in the earliest sources is E, most editions lower these shrill dissonances to E-flats. Given the absence of any E's or E-flat's in the LH figures, the E's are a defensible and logical reading, certainly having more character than the usual E-flats. As there is no manuscript, this remains a subjective choice.

The finale seems to end with the exuberant fanfares of mm.240-244, but Mozart has yet another surprise: transposing the initial theme down an octave, the LH playing in the lowest register of that period's instruments. The *una voce* pedal of Stein's piano must have been very effective! On modern instruments this effect is impossible if there is too much "right pedal." The bass slurs do not necessarily indicate finger-pedaling. The UC pedal may be depressed at m.245, but the RH line must not be too weightless; a truly whispered tone is indicated only by the *pianissimo* of the last two measures. What an astonishing range of emotion and scoring is heard in K.309! Exuberance predominates, but intimate sensibility is never far away and, at the end, clearly triumphs.

7 ORNAMENTATION IN THE THIRD MOVEMENT, K.309

m.

1   The onbeat *appoggiatura* becomes an approximate sixteenth note. The two notes after the suspension are definitely *non legato*.

10 The compound *appoggiatura* sounds motivically logical when played before the beat, but beginning the ornament on the beat is perhaps a welcome change of emphasis.

15 Because the melody unexpectedly leaps upwards after the trill, clarity is important. A light three-note *Schneller* is sufficient.

20 The *appoggiatura* is played as in m.l.

36 Each turn should begin immediately after the initial note sounds.

63 This *Schleifer* would sound lugubrious if it does not end on the beat.

66 The *appoggiatura* is piquant, not melancholy, and is best played very quickly before the beat.

76 The uppermost notes of this arpeggiated chord, and those beginning in m.86, sound on the beat.

116 These *appoggiature* become very light grace notes. Played on the beat they are technically easier but sound rather wooden.

136 Perhaps a five-note trill beginning on the principal note, without a termination, is best.

198 The trill does not need a termination and probably lasts until the second quarter-note beat.

ADDITIONAL ORNAMENTATION in such a hyperactive piece is rarely desirable. Bass chords that are strongly accented, as in mm.44, 65, 73, 186 may be energetically arpeggiated. Malcolm Bilson alters m.92 in a charming fashion.

SONATA IN D MAJOR, K.311

OTHER K. LISTING	K.284-c
DATE OF COMPOSITION	October-November 1777
TOTAL DURATION	17 minutes (with first repeat in i)

Whereas K.309 enjoyed many references in the Mozart family correspondence, K.311 shares the fate of most of Mozart's piano music and is hardly mentioned. Some authorities, including Landowska,[20] maintain that the musical portrait of Rosa Cannabich is the slow movement of K.311, not K.309. More useful for the interpreter is that he understands the formal experiments Mozart continued to explore in this sonata. In K.309 the first movement followed more or less usual structural lines and the two remaining movements were decidedly unorthodox. In K.311 we find the reverse; the first movement is unorthodox and the two remaining movements assume more usual forms. In these sonatas Mozart seems to celebrate life with sensual exuberance. These pieces throb with the energy of a young man exulting in his newly found, short-lived, independence. Yet it can be argued that both sonatas sound more natural on eighteenth or nineteenth century instruments than on modern grand pianos.

FIRST MOVEMENT	*Allegro con spirito*
FORM	sonata
APPROXIMATE TEMPO	$\downarrow$ = M.M. 134
DURATION	5 minutes (with first repeat)
SUGGESTED LISTENING	Serenade in D, K.204/213-a i
	Violin Concerto in G, K.216 i
	Violin Concerto in A, K.219 i

8 INTERPRETATION OF THE FIRST MOVEMENT, K.311

The entire movement exudes *joie de vivre*. Though there are occasional shadows passing over this sunny landscape, mystery and conflict are far away. These ebullient spirits generate a preponderance of *non legato* and *staccato* playing, which will not appeal to "incurable romantics." For instance, in the third measure, one usually hears the second beat F-sharp carelessly joined to the following *appoggiatura*, creating a disagreeable braying effect. All the bass notes in this measure and the fourth beat's RH eighth notes are definitely not *legato*, though not necessarily as short as the *staccato* eighth notes of m.2 or in the bass of m.7.

In the initial measures, a clear conception of which phrases could be played by stringed or wind instruments lends the playing more definition. Many play a *crescendo* in the sixteenth notes of m.10, but this is a mechanical effect suggesting vacuum cleaning. Mozart's *forte* in the first beat of the following measure clearly indicates increased activity there. In the bass of mm.13-14, the funny bassoon line is neither *legato* nor *staccato*, and in each measure, the sixth eighth note (not the fifth!) is emphasized.

At m.16 the second theme group begins in a gentler mood. The bass is no mere accompaniment, the slurs implying the shapes of the harmonic shifts. Exaggeration of dissonances or shortening of resolution notes disturb the gracious RH melody. The *forte* in m.24 begins with the RH's second sixteenth note, not the frequently heard thud on the first beat. The RH here evokes stringed instruments, the LH woodwinds. During the entire second theme group, any heavy accenting has a deadening effect. Pedaling is unnecessary throughout the whole exposition, with the possible exceptions of the initial chord and the quarter-note chords of mm.16 and 37.

The exposition's two final measures present gentle suspensions, true *sospiri* (sighs), derived from the similar pattern in the second theme. This sighing motif dominates the development section until m.58. Dabs of pedaling could be interjected to prevent a hiccupping effect; Konrad Wolff[21] observed that shortening the resolution of each suspension is not welcome here. The dynamics should be conceived in orchestral terms, the *fp* in m.41, a threatening "woodwind" chord interrupting the sighs of the violins. In mm.40, 42 a *crescendo* creates a false sense of drama. Measure 43's *forte* is not as strong as the outburst in mm.48-53, the climax of the movement. The fleeting darkness of B minor at m.54-55 is quickly erased by a lurch to G major.

Measure 58 seems to announce the recapitulation, but instead we hear the sentence that began at m.28! After the entire sentence is restated in G major we yearn for a return to the stability of D major, but in m.66 Mozart takes us through a whirling sequence, unmistakably suggesting a dog chasing its own tail. Unfortunately, this often sounds like the grimmest sort of Czerny étude. In this delightfully slow explosion of energy the player must carefully consider the tonal weight of each figuration. At mm.74-75 this strangely futile bustle most unexpectedly evolves into the concluding phrase of the exposition's first theme group. We still await a restatement of the initial theme of the movement, yet at m.78 the second theme group returns. Only in m.99 does the movement's opening reappear, but it is interrupted after six measures and spins off on another tangent. After all these surprises, Mozart plays a final joke by ending the movement conventionally, with the last four measures of the exposition. The *piano* of the last two measures is more teasing than tender.

Given the movement's capricious form, the surprise elements may be lost on a second hearing of the development and recapitulation sections. Conversely it could be argued that precisely because of the unusual structure a second repeat is welcome. This remains a totally subjective matter.

9 ORNAMENTATION IN THE FIRST MOVEMENT, K.311

m.

1   The initial *arpeggio* is usually played very quickly and ends on the beat. Landowska[22] observed that in the manuscript there is no *arpeggio* indication but a clear indication of an *acciaccatura* between the F-sharp and the A. The dissonant G certainly gives the opening chord a peppery emphasis, though the effect is not particularly Mozartian. When repeated at m.99, an *arpeggio* after the preceding trill would sound confused. The onbeat *appoggiature* that follow in the second half of these measures become sixteenth notes, with the notes after each suspension slightly detached.

4   The first *appoggiatura* falls on the beat; a sixteenth note sounds cheerful whereas an eighth note suggests inappropriate pathos.

7   Some artists play the upper auxiliary before the trill or even on the beat, but in such a triadic motif, it is surely better to begin the trill with the principal note (see Neumann[23]).

13 This onbeat *appoggiatura* implies a slight accent more than any loosening of meter.

16 The *appoggiatura* becomes a light grace note before the sixteenth notes.

19 After the preceding suspensions, this *appoggiatura* sounds more charming played as a prebeat grace note.

21 The trill is more spritely if played as a three-note *Schneller* than the usually heard turn.

23 The upper auxiliary could be played as a very quick grace note before the trill, which, depending on the instrument and the player's technique, consists of three or five notes plus termination.

31   Due to the slur, this trill must begin with the principal note. A five-note turn sounds lumpy. Seven notes, without a termination, with the fingering 2-3, is perhaps the best solution.
110 The uppermost note of each chord sounds with the bass.

In such an orchestral piece, few phrases invite ADDITIONAL ORNA-MENTATION. Perhaps when the exposition is repeated, the melody in mm.32-35 could be slightly altered. The chords in mm.37 and 56 should be arpeggiated like those in m.110. Some may be tempted to add decoration during the rests of mm.56-58, but surely the rests are rhetorical gestures, like question marks, which must remain suspenseful silences.

SECOND MOVEMENT	*Andante con espressione*
FORM	binary
APPROXIMATE TEMPO	♪= M.M. 84
DURATION	5 minutes
SUGGESTED LISTENING	Serenade in D, K.204/213-a v
	Haffner Serenade, K.250 viii
	Sonata for Piano & Violin in A, K.305/293-d ii
	Lied "Das Veilchen," K.476

10 INTERPRETATION OF THE SECOND MOVEMENT, K.311

This movement, like the *Andante* of the previous sonata, may sound innocuous to modern ears, but the openhearted tenderness evinced in both pieces evokes an interior world quivering with intimate feelings. This *Andante* is not difficult for a pianist who has a good sense for vocal line and fine range of tone from *mp* to *pp*. Though there are few contrasts in the piece, the interpreter must possess a very alert sensitivity to tiny shifts in emotion, otherwise the repetitive elements in the piece may overwhelm the inner discourse.

Aspects of variation, rondo, and sonata forms can be found here, though basically the piece is in binary form, the second section beginning in m.39, the *Coda* in m.90. The sense of equilibrium in the movement is uncanny. The repetition is delayed until the end of the section.

Whichever tempo is chosen, a pedestrian pace results if second quarter-note beats are emphasized. In the initial theme the articulation and phrasing are as subtle as they are exact. The first note of each slurred group is the strongest. In the opening measure the two RH B's at the end of the slurs must be detached. In the next measure the fingers must not "lazily" join the two slurred note groups. Slurred over the bar-line, the cello bass line is calmer. The upbeat to m.4 becomes droopy if slurred to the subsequent first beat. Depending on the instrument and performance space, the slight breaks between slurs may be smoothened by dabs of pedaling. All of these tiny nuances and "bowings" are not fussy details, but essential elements in this refined monologue.

The *forti* in mm.3, 7 are not noisy, but suggest that woodwinds have joined the stringed instruments. The wedged chords in these measures sound best with detached pedal strokes. In mm.8-11 finger-pedaling of the bass line is marked. Perhaps this also applies to mm.17-24, a wonderful melody so full of wistful longing, the interpreter may be tempted to let the tempo sag. This reduces sentiment to sentimentality. If the player's phrasing (generally the first note of each slurred group is the strongest) and breathing remain natural, surprisingly little *rubato* is necessary to give an affecting account of this movement.

In m.29 the LH can take some of the lower notes of the upper staff's octaves, which should sound as if the first and second violins of our imagined chamber orchestra were playing. The writing in the second half of m.87 and throughout m.89 is tricky. The lowest bass notes must be held for an eighth-note beat and the pedal changed again on the second sixteenth-note beat. Otherwise the *tenuto* bass line will be interrupted or the melody will become blurred. David Rowland speculates that the knee levers of the Stein piano may have inspired this unusual writing:

> "The downward stems of the left-hand accompaniment cannot be realized literally without the sustaining device ... in the works of other composers left-hand accompanying figures which exceed the span of a ninth or tenth occur very seldom before the 1790s ... These accompaniments are quite rare in Mozart's music too..."[24]

Given the vocal quality of the entire movement, it is best to avoid using the UC pedal until the *pianissimo* of the final two measures.

11 ORNAMENTATION IN THE SECOND MOVEMENT, K.311

There are several "border-line cases" in this *Andante*, for which no aesthetic or academic solution will satisfy every listener or player. A certain interpretation may sound expressive when played by one pianist, heavy and uninspired played by another. Experimentation often leads to a solution that sounds natural and spontaneous.

m.

1   This sort of ornament, a *Zwischenschlag*, recurs frequently throughout the movement. It should be played very lightly. An onbeat *appoggiatura* would sound wooden. Neumann[25] and Rosenblum[26] also refer to this prebeat interpretation.

8   Due to the slur, the trill begins with the principal note and should consist of five notes plus termination. A five-note turn creates a soporific effect.

9   The onbeat *appoggiatura* could be slightly longer than a sixteenth note. The two sixteenth notes after the suspension are more expressive if slightly detached.

10   The trill would sound pedantic begun with the upper auxiliary on the beat. Perhaps the auxiliary could be played as a grace note before the trill. Five notes and a termination are desirable.

16   As this trill begins a *cantabile* phrase, it begins with the principal note. A three- or five-note trill without termination suffices, as the final note of the measure sounds like a termination.

17   This trill is like that in the previous measure. Each A in the melody must have a slightly different inflection.

20   The *Schleifer* should be played quite lightly and ends on the sixth sixteenth-note beat.

22   The compound *appoggiatura* is best played before the first beat, for the G-sharp sounds bizarre above the bass G.

27   This trill definitely begins with the principal note. The termination (notated in some editions) is with G-sharp.

33   These lovely fluttering trills, consisting of five notes, must obviously begin with the principal note. If one chooses not to play a termination, seven notes may be welcome. Not all these ornaments require the same rhythmic impulse; in some, the first note might be slightly prolonged.

37   This is a conventional cadential trill and must begin with the upper auxiliary note. The termination should be clear and not end with an accent.

40   The turn is not quick.

43   The turn must begin as soon as possible. The *Zwischenschlag*

provides a puzzle. It is played here by both hands, and it would seem most logical to retain the interpretation as in m.l. However, Neumann maintains "the inserted turn may preempt all the inter beat space and ease the *Zwischenschlag* onto the beat."[27] This remains a possibility open to discussion.

76   The *appoggiatura* is to be played very lightly, but its placing is a very subjective matter.

79   This *appoggiatura* is also very light, but in a line with so many suspensions, it is perhaps more charming played as a grace note before the second eighth-note beat.

81   The turn can be played in various ways, but in any case the thumb must not thud on the G.

84   A three-note *Schneller* seems preferable to the usually heard turn of four or five notes.

THIRD MOVEMENT	*Rondeau: Allegro*
FORM	rondo
APPROXIMATE TEMPO	♩.= M.M. 88
DURATION	7 minutes
SUGGESTED LISTENING	Violin Concerto in G, K.216 iii
	Sonata for piano & violin in A, K.305/293-d i
	Flute Concerto, K.314/285-d iii
	Lied "Komm, lieber Mai," K.596

12 INTERPRETATION OF THE THIRD MOVEMENT, K.311

The infectious appeal of this piece is so strong that, unlike most finales of Mozart's earlier sonatas, it can make a fine impression even when played on its own. The pianist should be quite accomplished before attempting this piece, a veritable explosion of joy, which must not become a technical hurdle race.

Formally there is astonishing ingenuity. The structure is of the rondo pattern ABACABA ("A" being mm.1-40, "B" mm.41-85, "C" mm.119-173). Despite obvious rhythmic differences, the opening of the *Rondeau* reminds us of the first measures of the first movement. The upper line of the bass in the finale also recalls the bass at the beginning of the *Allegro con spirito*. In the course of the finale, this motif is inverted at mm.31-32 and becomes the nucleus of the B theme at mm.41-43. In its descending form the motif is frequently heard throughout the entire sonata; initially at m.28 of the first movement and m.29 of the *Andante*, then continually repeated. Like the finale of the other Mannheim sonata, this piece has the textures of a piano concerto. Certain themes show the expertise of a composer who has already completed major orchestral works, whereas other moments sound like a virtuoso pianist improvising at the keyboard. Landowska makes a fascinating parallel between this finale and one of Mozart's very last compositions:

"this rhythm ... is a fusion of a *sicilienne* with the Ländler, or Viennese waltz ... (which) we find once more in the Lied 'Komm, lieber Mai' (K.596) ... This tune became popular and is sung by every child around Salzburg."[28]

In such an exuberant atmosphere, good breathing and precise observance of detail are essential. Throughout the initial theme the *staccati* must be accurate if the effect is not to seem more inebriated than cheerful. In the second half of the theme the rests are certainly as important as the notes. The rhythmic difference between the chords on the first beats of mm.26 and 28, for example, is rarely heard, yet how many conductors would tolerate such nonchalance from an orchestra? Similarly, if the preceding chord is distended by careless pedaling, the beginning of the B theme in m.41 will not sound rhythmic. During the high-spirited conclusion of the theme (mm.32-40) the LH should not play *legato*. Throughout, the player must have a clear idea of which instruments could be playing.

What genius is evident in this "B" theme, where polyphonic craft blends with folk-song simplicity! The pianistic sentence beginning at m.56 loses its exuberance if pedaled. The slurs over groups of RH sixteenth notes do not indicate a *legato* touch but emphases on the first note of each group. The robust RH octaves of mm.72-73 and the subsequent sixths need no pedaling when the arms and wrists are relaxed and active. In mm.79-85 the writing suggests woodwinds, playing with exact rests. Depending on the instrument, the player might consider pedaling the *forte* chords in mm.112-118, where the atmosphere becomes theatrical.

B minor was a most unusual key for Mozart. The drama of this moment should, however, not tempt the player into careless articulation. Droopiness results if the first beats of mm.121,123 etc. are slurred. Pedaling can be relevant during the frenzied *forte* outburst at mm.127-138, but on most modern instruments the sound will be clearer when the pedal is changed as frequently as possible and not completely depressed. The LH leaps in mm.133-137 are not difficult if the passage is memorized in a slow tempo. The wild *non legato* bass line sounds like a dialogue between oboe and bassoon.

At m.139 the safe terrain of G major is reached. During this delectable interlude for woodwinds, the player must not relax so much that note and rest values become careless. The modulations in the sequence at mm.157-167 demand imaginative treatment, suggesting three different characters in a scene from an opera. In mm.168-172 we hear a *tutti* gesture frequently encountered in the concerti. The pedal, preferably only partially depressed, can certainly be used to lend orchestral weight in this surge to the soloist's big moment.

However, this is an *Eingang*, not a *cadenza*. The pianist must savor extreme effects here. The upward reaching triadic figure and the subsequent twisting passage in sixteenth notes are more searching than brilliant, whereas the subsequent *Presto* indication specifies that the chromatic scale is to be very quick; prolongation of its final note would spoil the effect of the suspenseful rest. The final *Adagio* interrogations can be played freely. See next section.

In the final "A" section, the RH thirds at mm.246-248 give a lot of trouble. They should sound like two oboes and will be more fluent if the LH plays some of the lower notes. The NMA[29] editors observe that in the second half of m.267 (upper staff) the manuscript has G, not the frequently heard A.

Unlike K.309, this finale ends in a trumpet-like burst of optimism, a festive conclusion to one of the most immediately appealing sonatas of the entire piano repertoire.

13 ORNAMENTATION IN THE THIRD MOVEMENT, K.311

m.

1   The three *appoggiature* in the upbeat and during this measure are all light prebeat grace notes.

5   The first *appoggiatura* becomes a quite strongly accented sixteenth note, falling on the beat.

21   Standardized timing would spoil the capriciousness of this cheeky turn, which returns in different guises. Sometimes it is more appropriate to begin the ornament before the second eighth-note beat; at other times, on or after that beat.

27   The compound *appoggiatura* acquires more character if played on the beat, creating a gritty dissonance *à la turque*. Playing it before the beat is also possible but requires a very relaxed, quick wrist movement.

76   The *appoggiatura* is best played before the beat. The trill is

clearest as a three-note *Schneller*.

119 This trill is often begun on the beat, yet the agitation of the
passage is increased if one plays a three-note *Schneller* ending
on the beat.

123 There are various ways to play this trill. Beginning on the upper
auxiliary is a possible gritty effect. In any case a termination
would reduce the tension of the line.

172 The initial chord of the *Eingang* is best arpeggiated and pedaled. In the *Adagio* phrase the two *appoggiature* are probably
meant to be accented, an effect more teasing than pathetic.
Making the *appoggiature* comically short is also possible. Perhaps the second of the subsequent turns is somewhat slower
than the first.

ADDITIONAL ORNAMENTATION is truly unimaginable in this piece.
Arpeggiating the dramatic chords on the first beats of m.118 and 172,
as well as the two last chords of the movement, is recommended.

VIII

SONATA IN A MINOR, K.310

OTHER K. NUMBER	300-d
COMPOSITION DATE	1778
TOTAL DURATION	18 minutes (with expositional repeats in the first and second movements)

1 A TURNING POINT IN MOZART'S LIFE

On March 7, 1778, from Mannheim, Mozart wrote to his sister[1] of the coming trip to Paris as if he were leaving for a distant continent. The same day his mother, Maria, wrote Leopold[2] expressing her dread of the venture. Worried about his son's future and determined to get him away from Aloysia Weber, Leopold insisted that success in Paris was essential.

Mozart and his mother arrived in the French capital on March 23. The rigors of the trip and the Spartan circumstances of the Mozarts' Parisian lodgings did not contribute to the health of Maria Mozart. Complaints of cold, bad food and loneliness fill her letters, while her son pursued hectic rounds of visits to aristocrats and musicians. Though many recalled his youthful triumphs twelve years before, there were few students or major appearances, and, worst of all, no contract for an opera. Europe's operatic capital was caught up in the "Gluck-Piccini war" and there was no interest in an opera by young Mozart. The composer's life would probably have taken a very different direction had he been given the chance to write an opera for Paris. He had the chance to become organist to the court of Louis XVI but rejected that opportunity, perhaps because he was afraid of losing Aloysia, but more probably[3] because the prospect of his family leaving Salzburg to join him in Paris meant a future of endless mutual dependency.

To be 22 and to have so little security was not only galling, but also distressing. Previously Mozart had related his disappointments to Leopold with humor, laced with sarcasm, but in the Parisian letters frustration and cynicism predominate. Mozart wrote indignantly of how everyone still persisted in regarding him as a *Wunderkind*. The mindless superiority of the aristocrats became utterly unacceptable to him. Only eleven years later, that same city saw the eruption of the revolution that would eventually spell the doom of aristocratic power throughout Europe.

On July 3, Mozart's mother died. The young man's letters in the subsequent months are fascinating from the psychological and socio-logical-historical points of view. Initially he did not even dare inform Leopold that Maria had died. Subsequent references to his mother's death are either lacking or are formulated in cliché-ridden terms.[4] Wolfgang wrote Aloysia Weber a long letter in which he did not even mention his mother's death.[5] However, he must have deeply missed his mother – though she had practically always taken Leopold's side in any conflicts – if only because she was a buffer in his complicated relationship with his father. The lack of a loving and undemanding parent was, to a degree, eventually tempered, later in Vienna, by Mozart's affectionate relationship with his future mother-in-law.

Baron Melchior Grimm, Mozart's chief benefactor in Paris, warned Leopold that Wolfgang's chances of success there were meagre. Leopold ordered his son to return to Salzburg. He presumed this would be acceptable because the Archbishop had granted Wolfgang a higher rank and more freedom to travel. But Wolfgang still hoped that Aloysia Weber would accept him. In November he returned to Mannheim and the Weber family. Leopold became vitriolic, adding emotional blackmail to his pressure tactics. Aloysia rejected Mozart; if she had accepted him, it is most unlikely that he would have returned to Salzburg. He would have evaded the power not only of the Archbishop, but also the domination of Leopold who, widowed, became even more interfering and domineering than before:

"Usually a parent's power is diluted when the prodigy enters the world of his chosen field and becomes attached to his teachers and mentors. Leopold played both roles – parent and mentor – for an unusually long period in Wolfgang's life, and consequently the inevitable breaking away was profoundly difficult for both father and son."[6]

Back in Salzburg, Mozart found himself in a personal and professional *cul de sac*.

2 A MASTERPIECE AND A MINEFIELD

No one who hears the A minor Sonata doubts that it is a masterpiece. Everything about this piece is original. For the player it presents a minefield of problems and paradoxes. Arguably no other piano work by Mozart inhabits such a subjective world. The black force of the sonata can be traced in later masterworks like the Piano Concerti, K.466 and 491, A minor Rondo, K.511, or B minor Adagio, K.540, but in all these compositions a degree of fatefulness or acceptance, however tenuous, seems to restrain the negative forces. In the A minor Sonata, strife and fury prevail. In all the movements, themes anticipating nineteenth-century romanticism are tossed in a wild salad with other ingredients, which evoke the baroque as much as Mozart's time. This periodless maelstrom of inspiration spans three centuries of musical experience and expression, making the A minor Sonata a true hybrid in the piano literature.

Hybrids are fascinating, but they are not easy to live with. Because of its turbulence, this sonata sometimes attracts souls much more at home with the romantic repertoire. Their interpretations may sometimes get closer to the heart of the score than schoolish performances, but theatrical presentation alone is not sufficient to communicate the special musical and emotional world of this sonata.

The clear manuscript indication "Paris, 1778," proves that the sonata was written during that period, so fraught with professional disappointments and personal tensions. K.310 is even more extraordinary if we consider the other works Mozart created in Paris, the Concerto for Flute and Harp (instruments for which Mozart had little enthusiasm), the Symphony, K.297, and the ballet *Les petits riens*. In all these pieces elegance and craftsmanship arguably prevail over original features. The Variations for Piano on "Je suis Lindor," K.353, rich in charm and brilliance but emotionally somewhat bland, also date from the Parisian stay. The Sonatas, K.330-333, and the Variations, "Ah, vous dirai-je, Maman," formerly attributed to this period, were conceived later.[7] There were also two sonatas for piano and violin written in Paris; the one in E minor, K.304, touches the dark world of the A minor Piano Sonata but is much more restrained in scale and expression.

Robbins Landon gives an eloquent description of the piano sonata:

> "Here we have the true essence of Mozart: uncompromising, serious ... nothing to do with the frivolous and ... decadent society in the midst of which, unbelievably and amazingly, it was written ... music out of its time and place, misunderstood by his contemporaries, a music frighteningly alone in its period."[8]

The key of A minor rarely predominates in Mozart's music, but it is interesting to note that Sandrina's "Ah, dal pianto" from *La finta giardiniera* and the Rondo, K.511, for piano solo, both in this key, are laments.

The "scoring" of the piece is unusual too. Though at times a single keyboard instrument seems incapable of expressing the explosive orchestral tensions, in other passages the refinement of the Stein fortepianos, which Mozart had discovered during the previous year, is evident. This dichotomy in sound textures poses many challenges to the pianist, but it is precisely the piece's emotional range and timeless potency that make K.310, of all Mozart's piano solo works written before his move to Vienna in 1781, the most appropriate on a "modern" instrument.

Often young talents want to play this sonata, usually with disastrous results; this is definitely "material for adults only." Mozart's inspiration may seem white-hot here, but an unthinking, youthful dash through the piece seriously diminishes it. Nothing in the structure or notation implies that Mozart wrote it down with haste; indeed, the slow movement has exceptionally detailed markings for that time.

The A minor Sonata seems to anticipate stormy masterpieces of the nineteenth century. Richard Rosenberg[9] makes interesting parallels between the sonata's opening motif and passages in the last movement of Beethoven's Opus 27/2 (familiarly known as the *Mondscheinsonate*) and the last scene of *Die Walküre* by Wagner. Recalling Mozart's complex feelings concerning his parents during his stay in Paris, it is curious to note that when Wagner used this motif, Brünnhilde is pleading with her father Wotan "Was it so shameful, what I have done, that you must punish my deed with endless shame?"

Psychological associations aside, there can be little doubt that the A minor Sonata is one of the few works in which Mozart revealed a private hell. There are moments of grace and light, but rage and terror generally prevail in this nightmarish landscape.

FIRST MOVEMENT	*Allegro maestoso*
FORM	sonata
APPROXIMATE TEMPO	♩ = M.M. 118
DURATION	6 minutes (with the first repeat)
SUGGESTED LISTENING	Symphony in G minor, K.183, i & iv
	La finta giardiniera: "Crudeli, o Dio," "Ah dal pianto" (nos.21-22), "Verrei punirti indegno" (no.13)

3 INTERPRETATION OF THE FIRST MOVEMENT, K.310

Few compositions by Mozart, and certainly none of the other solo piano works, begin as explosively as this. Baroque writing is evoked in the *ostinato* bass and in the RH's defiant dotted rhythms. Even on a fortepiano the RH would barely be audible above such a thundering bass, unmistakably suggesting galloping horses, but on a modern instrument the danger of imbalance becomes so obvious that too many players opt for ludicrously light LH sound. Although over-pedaling is an obvious danger here, total avoidance of pedaling renders the opening more disgruntled than defiant. The best results on a modern instrument are achieved if the right pedal is half-depressed and changed on every quarter-note beat. Holding the pedal longer causes sounds more easily associated with motorcycles than with heroic struggles.

The tempo indication may seem enigmatic. A statement by Konrad Wolff is relevant:

"The opening Allegro of a sonata or concerto, in the terminology of Mozart's elders and contemporaries, was usually classified as *Allegro moderato* when relatively slow, as *Allegro maestoso* when somewhat faster, and as *Allegro con spirito* when fast. The attributes *maestoso* and *con spirito* here did not refer to the character but to the speed of the music."[10]

The initial LH chords must not sound *staccato* and are played with the arm feeling quite heavy, and the fingers barely leaving the keys. The RH theme should be extremely energetic, each note shaped with an active arm stroke, the dotted rhythm better exaggerated than approximated. If the slurs at the end of mm.2 and 4 are extended over the barlines, the gasping effect of these moments is spoiled. In the first half of m.5 a conspicuous *diminuendo* in the RH, though frequently heard, is artificial. The descending, cello-like triadic motif of the LH is *non legato* and unpedaled.

A deep breath must be felt before the following phrase. The *staccato* thirds should sound as if played by violins or oboes, detached but not choppy. In mm.6-7 the RH quarter-note suspensions are resolved by eighth notes, which practically all pianists transform into quarter notes due to careless pedaling. This seriously diminishes the ominous anxiety of the phrase. Only the lowest notes of the bass chords have to be joined by the hand, but the grinding seconds of the initial bass chords should be evident. In m.8 some pedaling is appropriate, though the RH slurs should not be linked to each other by the hand. A *crescendo* here is both incorrect and banal.

The opening theme returns, sounding even more frantic. The sixteenth notes in m.9 are played with a forceful *non legato* whereas those in m.11 are slurred and require less finger articulation, implying a momentary lessening of tension. But this F major is too short-lived to offer any true relief from the prevailing turbulence. Where the music seems to lurch to D minor in m.13, the second and sixth RH eighth notes should not be bound to the subsequent tones. At mm.14-15 the fury seems to abate, but again the respite is momentary. It is crucial that the diminution of tone, evoking exhaustion more than any relaxation, does not begin before m.14. As noted elsewhere in this book, many players misunderstand Mozart's use of the term *calando*. Examination of numerous other works makes clear that reduction only of sound, and not of pace, is Mozart's intention.[11]

Any hope of peace is banned in m.16 where the bass *forte subito* in the first beat is followed a beat later by another *forte* in the upper staff. Mozart's notation of all these exact shifts are clearly indicated in the manuscript.[12] Similarly the *piano* in the second beat of m.18, suggesting depletion more than relief, and the *forte* on the first beat of m.20 evoke abrupt changes of emotion, not to be softened by *rubato* or tapering of dynamics. The RH sixteenth notes of mm.17 and 19 are *non legato*. Discreet pedaling may enhance the clattering cadential pattern of mm.20-21, but the LH's octaves and rests must be shaped with razor-sharp precision.

Nothing heard previously prepares us for m.23, the beginning of the second theme group, music that belongs to another emotional world, its eighteenth century elegance seeming ghoulish in this context. Robert D. Levin found in the "chatter of sixteenth notes a manic quality not unrelated to certain moments in Poe or Dostoevsky."[13]

The abrupt change in emotion, style and touch can easily make the pianist feel insecure, but the thin texture of these measures should not inspire a superficial, tinkling approach. Even if the arms are less active here, the hands and wrists should remain flexible, the fingers producing a healthy varied sound.

A rhythmically exact shaping of the LH is essential to give the entire theme stability. Measures 28-29 are slurred in the upper staff, implying not only a more liquid touch, but also emphasis of the first beats, whereas the LH notes on the second quarter-note beats are gently detached. The difference between slurred and unslurred RH sixteenth notes is as much a matter of phrasing as of touch. When slurred, no two subsequent notes should have the same tonal weight, whereas the absence of slurs, as in m.30, indicates *non legato* energy and a less lyrical approach.

The note repetition in the first beat of m.40 sounds clearer if both C's are played by the RH thumb, but any accenting would of course be disturbing. The RH articulation of the fourth beat in mm.40-41 seems ambiguous. When this three-note motif is first stated in the bass of mm.35-36, most editions mark both eighth notes *staccato*, but when the motif is repeated in mm.40-41, only the final RH eighth note is detached. This discrepancy is due to the crowded notation in the manuscript, which left little place for articulation marks. It seems advisable to detach both eighth notes whenever this motif recurs. In m.44 the RH wrist must remain very supple, without the slightest prolongation of the "second violinist's" sixteenth notes.

During such an extended, "busy" passage (though harmonically there is little drama here) the pianist must avoid holding his breath, for this can seriously disturb the rhythmic thrust. Obviously the lack of dynamic indications does not mean that everything is to be played within the same level of sound; between the *piano* at m.22 and the accent in m.54 much happens, though extreme changes of dynamics before m.43 seem unlikely.

Even in the most cheerful phrases the player must maintain total alertness. One sometimes hears the exposition's final measures played as a *diminuendo*, but this is surely inappropriate, with LH sixteenth notes writhing in a strong register and the RH dotted chords clanging remorselessly. This violent writing is more vigorous than the coagulated sound of the opening. Given the rapidity and contrast of events in the exposition, it would create a confused and hectic impression if the performer plunged into the development section without repetition of the exposition.

Though the C major at the beginning of the development section evokes a much gentler sound, the tempo must continue to surge nervously forward. The harmonic shift in m.53 is chilling and without accents. The inaccurate but "traditional" *legato* interpretation of the unslurred RH eighth notes creates a whining effect. In the following two measures the thudding accents predict storms. Indeed, catastrophe breaks loose in m.56. Perhaps it is best not to begin this *forte* too loudly, but with a massive *crescendo*, for the destination of this surge is marked *fortissimo*, a rare indication in Mozart's music. This arduous sinking into the lower regions of the instrument should be terrifying. "Half" or "*vibrato*" pedaling is useful in mm.56-57.

The rest of the development is as dramatic as it is unpianistic. The RH polyphonic writing first encountered in mm.59-61 is technically difficult; not only pianists, but even scholars[14] have observed this! The jerky polyphony is best played if the RH moves more energetically horizontally than vertically. It is advisable to change the pedal on each quarter-note beat here. The RH can release the highest and lowest notes as soon as the pedal has been changed on the fourth quarter-note beat, facilitating a full tone on the grinding first beats.

The chilling *pianissimo* at mm.62-65 was probably played in Mozart's time by using the moderator or *una corda* pedal. If the player uses the UC pedal on a modern instrument, the tone must still carry.

The thrusting D minor of m.70 predicts the hellish fires evoked in *Don Giovanni*, written nine years later; mm.74-79 are perhaps the wildest piano music Mozart ever wrote. The RH writing is so crazed that the pianist may become careless of the bass where no quarter notes or upbeat sixteenth notes should sound *legato* and the rests must have an inexorable precision. Any *allargando* or *ritenuto* effects in the chromatic scale that hurdles to the recapitulation would be vulgar. Some older editions print a second D-sharp at the end of m.79, but this is spurious (E. and P. Badura Skoda[15]).

In the recapitulation everything seems even darker than in the exposition; agonized variants appear in the first theme group and, as expected, the second theme group is cast in minor mode. The pleading *calando* in mm.94-96 should be shaped with a maximum of intensity and without a trace of *rubato*. The last four eighth notes of the upper line in m.96 are to be played with an exhausted *non legato*, not a droopy *legato*.

A fine pianist himself, Mozart was certainly aware that the chords at m.106 could not be played *legato* with the hand, but too many players try to bind the chords with ugly pedaling. It is best to view this moment in orchestral terms; like mm.6-7, the lowest bass notes are played *legato* and the repeated thirds *non legato*, a coordination that is not difficult if the LH thumb and wrist are sufficiently relaxed.

Two measures of jagged diminished seventh figures erupt at mm.126-127. A *caesura* before m.126 is natural, but the hands must pounce, panther-like, on the first beat of m.127, where any hesitation would seem unrhythmic. In m.129 some pianists choose to reduce the sound to a "theatrical hush," which totally ruins the thrust to the cadence. The following measure could perhaps begin somewhat softer, but, in such an furious context, sudden *piano subito* effects bring silent movie sound tracks to mind.

At the end of the recapitulation both pianist and listener should feel utterly devastated. A return to the beginning of the development section at this point hardly seems conceivable. Would reliving all those catastrophes enhance their dreadful message?

4 ORNAMENTATION IN THE FIRST MOVEMENT, K.310

m.

1   The initial *appoggiatura* should be quick, certainly no longer than a sixteenth note. To play it before the first beat is an appropriate rendering, as this crucial ornament, far from being decorative, forms a violent upbeat to the opening. Neumann describes a different rendition: "an *acciaccatura*, the simultaneous striking of both notes and quick release of the *Vorschlag*."[16] This seems a peculiarly baroque effect on a modern instrument but could be effective on some old instruments. Neumann also presents some convincing arguments for the *appoggiatura* being played on the beat, but ultimately both he[17] and the Badura Skodas[18] prefer this ornament played quickly and strongly before the beat.

2   This *appoggiatura* is usually played on the beat as a sixteenth note or even quicker. Neumann[19] does mention the interesting, highly unusual possibility of playing the ornament before the beat.

4   This onbeat *appoggiatura*, not written as an eighth note in the manuscript, clearly must be shorter. Some editions erroneously print an eighth note, probably due to the suspensions in mm.10 and 12, but these have a different notation and function.

9   See the entry referring to m.1. A prebeat interpretation necessitates a theatrical *caesura* before the ornament, strengthening the thrust of the upbeat.

15   This *appoggiatura* becomes an approximate sixteenth note on the fourth quarter-note beat. The first two notes of this beat do not have to be equal in duration and the last two are best played in an exhausted *non legato*.

22   The *arpeggio* is very quick, the uppermost note sounding with the bass, and all the notes played *tenuto*. If the thumb is not too stiff, and the hand motion begins with a low wrist, this is not difficult.

33   These onbeat *appoggiature* sound more functional if slightly accented and played as approximate sixteenth notes.

34   Such a cadential trill is usually begun on the upper auxiliary. Because the termination seems to evaporate into nothingness, it is essential that the player imagines the trill resolving in the bass at the first beat of the following measure.

39   The *appoggiatura* becomes a slightly accented sixteenth note on the second quarter-note beat. As the phrase is not *legato*, the trill may begin with the upper auxiliary, played as a light

grace note or on the beat.

42   These trills should definitely begin on the principal note, though they are frequently begun on the upper auxiliary, creating an unclear and inappropriate effect. If the player has a supple hand and active fingers, a trill of five notes, plus the notated termination, is preferable to a three-note trill.

43   See m.42.

49   See m.22.

70   Sounding against such an active bass, these trills confuse the line if begun with the upper auxiliary. Neumann[20] is also emphatic about this. Given the stormy context, a three-note trill plus termination is both dramatic and clear. The thumb playing the quarter note under each trill must not be tense.

74   The trill is like that in m.70. In the bass especially, it would be less desirable to begin on the upper auxiliary, even if it were played as a grace note.

80   Some editions have an *appoggiatura* before the first beat, but this is spurious (see previous section).

In a piece bursting with so much turmoil, ADDITIONAL ORNAMENTATION is scarcely conceivable. The bass chords in mm.57,119 (third quarter-note beat), 126, and the RH chord in m.128 (fourth quarter-note beat) could be energetically arpeggiated to heighten the music's surge. In the manuscript the final chords of m.133 are not arpeggiated as in m.49. Presumably the arpeggiation should be repeated, but it is arguable that these last chords sound more daunting if not arpeggiated.

SECOND MOVEMENT	*Andante cantabile con espressione*
FORM	sonata
APPROXIMATE TEMPO	♪ = M.M. 80
DURATION	8½ minutes (with first repeat)
SUGGESTED LISTENING	Symphony in C, K.551 ii
	Così fan tutte: Ferrando's aria, no.17
	Piano trio in C, K.548 ii
	Rondo in A minor, K.511, for piano solo
	Piano Concerto in E-flat, K.271 ii

5 INTERPRETATION OF THE SECOND MOVEMENT, K.310

This *Andante* presents the pianist with major challenges, the lavishly detailed text including many unexpected inflections that easily confuse the player. In this piece "to not lose sight of the forest for the trees" requires considerable musical maturity and experience. Youngsters should be dissuaded from studying this movement, which is interpretively more difficult than many slow movements of Beethoven's sonatas.

No single pace would do justice to the wide range of emotional and musical happenings; the tempo suggested above is a suitable basic pulse, but sentences like mm.19-31 need a somewhat calmer pace whereas most of the development section calls for a more urgent thrust.

The dynamic markings in the first four measures create an impulsive atmosphere, the *fortepiani* presumably indicating the strongest beats, not heavy accents. Though each tone should be imagined vocally, the melody is not to be played with a consistently *legato* touch. In m.1, for example, the sixteenth notes become more affecting if gently detached and pedaled. Conversely the first beats of mm.2-3 are based on suspension figures which are to be played *legato* even when notated without slurs. In the manuscript it is clear that the *crescendo* of m.3 is mainly in the last quarter-note beat, where normally a *diminuendo* would be expected. The *forte* in m.4 should not be taken too literally, but it contradicts the frequently heard coy *piano subito* on the first beat. If the fingers remain close to the keys during the *portato* thirty-second notes of m.4, pedaling is irrelevant. The wedge above the first RH note in m.7 may seem unnatural, but if one plays *legato* here, the melody becomes more droopy than yearning. This wedge does not imply an accent, but a clear separation from the slightly emphasized C-sharp which follows. This gives the rest of the measure more nervous energy, where, as in mm.3 and 6, a *diminuendo* would normally be implied.

In the expansive theme beginning at m.8 the lower notes of the bass line can be finger-pedaled. Because of the busy melodic detail, pedaling must be discreet. Many of the dynamic indications should not be interpreted too literally. The *crescendo* in m.9 seems premature and probably applies to the subsequent descending melodic line. The *fortepiani* in m.11 probably do not indicate accents but slight emphases or prolongations heard against a stable bass.

Too many players let the short cello-like transition in m.14 sag in direction and sound. The tempo may surge forward in mm.13-14, as *piano* appears only in m.15 in both staves. A violin should be imagined playing the repeated notes; on a modern piano they will sound aggressive if played too *staccato*. Though in mm.15-16 some *Urtext* editions indicate the RH with dots and the LH with wedges, there is no discernible differentiation in the manuscript. After all the expressivity of the preceding sentences, the player may feel uncomfortably exposed here, especially as during this theme, until m.19, pedaling is unthinkable. The two-part writing for the LH in mm.17-18 is not difficult if the wrist and the thumb remain loose.

The *fortepiani* of mm.19-20 could be interpreted not only as emphases but also as *rubati*, with slight prolongations on the quarter beats and some quickening in the subsequent three RH notes. The dynamic scale of mm.15-23 remains more intimate than theatrical; the *fortepiani* in mm.22-23 are slight accents (the upper octave notes must not become shrill), a syncopating effect that creates an atmosphere that is more uncertain than dramatic. The *crescendo* in m.23 should be played *non legato*, the pedal changed on each chord.

Intriguing ambiguity is found in m.27. The RH chord may seem straightforward, with the two uppermost notes held over into the next measure, but the notation for the lower parts lacks rests in the second and third beats. Mozart was usually careful about such matters and the omission of the rests may indicate that this chord should be arpeggiated, an effect which in any case sounds eloquent not only on "authentic" instruments, but also on modern ones. Most editions state or imply that the thirty-second notes in the last quarter-note beats of mm.26-27 are *legato*, but it would seem much more likely that Mozart simply presumed that the player would detach all the thirty-second notes in these measures. Such contrasting articulation of notes having the same rhythmic value is not a typical Mozartian device, but this remains a rather subjective issue.

The trill at the end of this sentence ends in *sforzandi* on the first beat of m.29. Mozart's omission of a *forte* indication in m.28 certainly does not forbid a *crescendo* to the subsequent measure's emphasized first beat; after all, trilling with both hands hardly suggests diminution of sound. In the manuscript the trills of m.83 are clearly marked *forte* and, harmonically, it is logical that this measure is played more strongly than m.28. Not all editions place the *piano* of m.29 in the second quarter-note beat, as in the manuscript.

In the exposition's tender, final three measures the harmonic shaping of the LH needs attention. Though the cadential *forte* may be relative, often this conclusion is played too softly. The energy in the sound should last until the last chord; both the return to the opening and the beginning of the development section take on more magic when the cadence in m.31 does not fade into mysterious whispering. The development section's beatific C major reminds us of the same startling moment in the first movement; here too the stability of the major mode and the melody must be shaped with warmth, the right arm moving freely to produce generous tone and phrasing, the LH remaining very still. However contemplative this moment may be, the sweep of the entire movement is lost if the tempo becomes funereal. In m.36 a D minor chord darkens the scene. This can be abruptly arpeggiated but on no account prolonged. The RH melodic line splinters into breathless ornamental patterns, which are not remotely decorative. The last two sixteenth notes of m.36 sound more fateful if pedaled and played *non legato*, like the parallel moments in mm.33-34.

Measure 37 announces a spiritual nightmare. The first five RH eighth notes are an aching inversion of the first movement's opening motif. The responding thirds do not console but seem to plead for release. This doomed dialogue evokes romantic morbidity more than eighteenth-century *Sturm und Drang* hypersensitivity.

Pedaling on each eighth-note beat seems advisable, as well as finger-pedaling the lowest bass notes. In the first two statements of this terrifying sequence there is no *crescendo*, only thudding accents on the first beats of mm.38 and 40, the manuscript having *forti* under both staves. In the final statement we arrive in an inexorable D minor, the most furious key in Mozart's harmonic vocabulary.

Startling and novel as the hammered *ostinato* beginning in m.43 may seem, the device was not Mozart's invention; Landowska,[21] Girdlestone[22] and Levin[23] see the influence of Johann Schobert in this sentence. Schobert's music had been much played in Paris, where the composer had died of mushroom poisoning some 21 years before Mozart conceived this sonata. Very similar to this hectic climax is the second movement of Mozart's Piano Concerto, K.39, a transcription of Schobert's Sonata Opus 17 no.2. In K.310 these seven measures are so furious that the power of modern instruments is certainly welcome. The player must be very careful to avoid stiffness in the RH thumb during the repetitions, as this will create a nasty tone on any instrument, as well as endanger the accuracy of the leaps. Some editions suggest changing the fingers on the repeated notes, a nineteenth-century tradition which is redundant on modern instruments.

It is interesting to note that however cataclysmic these phrases may sound, unlike at the climax of the first movement, there is no *fortissimo* indicated; Mozart, the natural pianist, knew that these textures, thickened by pedaling, would have enough power. The big wedges over the eighth notes in mm.43 and 47 give a Beethovenian impression of terrible energy and weight. Even some major recording artists shy away from the howling frenzy of this long sequence and play a *diminuendo* in mm.47-49, whereas Mozart clearly indicated that relief comes only in m.50, where, as in the first movement, the *calando* denotes only *decrescendo*.

The interpretation of upbeat thirty-second notes (for example, before the second quarter-note beat of m.46) is a subjective issue. Some prefer to avoid a polyrhythmic clash with the RH and play triplet sixteenth notes. In Schobert's piece, referred to above, similar upbeat notes in the bass heard against a RH *ostinato* in triplets are clearly indicated as triplet eighth notes. This approach is certainly clear for the listener and easier to play. However, other musicians maintain that a literal rendition of such polyrhythmic passages is the intention.

The intimations of F major in mm.50-51 suggest that the nightmare may be resolved, but in m.51 there is a chilling lurch to minor mode, followed by heart-rending *pianissimo* sighs of total depletion.

After all this, a virtually unvaried recapitulation could be expected, but Mozart transforms mm.8-14 of the exposition into a tender, but expansive, *aria*. The dynamic indications of mm.61-65 reverse those of the exposition; these are not accidental but, played as indicated, become totally organic. Mozart also expands the rhetorical ascending motif of mm.19-20 in mm.72-74, the yearning expressed in the exposition becoming even more poignant here.

The movement lays bare a world of naked pain and fragile hope. After so many trials and dangers, the final stability seems vulnerable.

6 ORNAMENTATION IN THE SECOND MOVEMENT, K.310

m.

1 The *appoggiatura* is played very lightly before the beat. An onbeat rendition seriously distorts the melodic line.

3 Played too slowly the *arpeggio* evokes false pathos, but if too quick, it disturbs the warmth of the phrase. The uppermost note sounds on the fourth eighth-note beat.

5 The pair of notes after the onbeat *appoggiatura* may be more expressive if slightly detached.

6 The trill is best begun on the principal note, perhaps slightly prolonged but not accented. A trill of five notes plus termination, or seven notes without termination is possible.

7 The first *appoggiatura* sounds on the second eighth-note beat and is not unaccented. The subsequent turn should not be too

fast, with the final A on the fourth eighth-note beat. The onbeat *appoggiatura* indicated before the trill could become a sixteenth note. The gentle fluttering of the trill should not be rapid.

8   This trill can become a four-note turn, beginning on the upper auxiliary, as suggested in many editions, but a five-note turn is perhaps more correct.

9   The onbeat *appoggiature* do not have to be of the same duration. Pedaling, not the fingers, should connect the resolution note of one suspension to the *appoggiatura* note of the next.

12   Given the rapidity of this phrase, the first trill becomes a three-note *Schneller*, preferably with the third note sounding on the second sixteenth-note beat. The two subsequent trills sound unclear with the same rendering and are usually played as prebeat *appoggiature* (Eva Badura Skoda[24]).

13   If played on the sixteenth-note beats and heavily accented, these ascending *appoggiature* can sound unsuitably baroque. Neumann is adamant that in such an instance "the intrusion of onbeat ornaments ... would usurp the accents destined for the principal notes."[25] If one prefers an onbeat interpretation, the *appoggiatura* must not be accented. The *appoggiature* may vary in length.

17   Beginning and ending with the principal note, the trill should be very light, not too quick, and has no termination.

19   A five-note turn is more correct and will not sound hurried if begun before the second sixteenth-note beat.

20   The turn resembles that in m.7.

21   The trill could begin with the upper auxiliary or the principal note.

24   See mm.7 and 21.

25   The usually heard four-note turns, beginning on the upper auxiliaries, often recommended in reliable editions, are certainly easier but seriously muddle the line. After all, the *fortepiani* suggest that the first note must be emphasized. To emphasize the upper auxiliary on a weak beat is an unlikely effect. Therefore a more appropriate rendition would be to play five-note turns, if necessary, beginning before the beat, or a three-note *Schneller*.

27   As mentioned in the previous section, the RH chord is arpeggiated.

28   The RH trill would normally begin on the upper auxiliary, but given the proximity of the lower RH line, both trills are clearer if begun on the principal notes. The RH trill must not slow down before the third quarter-note beat, where the LH trill begins, in-

troduced by a prebeat *appoggiatura*. As noted in the preceding section, these trills form a *crescendo* to the following measure.

29   Presumably the RH accent falls on the first beat, not, as in some editions, on the second sixteenth note. There will be less haste if the turn begins before the second sixteenth-note beat. In the trill at the end of the measure, beginning on the upper auxiliary sounds pedantic.

30   The turn can best become a very light *Schneller* (three-note trill) between the two groups of thirty-second notes.

33   The onbeat *appoggiatura* gains expression if it lasts slightly longer than a sixteenth note. The two tones after the suspension are best played *non legato* and pedaled.

36   Unlike Neumann,[26] I am convinced that the first three *appoggiature* should sound on the sixteenth-note beats; a prebeat rendition sounds unsuitably jaunty. These *appoggiature* may loosen the meter by varying in duration. The *appoggiatura* on the third quarter-note beat resembles those in mm.33-34. The last two notes of the measure are more soulful if played *non legato*.

37   The trill should consist of five notes and a termination. A four- or five-note turn, though frequently heard, sounds much too affable at such a grim moment.

39   The initial *appoggiatura* is best played before the beat, as the first RH third forms a suspension.

41   As the first beat of this measure resembles m.39, the trill should begin on the principal note. The fatalistic tone is perhaps enhanced if there is no termination.

44   Although one sometimes hears these trills begun on the upper auxiliary, bass trills in Mozart's time generally began on the principal note. In such a turbulent context, each trill will be clearer if the initial note is slightly prolonged.

51   This poignant trill definitely begins on the principal note and should not have a termination.

62   The onbeat *appoggiature* should be played as lightly and quickly as possible.

66   This turn consists of five notes but it will sound clumsy if not begun before the third quarter-note beat.

74   Given all the turn-like figurations here, the urgent trill is better played as a five-note trill without a termination than as a five-note turn.

85   Here better indicated as a trill than as a turn in m.30, the ornament remains a three-note *Schneller*.

A movement so rich in expressive ornaments hardly needs more. If one chooses to repeat the exposition, some variation is conceivable in the RH line of mm.9 and 11.

THIRD MOVEMENT	*Presto*
FORM	more rondo than sonata (see Chapter VIII, section 7)
APPROXIMATE TEMPO	♩= M.M. 88
DURATION	3½ minutes
SUGGESTED LISTENING	Piano Concerto in D minor, K.466 iii
	Idomeneo: Elettra's arias "Tutte nel cor vi sento" and "D'Oreste, d'Ajace," Chorus "Corriamo"
	Symphony, K.550 iv

7 FORM AND SUBSTANCE IN THE THIRD MOVEMENT, K.310

Because the whirl of this piece can readily confuse the listener, the player should examine the unusual form of this forbidding finale, a shadowy world, where conventional rondo or sonata forms seem to blur. Obsessive repetition predominates; all the major themes are based on series of descending sequences, in seconds or thirds. These unifying aspects are continually offset by a formal ambiguity, which keeps the listener guessing as to what is coming next. For a truly convincing interpretation of any piece, a sense of surprise is welcome, but here the surprise element is like a constant threat, as if the form itself has assumed a monstrous power.

The swirling first theme group ends in m.20. The next sentence, mm.21-28, is perhaps the only truly positive moment in the entire finale. Then, without any transition, at m.29 we hear a ghostly echo of the initial theme, the churning figurations pulling inexorably toward the center of the keyboard. An uncertain lurch to C major is heard at m.33, providing little relief; four measures later there is a bitter *forte* eruption. This sounds both new and familiar because the RH line in mm.37-40 is a tense variant of the more amiable phrase heard in mm.25-28, the bass heaving with destructive energy. The rugged parallel motion of both hands was daring in Mozart's time. Thrusting eighth-note figurations cannot save these tortured phrases from the inexorable pull of the bass.

Beginning in m.64, the first theme, now in icy octaves, is heard in the bass. At m.72 the material from mm.37-41 is inverted between the hands. The slithering motifs from mm.56-57 return at m.87, but with less energy, descending in a weary sequence to a ghostly sentence, mm.99-106, where all the tension seems paralyzed, the RH motifs futilely struggling to escape the dominant harmony. A *crescendo* in mm.96-98 is logical though most pianists let the line drift away here. This robs the subsequent eight measures of tension. At m.107 the opening theme is heard in the tonic key, giving the following section, despite all its turbulence, a sense of recapitulation. In terms of rondo form, mm.64-106 could be described as the "B" section and mm.107-142 the "second A" section. At m.127 the fateful theme from mm.37-41 returns with an even more violent bass.

At m.143 we are astonished to find ourselves in the pacific key of A major, but the ensuing theme seems more displaced than consoling. The restless seconds of the opening theme are still evident but now with little harmonic motion. There is brittle cheerfulness, like a soldier whistling in the trenches of some ghastly battlefield. These 64 measures (both repeats should be observed) are calm, but the tranquility is vulnerable. The RH melody has the simplicity of a folk song, perhaps even the harmlessness of a *Musette* played on a hurdy-gurdy. The section seems more like a "C" section of a rondo than the development section of a sonata.

In m.174-b there is a lurch back to the opening theme, stated in its entirety, a third "A" section. At mm.194-197 the RH theme from mm.21-24 returns, transformed into frantic gasps. The energy stalls in the three repetitions of m.199; what total despair is expressed here, like someone hitting his head against a wall. At m.203 a restatement of the "B" section begins, now in the remorseless tonic key. The fateful theme of mm.37-41 is repeated obsessively four times. Again the few ascending figurations cannot counteract the bassward pull.

The grim message of the furious *Coda*, beginning in m.245, is evident. Hope has vanished. All the defeated diatonic phrases suddenly explode into furious triadic figures and pounding repeated notes, strongly recalling the most frenzied moments of the first two movements and thereby enhancing the sense of inexorable doom permeating the entire sonata.

8 INTERPRETATION OF THE THIRD MOVEMENT, K.310

Maturity is needed to project the uncompromising grimness of this desolate emotional landscape. The pianistic demands are not modest and a sure topographic sense of the keyboard is essential. But technical proficiency alone conveys little of the movement's awesome power. The tempo indication contributes to the wild atmosphere of the piece. Though *presto* is often translated as "quick," a more useful connotation for the performer is "hasty." Here a frenzied nervousness, not mere speed, must project the struggle and stasis (see previous section) pulling against each other in every theme. About this finale Konrad Wolff commented:

> "It is essential for the pianist ... to experience the tensions in Mozart's music as well as their subsequent releases in his or her own person; an attitude opposite to what one ought to experience during the playing of a perpetuum mobile ... it is surely no coincidence that Mozart did not write these types of movements."[27]

Extreme emotions are best projected with as much clarity as intensity. Here there is more variety of detail than is apparent during a casual reading of the music. The fourth measure is an intriguing example of the subtle effects of articulation on motion and sound. In the manuscript Mozart does not slur the RH *appoggiatura* on the first beat, but this does not imply detaching; in that period all *appoggiature* were to be played as if slurred. However, the RH should not play the latter half of mm.8 and 15 *legato*. Slight detaching contributes to the exhausted atmosphere evoked here. At mm.5-7 the RH line is more expansive though the LH no longer has *tenuto* bass notes. Such *piano* moments need little pedaling. Even where more tone is required, as in mm.17-19, the pedal can best be changed twice in each measure, the ruthless wedged RH writing obliterating the panting articulation heard at the beginning.

Not only in the first theme, but throughout the entire movement, the pianist must guard against an unheeding *perpetuum mobile* effect, as if the music is moving in comfortably regular pairs of measures. A perceptive musician must pace these agitated motifs with varying impulses, of two, four, even eight measures.

Especially when playing in a big hall, it is tempting to make a single pedal stroke in each measure during the wild theme first heard at mm.37-40, but two pedal strokes are usually preferable, giving a more nervous, less bombastic thrust to the phrase. Neither hand should play *legato* during mm.37-43. Mozart indicated no slurs in mm.52-55, whereas the two subsequent pairs of measures are slurred. This is no mere oversight, for it creates a chilling contrast in dynamics as well as articulation, mm.56-59 suggesting an ominous *crescen-*

K.310

do from *subito piano* to *forte*. The bass line of mm.60-62 is not *legato*.
When the first theme returns in octaves at m.64, one pedal stroke
in each measure is possible, but during mm.72-86 the pedal should
be changed on each quarter-note beat. Presumably Mozart did not
intend contrasts of articulation between the two lower lines in mm.87-
94, where more slurs would have created a messy visual impression.
Conversely none of the eighth notes are slurred in mm.95-98, another
dead moment of *non legato* severity. During mm.99-104 the fingers
should not bind the RH's writhing figures to each other, but the single
slur over mm.105-106 creates a slithery transition to the initial
theme.

Idyllic as it may be, the *Musette*-like interlude beginning in m.143
should not inspire too much relaxation of tempo and alertness. As
noted in the previous section, this episode casts only fleeting light on
a dark scene. Perhaps this curiously naive A major theme is more a
yearning for optimism, or a vague memory of it, than optimism itself?
A conspicuous reduction of tempo here would be a sentimental effect
and create a disturbing "gear change" when the initial theme returns
in m.175. Obviously the *piano* indicated at m.143 should have a
different quality from the preceding *piano* phrases. The UC pedal
could be used throughout the entire section. The thirds are to be
shaped as written, sometimes slurred, sometimes not. Sufficient tone
in the upper line, sensitive phrasing, pedaling and a supple wrist are
essentials here. Slurring the second beat of mm.144-145, for example, makes the touching theme sound banal. The two-measure slurs in
mm.159-166 should be articulated by the hand. This enhances the
nervous unease of this transition.

In the *Coda*, beginning at m.245, the player must not let the fingers join any of the eighth notes, which, in our imaginary orchestra,
are vehemently spat out by the wind and stringed instruments.

Throughout this movement the pianist should take care that his
breathing is not inhibited by the relentless drive of the music. Commenting on this finale, Landowska referred to the "short, halting
breath, a rare instance in Mozart's music."[28] Breathing should not
result in artificial fluctuations of phrasing; slight *caesurae* before
mm.29, 64, 203, 226, 233 and 239 may be acoustically and emotionally necessary, especially in a large hall. But if such effects draw too
much attention to themselves the horror of the piece is diminished.

Due to the unrelenting tension of the material and the numerous
leaps, this finale often "goes off the rails" even when played by famous artists. Obviously in treacherous sequences like mm.37-40 and
72-76, the eyes should focus on the hand playing the leaps, with the

other hand's line securely memorized. Pianists should also avoid tension in the knees and lower back, natural responses when playing such a composition.

In all three movements there are moments when the listener should feel that the piano is almost exploding. This is no music for domestic consumption and the piece requires a fairly powerful instrument. I cannot agree with László Somfai's comment that:

> "It is perhaps no exaggeration to say that of all Mozart's sonatas, this is the one which the fortepiano of Mozart's day enjoys the greatest advantage over the modern concert piano." [29]

On the contrary, a modern instrument, played with perception and taste, is very welcome in this masterwork.

Had K.310 – such an original and essentially timeless piece – been the only piano sonata Mozart ever wrote, he would still be an acknowledged master of the genre.

9 ORNAMENTATION IN THE THIRD MOVEMENT, K.310

m.

4   This *appoggiatura* clearly should sound on the first beat, but its duration is less obvious. Virtually all pianists play it as an eighth note, a rendition that creates an excessively regular cadence. These *appoggiature* are not motivic, but dissonances of variable significance. Perhaps in m.4 the *appoggiatura* could be played shorter than an eighth note, whereas in m.8 what appears to be the same ornament gains weight if played slightly longer than an eighth note, "robbing some time" from the resolution note. In m.8, the two notes after the suspension can be played very lightly *non legato*.

25   This *appoggiatura* should definitely be played as a grace note, lightly and quickly, before the beat.

27   Given the importance of motivic delineation here (see section 7, this chapter), the trills are best played as three-note *Schneller* beginning on the beat.

144   Playing all the *appoggiature* in this theme as exact eighth notes results in puerility, not purity. A slightly longer *appoggiatura* seems appropriate in this measure, without any *rubato* in the bass, of course, but the subsequent *appoggiature* do not necessarily have the same duration.

155   The duration of this onbeat *appoggiatura* is subjective. Virtu-

ally all pianists play it as an eighth note but, as in mm.4 and 8, but as in mm.4 and 8, it could be shorter or longer.

157 As the trill is on the leading tone, it would be unwise to begin with the upper auxiliary. A five-note turn, with the initial principal note slightly prolonged, is sufficient.

163 This trill can only indicate a very light three-note *Schneller*, beginning before the first beat.

IX

MOZART IN VIENNA
VARIATION SETS WRITTEN BEFORE 1785

1 MOZART'S FIRST YEARS IN "THE LAND OF THE CLAVIER" (1781-84)

During the nineteenth century it became fashionable to presume that the last years of Mozart's life were totally miserable. Such misconceptions affect not only how Mozart's character has been regarded, but also how his music is interpreted. Actually most of Mozart's time in Vienna was marked by success and contentment. The composer circulated freely among the nobility, new bourgeoisie, Freemasons, theater people, and the working class. Most significant was Mozart's love for his wife, Constanze Weber. Few major composers have enjoyed such a satisfying marriage.

Mozart became one of Europe's first eminent self-employed musicians, with, at least until 1789, considerable earnings from concerts, teaching and, to a lesser extent, publisher's fees. During his years in Vienna, he earned more than the vast majority of musicians. What he wrote Leopold on June 2, 1781, was prophetic:

> "Vienna is certainly the land of the clavier! And, even granted that they do get tired of me, they will not do so for a few years ... in the meantime I shall have gained both honor and money." [1]

Unfortunately Mozart pursued a life style that was difficult to sustain and he did not achieve financial security from his triumphal first years in Vienna. Given his lack of a stable income and the economic depression of the late 1780's, he inevitably fell into periods of indebtedness.

No one would want to be without the violin concerti, the first eight piano sonatas, *La finta giardiniera*, *Idomeneo* and many other masterpieces like the *"Jeunehomme"* Piano Concerto, all written before Mozart's move to Vienna, but it is undeniable that he produced most of his greatest music during the final decade of his life. That he ventured only occasionally from the capital also indicates that he was generally content with his personal and professional existence.

On March 16, 1781, Mozart arrived in Vienna, very eager to rid himself of his Salzburg commitments. He had been in Munich for four months, rehearsing *Idomeneo*, reveling in the success of that masterwork, which displays a confident new musical language. Though the preceding years in Salzburg had probably been the least eventful in Mozart's life, his talents certainly deepened.

Young Mozart's dallying in Munich particularly vexed Archbishop Colleredo, who had taken virtually all his musicians to Vienna to impress the salons of the aristocracy. By the time Mozart finally arrived, nerves were frayed. The celebrated "kick up the backside" administered to Mozart by one of the Archbishop's officials became Mozart's welcome excuse to escape from Salzburg.

The Weber family had moved to Vienna and the young man stayed with them for a time. He promptly fell in love with Constanze, sister of the adored but inaccessible Aloysia. This time his feelings were reciprocated, but Leopold again disapproved. It is unlikely he would have regarded any woman as a worthy mate for his son.

In "the land of the clavier" every self-respecting home had a keyboard instrument, but because Mozart demanded a considerable fee, it was not always easy for him to find students. A turning point in the composer's development was the premiere of *Die Entführung aus dem Serail* on July 16, 1782. Not only was the opera a huge success in Vienna, but it remained during Mozart's lifetime his most performed stage work. As well as presenting a very enlightened attitude to cultural differences between East and West, *Die Entführung* poses significant questions about human relationships. Not only the public, but also Gluck, the senior opera composer of the day, and the emperor lauded the piece.

In the flush of this success, Mozart married Constanze on August 4. She brought much joy into his life. Mozart adored her and found it difficult to be separated from his wife for more than a few days. According to the mores of the time, he had to give lessons to female students at their homes. Not a few of these ladies became infatuated with their teacher, but after meeting Constanze, Mozart was apparently monogamous, another aspect of his character that has been slighted by some biographers. The young couple were very active socially, their household bustling with visitors, servants, babies (though only two of the six children were to survive), and, of course, music. In addition to the numerous concerts he gave on Sunday afternoons in Vienna, Mozart joined a group at the home of Baron van Swieten to study the works of the old masters, particularly J.S. Bach and Händel. In the summer of 1783, the young couple paid the customary visit to

Wolfgang's family in Salzburg. During their three month stay there, Mozart composed almost nothing. After that, Mozart had little to do with his family. Communication with his sister broke down completely and Leopold must have realized that he had lost his grip on his suddenly independent son. On their way back to Vienna, the young couple stayed at Linz, where Mozart (liberated from the claustrophobic world of Salzburg?) was so charged with energy that he completed the *Linzer-Symphonie* in four days, something of a speed record, even by his own standards.

Mozart felt so optimistic about his future that in early February 1784, he began a catalogue in which he entered virtually all the compositions he completed from that time until his death. He was enjoying increasing recognition as a composer as well as a virtuoso pianist. The only blemish on this happy time was a recurrence of rheumatic fever, the disease that was to cause Mozart's death seven years later. On September 28, the Mozarts moved to a lovely house, now the Mozart Museum in Vienna. Complete with a billiard room, this home was a luxurious residence for a musician at that time. The Mozarts remained there until April 1787, marking an exceptionally harmonious period in the composer's life. On December 14, he was initiated as a Freemason.

Brief biographical information is continued in the first section of Chapter XV.

In the period 1781-84, Mozart completed numerous works for piano solo; the five sonatas, K.330-333, and 457, four sets of variations, K.26 5,353,398 and 455, as well as other works, among them the Fantasy & Fugue, K.394. That he may have written some of these masterpieces for his students, certainly does not diminish their value.

2 THE REPUTATION OF MOZART'S PIANO VARIATION SETS

Mozart frequently improvised sets of variations on the fortepiano, harpsichord and organ. And from his childhood until the year of his death, he also wrote works in this genre. Yet few aspects of Mozart's output have remained as obscure as the keyboard variations. How many piano students are acquainted with more than one or two of these pieces? The variations rarely appear on concert programs. Scholars too have not given these compositions much attention. In his classic Mozart biography, Alfred Einstein[2] barely refers to any of these works. The variations have often been dismissed as casual entertainments, making too many concessions to the musical fashions of the day, yet even in these unassuming pieces, Mozart's astonishing inventiveness and structural certainty are apparent.

Beethoven and Brahms were to perfect variation form in the following century, but Mozart's works in this genre do not deserve their relative obscurity. It is baffling that piano teachers do not more frequently assign these delightful pieces, which provide an ideal introduction to many basic aspects of piano technique, to their students. Surely it is more enjoyable to become acquainted with broken octaves, trills, repeated notes etc. in these short, distinctive miniatures than in the generally dispiriting etudes of Czerny, Clementi, Cramer and their imitators?

In the last six sections of this chapter, three of the most popular variation sets will be discussed in considerable detail: the "Ah, vous dirai-je, Maman" Variations, K.265, the Paisiello Variations, K.398, and those on "Unser dummer Pöbel meint," K.455. The *Duport* Variations, K.573, are included in Chapter XIX. Unfortunately, there is simply not enough space within the scope of this publication to consider all the other variation works in depth. However, a brief survey of the variation sets written before 1785 follows.

3 VARIATION SETS WRITTEN BEFORE 1778

The Mozart family's stay in the Netherlands during the winter of 1765-66, was prolonged by the serious illnesses of both Wolfgang and his sister. The Eight Variations on a Dutch Song by C.E. Graaf, K.24/Anh.208 derive from this time. This was the first of the child Mozart's longer compositions for piano solo to be published. The choice of instrument is here of major importance. A modern concert grand piano may sound elephantine in this music, but that does not justify the claims of harpsichordists on the piece. Only the fifth variation, in dotted baroque style, sounds natural on their instruments. A fine fortepiano or a piano from the mid-nineteenth century is most suitable for these variations. It is interesting to note that even in this work, written when Mozart was only nine, the penultimate variation is in slower tempo. Though the Alberti bass[3] finale may seem unassuming to us, it exudes pride in the discovery of a device that apparently delighted the child composer. Many years later, Mozart used Alberti bass patterns throughout the entire slow movement of the Sonata in C, K.545. The delightful variations, very suitable for children, last about six minutes.

The Seven Variations on "William of Nassau," K.25, can seem somewhat less inspired than the previous set, but young Mozart's conception of virtuosity is touching, the double thirds in the first variation and the double intervals in the sixth being the obvious devices of a player whose hands cannot yet cope with octaves. The set lasts about 6½ minutes, and like K.24, is not well suited to large modern instruments.

Despite a later dating in the older Köchel catalogues, the Six Variations on "Mio caro Adone," from the opera *La Fiera di Venezia* by Antonio Salieri, K.180/173-a, were composed in 1773. Only the third variation, in which Mozart reduces Salieri's awkwardly shaped melody into an expansive line, is especially communicative. The finale is perfunctory, as if Mozart had wearied of a theme he did not find particularly enticing. The composition possesses more craftsmanship than spontaneity, but there are amusing touches in each variation.

The Twelve Variations on a Minuet by J.C. Fischer, K.179/189-a, date from 1774. From the family correspondence we know that Mozart frequently performed this set. The second variation displays a piquant sense of "orchestration" at the keyboard. In the ninth variation the RH repeatedly crosses the LH, a curious stunt, the reverse procedure being more usual. Variation 10 is a proud display of grown-up octaves, and hereafter all of Mozart's variations include at least one variation with octaves. The finale is much more effective than those of the two previous sets. However, the blend of boyish energy and courtly elegance in this work seems to have little appeal to players of modern instruments. Perhaps the length of the piece, lasting some 18 minutes if all the repeats are observed, is another deterrent.

Readers should also not ignore the final sections of Chapter VI, which discuss the masterly variations that form the finale of the D major Sonata, K.284. Arguably these variations, together with the first movement of the A major Sonata, K.331 (see Chapter XI) and the Gluck Variations, K.455 (sections 10 and 11 of this chapter), are Mozart's finest achievements in the genre.

4 THE TWO VARIATION SETS WRITTEN IN PARIS

Historians formerly presumed that the variations on "Lison dormait," "Je suis Lindor," "Ah, vous dirai-je, Maman," and "La belle Françoise" were composed in Paris, but analysis, especially of the music paper Mozart[4] used has made it clear that the latter two works were composed in Vienna during 1781-82. The "Ah, vous dirai-je, Maman" Variations, K.265, are discussed in sections 3 and 4 of this chapter.

During his disastrous Parisian stay in 1778, Mozart wrote two of his sunniest sets of keyboard variations. The Nine Variations on the Ariette "Lison dormait," K.264/315-d, are noticeably virtuosic in style and were obviously intended for the composer's use. The player is put through a hurdle-race of pianistic challenges. Virtually all pianists in this century have apparently concluded that the results are not worth the effort, but it is baffling that such a fine, witty piece is performed so infrequently.

The catchy theme is from the *Comédie melée d'ariettes*, "Julie," by Nicholas Dezède. Michaut the woodcutter sings this melody as he gazes upon the sleeping girl lying in the meadow, speculating about the delights he is about to share with her.

Energy and especially humor are required throughout this piece. The player could consider playing short *Eingänge* at the *fermate* occurring in the sixteenth measure of most variations. Variation 4 provides a variety of very funny and picturesque mood-paintings. The sixth variation is one of the most delightful pieces in broken octaves imaginable, though the LH broken octaves of the following variation can sound ponderous on modern instruments.

The *Adagio* variation is full of stylistic and textual problems, receiving three pages of explanation in the *Kritische Berichte* accompanying the NMA.[5] Perhaps, like a delicate fish being smothered in a heavy sauce, the theme is here overwhelmed by too much elaboration. There are some fine examples of Mozartian *rubato* here, the RH line taking rhythmic liberties, with the LH maintaining a steady metric pulse.

Variation 9 is a veritable circus of tricks, including what seems like a *glissando* in double sixths, though this can obviously be played by both hands. On the instruments of Mozart's time, such a *glissando* could be played by one hand quite easily. Complete with baroque-like preludizing in the *cadenza*, anticipating the Fantasy, K.394, this finale is as exuberant as it is funny. The entire showpiece lasts about 15 minutes and, for a pianist gifted with a fizzy technique and a robust sense of humor, is an absolute delight.

The Twelve Variations on "Je suis Lindor," K.354/299-a, are based on a theme from the *opéra comique*, *Le Barbier de Séville*, probably by one A.L. Baudron. Virtually all aspects of Mozartian exuberance and subtlety can be found in this rich work, which deserves more hearings than it receives. Variations 5 and 6 are marvelous miniature studies for broken octaves, where the hands must move economically between the black and white keys. The congenial minuet in Variation 8 explodes in a short but showy *cadenza*. Variation 9 is a mini-drama cast in E-flat minor, a key Mozart rarely used, the emotions ranging from melancholy to bitter defiance. The *tremolo* octaves of Variations 9 and 10 arguably sound better on fortepianos than on modern instruments. Perhaps it is the somewhat archaic elegance of the *Molto adagio* that discourages pianists in this century from performing this impressive work? Lasting some 18 minutes, these variations may not be easy, but any musical, technically well-equipped pianist should find them attractive.

5 THE OTHER VARIATION SETS FROM 1781-84

Written in July 1781, the Eight Variations on a March, "Dieu d'amour," from *Les Mariages Samnites* by Grétry, K.352/374-c, were presumably intended for teaching purposes, as the piece makes modest demands on the technical capacity of the player. A reasonable fluency in broken octave playing is required in the third variation, however, and a certain rapidity of trilling is desirable in the fourth. The writing for the LH creates no problems. The first six variations possess more fantasy than the staid *Adagio* and the unassuming final variation. As in the Salieri Variations, K.180, one feels that the theme did not sustain Mozart's inspiration.

The Twelve Variations on "La belle Françoise," K.353 (300-f), are also rarely heard. Though it offered no virtuosic display, Mozart was fond of the piece, playing it in Germany during his last tour (1789-90). The innocuous tune seems to inspire a veritable gallery of women's portraits ranging from giggling maidens to middle-aged melancholics. This richly characterized set, lasting some 14 minutes when all the repeats are taken, is technically not much more demanding than the frequently heard K.265. Any moderately proficient student with a refined approach to the instrument and a rich imagination can enjoy this adorable work.

The Eight Variations on "Come un agnello" from *Fra i due litiganti* by Sarti, K.460/454-a, pose a quandary. In a letter dated June 9-12, 1784,[6] Mozart wrote:

"Sarti is a good honest fellow! I have played a great deal to him and have composed variations on an air of his, which pleased him exceedingly."

The premiere of Sarti's opera was in Milan in 1782, and the piece was staged in Vienna the following year.[7] However, there is no mention of the piece in Mozart's own catalogue. Only the theme and two variations exist in manuscript. These do seem utterly Mozartian, but the version with eight variations, first published in 1803 is considerably different. Variations 3 and 6, as well as the concluding *Allegro*, all contain un-Mozartian elements. Much has been written defending and contesting the authenticity of the piece. Most experts vouch only for the theme and first two variations in the first version. Unfortunately, too many musicians labor under the misconception that the second version is by Mozart.

TWELVE VARIATIONS ON "AH, VOUS DIRAI-JE, MAMAN," K.265

OTHER K. LISTING	K.300-e
COMPOSITION DATE	probably 1781-82
APPROXIMATE TEMPO	♩ = M.M. 109-112
TOTAL DURATION	13 minutes, with all repeats
SUGGESTED LISTENING	12 Variations for Piano & Violin on "La Bergère Célimène," K.359/374-a
	Sonata, piano & violin, K.379/373-a iii

6 INTERPRETATION OF THE VARIATIONS "AH, VOUS DIRAI-JE, MAMAN," K.265

That this piece retains immense popularity is largely due to its theme, a cheerful tune known to all children in northern Europe and America. It is ironic that the origins of such a famous theme remain obscure. In the commentary supplementing the NMA edition[8] we discover that the theme is not by Nicholas Dezède, as stated in numerous sources, but was published as early as 1761, and during the 1770's became extremely popular in Paris. As noted in the previous section, K.265 dates from Mozart's early years in Vienna, not from his Parisian stay in 1778, and was first published in Vienna in 1785. Since then, these variations became, like Beethoven's *Für Elise* and Chopin's E-flat Nocturne, one of the pieces that virtually every player of the piano knows. In 1914, Ernst von Dohnányi based his Variations on a Nursery Rhyme for piano and orchestra on the same theme.

Like the equally well-known C major Sonata, K.545, these variations were surely intended for Mozart's piano students. Both pieces are unusually easy to read, suiting pianists of modest attainments. Some variation works by Haydn and Beethoven may be technically easier, but K.265 does provide an ideal introduction to variation form. Despite the straightforward quality of the material, the player of K.265 should have a keen sense of characterization and "instrumentation at the piano." Combining sensitive harmonic shaping with rhythmic control throughout the variations is not easy. The sparsity of the writing shows up the player's slightest lapse in concentration.

THE THEME consists almost entirely of quarter notes and its naive quality is ruined if the player lets his fingers lazily bind notes that are not slurred, creating bizarre, drunken effects. Unfortunately such misinterpretations can be found in numerous older editions. Nineteenth-century editors, uneasy with such "plain" material, added articulation and dynamic marks that grossly distorted the original text. An *Urtext* edition is absolutely necessary for the study of this piece. Except for the suspensions of m.16, the appropriate touch throughout the theme is a sensitively inflected *non legato*, not a choppy *staccato*. Pedaling obviously depends on the instrument and performance space. If used, the pedal should be changed on each quarter-note beat. Conspicuous accenting of the first beats should be avoided. Heedless thumping of repeated notes and sentimental slowing down at cadences are too frequently heard. The custom of repeating only the first sentence is to be shunned, as the piece is perfectly balanced when all repetitions are respected.

VARIATION 1 is a subtle dialogue between the hands or, metaphorically, between a violin/flute and a cello. The long slurs and the rests in the bass line are as important as the RH's busy patterns. The resolution notes of the suspensions in mm.4-7 should be clearly separated from the subsequent notes, without a trace of accenting. Repeated RH figurations should not be stated with the same volume, but shaped according to the harmonic progression.

The player should not wait before launching VARIATION 2. Here we encounter a standard Mozartian device of reversing the rhythmic activity of the first variation between the hands. Children, who often find this LH writing quite difficult, must not assume a "battle position" bowed over the keys, for this blocks free movement of the arms. The cheerful bustle of this variation is easier to obtain when the LH thumb does not tense. The fifth finger should not feel like an anchor here, but like a trampoline. Much care should be given to the balancing of tone in the RH writing, evoking three wind instruments.

In the good humored VARIATION 3, the prevailing *non legato* articulation of the upper line is easier if the fingers play close to the keys and the wrist remains supple. Care must be taken to avoid lopsided weighting of second quarter-beats.

For many, VARIATION 4 often becomes a hurdle race. Too often the pianist tries to play the LH too *legato*. Actually this line is more like a bubbly bassoon solo and should certainly not be pedaled. The longer RH notes need attention and healthy tone. On large modern instruments, this variation can become leaden if not played with considerable dexterity. Because the first four variations share a similar cheerful character, a slight pause is perhaps welcome before continuing to the next variation, which has a very different atmosphere.

VARIATION 5 is frequently spoiled by injection of misplaced pathos, whereas the tone is surely humorous. Woodwind instruments are evoked in this delightful piece, in which the rests should be accurate. Yet shortening of note values can suggest the clucking of chickens, hardly a desired effect! In mm.9-20, the melody has slurring over the bar-lines, clearly indicating that the first beat notes are softer.

VARIATION 6 may look like a daunting exercise by Czerny, but it shares the lighthearted good spirits of the first four variations. The triads deserve rhythmic alertness and the sixteenth notes sound best played *leggiero*, without excessive lifting of fingers. Too many players spoil this delightful piece with coarse tone and unnatural dynamic contrasts.

VARIATION 7 has an extrovert atmosphere but is not rough. The LH octaves will be heavy if both notes sound equally strong. Cloying *ritenuti* in mm.12 or 16 are to be avoided. A silence lasting an entire measure is desirable before continuing to the next variation.

Even if it is in minor mode, VARIATION 8 does not need deep-breathing drama or a slower tempo. A certain remoteness seems implied here, and the polyphony sounds more eerie if not pedaled. The half-notes in the RH's upper line need the most attention in this splendid little *fugato*. None of the eighth notes should sound *staccato* but are best shaped as *portato* woodwind lines.

The bareness of VARIATION 9's textures is curiously modern. The theme seems stripped to a skeletal outline, the enigmatic tone not fleshed out by any pedaling. This variation may suggest a child playing toy instruments, but the mixture of different touches and polyphony is not easy for most children. Pianists should be encouraged to sing, as well as play, each voice individually.

VARIATION 10, on the other hand, is a musically straightforward explosion of jubilant energy. Budding virtuosi will revel in the hand crossing and bustling traffic. Except in m.16, pedaling, changed on each beat, is welcome. Again the pianist should take care, especially when playing larger instruments, that the bass octaves do not become too heavy. If the player's spine and hips are tense, the variation becomes very difficult.

VARIATION 11 evokes string quartet writing, with beautifully nostalgic melodies for the first violinist. A ponderous pace with four impulses in each measure would kill the wistful charm of this elegant piece (approximate tempo ♪ = 84). In mm.9-16 some Mozartian *rubato* is possible, a certain loosening of the rhythm in the RH line with the LH continuing to play with an absolutely steady pulse. Pedaling of the quicker figurations must be very carefully judged. The two *fortepiani* suggest weight more than conspicuous accents.

On a fortepiano VARIATION 12 sounds wonderfully lively (approximate tempo ♪ = 120), but on a modern instrument it can easily become heavy-going. A monotonous *forte* kills the sunny energy of this finale, where lightness of touch and minimal pedaling are necessary. A diminution of sound at the end of the *Coda* would surely be artificial. There seems to be a redundant measure in the final flourish, creating a cheeky effect at the end of a piece that is a delight from the first note to the last.

7 ORNAMENTATION IN THE VARIATIONS, K.265

THEME

m.

7   Some pianists play a turn here instead of a trill. Indeed the André edition (1792) printed a turn here, whereas the first edition by Torricella (1785) had no ornaments indicated here or in m.15.[9] The dotted rhythm is clearer when the five-note turn or three-note trill ends on the second quarter-note beat.

VARIATION 2

1   Some editions have a trill on the first RH note of Variation 2, but this seems to be a misreading.

11   A three-note *Schneller* suffices here and in m.15, ending on the beat.

17   The upper auxiliary could be played as a quick grace note before the trill. Beginning the trill with the upper auxiliary on the beat creates an unpleasant octave with the bass. Depending on the chosen tempo and the player's technical ability, a three- or five-note trill, plus the termination, can be played.

VARIATION 3

2   A three-note *Schneller* with the final note on the second beat is
     preferable here and in the following measure.

8   This trill begins with the upper auxiliary sounding on the first
     beat and ends together with the third bass note.

VARIATION 11

5   In the second eighth-note beat, a five-note trill, beginning on
     the principal note and without termination, is preferable to the
     frequently heard three-note *Schneller*. The three subsequent
     onbeat *appoggiature* do not necessarily have the same duration.

7   A pleasant *rubato* effect is created if the onbeat *appoggiatura* is
     slightly longer than a thirty-second note, with the three subse-
     quent notes played somewhat quicker than indicated.

11   The final note of the first turn can sound on the second eighth-
     note beat. The second turn is probably best begun somewhat
     earlier than the first, with the *appoggiatura* G sounding on the
     last eighth-note beat.

VARIATION 12

1   The tempo necessitates a trill with only three notes plus termi-
     nation. Perhaps the upper auxiliary could be played as a grace
     note.

It is arguable that ADDITIONAL ORNAMENTATION would spoil, not enhance the lean textures of the piece. However, when repeating the
Adagio variation, there are numerous possibilities for decorating the
melody in mm.9-16, and an ascending *Eingang* in m.16 could be
played in place of the marked descending scale.

SIX VARIATIONS ON "SALVE, TU DOMINE" BY PAISIELLO, K.398

OTHER K. LISTING	K.416-e
COMPOSITION DATE	1783
APPROXIMATE TEMPO	♩ = M.M. 100/104
DURATION	8 minutes
SUGGESTED LISTENING	*Nozze di Figaro*: Figaro's aria "Se vuoi bal-lare," Act I, no.9
	Variations for piano, *Ein Weib ist das herrlichste Ding*, K.613

8 INTERPRETATION OF THE PAISIELLO VARIATIONS, K.398

Why is this delightful composition so infrequently heard? It certainly does not lack pianistic allure; *The Mozart Compendium*[10] rightly describes K.398 as a "showy concert vehicle." In formal terms, the piece is the most original of all the variation works Mozart wrote for piano. Any complaints of repetitiousness regarding other piano variations by Mozart are definitely not relevant to this piece. Is it perhaps the very combination of brevity and technical difficulty that intimidates less accomplished players? The rapid changes of character also demand a mercurial imagination and confident pianism.

On March 23, 1784, Mozart performed a program that we would consider impossibly long; the *Haffner* Symphony, two arias from *Idomeneo* and *Lucio Silla*, the Piano Concerto in D, K.175 (with the composer as soloist), then a short fugue "because the Emperor was present and then variations on an air from an opera called *Die Philosophen.*"[11] These variations were so successful that Mozart was recalled with stormy applause and then played the variations on "Unser Dummer Pöbel meint." Presumably both sets of variations were improvised at the moment. That musical orgy concluded with the Concert Rondo for soprano, K.416, and a repeat of the *Haffner* Symphony's finale!

Giovanni Paisiello (1740-1816) is today little more than a name in music history books, but he was much appreciated in his time, and Mozart attended numerous performances of Paisiello's operas. *Die Philosophen* (also *I filosofi imaginarii*, or *Gli astrologi*) was a light opera that enjoyed considerable success. Presumably Mozart saw it in Vienna in 1782, but since then the piece has fallen into total obscurity. The aria "Salve tu, Domine," Act I, no.8, is sung by a certain Giulio. The text is in a mixture of Latin and the vernacular: "Sir, the Phontidas of Argas sends me to salute you ... if you did not respect his learning I would not dare to come ... in his name I appear before thee..."[12]

The THEME suits the mock seriousness of the text. The first eight-measure sentence is abruptly interrupted in m.9 by a perky "bugle call" motif, falling at m.11 into a comically jerky cadence. A wistful lyrical two-measure phrase follows, is repeated, then abruptly ends in more jerky dotted figurations. In m.17 the "bugle call" motif makes an assertive return, heard against LH octaves moving in a rhythm that comically evokes both duple and triple meter. After the *fermata* the theme seems to evaporate into question marks.

There are no dynamic markings in the entire text and no tempo indication at the beginning. This gives the player both freedom and responsibility. If one considers a tempo that is lively but not garbled for Variation 6, which has the quickest passages, the result would be an unrushed *Allegretto* that does not spoil the humor of the theme. While the theme's first eight measures are clearly *non legato*, pedaling, changed on each quarter-note beat, can give body to the tone. The "bugle calls" are more amusing if played without pedaling, whereas the lyrical phrase of mm.12-16 requires a melting *legato* touch. On a modern instrument the drunken march of mm.17-20 is best played with short pedal strokes on each quarter-note beat and no thumping of the bass octaves. The cadences at mm.11-12 and mm.19-20 should end resolutely. A *decrescendo* would render the last three measures redundant.

VARIATION 1 consists largely of RH embroidery, but in the latter half the LH has some dashing moments. The technical challenges should not dilute the high spirits. In mm.1-8, the RH melody notes can be played with more tone than the ornamental notes, but this should not result in accents. As in the theme, mm.9-12 are more humorous than vigorous, with any strokes of pedal as short as possible. The *Urtext* editions have divergent placing of the RH slurs in m.14; surely it is more logical to imagine a new RH impulse beginning simultaneously with the LH sixteenth notes. A *non legato* touch, energetic and unpedaled, is suitable in mm.17-19. The player must memorize the RH here, for the leaping LH line needs visual preparation. Some *Urtext* editions have the sixteenth and eighth notes in m.20 slurred, but this does not seem appropriate.

VARIATION 2, with both hands jumping about the keyboard, creates an exciting sound and spectacle. This pianistic device was to become widely imitated later (in Schubert's *Wanderer-Fantasie*, Mendelssohn's *Variations Sérieuses*, countless pieces by Liszt etc.), but Mozart's audience must have been astonished by the novelty of such display. This variation is not difficult if first learned with the hands playing simultaneously, not in the syncopated rhythm. When the typography of each harmony is clearly imprinted on the memory, the player does not have to worry about the leaps. During this short *tour de force*, the player should avoid holding his breath and not tense his wrists or knees, for mobility and balance are essential. The hands should move as economically as possible and there is minimal pedaling. In the last sixteenth-note beat of the second measure, some pianists, perhaps rightly, repeat the previous RH third, contradicting the line's descent of a sixth given in most editions. In mm.17-20 the lopsided bass makes the drunken march sound even more comical.

In VARIATION 3, more than "half-pedaling" is not desirable on modern instruments. The lyrical phrase of mm.12-16 is ingeniously varied, vacillating more than ever between contemplation and humor. Pedaling in mm.17-19 would make the march seem more drowned than drunken. Suiting the tongue-in-cheek theme, the variations become increasingly capricious. Only the first three are conventional in form. For the rest, one could speak of deconstruction as much as of structure. The theme is incomplete in the last three variations, which blossom into whimsical, even wild improvisations.

VARIATION 4 touches very different emotions, but if the tempo slackens, the dark atmosphere becomes overly pathetic. Mozart weaves mournful decorations around the theme's first sixteen measures. The upper violin line is so noticeable that the LH's viola and cello lines can easily be slighted. Articulation is a challenge throughout this variation; the notation seems incomplete, the *Urtext* editions giving conflicting readings. Certainly there are no "melting *legato* lines" here, but short, anxious groups of notes. In mm.2,4 the RH aching quarter notes are probably *legato*. The articulation in the next sentence, mm.5-12, is conjectural. The bass in mm.9-12 should be a weary *portato*, not a formless *legato*. In mm.12-16 differentiation between suspensions and three-note groups is desirable, with the RH leaving the keys at the ends of slurs, and dabs of pedaling preventing actual breaks in the sound. What a surprise m.16 is, a return of the original theme, now syncopated and in the unusual key of A-flat. Has the foregoing *minore* been so serious after all? This phrase could be assertive or exotically muted, but the tone grows in mm.23-26 during abrupt modulations, coming to rest on the dominant during a fairly elaborate *Eingang* at m.27. This should not be played too deliberately, the *Adagio* indication suggesting breadth more than turgidity.

VARIATION 5 begins predictably, but both the lyrical phrases and the march vanish. Accents on the second quarter-note beats should be avoided. The upper voice in the theme has a full sound, the trills never dominating. The text of mm.22-23 is unclear; some players trill during the first beats of these measures. Others interpret the indicated quarter notes literally. Arguably the shifting bass line has more impact if the trills are interrupted. Too much pedaling can deflate the energy of the *Eingang*. From Mozart's detailed notation it is obvious that the ascending scale is not to be played with a mathematical interpretation of the note values, but as a brilliant *accelerando*, expiring into silence (the *fermata* placed above a rest). The preceding diminished-seventh *arpeggio* may be free, certainly less rapid.

VARIATION 6 offers not only virtuoso high jinks but also startling formal innovations. It elaborates the first eleven measures of the theme, then repeats mm.9-10. The rotational writing in both hands is a delightfully flamboyant effect and far from easy. Visual preparation is important, with the eyes on the RH until m.9, on the LH from mm.9-13, etc. The fingers should remain as close to the keys as possible and the wrists able to make extremely quick horizontal movements. The gradual sinking to the low register is humorous on a fortepiano but easily becomes sludgy on a modern instrument. The pedal should be merely touched now and then; the lower the register, the less pedaling is needed.

The music is interrupted by a third *Eingang*. This seems to possess the diversity and length of a *cadenza* but lacks the thematic references of a true *cadenza*. The combination of brilliant passages and rowdy humor form a splendid étude for anyone planning to perform Mozart concerti. There are many dynamic possibilities here, but not all the passages should be played with the same energy. The numerous *fermate* obviously do not have the same duration but should seem like suspenseful question marks. Given the presence of thirty-second notes, passages in sixteenth notes are not to be rattled off with maximal rapidity.

At m.17 the "bugle call" returns with jaunty LH broken octaves. The same phrase is repeated an octave higher with flippant ornamentation. A comically repetitious *Coda* based on the most unprepossessing module (mm.11-12) of the theme begins in m.25. Rhythmic exactness of the numerous rests contributes to the humor of all the repetitions. Most pianists play the final seven measures softly, but given the harmonic development and the low register, a *crescendo* in mm.31-32 is certainly possible.

The Paisiello Variations are technically among the most difficult compositions Mozart wrote for piano solo. Exuberant and unpredictable, the piece gives a vivid impression of how Mozart must have improvised at the piano, delighting his audience and, no doubt, having a fine time himself.

9 ORNAMENTATION IN THE VARIATIONS, K.398

THEME
m.
2   These trills are extremely difficult to play if the thumb holding the lower RH notes is tense. A four-note onbeat *Pralltriller*,

beginning on the upper auxiliary and without a termination, sounds suitably bright and clear.

13   The *appoggiatura* is played as a very light grace note, before the beat.

VARIATION 3

1   The *arpeggio* is played very quickly, with all notes held, the uppermost note sounding on the first beat.

14   The *appoggiatura* seems more natural played as a grace note before the beat. An onbeat rendering creates a sneering effect that hardly seems appropriate.

VARIATION 4

27   The three initial *appoggiature* are best played weightily on the eighth-note beats but do not have to assume the same note values. The compound *appoggiatura* before the trill can best sound with the bass's third. The length and dynamic direction of the trill is totally subjective.

VARIATION 5

All the trills in this variations begin on the principal note. As noted in the previous section, trilling during the first beats of mm.22-23 is a subjective choice. The LH trills are softer than the RH ones.

VARIATION 6

16   The descending series of turns should not sound hectic and can be free in tempo. Each turn must begin as soon as possible after the principal note has sounded. The final "chain trill" is rapid, each trill approached from the lower auxiliary and without the frequently heard accenting.

In a piece bursting with so much character and invention, is ADDITIONAL ORNAMENTATION needed? Some important chords certainly sound better if energetically arpeggiated; for example, the dominant sevenths in m.27 of Variation 4 and m.24 of Variation 5, and in the final *cadenza*, the chord on the first beat of m.16 and the four subsequent bass triads. Ingrid Haebler[13] adds a delightful turn to the *fermata* B-flat of Variation 4.

VARIATIONS ON "UNSER DUMMER PÖBEL MEINT" BY GLUCK, K.455

COMPOSITION DATE	1784
APPROXIMATE TEMPO	♩ = M.M. 60
DURATION	14 minutes
SUGGESTED LISTENING	*The Pilgrims to Mecca* (by C.W. Gluck): no.3 "Les hommes pieusement..." Piano Concerto, K.453 iii Sonata for Piano & Violin, K.481 iii

10 INTERPRETATION OF THE GLUCK VARIATIONS, K.455

Mozart improvised variations on this theme during the historic concert in 1784, when his playing, conducting and compositions were acclaimed by the emperor and Gluck (see this chapter, section 8). From Mozart's own catalogue we know he completed the set of ten variations on July 25, 1784.

Gluck's piece was his last and most successful attempt at creating a comic opera. The piece, which had its premiere in Vienna in 1762, became known under a rather wild variety of names, *La Rencontre imprévue*, *Les Pèlerins de la Mecque*, *The Pilgrims to Mecca*, etc. It is obvious that Mozart imitated certain elements of Gluck's score when writing *Die Entführung*. Both pieces have "Turkish" elements and even share a servant named Osmin! The jaunty theme, "Les hommes pieusement..," is sung by the Calender, an Islamic holy man who lives from alms, though his existence seems not particularly devout:

"Men piously take us for Cato. They imagine foolishly that we live in poverty. Many believe we do! The good folk do not know how many attractions our lot holds for us, how worthy it is of envy. A kitchen supplied with a hundred different dishes, and a cellar full of the priciest wines. It's the lovely life, of the good old Calenders." [14]

The German translation of this text began, "Unser dummer Pöbel meint...," and this is how Mozart listed the piece in his catalogue.

Only five months before the Variations, Mozart had finished the finale to the Piano Concerto, K.453, which shares with these variations the same key and a similar character. Both are also marked *Allegretto* and *alla breve*. In the variations' theme, a pace faster than

♩ = 126 evokes an *Allegro* pace. Perhaps more important than the choice of tempo is the necessity of keeping the second and fourth quarter-note beats light. Certainly on a large modern instrument the player must take care not to play the octaves too heavily. Energy and *joie de vivre* characterize this jaunty theme; daintiness should be avoided. The dynamic contrasts evoke changes in scoring more than in volume. Tchaikovsky orchestrated such details beautifully in his arrangement of the piece in his Fourth Orchestral Suite, *Mozartiana*, Opus 61. The length of the pedal strokes is determined by the instrument and acoustics, but even on repeated notes, the pedal should be changed with each quarter-note beat. The thirty-second notes in mm.5 and 7 have more humor if not joined by the hand or pedaling to the subsequent *piano subito* measures.

Given the brevity of the theme and the presence of some through-composed variations later in the piece, it certainly seems best to observe all repeats. It is also imperative that the player use an *Urtext* edition. Older editions mangled the dynamics and articulation of this piece unmercifully.

The slurring in VARIATION 1 is interesting. The dynamic direction and articulation, with the RH stressing the fourth quarter-note beats in mm.5 and 7, differ noticeably from the theme. When the RH has such busy figurations, the bass is too often played in an unthinking way. For example, a lopsided effect is created if the LH emphasizes the second or fourth quarter-note beats in mm.1-2, 9-10. Beginning in m.5 the quarter notes of the lower bass line can sound like a cellist playing *non legato*. Pedaling is best avoided throughout.

VARIATION 2 is the usual brilliant piece for the LH. If the thumb is very loose and the elbow free, this variation is not really difficult. On a large modern instrument especially, the variation can sound like hard work if the RH does not project more strongly than the LH.

VARIATIONS 3-9 have no dynamic indications, thus posing some intriguing alternatives for the performer. VARIATION 3 seems to be more delicate than the preceding pieces. Tchaikovsky's light scoring in *Mozartiana*, with a flute playing the melody, is a splendid example for the pianist. The slurring is detailed. Stressing the first note of each slurred group is certainly more important than separating slurred groups.

In VARIATION 4, phrases that seem similar do not always assume identical dynamic direction or intensity. The atmosphere is more playful than bombastic. Throughout the entire variation the player's arms must remain very free, as the tonal quality of the half notes needs much attention. Whenever sixteenth-note figurations are present, violins or celli are evoked; pedaling, therefore, should be avoided.

In VARIATION 5 the manner of articulation of the repeated notes is a quandary. In the manuscript there are none of the *staccato* indications found in later sources.[15] This is no mere detail, for if these notes are pedaled the character of the piece changes totally. In either case, the repeated notes, played with the fingers very close to the keys, must not be accented. The scoring of this somber interlude, bringing both wind and stringed instruments to mind, is so rich that colors, more than overt dynamic contrasts, must be evoked. As long as the tempo seems to move in two, and not four, impulses to a measure, a slightly more deliberate pace will not be unnatural.

With VARIATION 6 the jauntiness of the theme returns and perhaps the same dynamic structure is heard here. Thumping the second and fourth quarter-note beats or shortening the rests destroys the delectable humor of this piece. Again the basic touch is *non legato*, without pedaling.

VARIATION 7 is a highly original *fugato* piece, the chorale style creating a more spiritual atmosphere. The texture suggests the conversation of four persons, with a considerable variety of emotion and experience. Pedaling can be used on *portato* quarter notes and avoided with any eighth notes. The unorthodox triplet in the upper voice of m.4 (a C between the E and A) is found in the manuscript.[16]

Virtuosi, budding or full-grown, revel in VARIATION 8. On a modern instrument the pedal strokes should not extend entirely through each quarter-note beat. The highest note in m.2 is given in the two oldest sources as G,[17] but in others as E. Both renditions are heard; the choice remains subjective. During this explosion of energy the LH octaves should be set down sensitively, sometimes the thumb's notes are stronger, at other moments the lower notes can be emphasized. The only manuscript copy of the variations breaks off at m.10. For the remainder of the piece, editors have to rely on the first editions.

At m.20 the RH flies into a frenetic and comically repetitious improvisation, a long *Eingang* more than a *cadenza*. Many players are tempted to depress the pedal for both measures of diminished seventh harmony, a foreign effect that brings Liszt to mind; changing the pedal on each quarter-note beat is vastly preferable. Obviously there is considerable dynamic freedom in this brilliant passage. A *diminuendo* is conceivable in mm.23-24, but would be unnatural in the long descending sequence.

VARIATION 9 is definitely the most challenging of the set. Without eloquent phrasing and much concentration, this dignified aria can easily seem loose and repetitive. A dirge-like pace suits neither the character of the variation nor the *alla breve* indication; ♪ = 88 is an approximate tempo which gives the long notes some serenity. When the correct slurring is observed, the phrasing takes on more vitality. In the first two measures, the highest RH notes are not emphasized, but in m.3, where a slur begins with the high E, this note is the strongest of the measure. Similarly the RH notes on the third quarter-note beats in mm.5, 6, 27, 30-31 are to be stressed, but with care; for example, the stress in m.6 is harmonically stronger than the gentle suspension of m.31. The instrument and performing space influence the use of pedaling for bridging any holes in the melodic line, but the hand should leave the keys before a slurred group begins. On the low chords first heard in m.17, but repeated three times later, the NMA editor comments:

> "Only the top note of the chord is dotted, in both the autograph and the earliest editions, probably indicating that it should be played *arpeggiando*." [18]

Again the player should remember that in a piece in which the LH has so few notes, the bass must never plod mechanically but be sensitively formed to underline the harmonic and rhythmic direction of the phrase.

Throughout the entire variation the projection of these elaborate lines will be easier if the pianist does not bend over the keys. An alert body posture, not myopic stiffness, contributes much to organic presentation of such rhythmically complicated phrases. Unfortunately the *Adagio* indication encourages too many players to strive for tragedy in a sunny landscape. But surely even the A minor of m.17 is merely apprehensive, not threatening. The wondrous final five measures, inward yet remote, curiously anticipate moments in Beethoven's last string quartets. These are easier to play when the pianist leans slightly to the left side of the keyboard.

VARIATION 10 is in quicker tempo (approximately ♩. = 72), very like a piano concerto finale. The player will be able to judge character and color easily if he clearly differentiates between "orchestral" and "solo" phrases. Pedaling is unnecessary during the first 16 measures. In the comical dialogue of instruments or characters in mm.9-16, the dynamic contrasts should be introduced without ponderous agogic effects.

The brilliant passage beginning in m.52, indicated as a *cadenza*, is actually an *Eingang*. A considerable *ritenuto* in m.57 would not be a suitable introduction to the following theme. If the player's spine is free, the swift crossing of hands in this second section is not difficult, the sequence becoming a masterly deconstruction of the theme's initial motif. A long *crescendo* is implied in mm.86-93, with its dramatic descent to the lowest note of the pianos Mozart knew.

A *fermata* on the high C in m.97 is not advisable, but the ensuing silence could be lengthened. Arguably, during the ten subsequent measures – a masterful delay of the theme's return – the rests can be interpreted with more freedom than the notes. Some broadening of tempo in mm.109-112, unmarked but surely intended, makes the return to the theme's initial tempo more natural.

At m.119 we suddenly realize that this repetition of the theme functions as a *Coda*. In m.119 the second and fourth quarter-note beats are to be weighted slightly more than the conventionally strong beats. But surely the dynamic level is modest, the atmosphere more nostalgic than energetic. The *non legato arpeggio* figures on the third quarter-note beats of mm.120 and 124 should not be pedaled. In m.130 Mozart indicated a crossing of hands that many players may find extremely uncomfortable. This is much easier if the LH plays the sixteenth notes from the second quarter-note beat of m.130 onwards, the RH playing the two "oboe" lines of the upper staff. Why do so many pianists play a conspicuous *diminuendo*, an unnatural effect when the bass line descends so low? In the two final measures, one could play either an exuberant *crescendo* or a smiling *decrescendo*. A *caesura* before the final chord is more suitable than a weary *ritenuto*.

11 ORNAMENTATION IN THE VARIATIONS, K.455

THEME

m.

4   The onbeat *appoggiatura* sounds much livelier if played quicker than an eighth note.

VARIATION 2

1   Given the thematic line, the compound *appoggiatura* must end on the beat and is played as quickly as possible.

9   All of the *arpeggio* notes are held.

VARIATION 3

2   A *Schneller* of three notes, ending on the first quarter-note beat, is the best solution.

VARIATION 6

1   All the trills in this variations begin on the principal note. It is much easier to avoid mechanistic *crescendi* during these trills if there is no pedaling.

VARIATION 7

18 These trills begin on the principal note and consist of three or five notes plus the indicated termination.

VARIATION 9

1 Most authorities maintain that these trills are best begun with the principal note, in which case, the first note may be slightly prolonged but not accented. If one chooses to begin with the upper auxiliary, that note would be more accented.

4 The turn should not seem quick.

15 The turn begins with the upper auxiliary, just after the second quarter-note beat.

28 Another subjective ornament, the turn could end on the fourth eighth-note beat.

41 If a brusque effect is desired, the *appoggiature* are on the sixteenth-note beats. Grace notes played before the beat achieve a lighter effect.

44 The trill begins on the slightly prolonged principal note. The line is smoother if there is no termination.

VARIATION 10

109 Given the rapidity of the preceding notes in m.108, the compound *appoggiatura* before the trill must begin on the first beat. The trill should have a concerto-like brilliance, played as quickly as possible with much emphasis of the upper notes. The G of the following measure could be interpreted as the termination of the trill.

122 To play the *appoggiatura* on the beat in such a series of sixths would sound horribly wooden.

127 The *appoggiatura* is on the fourth quarter-note beat, and can be slightly accented.

ADDITIONAL ORNAMENTATION seems virtually inconceivable during this piece, except perhaps in mm.33 and 37 of the *Adagio* and m.32 of the last variation. All the RH chords in Variation 4 should be energetically arpeggiated, as well as the first beat chords in mm.41-42 of the *Adagio*, and the chords in mm.51,105,111,133 of the final variation. It has already been noted that the chords in mm.17 and similar moments of the *Adagio* are to be arpeggiated.

The reader is reminded that three other sets of variations are discussed in detail elsewhere in this guide:

– the third movement of the D major Sonata, K.284, in the last two sections of Chapter VI

– the first movement of the A major Sonata, K.331, in the first two sections of Chapter XI

– the *Duport* Variations in sections 2 and 3 of Chapter XIX

X

SONATA IN C MAJOR, K.330

OTHER K. LISTING   K.300-h
COMPOSITION DATE   probably 1782-83
TOTAL DURATION   17 minutes (expositional repeats in i and iii)

1 BACKGROUND OF THE SONATAS, K.330-332

The first Köchel catalogue gave 1779 as the composition date for the sonatas K.330-332. Later Einstein[1] agreed with Saint Foix's presumption that the three sonatas dated from Mozart's stay in Paris. Most editions published before 1986 give Paris as the locality and 1778 as the date of composition. In his book on the different sorts of paper Mozart used, Alan Tyson remarked:

"The dates of K.330-332 are still unresolved. These sonatas are mostly on a rare paper, matched only by that of three orchestral minuets K.363, which are also undated. I now think Mozart may have written them [like K.333] during that Salzburg visit in the summer of 1783, again with the teaching that lay ahead in Vienna in mind. (The right hand is written in the soprano clef ... evidence of their use as teaching material?)"[2]

A possible clue in Mozart's correspondence may shed some light on the issue. On June 9, 1784, he wrote Leopold:

"I have now given Artaria three sonatas for clavier only, which I once sent to my sister, the first in C, the second in A, and the third in F."[3]

Artaria did publish the three sonatas as Mozart's Opus 6, but it is interesting to note that in the same letter Mozart also wrote "I have given three others to Torricella, the last of which is the one in D, which I composed for Dürnitz in Munich." Indeed in the same year, another Viennese publisher, Torricella, printed the *Dürnitz* Sonata, K.284, the Sonata for Violin & Piano, K.454 (dated April 21, 1784), and the Piano Sonata, K.333, which, according to Tyson,[4] can be dated conclusively to 1783. Mozart's reference in that letter to the D major Sonata may indicate that of the six pieces it was the only one not of recent composition.

Some historians conclude that Mozart may have intended K.330-332 for amateurs, whereas the Torricella sonatas were more for performers. Amateurs in 1784 must have been technically well equipped if they could cope with the pianistic demands of K.331's variations or K.332's finale!

2 SPECIFIC CHALLENGES REGARDING TEMPO & DYNAMICS

In previous sonatas, we have already seen how Mozart used nouns and adverbs when qualifying a tempo. But one cannot help speculating on the tempo notation here. When we examine other works where Mozart indicated *Allegro moderato*, we quickly realize aesthetic and practical problems can arise if the initial tempo is too quick. A splendid example is the famous final section "Du, du, du" of the Queen of the Night's aria in the first act *of Die Zauberflöte*. This too is marked *Allegro moderato*, but how often one hears this begun at a breathtaking pace that necessitates abrupt reductions of tempo! Similarly, in his church music Mozart wrote several movements with the marking *Allegro moderato*. In all of these, a brisk pace would undermine the gravity of the sung texts. We can deduce that Mozart wrote *moderato* not only as a warning to performers that a hasty tempo could make some elements in the piece unplayable but also to prevent distortion of the piece's spirit.

It is interesting to recall that the only other first movement of a piano sonata that is in 2/4 meter is in K.281. Metrically the two pieces are similar, with the quickest passages being in thirty-second notes. But in this C major Sonata we are in an introverted world of subtle emotions. The *Allegro moderato* of K.330 is more like a quiet monologue whereas K.281's first movement is robustly extrovert. During the development section of K.330's first movement, the music fluctuates between positive and negative poles, but the changes are more internalized than dramatic. Even on recordings by renown artists the first movement is often rattled off at a tempo that renders the exposition superficial and obscures the rich *chiaroscuro* contrasts of the development section.

Among Mozart's piano sonatas, only K.545 requires less dexterity than K.330. Also because of this, millions of pianists know and love the earlier sonata, which Einstein described as being:

"a masterpiece, in which every note 'belongs' – one of the most lovable works Mozart ever wrote."[5]

Though many recordings of this sonata are available, few are truly convincing. The fortepianist Malcolm Bilson[6] and Clara Haskil,[7] playing a modern instrument, do convince, though their interpretations are conspicuously different. However, both chose a similar tempo for the first movement, resulting in fine-grained performances.

A special aspect of the sonata is the astonishing amount of phrase repetition and decoration. If the pianist cannot delight in this, he should avoid the piece. The lack of overt emotional and dynamic contrasts, especially in the first and third movements, demands of the player a sensitive motivation for each note he plays, just as the general lack of pedaling requires a supple touch and phrasing.

The dynamic indications in K.330 taken from the first edition (hereafter abbreviated as FE) are most suspicious, but fortunately the manuscript has been rediscovered in Krakow, Poland, so that it is possible to see which dynamic indications were added to the proofs of FE. Unfortunately most publishers (a laudable exception is the *Wiener Urtext Ausgabe*) are unwilling to limit the dynamic indications to those found in the manuscript. When included in small print or placed between brackets, the numerous FE indications can be differentiated from the manuscript indications, but their mere presence lends them a questionable validity. We will never know whether Mozart made these additions himself. Many seem dubious, others irrelevant, even erroneous, but virtually no player can help being affected by what he sees in the score. The dubious dynamic indications in the first movement of K.330 form a conspicuous hindrance to a natural exposition of the music. It is interesting to note that Haskil in her beautiful recording rarely pays any attention to the FE indications.

FIRST MOVEMENT	*Allegro moderato*
FORM	sonata
APPROXIMATE TEMPO	♩ = M.M. 63
DURATION	7 minutes (with expositional repeat)
SUGGESTED LISTENING	Piano Concerto, K.414/385-p i
	String Quartet, K.387 i
	Quartet, oboe & strings, K.370/368-b i

3 INTERPRETATION OF THE FIRST MOVEMENT, K.330

The intimate tone of the opening often tempts the player to assume an introverted posture, leaning too close to the keyboard. This blocks freedom of breathing and arm movement. Similarly a rigid positioning of the body opposite the middle of the keyboard hardly suits the dancelike pace of this piece. Frequently in this movement, the player should incline to the right side of the keyboard, without leaning closer to it.

At the outset the NMA[8] suggests a *forte*. Bright optimism certainly seems more appropriate than vague delicacy. Pedaling is unnecessary throughout this theme. Excepting the accents in mm.31, 34, and 38, there are no dynamic indications in the manuscript until the *Codetta* at mm.54-58. Certainly the regrettable FE *forti* and *piani* during the first theme sound willful if played as abrupt changes in volume.

Small inflections in the melodic lines are not always self-evident in this piece. Even if it is on the first beat, the very first melody note should sound like a light upbeat. The second note, the first of a slurred group, receives more emphasis. The final RH notes of mm.5-6 are energetic, whereas those of mm.9-10 are light. Too many players give all the first beats of the melody the same emphasis, whereas mm.2,4,6,8 are lighter.

The LH phrasing indicated by the slurs in mm.8,16 and 19-24 should be warmly shaped. In m.8 the first group of three slurred eighth notes is played by an imaginary cello, the subsequent four notes by a viola. Good quartet players would never shorten the bass notes of mm.12 and 14, which many pianists play with a jarring *staccato*. Some editions place *staccato* dots over the LH eighth notes of m.13 and wedges over the first two LH notes of m.17. Clear functional differentiation between dots and wedges is rare in Mozart; here, neither the *staccati* nor the wedged notes should be too short. Otherwise they become too emphatic in this cheerful context.

After a high-spirited transitional sentence at mm.12-18, in m.18 the comical cello upbeat to the second theme group is, of course, to be played *non legato* and without pedal. A lovely stability under the cheeky melody is created if the LH's lower notes in mm.19-24 are finger-pedaled but not accented.

The FE dynamic contrasts in mm.19-30 seem even less probable than those in the opening theme sentence and are surely best ignored; this should not mean, however, that all these delightful, laughing phrases are to receive the same sound. The LH triplet sixteenth notes, starting at m.26, can be played very *non legato*, as if the keys were too hot to touch, but the tone should never overwhelm the melody. Humor is based on details; the manuscript *sforzando* in m.31 can be quite strong and perhaps introduced by a *crescendo*, whereas the *sforzando* in m.35 merely indicates an unexpected, comical accent, not as weighty as the emphases in mm.31 or 38. Measures 35 and 37 sound unmistakably like giggling.

The FE dynamic indications in mm.40-41 seem especially artificial and, in my opinion, can best be ignored. More tone is welcome in the two subsequent measures. The FE *piano* contrast in m.44 is logical, but the next measure's *crescendo* is surely slight and the *forti* in mm.46, 52 relative. The FE *forte* in m.48 can only refer to the RH quick notes, not to the first beat. At the manuscript's *forte* in m.54 there is a striking change of motif and texture, as if our imaginary string quartet were playing *unisono* for the first time. In mm.54-57 the second quarter-note beats are light. In the final measure of the exposition, the first eighth-note beat is not *staccato* and could be pedaled to the following chord.

The entire exposition is based on frequently repeated two-measure motifs, separated by rests. If the player projects all the rests in the same way, the performance will become segmented. The rests in mm.2, 5, 20 and 43, for example, are less deeply breathed than those in mm.4, 6, 22 and 44.

In the development section, the phrases become considerably longer. The entire section has two sentences, mm.59-66 and 66-88, the latter going through at least eight emotional transformations. Yearning triadic figures, sorrowful suspensions and nervous syncopations predominate in these quasi-operatic melodies. The manuscript's *sforzandi* in mm.62-63 conjure up restlessness with slight emphasis on what would normally be the lighter beats. With regard to the other dynamic indications, I would advise a skeptical approach.

During the emotional outpourings of mm.69-85, there are many alternatives to the capricious readings of the FE. Bilson, for example, makes a big *diminuendo* in m.70 and plays the following six measures very softly, whereas Uchida[9] makes a *crescendo* in mm.67-70 and plays with full tone until m.75. The RH slurs in mm.75-76 indicate fatalistic sobs when played as written, with a slight separation between the second and third notes.[10] A singer would perhaps sing the same vowel on the first two notes and another syllable on the third. For the pianist a slight separation enhances the fatalism of this rhetoric.

Obviously the FE *forte* in m.90 belongs two measures earlier, another instance of how unreliable these indications are. The *Coda* beginning in m.145 is a bittersweet reflection of the development's opening and ends the movement with a rather ambivalent, introverted impression, predicting the following movement's quiet intensity. As there are slurs extending over bar-lines elsewhere in the first movement, there is no justification for joining the RH sixteenth notes on either side of the bar-lines in mm.145-148. The *sforzandi* in mm.148,150 are slight, like those in mm.62-63, and the FE *sforzando* of the final measure is utterly redundant.

4 ORNAMENTATION IN THE FIRST MOVEMENT, K.330

m.

2   The trill sounds fussy if begun on the upper auxiliary. Some, including myself, find that the lower auxiliary B would sound clumsy here. Clearest is a five- or seven-note trill, with the subsequent thirty-second notes forming the termination.

7   The *appoggiatura* is definitely to be played as a grace note. Neumann[11] takes much trouble to establish the priorities in such cases. Though many recording artists play the *appoggiatura* on the beat, obviously the melodic note, the upper G, should be stressed by sounding on the beat. Rosenblum[12] gives an excellent survey of attitudes from methods of the period and states that this ornament is an example of "another step in the evolution of ornament performance during the Classic period." The trill later in the measure has three notes, begins on the beat, and the subsequent thirty-second notes form the termination.

17   Of the onbeat *appoggiature* the first could perhaps be slightly prolonged, "robbing time" from the subsequent thirty-second notes.

19   This *appoggiatura* has puzzled pianists for generations. Neumann[13] discusses this case at some length and concludes that the ornament in m.19 should be played as a grace note, in contrast to the onbeat suspensions heard in the second beats of m.19 and in 23. A more likely rendition is to play the *appoggiatura* as quickly as possible (no more than a thirty-second note) on the beat.

26   The trill consists of three or even five notes plus the termination. Given the breezy character of this phrase, it could be preceded by the upper auxiliary as a grace note.

27   The *Schleifer* is jaunty, not melancholy, and therefore ends on the first beat.

37   About this subjective trill Rosenblum[14] writes, "Some favor the importance of the line and start the trill on E; others favor the dissonance provided by an upper-note start, particularly since

the preceding *staccato*, the fresh articulation on the downbeat, and the dotted rhythm all add to a momentary prickly effect." Certainly both readings are plausible.

41   Though one often hears this onbeat *appoggiatura* as a sixteenth note, it is more vivacious when played quicker.

47   This *appoggiatura* and that in m.54 are on the beat and can be slightly emphasized. Due to the slur, the trill must begin on the principal note.

65   The slurred trill begins on the principal note, which could be slightly prolonged. Five notes, not three, are welcome before the indicated termination.

66   Playing these *appoggiature* and that in m.71 as very light grace notes makes their effect much more charming than the usually heard onbeat rendition.

78   Both *appoggiature* are played on the beat, but their duration is very subjective. The ornaments are more expressive if not joined by the fingers.

129   These three-note trills are impossible for anyone who has assumed a hasty tempo or does not have a quick wrist. Often upper auxiliary grace notes are played instead of trills. A more interesting alternative is to play grace notes in m.129, three-note *Schneller* in the next measure.

ADDITIONAL ORNAMENTATION seems irrelevant throughout the piece. The bass chords in mm.25, 31, 112 and 118 could be arpeggiated. Malcolm Bilson and Gustav Leonhardt[15] arpeggiate the final chord, a poetic touch that calls for repetition of the lowest bass note.

SECOND MOVEMENT	*Andante cantabile*
FORM	sonata
APPROXIMATE TEMPO	♪ = M.M. 104
DURATION	4½ minutes (with no repeats)
SUGGESTED LISTENING	*Entführung aus dem Serail:* Belmonte's 3 arias
	Sonata for Violin and Piano, K.378 ii
	Lied "Verdankt sei es dem Glanz," K.392/ 340-a

5 INTERPRETATION OF THE SECOND MOVEMENT, K.330

For musicians who like imagery, the first movement could perhaps be seen as a young couple courting; in this *Andante*, their love seems fulfilled, though at times thwarted. The double qualifications *cantabile* and *dolce* demand an intensely *legato* style, which makes this one of the most immediately appealing pieces Mozart wrote for the piano. One should be very careful not to choose a sluggish tempo, as this can result in nervous *rubato*, more seasick than eloquent. Conversely a tempo that is too quick can result in lovely detail being lost.

However vocal the melody seems, the "scoring" strongly evokes a string quartet. Therefore the balance of the nonmelodic parts needs much aural sensitivity. It is easier to balance the tone among the voices in the few overtly polyphonic phrases than in more homophonic ones.

Emotion should not be confused with spinning long, gooey *legato* lines, which express little more than beautiful sound. In an atmosphere of such heightened sensitivity, details are important. For example, one rarely hears the separation of the RH second quarter-note beat's note in m.1 from the three subsequent notes, a slightly nervous breath, which is much more expressive than playing the entire measure as if it had a single slur.

The motif of four repeated notes, heard at the beginning, is a unifying element throughout the movement, returning in mm.20-28, 36-40 and 60-64. The player must respond to the changing contexts of this motif, sometimes static, sometimes urgent. One can learn much from this magnificent theme; how a true *legato* means that no two consecutive notes have the same intensity, how each suspension should have a different weight, how carefully the *legato*, *portato*, *non legato*, and *staccato* inflections must be differentiated. All of this can be studied away from the piano, with the pianist trying his best to sing as expressively as possible (for most pianists, admittedly an exercise to be performed in solitude!).

If the player feels inhibited by the proximity of the hands throughout this movement, he might practice with the RH line an octave higher. This can give a sense of more breadth in the body, and therefore, perhaps, in the spirit. Above all, the player must take care not to give all the first beat suspensions the same weight.

Most analysts of the piece describe the section beginning in m.20 as a middle section of a ternary form. But given the prevalence of the repeated four-note motif and many similarities of melodic layout between mm.1-8 and mm.20-28, mm.8-20 and mm.28-36, it would be inaccurate to view this section as an event unrelated to the exposition. Of course the abrupt shift from major to minor mode, from warm tenderness to utter desolation, reminds us of Schubert, making this development section seem like music from another world. In Mozart's music, F minor usually expresses utter hopelessness; in the slow movement of the Sonata K.280 and some passages in K.533-494 we hear a similar desolation. After eight measures in this dangerous key, A-flat is reached in m.27. But the relief is fleeting, wiped out by a lurch back to F minor three measures later.

The manuscript's *pianissimo* indicated at the beginning of the development is unusual in Mozart. This ominous sound is most easily caught by using both the *una corda* pedal and a touch that is not too shallow. On her recording, Lili Kraus[16] plays the LH "cello" line with minimal pedaling, the result sounding like hesitant heartbeats. This is difficult to maintain during the *legato* RH sixths of m.21, for example. Perhaps the best solution here is to change the pedal on every eighth-note beat, giving a grim irrevocability to this unique passage. If the first beat bass notes are prolonged, the texture loses its eerie quality.

In the shift to optimism at m.25, there should be no more UC and the pianist should play with a warm sounding arm *legato*. These eloquent quartet textures require attentive articulation. Measures 32-34 are a splendid contradiction of the misconception that Mozart's slurs never extend over bar-lines. What an expressive duet this is; the violin line interrupted by the bar-line before its sorrowful suspension, while the cello line surges optimistically over the bar-line. A noticeable *diminuendo* in m.35 should be avoided (the *piano* is not in the manuscript), for this is the climax of the entire movement and a premature *decrescendo* makes the subsequent phrase seem redundant.

The valedictory phrase of mm.36-40 is not in the manuscript, but from the FE. This and the addition of four more measures at the end of the movement heighten the emotional potency of both sections and, with their repetitions of the initial motif, lend even greater structural unity to the whole movement. These additions were surely by the composer,[17] like similar changes to K.284,332 and 457. However, this does not prove that Mozart added all the frequently peculiar dynamic indications in the rest of the FE.

The grinding dissonance on the first beat of m.39 can be played quite softly on a modern instrument and still be startling. Fortepianists often resort to excessive *rubato* here, as if their instruments cannot respond sufficiently to the sensitive shifts in these heartfelt introspections.

After the recapitulation, there is a brief *Coda* in mm.60-64. As in the development, use of the UC is advisable, but with such ethereal music, one should not bend over the keys. Sitting back removes arm weight from the hands and creates an attitude of "listening as much as playing."

What of the repeat signs in the exposition and development sections? One recording artist who plays no repeats in the entire movement is Gustav Leonhardt. My conclusion is that this movement has a natural shape when all repeat signs are ignored.

6 ORNAMENTATION IN THE SECOND MOVEMENT, K.330

m.

1   The turn is best begun after the second quarter-note beat.

5   The *appoggiatura* should be a quick, light grace note before the beat.

8   The *appoggiature* here and in mm.11, 24 express pathos and should fall on the eighth-note beats. Their actual duration is a subjective matter; one may become a sixteenth note, another slightly longer. Each suspension calls for a different weight of tone.

15   Beginning the trill on the upper auxiliary would break the emphatic line created by the repeated E-flats. A slight pause on the first note is expressive and the trill should not be too rapid. The subsequent F becomes the termination.

25   The *appoggiature* will sound skittish if played as grace notes. Their duration does not have to be uniform; playing all three as sixteenth notes would create a lugubrious effect.

26   The last note of the turn is best played on the second quarter-note beat.

35   The *appoggiatura* sounds on the third quarter-note beat. The last two sixteenth notes of the measure are more dejected, and expressive, played *non legato*.

Additional ornamentation is unnecessary in a movement so generously ornamented by the composer. In such a *cantabile* piece it is not difficult to imagine alterations and additions to melodies, but these would be relevant only when a section is repeated. As observed above, the desirability of repetition is debatable.

THIRD MOVEMENT	*Allegretto*
FORM	sonata
APPROXIMATE TEMPO	$\quad$ = M.M. 80
DURATION	6 minutes (with repeat of exposition)
SUGGESTED LISTENING	Concert Rondo for Piano and Orchestra, K.382
	Piano Concerto, K.414/385-p iii
	Rondo for Strings & Winds, K.373

7 INTERPRETATION OF THE THIRD MOVEMENT, K.330

This sunny finale takes us into the world of the *Singspiel* or the *opera buffa*. Whereas the first movement evoked the *galant* conversation of a string quartet and the slow movement seemed periodless in its musings, this exuberant finale brings us back to earth, to amusement and festivities. The textures are orchestral, though suggestive of a street band rather than a large symphony orchestra. On a big modern instrument these high spirits can easily sound heavy, even coarse. A genteel touch and minimal pedaling are necessary.

Musically this movement is quite straightforward, but there are two hazards for the unwary player. One is rhythmic steadiness. On recordings it is surprising how many well-known artists adopt a disconcerting stop-go approach, with numerous *accelerandi* and *ritenuti* making the music sound artificially complicated. The other challenge, choice of logical dynamics, we have encountered in the previous movements. None of the dynamics printed in the *Urtext* editions are from the manuscript. Even the *piano* at the beginning is questionable; surely a cheerful, extrovert sound is more logical here. At the beginning of the recapitulation, the FE has *sotto voce*, but according to Frederick Neumann, this denotes *mezzoforte* in Mozart, not *più piano*.[18] It is difficult to believe that these indications were added by the composer. The *piano* indicated in m.22 certainly refers to the previous measure. The *crescendo* in m.25 and the *forte* in m.59 seem unlikely effects.

Lively articulation brings out the good humor of this piece. In the first four measures the LH plays *non legato*, whereas the mellow eighth notes in mm.5-6 are *legato*. In mm.1 and 5, the RH eighth notes on the second quarter-note beats end slurred groups; though they should not be bound to the subsequent eighth notes, if they sound overtly *staccato*, the melody seems somewhat fussy. The bass in mm.9-12 inhibits many players, if only because it is technically more difficult than anything else the LH has to play in this sonata. The passage is not so hazardous if played *non legato*, unpedaled, with the thumb and wrist relaxed, and the eyes on the LH, not on the music. The first beats of mm.l6 and 18 often sound ugly due to heedless RH accents and nasty shortening of the LH thirds. Nowhere in the first theme is pedaling necessary.

At mm.21-28 the bass should be played as *leggiero* as possible, but some artists attempt a *staccato* here, which sounds pedantic, especially on a modern instrument. The whole theme is gently coquettish and there is no need for artificial dynamic contrasts. A strong *forte* in m.29 seems belligerent, a slight *crescendo* in mm.30-31 more natural. In m.39 the bass is no longer slurred, inferring that the seven previous measures could be finger-pedaled. Playfulness, not roughness, is surely evident in the exuberant sentence that begins at m.47. From m.61 until the end of the exposition, to enable free movement of the left arm, the player should lean slightly to the right side of the keyboard, without bending over the keys.

The first measures of the development section (not the middle section of a ternary form, as maintained by some commentators) are subtle variants of the first two measures of the exposition. Lighter moments in Mozart's operas come easily to mind (for example, most appearances of Papageno in *Die Zauberflöte*, Figaro in *Le Nozze di Figaro*). The unexpected C minor of mm.87-91 is more a passing cloud than an actual storm, the RH's recitative-like fragmentation based on the dialogue of thirds and suspensions so evident earlier in the section.

The last eight measures of the *Coda* are missing in the manuscript. What a frivolous farewell this is, almost like a music hall routine. R.D. Levin commented:

"... we encounter a detail that is the essence of Mozart's delectable childlike spirit: he overextends the coda idea like a child that wants just one more candy..."[19]

The impetuous quality of all these good-natured themes is diminished, in my opinion, if the second repeat is observed.

8 ORNAMENTATION IN THE THIRD MOVEMENT, K.330

m.

2   The *appoggiatura* is practically always played as an onbeat sixteenth note, but it is livelier if played quicker. An alternative is to play it as a quick *Zwischenslag* before the beat.

4   The trill is best played with three or (depending on the instrument) five notes, beginning on the principal note and without a

termination. The thumb playing the lower line must remain totally loose throughout the trill.

21 The turn begins just after the second quarter-note beat.

33 The *appoggiatura* becomes a quick prebeat grace note.

39 One usually hears these trills begun on the second quarter-note beats, with three notes and no termination. However, this can sound more muddled than cheerful. A prebeat rendition is also possible, with the final note on the second quarter-note beat. It is essential that the first beats during this phrase are light.

54 This onbeat *appoggiatura* has more character if accented and played very quickly.

60 Due to the slur, the trill begins on the principal note and has five notes, not three, plus the indicated termination.

61 This *appoggiatura* could be played on or before the last sixteenth-note beat. More important than timing is nuance. If the ornament is not extremely light, the figure seems lopsided.

69 With the LH taking the middle-voice D's during the initial four measures of the development, it is not difficult to play a five-note turn, but a three-note *Schneller* is more humorous.

73 Here a turn definitely sounds cumbersome; a three-note *Schneller* is preferable.

170 The final chords are more festive if vigorously arpeggiated.

XI

SONATA IN A MAJOR, K.331

OTHER K. NUMBERING   K.300-i
COMPOSITION DATE   probably 1782-83
TOTAL DURATION   16 minutes (most repeats omitted)

1 FACTS AND FANTASIES: SONATA OR SUITE?

The A major Sonata was published in 1784, with the Sonatas in C and F, K.330-331. It is now assumed that these sonatas date from a later period than Mozart's Parisian stay in 1778 (see first section of Chapter X). As all manuscripts of K.331, with the exception of the *Rondo's* conclusion, have disappeared, it is more difficult to refute the debatable elements of the first edition (hereafter FE).

The popularity of this sonata has inspired some peculiar flights of fancy. Many commentators have been misled by the Parisian accreditation. Dennerlein,[1] for example, maintained that this sonata and the A minor Sonata, K.310, formed a pair, the A minor being a lament conceived just after the sudden death of Mozart's mother in Paris, the A major being a memorial to her written soon afterwards.

The direct appeal and unusual form of K.331, "this most famous of all eighteenth-century sonatas," as H.C. Robbins Landon[2] termed it, has stirred a wide range of reactions. Albert Einstein commented:

"... the work that has given so many people their first impression of Mozart. It is, however, not typical but exceptional; it is in a way a counterpart to the Munich Dürnitz Sonata in D, but it places the variations at the beginning, and accordingly casts them in briefer and less virtuoso forms; it contains instead of a polonaise the most French of all dance forms; and it ends with a true *scène de ballet*." [3]

Others are less appreciative of this unique work. In 1956, Arthur Hutchings referred to Einstein's description, then made the surprising deduction:

"perhaps these facts explain one's feeling that the sonata, being more of its own time than of all time, is less attractive than its neighbours." [4]

Dennerlein[5] proposed that the latter movements are also variations, the *Minuet* forming Variations 7-8, the *Rondo*, Variations 9-12. Because of motivic development throughout all three movements, this theory is less peculiar than it seems.

Among Mozart's piano sonatas, only K.282 and K.284 have something of K.331's suite-like character. But the outer movements of K.282 and the first of K.284 are in sonata form, whereas in this A major Sonata not one movement is in sonata form. Is the sonata a suite of three genre pieces or is it a triptych, each movement needing the support and contrast offered by the others?

There are many resemblances to be found in all the movements, among them:

1. Exotic "Turkish" effects are not only present in the *Rondo* but also in the first movement, in the bass in mm.5-8, 17-18 of Variation 1, the sharp LH accents in the corresponding measures of the following variation and the exotic patina throughout Variation 3. In much of the final variation, the spicy *appoggiature* of mm.20-22 and the exuberant bass *arpeggi* of mm.5-6, 11-12 are very like the bass at mm.25-31 of the *Rondo*. Even in that very European dance, the *Minuet*, there is chromaticism of an exotic tint in mm.19-29 and ominous, foreign doubling of octaves at mm.20-23 in the *Trio*. Throughout the entire *Rondo*, the bass writing sounds frenetic, obsessively wild. In the *Coda* rugged bass *arpeggi* combine with frenzied RH bell effects to create a most un-European sound world.

2. One motif recurs constantly throughout the whole sonata. Its most noticeable appearance is at mm.18-23 of the *Trio*, but this pattern of five notes descending diatonically has already been heard in the first two measures of Variations 2,3,5 and 6. In the *Rondo* we hear this motif at mm.9-10,26-27,30-31,40-41, etc.

3. The variation theme, the theme of the *Minuet's Trio* section, and the two major themes of the *Rondo* are all based on the alternation of diatonic figures and thirds.

FIRST MOVEMENT	*Andante grazioso*
FORM	variation form
APPROXIMATE TEMPO	♪= M.M. 126-129
DURATION	7½ minutes (without repeats)
SUGGESTED LISTENING	Sonata for Piano and Violin, K.305/293-d ii
	Variations for Piano and Violin "Hélas, j'ai perdu mon amant," K.360/374-b
	Divertimento for Strings and Horns, K.334/ 320-b ii

2 INTERPRETATION OF THE FIRST MOVEMENT, K.331

THEME   No other single theme in Mozart's piano music has attracted as much commentary as the melody on which these variations are based. Ironically enough, cozy images of Mozart's mother singing this lullaby-like tune to her little boy are not mere sentimental imaginings; a Bavarian folk song that bears a remarkable resemblance to this theme had already been printed in a collection, the *Ostracher Liederhandschrift*, well known during the eighteenth century in central Europe. The English translation of the opening is "Be Happy, my heart! Do not think of any pain!" The theme apparently made a strong impression on Mozart's subconscious, as it appears in the *Minuet* of the G major Sonata for Violin and Piano, K.9, written when the composer was ten, and in the *Andante* of the D major Symphony, K.95/73-n, four years later. Traces of this folk song theme can be found in many of Mozart's later pieces. The same theme attracted other composers long after Mozart's death; Reger wrote his mammoth *Mozart Variations* for orchestra on this theme, and Mahler made a reference to it in the second *Trio* of his first symphony.

The tradition, begun in the nineteenth century, of playing this movement in a mournful fashion is difficult to erase. Such a heavy style hardly seems appropriate in a piece indicated *grazioso* by the composer. Many interpreters vary the tempo considerably from one variation to another, but if one assumes that the music is generally sunny, not riddled with schizophrenic conflict, it is not so difficult to find a tempo that suits the theme as well as the four subsequent variations.

As in K.330 and 332, there is no proof that the interpretive signs of the first editions are Mozart's. However, the dynamic indications and accents of the theme are welcome activating touches. The little *sforzandi*, sometimes more breaths than actual emphases, keep the listener from drowsing off during the lullaby. It is very important to note that the NMA[6] has slurs only over the first two notes of the theme. If the fingers make a tiny separation, on modern instruments preferably pedaled, between the second and third notes, the initial motif is not sleepy, but very awake. The sixteenth note must not sound *staccato*, of course, but only slightly detached from the next tone. The pedal should be changed on the third, fourth and sixth eighthnote beats. It is imperative throughout the theme that the hand does not bind the last eighth-note beats to the subsequent first beats, an unattractive drooping articulation that Reger indicated in his somewhat elephantine variations on the theme.

With clear pedaling and avoidance of excessive *legato*, this theme takes on a gentle lilt, suiting the *grazioso* quality Mozart indicated. The repeated notes should be varied in expression, like different words or syllables in a song. Care must be taken with the voicing of the chords; if the notes played by the LH thumb are too heavy, they not only disturb the delicate relationship between the melody and the bass line, but drag on the gentle propulsion of the theme. The dynamic level in mm.5-8 of the theme is not clear. Admittedly in all six variations these measures are marked *forte*, therefore it would seem logical if this phrase were played somewhat fuller than the opening four measures. However, the player is again reminded that even the *Urtext* editions of this movement are based on the first editions, not on a manuscript.

Beginning a piano sonata with variations was highly unusual, though Beethoven did it in his Opus 26. The suite-like character of both compositions and the atmosphere of the initial theme are curiously similar. There are other resemblances; the quickening of pace from the first variation to the second, the minor mode of the third, the playful changes of register in the fourth.

VARIATION 1 evinces more fantasy than most other opening variations of Mozart variation works. The suspensions and repetitions enhance the theme rather than merely decorating it. The balance of elegance and restlessness is a very subjective matter, but romantic *rubati* would be misplaced. Pedaling should be minimal. The five-note groups of sixteenth notes have two slurs, clearly indicating two impulses, not one, with a slight separation between the third and fourth notes and slight emphasis of the first and fourth notes. However beautiful the pianist's touch may be, playing these figurations as if each five-note group had a single *legato* slur sounds boring and clumsy. The slight detaching of the unslurred RH upbeats in mm.5-7 should also not be ignored. The *forte* phrases can be played with energy but without rowdiness. Hesitating in order to accomodate the LH leaps in mm.7-8 is misplaced.

VARIATION 2 embroiders the theme with trills and triplets. In this lively piece the articulation is evident. The first beats of mm.2-4 are to be very light and certainly not played *staccato*. The long slurs over the bass line surely indicate calmness of line rather than any need for pedaling or finger-pedaling. In the assertive *forte* phrase, accents on the LH *appoggiature* are possible. It is advisable that the fourth finger begins the difficult RH upbeat figures to mm.6-7.

VARIATION 3 is an "exotic" piece in minor mode, the theme flowing in sixteenth notes that ingeniously stray from the melody. This variation is more menacing than melancholy. Too often players slow down here, diminishing the surge of the entire movement. The slurs can be interpreted more as indications of emphasis than of touch. Without any accenting, the first beats of most measures are strongest, as in the theme. The *legato* octaves evoke smooth lines played by the first and second violins in the orchestra. On the keyboard this is a major challenge; the pianist's thumb must be as relaxed as possible, with a minimum of hand movement between black and white keys. A *legato* impression can only be maintained by changing the pedal on every eighth-note beat and playing the upper line of the octaves as expressively as possible. The LH line has more gravity (in both senses of the word) if the lowest notes are finger-pedaled. In m.12 avoid the frequently heard pause before the fourth eighth-note beat, a decadent effect caused by a faulty rendition of the RH ornament (see next section). As elsewhere in the movement, *rubato* can easily trivialize the content, but the phrases must breathe well.

Despite the apparent innocence of VARIATION 4, it is a challenge to avoid bumpy accents and achieve a fine balance in the scoring. It has already been noted how Mozart loved the showy device of crossing the hands. Here the LH must leap sometimes more than two octaves and play *legato* double notes. With the LH playing double notes in such a high register, the uppermost line rarely "sings" sufficiently. It is possible to avoid the crossing of hands: in mm.1-2, 4-6 the LH can move with lightning speed to continue the sixteenth notes beginning on the second eighth-note beats. The *sforzandi* in mm.11-12 can best be imagined as violin downbeats, not sharp emphases. The D-sharp in the third eighth-note beat of m.12 is bizarre. The editors of the NMA[7] refer to the more conventional version stated in the Breitkopf & Härtel edition, which deletes this note. When heard just after the LH's D, the D-sharp certainly does not seem likely. Unlike other compositions by Mozart or Beethoven, this dry-cleaning of dissonances does seem valid.

VARIATION 5 is a tender aria for soprano or tenor. The tempo must suggest breadth, not stasis. An approximate tempo of ♪ = 60 is natural. The atmosphere here is more pensive than melancholy, very much like Ferrando's tender aria in *Così fan tutte*, "Un aura amorosa," also in A major. As in that magnificent aria, overt shifts of tempo would upset the inwardness of the content. The interpretive indications here are so detailed and effective that they are presumably Mozart's. The player must observe every detail marked in the score, shape each RH motif with a truly vocal inflection. The LH line can be molded very expressively without a trace of *rubato*. Too much lingering or rushing destroys the heartfelt simplicity of this thoughtful melody, whereas metrical playing of all the RH thirty-second notes would be horribly unimaginative. Pedaling must not obscure any short notes; for example, two pedalings, not one, are essential during the last eighth-note beat of m.1 to prevent blurring. Where wind instruments are clearly evoked, as in mm.5 and 6, pedaling is not suitable. Presumably the wedged repeated notes in the fifth eighth-note beat of m.7 are to sound *portato*, like those in m.15. The tiny rests of mm.13-14 require deft hand- and footwork. Purists will maintain that the repetitions must be observed, as Mozart wrote two different concluding phrases for both sections of this variation. Arguably, in this composition, the charm of each variation seems lessened, not enhanced, by repetition. I prefer to play the second ending to each section.

VARIATION 6 becomes garbled if taken too quickly, stodgy if played too cautiously; an approximate tempo of ♩ = 122 is recommended. The change of meter, as well as of tempo, is a comic effect. But the comedy darkens already in mm.5-8, where the *Rondo*'s Turkishness is predicted, and these elements are reinforced in the *Coda*. These excited phrases sound very colorful on forte pianos, whereas on large modern instruments the sixteenth notes can sound dull if not played with sensitive shaping. In phrases like mm.5-8, the thematic outline can be evident without rough accenting. The RH writing is sometimes quite difficult technically, requiring a relaxed thumb, considerable horizontal flexibility in the hand, and active middle fingers. The bar numbering in some editions differ in Variation Six. The numbering here is from the NMA, which does not print the repetition of mm.9-18.

3 ORNAMENTATION IN THE FIRST MOVEMENT, K.331

THEME

m.

10 The *Schleifer* can begin on the first beat but presumably is more wistful than melancholy and is therefore best played lightly and quite rapidly. Some prefer a prebeat rendition of the ornament.

VARIATION 1

7 On a modern instrument the trill, beginning on the principal note, can be played with three notes (though five are preferable) plus the indicated termination.

VARIATION 2

1 These trills are like those in m.7 of the first variation. If desired, upper auxiliary grace notes could be added before some of these decorations.

5 The *appoggiature* are best played as quickly as possible before the eighth-note beats (see Neumann[8]). Playing them on the beat would be a strange effect, bringing Prokofiev to mind.

9 The indicated trill may become a mere upper auxiliary grace note *appoggiatura* or a three-note *Schneller* ending on the final eighth-note beat.

VARIATION 3

12 How often this conspicuous ornament is played incorrectly before the beat! The compound *appoggiatura* contributes a doleful dissonance to the fourth eighth-note beat, the first note, not the last, played simultaneously with the lower voices.

VARIATION 5

8 The turn should begin as soon as possible after the principal note if it is not to sound rushed.

13 This turn could be played just before or after the third eighth-note beat.

17 The energetic *arpeggio* is *non tenuto* and ends on the first beat.

VARIATION 6

1 The *appoggiatura* is better played as a grace note before the second eighth-note beat than as the usually heard onbeat triplet sixteenth note. Though requiring quicker hand movements, this interpretation has more vivacity.

4 Like Neumann,[9] I view the *appoggiature* as grace notes played before the beat.

5 The brusque LH *arpeggi* are to be played *tenuto*, with the up-

permost note sounding on the quarter-note beats.

8   The unusually low-lying bass triad[10] is another "exotic" effect, especially when arpeggiated, though not forcefully on a modern instrument.

15   The *appoggiature* resemble those in m.4.

20   Due to the upbeats and tempo, the compound *appoggiature* can only be played beginning on the beat and as rapidly as possible. This sequence of ornaments is not difficult if the upbeat sixteenth notes are clearly detached.

Some added ornaments are possible if Variation 5 is repeated, where Bilson[11] makes many beautiful alterations, notably in mm.4, 11 and 15. However, Lili Kraus,[12] without adding a note, plays so lovingly that the total lack of added ornaments becomes an irrelevant issue. Obviously the two final chords of the movement sound better if energetically arpeggiated. In any case, the rhythmic complexity of the piece should not be increased by any ornament that sounds more elaborate than expressive.

After much experimentation, I find that all repetitions in this movement could be omitted, but this is obviously a subjective choice.

SECOND MOVEMENT   *Menuetto*
FORM   ternary
APPROXIMATE TEMPO $\downarrow$ = M.M. 122 (*Trio* = 118)
DURATION   5 minutes (with some repeats)
SUGGESTED LISTENING   Serenade for Strings & Winds, K.320 ii
                        Sonata for Piano & Violin, K.377/374-e iii
                        String Quartet, K.387 ii

4 INTERPRETATION OF THE SECOND MOVEMENT, K.331

Any sensitive listener soon realizes that this movement is more than a courtly dance. Compared to the outer movements, this *Minuet* may seem like a calm oasis, but the atmosphere is volatile, not at all calm. Within a few beats, conflicts evaporate into resignation, and resignation explodes into conflict. We can imagine contemplative soliloquies, spirited dialogues, bustling group situations. There is a delicious ambivalence in this *Minuet*, which is particularly Mozartian, grace and unease existing side by side. Because of this dichotomy and the diversity of rhythmic figures, it is not easy to establish a stable tempo. The piece does not inhabit the world of Mozart's youthful minuets, but rather of the *Empfindsamkeit* composers, particularly Johann Schobert (1720-67). In mm.19-30 we seem to be at an opera, hearing a lovelorn tenor howling his torment.

Within the first section, ending at m.18, phrase lengths are as unpredictable as the emotional contradictions: pride, coquetry and yearning are all evoked in the first measures. There seems to be an enigmatic smile at mm.9-10. In the subsequent recapitulary sentence (mm.31-48), the second theme conforms to sonata principles by reverting to the tonic key. Throughout, sixteenth notes should be played lighter than the eighth notes.

As noted in Chapters III and V, a minuet including sixteenth notes becomes muddled if the tempo is too swift. The *Trio* could be played somewhat slower, but any reduction of pace should be barely perceptible.

Contributing to the variety of expression, the slurs need much attention. As the *Trio* has some slurs extending over bar-lines, there is no justification for the fingers joining a slurred note group to the first note of the subsequent measure when this is not indicated. Whether or not dabs of pedaling are needed to prevent tiny silences between successive slurs depends on the instrument, performance space and tempo. In mm.20-29 the arching cello lines need as much attention as the aching violin melody; *rubato* in the bass should be avoided. The RH upbeat sixteenth notes have more lift if they are not slurred to the first beats. In m.23 the suspensions are most searing when the resolution note of each suspension is gently separated – without sounding *staccato* – from the next note.

In the *Trio* dark and light images pass, floating on an unusually long stream of eighth notes. This is no mere accompaniment but a subtle entwining of melodic motifs. The opening sentence is sometimes idyllic, sometimes humorous. At m.17, there is an abrupt lurch to E minor. As in the *Minuet*, the *Trio's* middle section has a rather developmental character. Here, threatening Turkishness and the most dramatic appearance of the descending motif, noted in the previous section, disturb the previous tranquillity.

The writing in the *Trio* is a fine example of the original connotation of the term, indicating a piece for three players. The phrases with crossed hands remind us of VARIATION 4 of the first movement; here too it is conceivable to shift both hands, without crossing, up and down the keyboard. The uniform rhythmic flow is enlivened by the slurs, which prevent this wonderful episode from drifting into a misty sea. There should be some separation, covered by pedaling if desired, before the second quarter-note beat of mm.4, 6, 8 (presuming a new measure-numbering at the opening of the *Trio*); slight separations before the bar-lines of mm.4-5, 8-9 give the melody more breath. The grim octaves in eighth notes at mm.20 and 22 and the quarter notes at mm.21 and 23 should not be pedaled. Indeed they are the only conspicuous *non legato* elements in an exceptionally *legato* piece. The harmonic activity in mm.25-36 is striking, a poignant breathless RH theme struggling against the inexorably descending bass, sinking in m.31 to D minor, remote from the movement's tonic key. For five measures the music seems paralyzed, until in m.37 it slides back to the pacific D major. In the final section, descending motifs proliferate, creating a beatific calmness.

Given the movement and diversity of the piece, the performer must avoid sitting stiffly and thus impeding his ability, in the *Trio* for example, to play with crossed hands. Good breathing is easier when the body remains supple. Some repetitions could be omitted, though it seems advisable to repeat the first sixteen measures of both *Minuet* and *Trio*.

5 ORNAMENTATION IN THE SECOND MOVEMENT, K.331

Minuet
m.
1   Neumann maintains that the uppermost note of such *arpeggi* fall on the beat: "Arpeggios ... are only surface adornments to put the melody in pleasing relief, adding elegance, not substance."[13] The Badura Skodas[14] maintain that the *arpeggio* should start on the beat, though the uppermost note should be more emphasized than the first. Rosenblum[15] suggests that the *arpeggio* in m.1 could begin on the first beat. At m.13 a version of m.11's *arpeggio*, written in sixteenth notes, begins on the first beat, but perhaps diversity, not consistency, is what the composer intended here. In mm.41, 43 a contrast is clearly implied. When the first theme is recapitulated at m.31, a prebeat rendition sounds awkward without some rhythmic freedom before the first beat.
17   The *appoggiatura* is very short, but its position before or on the beat remains an intriguing question. Recording artists too are di-

vided on this issue. I believe that a grace note rendition will sound too much like the upbeat to this measure's second beat and that a slight dissonance on the third quarter-note beat is welcome.

19   These *appoggiature* should definitely be played before the beat.

40   The turn is best begun as soon as possible.

47   The trill could begin on the principal note or upper auxiliary. Clearly the termination is formed by the subsequent thirty-second notes.

Trio

9   The *appoggiatura* would sound jerky if played on the eighth-note beats.

ADDITIONAL ORNAMENTATION is conceivable in such a *galant* piece, especially during repetitions, for example; a *Schleifer* before the first beat of the melody in m.9, or an ascending F-sharp minor chord in the first beat of m.17, etc. Malcolm Bilson makes delightful changes in the *Minuet* melody at m.29. In the *Trio* one could consider some alteration of the repeated upbeat sixteenth notes in mm.25-29.

THIRD MOVEMENT	*Allegretto: Rondo Alla Turca*
FORM	rondo form
APPROXIMATE TEMPO	♩ = M.M. 126-129
DURATION	3½ minutes (with all repeats)
SUGGESTED LISTENING	Violin Concerto, K.219 iii
	Entführung aus dem Serail: Osmin's arias, (Act I, no.3 and Act III, no.19), Chorus of the Janissaries, (Act I, no.5)
	C.W. Gluck: *The Pilgrims to Mecca*: Overture

6 INTERPRETATION OF THE THIRD MOVEMENT, K.331

This *Rondo* is often abused by pianistic racehorses, who apparently believe that fleet fingers and motoric drive are all that are needed in this piece. Though articulation, phrasing and ornamentation are less complicated than in most other sonata movements by Mozart, reducing the *Rondo* to a pianistic exhibition of finger work robs it of its uniqueness. Wanda Landowska gave a marvelous description of the *Rondo*'s background:

"Musicians, poets, painters, dancers, couturiers, and craftsmen in every art were fascinated by the opulent and rare qualities of Chinese and Turkish taste ... Mozart proved it eloquently in his Rondo Alla Turca, which is truly a Janissary orchestra in miniature ... the pianofortes of the eighteenth century had numerous stops producing the sounds of bells, drums, and kettledrums, forming an ensemble known as musique turque." [16]

It is possible that the piece was strongly influenced by Gluck's *Pilgrims to Mecca*; a theme from that opera inspired the wonderful piano variations K.455 (Chapter IX). This *Rondo* definitely resembles the overture to Gluck's opera as much as the overture to Mozart's own "Turkish" masterpiece, *Die Entführung aus dem Serail*.

Despite its eccentric character and its appeal to children of all ages, this movement loses some of its "exotic" impact if played on its own. As noted in the first section of this chapter, there are definite motivic bonds with the other movements. After such a diverse *Minuet*, a movement in sonata or rondo form might have been rather heavy. Mozart chose to end with a balletic flood of energy, more shadow play than courtly dance. Oriental gestures, faces and costumes are easily imagined here.

If Mozart had wanted a whirling, frenzied pace, he would have indicated *Presto* or *Allegro assai*. This aspect is as often ignored by young students as by recording artists. Marty[17] rightly differentiates between the faster type of 2/4 *Allegretto* (this movement, the *Allegretto* section of the D minor Fantasy, K.397, etc.) and the more lyrical sort of *Allegretto* found in the variations on "Je suis Lindor," the third movement of the Sonata, K.330, the famous lied "Ein Veilchen" and the finale of the Sonata, K.576. The tempo given above is spirited but does not drown the dark colors in mere speed. Dennerlein even suggested that this movement was a "serious matter of bitterness and sorrows." [18]

Exactness of note values and rests is essential in the main theme. The RH eighth notes on the first beats of the first two measures are neither *staccato* nor prolonged. The quarter note on the first beat of m.4 should not be played *staccato* but just slightly detached from the next note. With such taut articulation the theme takes on menacing energy.

Shaping of the bass line is subjective. Too many editors assume that the first two eighth notes of each measure are slurred throughout the movement. If these notes are slurred in mm.1-2, it could be assumed that mm.4 and 33 take the same articulation. But it is less certain that mm.3,7 and 9 imitate the same articulation. And is the bass of the F-sharp minor section beginning at m.33 to be slurred? The NMA[19] does not give this indication and the bass of this section is sometimes played *non legato* throughout, arguably enhancing the nervous character of the interlude.

In the Janissary march theme ("B section," mm.24-32) the "Turkish cymbal pedal" of some antique instruments would be welcome, but on modern instruments, no pedaling is needed until the *Coda*. Because many children encounter their first octaves when confronted with this *Rondo*, the technical difficulty of the Janissary theme can seem awesome. Too often children are assigned this piece before their hands are big enough to cope with this passage, but in any case, relaxation of the thumb is more important than actual hand size. The passage can best be initially learned with the thumb (and the fifth finger) playing alone. Use of the third or even the fourth finger on black keys is not advisable in such an energetic *non legato* theme unless the player has large hands. The RH movements between black and white keys should be minimal.

In the F-sharp minor section the RH line is shaped by the bass's harmonic progressions. For example, mm.34 and 36 are more active than mm.33 and 35. The fourth RH sixteenth note of m.55 is often given as F-sharp, but the A above it is preferable.[20] A mechanistic performance of either line is most offensive, for this episode darts between danger and hope. It is no mere *étude*, but a good technique is certainly required if each note is to receive its individual weight. Konrad Wolff made a daring suggestion (not to be ventured during competitions!):

"I would not consider it a crime to play the right hand of the F-sharp minor episode (mm.32-40, 49-56) ... one octave higher than marked, at least at the repeat. Mozart might well have done the same thing himself, had this high register been available to him, for the passage certainly smacks of piccolo flutes."[21]

The RH broken octaves in the third statement of the Janissary theme at mm.88-96 give trouble to many players. A relaxed thumb is essential in navigating the leaps. Younger children often find this difficult as they are inclined to hold the middle fingers tensed in a stiff "octave mold," useless when negotiating sevenths and ninths.

In the rousing *Coda*, the drumming and jangling of the Turkish band return. In mm.96-108 and from m.116 to the end, pedaling is welcome, but with clean changes on each quarter-note beat. Editions differ in the first beat of m.122; should the RH play a four-voice A major chord or a mere sixth C-sharp-A?[22] Surely a sound fuller than a sixth is welcome at this climactic moment? All players of this *Rondo* should know Osmin's music in *Die Entführung*. The section is full of flashing violence, vividly like Osmin's threats to decapitate his enemies and make mincemeat of them.

7 ORNAMENTATION IN THE THIRD MOVEMENT, K.331

m.

1   The *appoggiature* are always played as slightly accented sixteenth notes on the beat. Neumann[23] also remarks that the notation evokes the dissonant character of the first note of each figuration.

5   The *Schleifer* should be played as quickly as possible, ending on the first beat, and definitely not slurred to the second beat.

23   The trill can be played as three or five notes before the termination. It is suitable here to play the upper auxiliary as a crunchy upbeat before the trill.

25   The bass *arpeggi* are to be played as energetically as possible, with the uppermost notes on the beat. One sometimes hears the *arpeggi* begun on the beat, but this is neither correct or natural.

97   This is a very interesting example of eighteenth-century musical shorthand. The *arpeggi* in the RH are surely to be played simultaneously with the LH *arpeggi*, but unlike those in the bass, all the RH notes are to be held. This difference is clearly evident in the two forms of *arpeggio* notation in the manuscript fragment that has survived.[24]

101   The *appoggiature* are played as quickly as possible before the beat, necessitating vigorous wrist movements.

109   The *arpeggio* ends on the second quarter-note beat. This phrase is like a flute solo and therefore the arpeggiated notes are not to be held.

XII

SONATA IN F MAJOR, K.332

OTHER K. LISTING   K.300-k
COMPOSITION DATE   presumably 1783
TOTAL DURATION   20 minutes (with expositional repeats in i and iii)

1 SONATA AND OPERA

It was generally presumed that Mozart wrote the Sonatas K.330-333 during his 1788 stay in Paris. But some researchers[1] have concluded that these sonatas were probably completed some five years later, when Mozart was living in Vienna. Each of these masterpieces inhabits its own world of sound and emotion. Whereas the previous Sonata, K.331, was enlivened by various dance elements, in K.332 we find ourselves in an operatic atmosphere.

With the triumphs of *Idomeneo* and *Die Entführung* behind him, Mozart must have found it deeply frustrating that during this productive period he received no commissions for a new opera.[2] But no other major composer created so many instrumental works permeated with the spirit of the theater. The F major Sonata may be regarded as one of these "operas without singers." Its vivacity of melody and relative lack of motivic transformation evoke the stage more readily than the concert hall. This contributes to the sonata's particular appeal, making it, as Alfred Einstein remarked:

> "... one of Mozart's most personal creations, with which one should not find fault simply because it is so little like Beethoven."[3]

As in *Nozze*, composed some three years later, the chaos of life is viewed with an affectionate tolerance for human weakness. Both *Nozze* and K.332 are splendid expressions of the Enlightenment. The opera's humanistic attitudes are clearly anticipated in this piano sonata. In both works the rush of events leaves the listener almost breathless. However, not all is cheer and joy. Abert commented on the D minor passage in the first movement...

"which with typical Mozartian unpredictability soars up, ghostlike, from the world of darkness."[4]

Such threatening moments enhance the theatrical tone of the sonata. The first two movements are not based on conventional sonata principles of contrast and development. In the *Allegro*, an almost dizzying succession of characters whirl onto the stage of the player's imagination. The *Adagio* seems like a quiet gathering of women, each with her own thoughts. The finale has a hyperactivity that reminds us of a comic opera finale. Only when the pianist has something of a fine Mozart conductor's sense of timing and a stage producer's alert delineation of character and plot, can both the player and listener exult in this delightful opera for the piano.

FIRST MOVEMENT	*Allegro*
FORM	sonata
APPROXIMATE TEMPO	$\downarrow$ = M.M. 138
DURATION	7 minutes (with exposition repeated)
SUGGESTED LISTENING	much of *Nozze di Figaro*; for example, the duets of Susanna and Figaro, Figaro's aria "Se vuoi ballare"

2 INTERPRETATION OF THE FIRST MOVEMENT, K.332

When hearing this music, one can easily imagine young people like Figaro and Susanna *(Nozze)* rushing about, trying to make sense of their hectic existence. Given the considerable diversity of note values, it is not easy to balance the elegance of triple meter with the thrust implied by the *Allegro* indication. Ideally the music should flow with one impulse, not three, in each measure. One unifying aspect is that three themes (mm.1-22, 41-56, 94-109) share a minuet-like flow. Coherence during this busy scene will be more evident when these themes do not differ noticeably in tempo.

Choice of a basic tempo remains very subjective. Among the forte pianists, Malcolm Bilson[5] certainly succeeds in characterizing each theme imaginatively. Among the players of "modern" instruments, Lili Kraus[6] captures the operatic spirit of this movement with exceptional flair. Whereas in the playing of Kraus and Bilson we savor each moment, many other pianists serve dull meals. It is not surprising that both Kraus and Bilson assume tempi that are more energetic than cautious.

The player is confronted with considerable textual quandaries in this movement. Many details in the 1784 first edition (hereafter abbreviated as FE) are not to be found in the manuscript. There is no proof that the added indications of dynamics, phrasing and articulation were Mozart's or even approved by him. Unfortunately the *Urtext* editions include these revisions, many of which seem irrelevant or misleading. Though these revisions are usually printed in smaller type, their presence on the page inevitably influences the interpretation. Editors often justify all the FE alterations because the FE ornamented version of the *Adagio*'s final section is certainly an improvement over the bare version in the manuscript. But it remains debatable whether the "interpretive enhancements" elsewhere in the FE are by Mozart.

Until recently the opening theme was often described by piano teachers as a "long *legato* line." Malcolm Bilson is explicit on this subject:

> "My most frequently cited example of neglected or wrongly executed slurs is the opening of ... K.332. Mozart's clear slurs over each bar (indicating, according to all 18th-century sources, that the first note is to be stressed, and the second note, shorter and weaker, corresponds to 'sighs')."[7]

This opening melody is violinistic and needs vibrant tone. But if the hand binds all the notes, the line loses shape. The RH should leave the keys before each bar-line. Dabs of pedaling may be desirable to prevent audible gaps in the line, but pedaling throughout the theme sounds soupy. Compromising romantic and more "authentic" practices, Konrad Wolff's[8] recommendation of pedaling the first two quarter-note beats and releasing the pedal with the third, creates a jerky effect. Depending on the instrument and performance space, the lower bass notes could be finger-pedaled. Use of the UC is not advisable, as this theme has a warm optimism that must not seem muffled.

In the manuscript[9] one slur clearly extends over the bass line of the first two measures. The NMA[10] includes this articulation, which suggests a calm accompaniment and a tempo that is not too sedate. During the responding phrase a yodeling effect is avoided in mm.5-6 if the first note of each slurred group is slightly stressed. The FE *crescendo* in m.9 and *forte* in m.11 seem unnatural to me but in any case are surely not dramatic. A sentimental *ritenuto* at the cadence in mm.11-12 is a regrettable tradition deriving from the nineteenth century. The rest in m.12 is a deep breath, too often shortened by careless pedaling.

At mm.12-19 a jaunty parody of military glory is heard, unmistakably anticipating Figaro's "Si vuoi ballare" from *Nozze*. If the FE *piano* is respected, the brass band humor of this phrase is dampened. The pianist should focus on rhythmic vitality here, not on trying to play softly. Again the phrasing is clearly indicated, the first note of each slurred group slightly emphasized. The cadence in mm.19-22 may fade away gently, but here too, slowing down is not welcome. The quarter notes before rests have more charm if slightly shortened but sound ridiculous if they seem *staccato*.

The *forte* in m.22 is Mozart's first dynamic indication in the manuscript, yet many pianists inexplicably ignore the drama of this moment. The slurring over the bar-line of mm.22-23 indicates that the upbeat to m.23 is strong; over-accentuation of the first beat of m.23 is like colliding with a wall. The subsequent first beats in this fiery *minore* are so obviously weighty, the FE accents hardly seem necessary. Or do they suggest slight rhythmic prolongation, a rhetorical effect noted in many eighteenth-century methods (Nagel, Türk and others[11])? Surely relaxation of tension during the second and third quarter-note beats cannot be the intention. Even on recordings the jagged RH triadic figures in mm.31-36 rarely sound distinct; on a modern instrument *"vibrato* pedaling" and a very energetic *non legato* touch are required. The RH thumb must remain loose and not linger on its notes. The restless bass line of mm.31-38 is best played *non legato*; its thrust would be diminished by any finger-pedaling of lower notes. Reduction of tone at the return to major mode at m.33 is another questionable romantic touch. Richard Rosenberg[12] noted that mm.37-40 anticipate the fiery third movement (mm.30-34) of the C minor Sonata, K.457.

An entirely different operatic character seems to appear at m.41, the unmistakably feminine theme resembling the opening of Zerlina's well-known "Vedrai, carino" from *Don Giovanni*. Until m.56 the RH slurs clearly indicate a seductive, flirtatious atmosphere. With the melody flowing in two-measure units, a monotonous emphasis of first beats sounds wooden. In the bass, unslurred quarter notes should not be played *legato*, but the manuscript does have a single slur for mm.53-54, missing in most editions. The FE *crescendi* in these phrases seem misplaced.

Feminine charms vanish at m.56 where the manuscript's *piano* marks a sudden lurch to breathless anxiety, even more ominous than the fury of mm.22-40. The LH quarter notes should be unpedaled and slightly detached. Pedal strokes could add weight to the symphonic *forti* of the mm.60-65. The accents clearly indicated in the manuscript take on different emotional connotations in each measure.

Students often make heavy weather of the following transitional passage. It should be noted that there are no slurs over the bar-lines at mm.65-66 and 66-67. The undulating double thirds should evoke two woodwind instruments, but if the RH movements are more vertical than horizontal, we seem to be hearing some grim piano étude. In the middle line, all the B's and C's and most of m.70 can best be played by the LH. With these adaptations, *legato* is achieved without resorting to the pedal, which would blur these oboe-like lines. Not all *Urtext* editions have accurate slurring here. In the manuscript, slurs in both staves clearly extend from m.67 to include the first eighth-note beat of m.68. In many editions the next slur in the upper staff extends from the second eighth-note beat of m.68 and apparently ends before the bar-line of mm.69-70. In the manuscript the writing in the upper staff is simply too cramped to permit the slur to include the first eighth-note beat of m.70, though that was surely the intention. In the bass a slur clearly extends from m.68's eighth note to the quarter note of m.70.

At m.71 some of our comic opera characters seem to have reappeared in a sunny phrase, which recalls both mm.14-15 and 41-42. Measures 71-82 should be conceived as two long sentences, not a series of gasps. Verticality can be avoided when the uppermost line is projected with healthy tone and sensitivity. If the repeated chords in mm.71 and 73 are not audibly separated, the result is deadening. Some editions still print G-sharp as the first bass note in m.80, an unjustified spicing found in many nineteenth-century editions. Note that in mm.75 and 81 only the first quarter-note beats are slurred. In m.82, the first beat accent is from the manuscript but is surely more comical than thunderous. Discreet half pedaling may be welcome at the fuller *forte* outburst that begins the surge to the *Codetta* at m.84, where the imaginary stage suddenly fills with people. Measures 86-89 are more difficult to play than they sound. Rushing in the second quarter-note beats should be avoided and the LH sixteenth notes are not perilous if the pianist can keep his thumb as relaxed as possible.

The exposition should be repeated. So much has already happened in our "mini-opera," only the most impatient listener would want to be pulled immediately into more new situations. Repetition of the exposition also enhances the unusual breadth of the development section.

The naive tune that opens the development section sounds familiar, probably because its rhythmic pulse reminds us of mm.71-74. Russell Sherman memorably describes this moment:

> "... a new-old melody, a fresh face with old bones, or an old face with a new hat. Most remarkable, perhaps the ultimate stroke of genius, is the absolutely placid emotional atmosphere which accompanies this extravagant calculus of ideas, wherein the plumage of so many themes is woven so quietly, so inconspicuously together."[13]

This calm sentence hovers for fifteen measures in the dominant key. The FE accents, referring to suspension notes that would be stressed as a matter of course, seem more like an anonymous editor's foolish attempts to "liven up simplicity."

At m.109 the music returns to the most enigmatic material from the exposition (mm.56-63), its second sentence considerably extended and cast in the minor mode. This is one of the longest sequences to be found in all of Mozart's instrumental works. Here the atmosphere becomes so theatrical that the listener can almost smell the make-up, candles and sweat of an eighteenth century opera performance. In larger performing spaces, it is advisable to change the pedal on each quarter-note beat throughout the entire sequence. The grim chords heard on the first beats of mm.118-122 form the climax of the entire movement.

The *dénouement* from the climax in m.122 to the recapitulation demands much perception. It is not obvious how much sound is appropriate in mm.123-126. To facilitate the *legato* playing, the RH double thirds can be divided between the hands as in mm.67-69. Similarly the B-flat in m.129 can best be played by the LH thumb. Five changes of instrumentation are evoked during mm.123-132. The rests, better exaggerated than shortened, are like question marks, each short phrase asking something new.

After all this ambiguity how reassuring it is to hear the smiling initial theme! The most striking feature of the recapitulation is the expansion of the sequence in mm.155-166. Mozart apparently forgot to repeat the RH major second in the first quarter-note beat of m.193. As this figure occurs elsewhere in the movement as a repetition, it is unlikely that at this moment a variant was intended. The C-sharp in the bass of the first beat of m.216, like the G-sharp in m.80, seems unnecessary, but it is found in FE and some fine artists prefer it to the more logical G of the manuscript. The rousing conclusion seems like a triumphant chorus accompanied by quite a large orchestra. There should be more tone here than at the end of the exposition, but pedaling any phrases with bass sixteenth notes evokes vacuum-cleaning more than joy. A *diminuendo* in mm.228-229 is a weary effect hardly suiting the energy of this conclusion. As in m.93, the second quarter-note beat of m.229 should not be prolonged or played stronger than the first beat. Pedaling may be welcome in the last four measures, but the hands must not play *legato*.

After all these characters and events have passed on our imaginary stage, a return to the beginning of the development seems anticlimactic to me and to many others, but this issue remains extremely subjective.

3 ORNAMENTATION IN THE FIRST MOVEMENT, K.332

m.

8   The bass line being most important here, this trill must be unobtrusive. A very light three-note trill (or four-note trill beginning on the upper auxiliary) is possible, the final note sounding on or after the fourth eighth-note beat. The subsequent D functions as a termination to the ornament and is therefore played considerably quicker than marked.

25   I agree with scholars like Frederick Neumann,[14] who maintain that beginning an *arpeggio* on the beat creates an unnatural syncopation, the uppermost note losing strength if it sounds after the beat. Mozart's unarpeggiated notation in mm.29, 161 and 165 is most probably a shorthand notation of the arpeggiation in m.25.

37   Here too the uppermost note of the *arpeggio* should sound on the first beat.

41   That both the LH *arpeggio* and the RH *appoggiatura* are to be played quickly and lightly is more important than their prebeat timing.

45   Beginning this compound *appoggiatura* on the second quarternote beat makes a stiff impression hardly suited to this wistful theme. Beginning the ornament sooner seems preferable.

73   The *appoggiatura* offers us a fascinating quandary. To play it as an eighth note on the first beat is the worst choice, as this

spoils the rhythmic contrast with m.75. If one prefers an onbeat rendition, the *appoggiatura* becomes the uppermost note of the triad, with the approximate duration of a sixteenth note. Neumann[15] differs, suggesting that a quick grace note, sounding before the beat, is more appropriate here and does not disturb the sequential line of repeated notes.

86   With the written termination in thirty-second notes a three-note trill beginning on the principal note is sufficient. A fine technique and a clear-toned instrument permit a five-note trill before the termination, but that can sound like some machine drilling. It is conceivable to play two of the four trills, the second pair for example, with the upper auxiliary notes played before the beat as energetic grace notes.

IMPROVISED ORNAMENTATION

There are few possibilities in this lively movement for additional ornamentation. Wanda Landowska[16] adds trills in both hands to the first beats of mm.78, 80, but unfortunately repeats this effect each time that phrase recurs, thereby robbing a humorous touch of spontaneity. Bilson adds an appropriate turn to the first quarter-note beat of m.143, and his gritty turn on the uppermost C-sharp in m.154 is an inspired rhetorical gesture. When m.190 is repeated, the last two RH notes could be D and B-flat. The RH chords in mm.92-93, 118-119 gain vitality when briskly arpeggiated.

SECOND MOVEMENT	*Adagio*
FORM	binary
APPROXIMATE TEMPO	♪ = M.M. 69
DURATION	5 minutes
SUGGESTED LISTENING	*Le Nozze di Figaro*: Countess's two arias
	Symphony, K.338 ii
	Piano Concerto, K.413 ii
	Andante for flute and orchestra, K.315

4 INTERPRETATION OF THE SECOND MOVEMENT, K.332

However straightforward the form of this movement may be, the emotional subtext remains enigmatic. Even among famous artists a considerable diversity of concepts can be heard in this *Adagio*. If the first movement seemed to evoke figures from Mozart's operas like Figaro and Susanna *(Nozze)*, or Zerlina *(Don Giovanni)*, during the first theme of this movement a more pensive character, like the Countess *(Nozze)*, seems to be on our imaginary stage. Here we sense the mercurial apprehensions, longing and disillusionment that form the undertow of life's experience.

The choice of tempo is a highly subjective matter. The breadth of a Beethovenian or romantic *Adagio* is clearly irrelevant. Perhaps Mozart's *Adagio* indication could be a warning to avoid a merely graceful approach. The forte pianist Alexei Lubimov[17] assumes a basic tempo that allows the music to move naturally, without any diminution of the piece's wistful tenderness. Playing a modern instrument, Lili Kraus also gets very close to the heart of this quiet "aria for piano." Her basic tempo neither drags nor rushes and she delineates the emotional subtext of each theme beautifully. Conversely Deskö Ránki[18] chooses a spritely *Allegretto*, which reduces the music to such optimistic *naivete* that the result seems a parody. Personality, instrument, touch, acoustics, even the time of day will affect the pace one chooses, but it is evident that both haste and morbidity should be avoided.

For players who have sensitive souls and an ability to make the piano sing, this *Adagio* is one of the most gratifying pieces in the entire piano repertoire. Virtually nowhere do two consecutive melody notes have the same intensity or color; even the shortest RH notes are vocally inflected.

While so much of the pianist's attention naturally focuses on the upper line, the bass must not be allowed to blur in absent-minded mumbling. Many editions give the bass line indiscriminate slurring, which encourages generalized, inattentive playing. In the manuscript, Mozart slurred each half of m.3, the last quarter-note beat of m.8, the second and fourth beats of m.9, as well as the second beat in m.10 and parallel phrases. The slurring in mm.16-17 draws attention to a short "cello" solo and, in mm.19-20, to an expressive "viola" line. This subtle use of slurs clearly indicates the places where the bass line is to be more actively shaped, though not necessarily louder. Finger-pedaling of the lower notes in the bass is a subjective matter, dependent on tempo, instrument and performing space. Frequent finger-pedaling does lessen the need for the pedal, which, during quicker figurations like the turns of the initial theme, should be avoided.

As vocal as the RH conception may be, an all-purpose *legato* touch drains the lines of vitality. Slurred note groups should be joined to each other only by the pedal, not by the hand. In the first two measures the fingers should leave the keys before the fourth quarter-note beats, the preceding sixteenth note being played very lightly. Presumably the melody in the first two quarter-note beats of m.1 is to be played *legato*, but if the sixteenth note after the first turn is joined by the hand to the subsequent dotted eighth note, the effect seems soporific. Depending on the instrument, discreet dabs of pedaling can prevent audible gaps in the melody.

In m.3 RH slurs are indicated over both halves of the measure and, in m.4, over each quarter-note beat, the third slur extending to the C on the final beat. Here too, joining these slurred groups to each other with the hand diminishes the lift and vitality of each individual gesture. Usually the first note of each slurred group of melody notes is the strongest, but molding these small note groups into an expressive line requires art. The longer notes must be played with sufficient weight if they are not to fade; the quicker notes have to be shaped with the care a fine singer would give them. The redundant FE accents in m.4 are surely not emphatic but to be played as normal *appoggiature*. The first beat of m.7 is not stressed in the manuscript, and the *piano* extending from the second quarter-note beat of m.7 to the cadence is an even more questionable FE revision.

For generations students have tried to play the innocuous LH beginning of the second theme at m.8 too softly or too *staccato*. The manuscript has no *piano* indicated in the latter half of m.8, and the repeated notes are not marked *staccato*. Absolute serenity is desirable in this brief transition. The atmosphere is not so different from the first theme. Indeed the short RH motif of m.9 is a quasi-inversion of the initial phrase, but there is less sophistication here, as if those cheerful women, Susanna or Zerlina, have taken the place of the melancholy Countess on our imaginary stage. Beyond a slight surge of energy in the last quarter-note beats of mm.8-9, 13-14, there should be no overt dynamic activity throughout this theme. It takes much control to maintain tempo during these calm measures. Nervous rushing, often heard when the LH plays alone here, is as unnatural as sentimental lingering.

The mood changes abruptly with the RH's thirds, the wistful reveries of a more complicated soul (maybe the Countess has returned?). Perhaps the manuscript's accents suggest loosening of meter more than mere accenting. In each quarter-note beat, the first third may be slightly prolonged, the others shortened. Linking the quarter-note beat slurs to each other, even with pedaling, spoils the rhetorical sighing effect. The stressing of the third quarter-note beat of m.11 is found in the manuscript but surely expresses resolution more than heavy emphasis. In m.12 an atmosphere of graceful resignation returns, the RH leaving the keys at the end of each quarter-note beat. The "viola" line on the third quarter-note beat of m.12 has an A that forms a piquant dissonance with the RH. The B-flat stated in many editions and the E-flat replacing the D at the parallel moment in m.32, are gentler, but neither the manuscript nor the FE have these more conventional harmonizations.

With the impulsive change of emotion during the second half of m.16, the FE *forte* (which could also be interpreted as a *crescendo*) does seem relevant. In the FE so many slurs are added to the RH thirty-second notes in m.17 that these can sound like hiccups; in the manuscript only the C-sharp and high D, and the subsequent C dropping to B-flat are slurred. The other notes are very clearly marked *staccato* and should be played as such. Surely the FE *forte* in the second half of m.18 indicates no more than a gentle increase of tone during the trill. Measures 19-20 form another of Mozart's wondrous soprano aria *codette*, to be played with warmth, not watery murkiness.

Though the themes of this first section ending in m.20 suggest a skeletal sonata form, no development section follows. The simplicity of binary form is itself expressive (as in Beethoven's Sonata, Opus 81-a, *Les adieux*, where the hyperactivity of the outer movements is also sharply contrasted in the calm symmetry of the central movement).

According to the manuscript, the second section is virtually unchanged, except for the usual shift of the second theme to the tonic key. Before Mozart sent the sonata to the Viennese publisher in 1784, he apparently realized that the two sections were too similar. Most of the RH decorations added in the FE are enhancements, but it must be restated that there is no proof that the composer approved these or other changes of articulation and dynamics. Virtually all modern editions give both versions of the second section, so it is easy for the player to compare the options; these are further discussed in the next section.

5 WRITTEN AND IMPROVISED ORNAMENTATION
IN THE SECOND MOVEMENT, K.332;
A COMPARISON OF THE TWO TEXTS

m.

1   To suit the tenderness of the line, the initial turn can best begin
just after the sixth bass note. Beginning precisely on the fifth or
sixth sixteenth-note beat can create a rigid impression. The frequent recurrences of this turn do not have to take an identical
rhythmic shaping; the languid, playful, even dramatic character
of different phrases are reflected in the timing of the ornaments.

7   The initial *appoggiatura* is preferably played before the beat.
The subsequent *appoggiature* in the second beat become *tierces
coulées*, sounding with the LH sixteenth notes, not before them.
Such sighs may vary rhythmically, as in an opera recitative,
some *appoggiature* becoming thirty-second notes, others somewhat longer.

11   Begun on the upper auxiliary, the trill sounds brittle. It has
suitable poignancy if played as a five-note turn beginning on
the principal note.

16   The *appoggiature* are definitely to be played before the beat.
Each of the subsequent trills has three notes (on lighter instruments, five) and a termination. Note that the upbeat notes before the trills are very impulsive sixty-fourth notes, not the
usually heard dreary thirty-second notes.

18   After the upbeat F, beginning the trill on the upper auxiliary
sounds pedantic. Beginning with the lower auxiliary is another
possibility.

19   Surely the trills do not have to be identical. One could be a
Schneller, the other a five-note turn. Ornaments beginning with
the upper auxiliary could muddle the line.

20   A vocal suspension is welcome here, the *appoggiatura* becoming an approximate dotted sixteenth note on the first beat. A
thirty-second note, though frequently heard, seems much too
frivolous for this nostalgic context.

22   A turn, trill, or compound *appoggiatura* could be added to the
melody in the third quarter-note beat.

23   Virtually all *Urtext* editions give both FE and manuscript versions of the second section. The FE's *appoggiature* on the first
and third beats are welcome. Their duration is not only subjective but does not have to be consistent. The fourth quarter-
note beat of this measure is an especially suitable moment for

Mozartian *rubato*, the melody becoming less metrical than the steady bass line. The manuscript's *appoggiatura* E on the third quarter-note beat seems more appropriate than the G in the FE.

24 The FE version is preferable, though its accents must not be exaggerated.

25 This outburst is more emphatic than the parallel phrase in the first section. The tension could be heightened by double-dotting the sixteenth notes before the second and third quarter-note beats.

26 The FE dramatic scale seems apt. A motorcycle noise will be evoked if the pedal is held too long during this passage. Landowska adds a beautiful slide between the two penultimate notes of the melody.

27 This most anguished measure of the *Adagio* seems to call for more ornamentation than in the first section. Mitsuko Uchida[19] adds a second high D-flat on the second eighth-note beat, a suitable rhetorical effect. There are many possibilities for additional ornaments during the second half of this measure.

30 The FE version of this and the three subsequent measures is definitely preferable.

34 The FE syncopation of the thirds is an interesting variant. It will seem wooden, however, if played too metrically. The articulation is also changed, a long slur replacing the short sighing slurs of the first section. Rosenblum too comments on "a suppler, more improvisatory rhythm"[20] here.

36 As the manuscript's descending RH figure in the second eighth-note beat is a fine variant of the ascending figure heard three times previously, the FE version seems redundant.

38 Perhaps the FE version is preferable in the first quarter-note beat, whereas the manuscript version is more expressive in the second. The lower auxiliary note could be introduced at the beginning of the trill.

39 Surely it is unimaginative to play this measure exactly as in the first section. Playing a *Schneller* (three-note trill) and a mere *appoggiatura* B-flat suits the nostalgic mood.

40 In the fourth eighth-note beat, an E-flat and a C could be inserted between the two RH notes, like a wistful sigh at the end of this valedictory phrase.

THIRD MOVEMENT   *Allegro assai*
FORM   sonata
APPROXIMATE TEMPO   ♩. = M.M. 96
DURATION   8 minutes, with the exposition repeated
SUGGESTED LISTENING   *Haffner* Symphony, K.385 iv
                      Nozze di Figaro: Overture, finales to both
                      acts

6 INTERPRETATION OF THE THIRD MOVEMENT, K.332

What could be more different from the *Adagio* than this surging
maelstrom of sounds and feelings? Robbins Landon eloquently describes the pianistic allure of the finale:

> "The bold chromatic sections, the octaves, the dashing figures that
> sound like the violins of a grand symphony will have appealed to the
> connoisseurs ... at whose soirees Mozart regularly appeared throughout
> the 1784 season." [21]

The brilliant opening theme and the development section's wild
sequences evoke a piano concerto, but the whirlwind succession of
musical ideas also conjures up a bustling opera finale, with players
rushing on and off the stage. Any pianist who sees this expansive
piece only as an opportunity to display his technical proficiency will
soon come to grief; a mercurial imagination is necessary to project the
quicksilver action of this theatrical movement.

Again it should not be forgotten that for Mozart, the adverb *assai*
connotes "very," not "rather." [22] A degree of haste is desirable in this
movement. If the initial chord is arpeggiated, it sounds more like an
upbeat than a grim downbeat. Prolongation of this chord, however,
has a braking effect on the thrust of the upper line. The RH's initial
flourish is perilous, not only because it is so exposed but also because
it does not lie easily "under the hand." There are various fingerings
possible in this passage. More important is the relaxation of the
thumb, which must be able to facilitate extremely quick horizontal
adjustments of the hand. Too much *staccato* or heaviness in the initial
LH eighth notes would be obtrusive, but, surprisingly enough, this
figuration, spanning a fifth (Motif A) before it seems to dissolve into
itself, becomes one of the most important threads uniting the entire
movement. Vigor, not volume, is welcome in the opening theme.

Stronger sound is required later, at m.36's opening to the second thematic group and during the development section.

The *dolce* theme beginning in m.15 obviously introduces another character, both flirtatious and uncertain, rather like Cherubino in *Nozze*. Unfortunately, too many editions have applied Mozart's *staccato* markings in the second half of mm.17 and 19 to the RH eighth notes of m.15, where the manuscript has none. Playing *staccato* in m.15 contradicts the *dolce* indication. In the manuscript the chromatic seconds of the hilariously jerky figure in mm.22-23 are not slurred. It is debatable whether the FE's slurs here and at all subsequent repetitions are improvements. The *staccati* will not sound choppy if the fingers stay close to the keys. The lowest notes of this bassoon-like interjection progress upwards over a fifth, its resemblance to Motif A camouflaged by the interpolated notes.

Throughout the entire first theme group there are at least five different characters rushing about on our imaginary stage, necessitating a very alert sense of timing. The rests in mm.22 and 26-27 contribute much to the sense of comedy. Use of the UC should be avoided until the wistful *pianissimo* cadence in mm.34-35. Mozart used *calando*[23] to designate diminution of volume, but not of speed. Any slackening of tempo in mm.32-35 would be debilitating.

The trumpet-like announcement of the second theme group at m.36 sounds curiously new, yet familiar. Motif A is now inverted (in descending form), followed in mm.39-40 by the ascending version of Motif A in the highest RH notes. The same motif underlines the descending line in both staves, extending from m.41 to m.44. The bass eighth notes in mm.39-40 should be light and slightly detached, in mm.46-47 like cello *pizzicati*.

The following C minor theme reminds us of the *Adagio*'s opening, some of the slow movement's hopeful figures drooping sadly here. This anxious theme is even more difficult to shape convincingly than the brilliant passages. In the manuscript Mozart clearly indicates that the RH eighth notes after the second beat of m.50 are to be played *staccato*, evoking an atmosphere that is agitated as well as melancholy. Heavy accents should be avoided and the bass played without any (finger-)pedaling. The rests, too often ignored, give the theme an anxious gasping quality. It is an understatement to observe that the FE dynamic indications in this theme are capricious.

Though the *forte* at the first beat of m.65 does not seem logical, Mozart's manuscript also has an explicit *forte* before the first beat in the bass. Apparently the composer wanted a jolting effect here, an unexpected character bursting onto the scene. The broken sixths in mm.68-69 lose their bubbly charm if the player's thumb is tense. The rest of the exposition is a playful affirmation of the dominant harmony. Perhaps the hyperactivity of the exposition and the expansiveness of the development make repetition of the exposition welcome, but this seems less imperative than in the first movement.

In the development section, Motif A is restated in the bass line of mm.93-95. At mm.96-97 it turns in on itself, unable to break away from the first few notes. What drama there is between the centrifugal and centripetal tension! There are many ways to shape the dynamics of these rushing passages, but repetitious, symmetric contrasts of *piano* and *forte* readily become artificial.

Because the final page of the manuscript has disappeared, from m.107 until the end, the earliest source is the FE. Therefore the ensuing dynamic indications do not have to be slavishly followed. A *decrescendo* in m.111, as on Landowska's recording, is logical, whereas the FE indicates *piano* only in the following measure. The surprising FE accents in mm.113 and 115 presumably suggest that the slurred upbeats are less strong than the long notes. The first RH D-flat in m.118 is tied over (in the FE), but is the rhythmic impulse not the same as in the previous measure? These measures are transformed in a joyous explosion of energy beginning at m.120. The RH's notes moving parallel to the bass line in mm.120-126 should be stressed.

A concerto *cadenza* is evoked in mm.124-147. Though Mozart explores new motivic territory here, *cadenzas* in his mature works always include some motivic references. At mm.137-38, mm.70-71 are recalled, and in the ascending RH passage at mm.139-142, the outline of the expansive phrase first heard in mm.54-57 is reversed. Obviously some rhythmic freedom is called for during these improvisatory phrases, but wild deviation from the basic tempo does not seem appropriate in such a finely knit movement. Unlike many editions, in the FE the second B-flat in m.127 is not tied but repeated, and that measure's eighth notes are not slurred, creating an ominous lurch to the eerie G minor that follows. The logic of the *forte* and *piano* indications in mm.135-139 is dubious.

The length of the humorous sixteenth-note passage leading to the recapitulation makes players nervous; if begun softly and played as a *crescendo*, it becomes delightful and structurally organic. To avoid an unrhythmic jerk at the beginning of the recapitulation, the last four or five notes of m.147 can be played by the LH. The next measure's chord would sound confused if arpeggiated as in the opening of the movement. It is natural that such a theatrical atmosphere brings surprises in this section too, the characters of our imaginary opera appearing in a different sequence. At m.169 there is a fine joke, the music suddenly lurching into the second theme group, with mm.22-35 returning only at m.232. The meter is unusual in mm.227-231, where the rests are more effective if prolonged.

The hectic activity vanishes at m.242, a tender recall of the exposition's wistful mm.32-35. A confused girl (Barbarina in the beginning of the final act of *Nozze?*) is the only character remaining on stage. This "fade-out" conclusion seems to suggest that all the turmoil has been not only like an opera, but also like a dream.

7 ORNAMENTATION IN THE THIRD MOVEMENT, K.332

m.

15   The *appoggiatura* is to be played very quickly before the beat.

16   Following the operatic style of the time, it is best that the *appoggiatura* is on the beat, and the resolution note F (without repetition!) on the second beat.

31   This ornament rarely sounds convincing because most players emphasize the second beat more than the first, creating a lop-sided effect. Probably the *appoggiatura* is best played as a prebeat *Zwischenschlag*. If played on the beat it must be extremely short.

53   A nervous five-note trill, beginning on a slightly elongated principal note and without a termination seems preferable to the academic sounding turn given in FE. If the two notes after the ornament are not played in a gentle *diminuendo*, the soulful character of the line is lost.

64   This *appoggiatura* is more mournful than that in m.31 and could become a quarter note on the second beat. An eighth-note rendition sounds like a hiccup.

73   This *appoggiatura*, and that in m.84, are like that in m.31.

199   The *appoggiatura* is like that in m.64.

226   This and the subsequent RH chords can be rapidly arpeggiated.

231   A few fine artists play this final affectionate *appoggiatura* as the uppermost note of an *arpeggio* ending on the first beat. A certain rhythmic freedom is welcome here.

The bass chords of mm.1, 7, 91 and all chords in mm.89-90, 226-229 can be vigorously arpeggiated. Further alterations of such highly organized material seem redundant.

XIII

SONATA IN B-FLAT MAJOR, K.333

OTHER K. LISTING   K.315-c
TOTAL DURATION   23 minutes, with first repeats i & ii
COMPOSITION DATE   about November 1783

1 BACKGROUND OF K.333

July 1784 saw the publication of Mozart's Opus 7, including this sonata, the Sonata in D, K.284, and the Sonata for Piano and Violin in B-flat, K.454. This opus was dedicated to the Count and Countess Kobenzl. The countess was Mozart's first piano student in Vienna. Until recently historians found it difficult to ascertain the composition date of this B-flat sonata. Alfred Einstein[1] maintained that K.333, like the piano sonatas K.330-332, was composed during Mozart's Parisian sojourn in 1778. The musicologist Alan Tyson devoted an entire chapter to the origins of K.333 in his *Mozart: Studies of the Autograph Scores*, commenting:

"In the course of his penetrating study of Mozart's handwriting during the decade 1770-1780 Wolfgang Plath concludes that the autograph was not written in Paris or even shortly after; the handwriting suggests to him a date of around 1783-84..."[2]

In an account as suspenseful as a good detective story, Tyson describes how he could deduce from the unusual sort of paper Mozart used when writing the sonata that the piece was most probably written in November 1783, when the composer had taken his young wife to Salzburg to meet his family, but his mind...

"... was already on Vienna and on the material that he needed for teaching and for private concerts and soirees. ... for on February 10, 1784 he wrote to his father that the whole of each morning was occupied in giving lessons; he repeated this on March 3 and added that 'almost every evening I have to play'... Between its composition in November 1783 and its publication in the summer of 1784 Mozart is likely to have made much use of the Sonata in B-flat."[3]

This sonata is more frequently heard than the other two piano sonatas in B-flat, K.281 and 570. Yet despite its tuneful appeal, K.333 often fails in performance. The curious blend of elegance and energy heard in much of this sonata can easily disintegrate into academic daintiness. As in the previous three sonatas, the lack of dynamic indications in the manuscript was amended in the first edition (hereafter FE). Many of the additions remain questionable.

Because suspension figures are so numerous throughout all the movements, some German writers have referred to K.333 as the *Seufzersonate*, the "sonata of sighs." Players with melancholic dispositions are often misled by all these suspensions and seek false pathos in the piece. This is most regrettable, as K.333, occasional dark moments excepted, is one of Mozart's sunniest creations for the piano. This sonata expresses life in undramatic terms yet, despite this minimum of *Sturm und Drang*, there are many contrasts and surprises in K.333.

FIRST MOVEMENT	*Allegro*
FORM	sonata
APPROXIMATE TEMPO	$\downarrow$ = M.M. 120, sometimes quicker
DURATION	8 minutes (with exposition repeated)
SUGGESTED LISTENING	String Quartet, K.387 i
	String Quartet, K.168 i
	String Quartet, K.172 i
	Flute Quartet, K.285 i

2 INTERPRETATION OF THE FIRST MOVEMENT, K.333

Although playing all the themes in this piece at an absolutely uniform tempo would sound grotesquely rigid, considerable taste is required to make any tempo fluctuations seem natural, and not haphazard. Haste could spoil the genial activity of this *Allegro*, but a tendency to drag is even more foreign to the general optimism of the piece. The opening theme is often played with misplaced melancholy. Lingering over suspensions and interjecting seasick *rubato* effects (before the first beats of mm.2 or 4, for example) display a superficial "expressivity" that is not suited to the high spirits of this music. Such misplaced melancholy can be evoked even in the upbeat to m.1, if this figuration is played as four *legato* sixteenth notes, the interpretation stated or recommended in most current editions. These four notes have a different character and shape from the upbeat figures before mm.3 and 5. The initial *appoggiatura* may or may not be very slightly prolonged (a debatable point, according to the methodologists of the time), but what seems more important is that the last two sixteenth notes before the bar-line should be played with a light, slightly detached touch. Authorities like Nikolaus Harnoncourt[4] and Ludiger Lohmann[5] refer to this interpretation of such figurations. This is no mere academic detail, as it becomes immediately apparent to any sensitive listener that a less *legato* interpretation opens the piece with a vitality very different from the droopy *legato* usually heard. Though the more articulated version is technically challenging to execute, this is no reason to ignore it. If the player's thumb is relaxed and the fingers remain close to the keys, the result is delightful.

A strong sense of line is essential if fragmentation is to be avoided. The first sentence, ending on the third quarter-note beat of m.10 must not be divided; "breaths" in the fourth quarter-note beat of m.5 or the first of m.8 must not become divisions in the sentence. Note that each of the first five measures has a suspension on the initial beat. Weighting all these inflections in the same manner would be soporific.

The string quartet texture of the entire first theme group is explicit. It is no coincidence that in 1783, Mozart completed several quartets. It is easy to imagine the LH lines being played on the viola or the cello and the RH phrases on the violin. The pianist should also consider how mobile most string quartet players are. Their body language is active and inter-active; if the pianist remains sitting, Buddha-like, opposite the middle of the keyboard throughout the piece, the vitality of this delightful discourse will evaporate.

The RH sixteenth notes in m.2 are surely energetic (a blend of *legato* and *leggiero*) and in m.4 a lighter *leggiero*. Many editions print a slur over the two RH sixths in the third quarter-note beat of m.9. The autograph is not clear here, as the leger-lines run into the staff above, and there was insufficient space to indicate the articulation. The NMA[6] implies that a slur on the third quarter-note beat may be intended. Also possible is a slur from the E-flat to the D and slight detachment of the subsequent notes in the upper line.

On a fine forte piano, the RH line at m.10, opening the transitional theme, becomes a lovely viola solo. This delightful contrast in color is less easily evoked on modern instruments. Strong accentuation of the RH *staccato* notes in the third quarter-note beats of mm.15-16 would spoil the playfulness of this delectable phrase. It is interesting to note that in the manuscript, Mozart indicated a clear separation of notes only in m.16 (and less clearly in the parallel passage at m.112). This is an intentional discrepancy in notation, as the upbeat to m.17 is surely livelier than the upbeat to the previous measure. Throughout the first theme group pedaling is not necessary. In m.23 the upper line reminds us of the opening. Some pianists curiously choose to play this measure delicately, but it is surely more energetic than the first theme. If the initial six-four chord is played too heavily, the opening of the theme can sound like a conclusion. In the manuscript this chord is marked differently in the recapitulation (see section 3). The atmosphere becomes overtly flirtatious here; therefore the slurs in mm.24-25, 29 and 32-33 need even less pedaling. In the repeated motifs of mm.25 and 33 the first note under each slur is slightly stressed. If this phrase is not played with charm, the result can sound like alpine yodeling. The LH slurring in mm.27-28 is not enigmatic if viewed as an indication of emphasis, with the first eighth note obviously being stronger than the final quarter note.

In m.39 the graceful world of dance and conversation suddenly yields to unrest and dark energy. The manuscript's first dynamic indications in the entire movement are found in mm.39-45, where Mozart obviously wanted an agitated atmosphere. Perversely some pianists play a *diminuendo* in m.39, ignore the *forte* indicated in the second half of the next measure and play m.43, clearly marked *piano*, even in the manuscript, with more tone than the previous measures. But it soon becomes clear that the brief excursion to minor mode was more a false alarm than a real drama.

It is advisable to play the lower note of the RH octave on the third quarter-note beat of mm.43 and 139 with the LH thumb. A sticky approach, with slowing down and pedaling, should be avoided here; the RH octaves suggest two horns and do not have to be played absolutely *legato*. In the final sentence of the second theme group it seems obvious that mm.54-58, the climax of the exposition, have more tone than mm.50-53. The *Codetta* theme at mm.59-63 is a wistful dialogue between the violin and cello, both lines absolutely equal and without a trace of first beat accentuation.

The development section is a big canvas painted in primary colors. Mozart begins with something of a prank. The initial motif of six descending tones is answered in m.65 by an enigmatic echo of the motif that erupted at m.39. This juxtaposition of wildly opposite elements predicts strife. In m.71 this bursts forth with vengeance. Some performers allow this wild sentence to lapse into whispered muttering, but surely this is an explosion of defiance thrusting forward on a frantic Alberti bass? During this long climax of the movement, the tone should remain quite full until m.85, where all the negative energy begins to gradually fade in a regretful sequence, the RH's soulful suspensions heard against nervous LH chords, unpedaled and slightly detached. When the bass line changes in m.89 to *arpeggi* striving futilely upwards, the intensity is again very operatic. Note that the eighth notes in m.93 are not slurred and can best be played with an exhausted *portato*. If this transition is well articulated, a *caesura* is more relevant than the frequently heard sentimental *ritenuto*.

To the expositional thematic material, the recapitulation adds even more enhancements; the motif from mm.46-48 is expanded in a operatically expressive sequence during mm.142-146, better shaped with variations of tone than with *rubato*. Another sequence follows, beginning in m.147, evoking winks, smiles and, in m.149, even belly-laughs. R.D. Levin writes eloquently of the *Codetta*:

"Mozart's deftness in following the grand concluding passage of mm.152-161 with an intimate five-measure epilogue is not merely disarming: it shows how easily he could reconcile – or at least link – his public and private personae." [7]

The manuscript *crescendo* in m.148 clearly indicates that this *Allegro* was intended for the forte piano, not the harpsichord. Yet the considerable challenge posed by this movement has less to do with choice of forte piano or modern instrument and more with the performer's sensibility. The piece inhabits a distinctly eighteenth-century emotional world, with grace and contentment more evident than conflict and anxiety. If the player chooses to paint the positive themes darkly and to exaggerate the stormier moments, the result will sound insincere. Conversely, an overly placid, aesthetic approach will deprive the music of its surprise elements. Any pianist who can balance the logic and spontaneity of this *Allegro* possesses a sure grasp of Mozart's language.

3 ORNAMENTATION IN THE FIRST MOVEMENT, K.333

m.

1   About the *appoggiatura* in the upbeat to the first measure Neumann[8] refers to Steglich's interpretation of such an *appoggiatura* becoming a slight prolongation. This seems a decadent effect. As noted above, this upbeat is different from that to m.3.

The two notes after the suspension should be very light.

21   In this animated phrase, the trill sounds more distinct if played as a three-note trill *(Schneller)* rather than as a turn beginning on the principal or upper note. The slurring indicates that the third quarter-note beat is emphasized, not the trill.

23   The NMA editors[9] maintain that the RH chord should be arpeggiated. In the manuscript Mozart's notation for the chord differs in the parallel passage of the recapitulation. Presumably the intention is to play the lower notes of the chord *tenuto*, but for how long the lower three notes of the chord are held remains an open question. In any case the uppermost note must sound with the bass octave.

26   Beginning the trill on the upper auxiliary would sound muddled, especially as in the recapitulation Mozart slurred the first two quarter notes. Three notes plus the notated termination suffice.

27   These onbeat *appoggiature* rarely sound like motivated enhancements of the line. The dullest possibility, unfortunately commonly heard, is to play them as eighth notes, but suspensions in this rhythm are written out in m.29-30. It is obvious that those in mm.27-28 must assume a different timing. In m.27 a very quick sarcastic *appoggiatura* seems appropriate. The *appoggiatura* of m.28 is obviously more gentle and somewhat longer than that in m.27.

35   In the manuscript this *appoggiatura* is clearly indicated as a quick ornament, on the beat and vigorous.

37   The *appoggiature* are presumably to be slightly accented with the two notes after each suspension played more lightly. The last beat trill is preferably begun with the principal note and has three notes (five on a lighter instrument) before the termination.

58   Beginning this trill on the lower auxiliary is possible, though an upper auxiliary beginning is more usual.

62   The turn requires very acute timing and a supple wrist. The ornament begins as soon as possible after the first beat B-flat (which is detached but very light) and ends on the third eighth-note beat. The frequently heard four-note turn beginning on the upper auxiliary is easier to play.

65   The first *appoggiatura* is played before the beat, the second is like the *appoggiatura* at the beginning of the movement.

76   Each trill is more dramatic if begun on the principal note. Be-

ginning with the upper auxiliary is also possible.

79 This trill must begin on the principal note, emphasizing its grinding effect. Three notes suffice if the first note is slightly prolonged; otherwise a five-note trill is also effective. A termination would disturb the line here.

80 The *appoggiatura* which sounds on the fourth quarter-note beat can be dramatically accented.

150 The surprising *piano subito* would sound confused if the trills become four- or five-note turns beginning on the upper auxiliary. The clearest rendition would be to play a three-note trill beginning on each quarter-note beat.

SECOND MOVEMENT	*Andante cantabile*
FORM	sonata
APPROXIMATE TEMPO	♪= M.M. 104
DURATION	7 minutes (with exposition repeated)
SUGGESTED LISTENING	String Quartet, K.172 ii
	String Quartet, K.168 ii
	Piano Concerto, K.453 ii
	Sonata for Piano & Violin, K.454 ii

4 INTERPRETATION OF THE SECOND MOVEMENT, K.333

It is interesting to compare Mozart's three piano sonatas in B-flat, products of very different periods in his life. All three slow movements are, predictably enough, in E-flat major, but there resemblances cease. The *Andante amoroso* of K.281 is youthful music, sensual and playful, whereas the *Adagio* of K.570, written some six years after K.333, embraces a broad range of human experience, viewed from a distance. The slow movement of K.333 is more serious than K.281, more immediate than K.570. The piece clearly shows the influence of Haydn's "Russian" string quartets of 1781 on Mozart's writing, which was gradually becoming more polyphonic.

All the themes in this *Andante cantabile* can be shaped with the expressive possibilities of a fine chamber ensemble of stringed and wind instruments. Everything in this movement must sing. Opera arias, like those of the Countess in *Nozze*, come to mind. Even all the accompaniment figures are slurred. A feeling for vocal phrasing and a fluent *legato* touch are absolutely essential. In this subjective music, some forte pianists play with an excess of *rubato*, which distorts the natural pace of the music. At the other extreme, Mitsuko Uchida,[10] on a modern instrument, takes a ruminative approach, which seems somewhat remote. Lili Kraus[11] is one artist who possesses the sensibility and generosity of projection inherent in this warm-hearted music.

The alert Richard Rosenberg[12] noted that the *Andante*'s opening motif was anticipated in the initial sixteenth notes of the *Allegro*'s m.14. Most pianists will be delighted to realize that virtually the entire theme, and indeed, the whole movement, can be pedaled. The strings of the instrument must be allowed to vibrate freely, though obviously pedaling of the shorter notes must not cause blurring. Except in the whispered conclusion, the UC pedal should be avoided, for its use neutralizes the desired intensity of tone.

A fluent tempo allows the first phrase, ending on the second quarter-note beat of m.4, to be shaped in one breath. The organic unity of the next phrase, ending on the first beat of m.8, must also be preserved. Breaking either line at moments that may seem like breaths (the third quarter-note beats of mm.3, 6, for example) gives the music a shallow pathos. Generally throughout this movement, the ends of slurred groups can be joined to the subsequent notes by pedaling.

The phrasing of the theme is evident, with gentle emphasis on the initial notes of each slurred group. The first measure is easier to play truly *legato* if the LH thumb plays the E-flat in the upper staff. A singing tone is more attainable when the fingers are not noticeably curved. In the manuscript the last two sixteenth notes of m.3 are not slurred and are more affecting if played *portato*.

In the transitional theme at mm.8-11, all the LH E-flats can best be finger-pedaled so that when the pedal is changed, the bass is still sounding. The emphases indicated on the first beats of mm.9 and 11 are not in the manuscript; obviously these suspensions are to be given more weight than the suspension on the first beat of m.10, but any overly theatrical effects sound unnatural. Agogic freedom here should be confined to the upper line, the bass remaining steady.

The FE's addition of a lower "second violin" part playing A and B-flat in the first quarter-note beat of m.15 is logical, as three-part writing prevails throughout this theme. For the articulation of the uppermost line in the third quarter-note beat of mm.14 and 16, and at the parallel moments in the recapitulation, the manuscript has four different lengths of slurs, but it seems unlikely Mozart wanted four different articulations. At m.64 in the manuscript, there was more space for marking a slur, apparently extending to the final eighth note. This articulation is probably the most appropriate in all four instances. The LH writing beautifully evokes cello and viola lines. The cello's repeated B-flats in m.17 are a daringly modern touch, as they seem like a continuation of the upper line transposed to the low register. However, these notes, with the addition of a fourth repetition, evolve into a melodic motif in the uppermost line of mm.21-22, 25-26. This motif of four repeated notes assumes dramatic guises in the development section.

In the FE *piano* and *forte* contrasts in mm.21-27, the motifs marked *forte* do have more energy, but crass contrasts sound capricious. One can better imagine alternating stringed and wind instruments. Similarly the FE's *crescendo* and *forte* after the first quarter-note beat of m.30 become unnatural if too conspicuous.

Impatient souls will be daunted by the prospect of repeating the exposition in a slowish movement, but the weight and range of the development section can obliterate the impact of the exposition if the latter section is not repeated.

In the opening measures of the development section the collapse into F minor is terrifying. Mozart's music rarely gravitates to the threatening world connoted by this key (see also Chapter IV, section 10). It is interesting to note that the slow movement of the string quartet, K.168, presumably written just a few months before this sonata, is also in F minor. Heavy suspensions and doom-laden note repetitions create an atmosphere redolent of danger and grief. The movement's opening measure is nightmarishly distorted in m.32. The motif of three repeated notes followed by a suspension, first heard in the upper line of mm.8-9, becomes agonized in mm.33-34. The hollow repeated bass notes that follow (double basses playing without *vibrato*) contribute to one of the most ominous moments in all of Mozart's music. Arthur Hutchings commented:

"... the rhythm and chromatic harmony just after the double bar in the slow movement is audacious beyond anything in the other Paris sonatas."[13]

We now know that Mozart did not conceive this piece as early as 1778, but, like Hutchings, we still wonder at the modern tone struck here, a premonition of the stark textures to be heard later in Beethoven's final string quartets and some of Schubert's songs.

The player may play each group of repeated notes in one pedal as long as unintentional *crescendi* do not result. In mm.37-40 there is a grim struggle to escape the fatality of the bass notes. During mm.41-43 there is a shift to the pacific key of A-flat major; however, the peace is slowly decimated in a fateful sequence, sinking wearily towards the bass. Obviously not all the first beat suspensions should be played with the same intensity. Each harmony evokes a slightly different emotion. At m.48, anguish is resolved in beatific dominant seventh chords. As if recovering from a particularly harrowing experience, the music stays in this single harmony for three entire measures. Lack of theatrical effects and supremely alert timing are required here.

Among the various modifications in the recapitulation, there are several phrases with *legato* sixteenth and thirty-second notes. Certainly on modern instruments these are in danger of sounding heavy or unclear if not played with a minimum of pedaling. When shaped with too much *rubato* these enhancements can sound like a parody of Chopin. Mozart took the trouble to write two versions of m.81, the first leading back to the beginning of the development section. One rarely hears this repetition. Lubimov's[14] recording is an exception, but his interpretation, interesting as it is, does not seem to gain from the second repetition. To experience the horrors of the development section after the recapitulation's gentle stability is a peculiar emotional progression.

It is significant that the final *pianissimo* is the only dynamic indication to be found in the manuscript. Dreamlike, all the hope and dread experienced in this incredible voyage fade gently away.

5 ORNAMENTATION IN THE SECOND MOVEMENT, K.333

m.

3   The *appoggiatura* is practically always played as a sixteenth note on the third quarter-note beat, but it could be slightly prolonged. Even more obviously than in the first measure of the *Allegro*, the last two sixteenth notes of the measure become more expressive if slightly detached.

5   Played as a sixteenth note on the beat, this *appoggiatura* seems banal, but played longer it sounds maudlin. I wrestled with the interpretation of this ornament for many years until I saw Mozart's manuscript, where a solution is evident. In metrical terms, there are two notes "too many," a C and a D before m.5. Of course these can be absorbed in the *Eingang*-like freedom

of this transition. Unfortunately the FE "rectified" what must have seemed at the time a metrical mistake. It is best to follow Mozart's original notation, with the additional C and D before the first beat of m.5. This may result in a slight delaying of the first beat of m.5, but the thirty-second notes do not have to be played metrically in this context.

6 In a *legato* line the trill must begin on the principal note. Trilling too rapidly would disturb the tender sentiment of the phrase.

7 Not all the onbeat *appoggiature* have to be played with identical timing.

10 This sighing *appoggiatura* is to be played on the beat. Clearly this ornament should not resemble the long suspensions heard in the first quarter-note beats of mm.9 and 11. An approximate dotted eighth note is lovely but without any *rubato* in the bass line.

12 The indicated turn is best begun as soon as possible.

14 The *appoggiatura* is definitely to be played as a light, quick grace note, before the first beat.

50 This is a moment for rhythmic freedom. The first quarter-note beat could be slightly expanded, but a *ritenuto* in the subsequent descending line, though frequently heard, is sentimental.

57 This onbeat *appoggiatura* is gently emphasized.

68 The turn is best begun just after the third eighth-note beat, with the bass inexorably steady.

70 This is an intriguingly subjective ornament. Mozart did not frequently write this type of *appoggiatura*, descending an octave. It is best played very lightly on the third eighth-note beat, the lower E-flat perhaps played just before the fourth beat.

ADDITIONAL ORNAMENTATION seems desirable only during the repetition of the exposition. Malcolm Bilson,[15] for example, makes charming alterations to the melodic line at mm.5, 16 and 20. Adding ornaments to the stark lines of the development section is unthinkable and, as the recapitulation is already rich in decoration, any additions there are irrelevant.

THIRD MOVEMENT   *Allegretto grazioso*
FORM   sonata, with rondo elements
APPROXIMATE TEMPO   ♩= M.M. 72
DURATION   7½ minutes
SUGGESTED LISTENING   String Quartet, K.159 iii
                      String Quartet, K.428 iv
                      String Quartet, K.458 iv
                      Quintet for Piano & Winds, K.452 iv
                      Sonata for Piano & Violin, K.454 iii

6 INTERPRETATION OF THE THIRD MOVEMENT, K.333

After the emotional *Andante*, Mozart shrugs off introspection; a youthful certainty of "all's well that ends well" seems to prevail throughout the finale. That there are few mysteries in this extrovert, confident piece does not diminish its stature. The exuberance and structure of the K.281's finale are recalled; the flood of characters and surprises is so rapid that the listener feels caught up in the finale of a comic opera or a piano concerto.

There have been many speculations concerning the structure of the movement; is it in sonata or rondo form? It would seem that the sonata form predominates, with the second theme (mm.24-36) following the sonata pattern by returning at mm.148-164 in the tonic key. But Mozart's delightful prank, inserting the first theme group at mm.41-56, misleads the listener into thinking the piece is progressing in rondo form.

Articulation in the first theme is a delicate matter. Though the first three RH notes are usually played as if the slur binds all three, it is not only more correct, but also more lively, to make a slight separation in m.1 between the D and first B-flat, and in m.2 between the G and A. This gives a dance-like lift to the theme, which will become sodden if played too *legato* or with any pedaling. In each pair of repeated notes, the second note must be very light.

To save time, Mozart wrote out the theme only at the beginning of the movement. Due to lack of space between the staves, the notation in the manuscript is not always clear. Slurring the first two quarter notes in the bass of mm.2 and 6 may seem likely but is to be found in the manuscript only at m.6. The ascending scale in m.8 can best be played *non legato* and *forte subito*; a *crescendo* here brings a motorcycle to mind. The upbeat RH eighth notes before the third quarter-note beats of mm.16, 18 and 20 are often slurred, as they are not marked *staccato*, but (as noted in other chapters) upbeat notes before *staccati* are usually to be shortened even if this is not indicated. Inflection must also be considered; if the upbeats are accentuated, the result is more vulgar than amusing. A cheeky *piano* seems much more appropriate in mm.16-28 than the *forti* or *crescendi* suggested in some editions.

At m.24 the RH line of the mischievous second theme begins on the third quarter-note beat; the LH line with the second eighth note. The humor is underlined by the unusual weighting of the third quarter-note beat in the subsequent six measures. The brilliant passages in sixteenth notes should be played with the harmonic sensitivity and rhythmic exactness of first violins in a fine orchestra.

After the delightful play of woodwind polyphony in mm.57-64, the strings return with a G minor theme that is more threatening than dramatic. The anguish of mm.65-70 recalls the F minor music in the development sections of the first two movements, but here the tension is transient. The bass being slurred, the LH's lowest notes are best finger-pedaled. The RH slurring is clear; the upbeats before mm.65 and 67 are not stressed, those before mm.66 and 68 clearly are. The hand should leave the keys before the fourth quarter-note beat of mm.65 and 67. The LH thirds of mm.69-70 are too often sleepily prolonged or abruptly shortened.

In mm.71-74 the music hovers between major and minor modes. Mozart plays another fine prank at m.76, where we hear an abrupt lurch to E-flat major and a grotesque, drunken duet for violin and cello. After lengthy harmonic stasis, the breezy good spirits evaporate into reminiscences of the first theme, cast in a remote C minor at mm.91-94. The harmonies remain restless, the uncertainty enhanced by the *non legato* eighth notes in the bass of mm.93-94, 97-98 and the gasping syncopations between the hands at mm.99-101 and mm.105-109. Any *forte* indications found in mm.98-99 cannot be traced in the manuscript and do not seem particularly appropriate, though surely mm.100-101 form a *crescendo* to the rhetorical climax of m.102.

After all these developments, concentration and poise are needed to play the return of the first theme at m.112 in the same tempo as at the beginning. Weighty orchestral chords at m.132 abruptly disturb the good humor of the theme. Some editions have a B rather than a B-flat in the chord on the second and third quarter-note beats here, a questionable alteration. The surprising lurch to C minor in the following measure is anxious, but any sense of danger quickly evaporates into passages of concerto-like exuberance beginning in m.137. At m.148 the second theme returns. This often sounds lopsided, as most players begin the sentence on the second quarter-note beat, whereas that note belongs to the previous sentence. All the sparkling passages that follow must be harmonically shaped, not rattled off with mechanical brilliance. The climax of this section at mm.158-163 requires the potent *non legato* of a concerto soloist, no fluttery domestic *leggiero*. The atmosphere becomes increasingly orchestral, with the woodwinds in mm.164-167 followed by the entire orchestra bursting into activity at m.168.

The *cadenza* clearly indicates that Mozart regarded the sonata as an important work. Whereas in some other sonatas he designated an *Eingang* as a *cadenza*, this is a true *cadenza*, with thematic references and considerable shifts of mood, like a series of portraits. Metric playing would be deadly here, but if *rubato* is not kept to a minimum, these engaging phrases can become maudlin. The composer's unusual indication *cadenza in tempo* also warns us against too dreamy an approach. The chromatic shock at m.177 is more startling if played with the full tone implied by the FE's *forte*. As in mm.168-171, the expansive *tutti* sequence at mm.189-193 needs powerful sound, but the pianist's arms must remain free, especially when playing modern instruments, if banging is to be avoided. The pedal should be changed on each quarter-note beat. Some dynamic freedom is welcome in the subsequent nervous sentence building up to the *fermata*. Mozart's *"ad libitum"* applies to the entire concluding paragraph of the *cadenza*. The notation of sixteenth, thirty-second and even sixty-fourth notes gives an indication of the pacing during these free gestures. The final sequence of four descending notes, in which the second note should be separated from the third, is stated eight times in three rhythmic variants. As in the final *Eingang* of the D minor Fantasy, K.397, this suggests a playful *ritenuto*, not metrical diminution of mathematical precision.

The *Coda*, exuberant but sometimes nostalgic, has a generosity of scale that anticipates Beethoven. The jubilant tone of mm.203-213 will be lost if there is tension in the wrists. As many of mm.206-207's dreaded RH repeated notes as possible should be played with the third finger, with the fourth finger perhaps on the first and last of each group; changing the fingers on each note here, as stated in many older editions, may produce sounds more appropriate to a shooting range than to a sunny finale. What a magical variant of the opening theme Mozart gives us in its final appearance, beginning with the upbeat to m.214.

Orchestral emphasis is achieved by separate pedal strokes for each of the final chords. In the upper staff of the last chord, the manuscript clearly has a sixth chord; the FE's doubling of the RH B-flat creates more academically correct textures. But this effect, certainly on modern instruments, can sound shrill, especially if the D is not strong.

7 ORNAMENTATION IN THE THIRD MOVEMENT, K.333

m.

10   Played as five equal notes the turn sounds muddled; the first beat E-flat should not be too short and is better played with the second, not the third finger.

31   The trill is as energetic as possible. Beginning it on the principal note is dull; a sharply accented upper auxiliary played as a quick grace note before the third quarter-note beat adds more bite.

35   In this tempo, the first note of the compound *appoggiatura* falls on the first beat. The trill should be as rapid as possible, with brilliant tone in the upper auxiliary tones.

73   This compound *appoggiatura* is startling, and is best begun on the first quarter-note beat, ending on the second.

91   The *appoggiatura* should be played lightly before the first beat and could be preceded by a *caesura*.

102   In the turn the last B-flat and C become eighth notes in the second quarter-note beat. Note that the subsequent quarter notes are rhetorically *non legato*, with two pedal strokes.

155   The trill is perhaps best begun on the principal note.

158   The *appoggiatura* becomes an accented onbeat sixteenth note.

171   The RH chord is not always notated correctly. The uppermost note should be a half note, the other three, quarter notes, a clear indication that the chord is to be vigorously arpeggiated. The uppermost note sounds with the bass and a pedal stroke is welcome.

197   If the player wants an *allargando* in this measure, it is not difficult to play each trill with five notes plus the indicated termination. If one plays without any broadening of tempo, three notes plus termination are sufficient. The upper auxiliary could be played as a sharp grace note before each trill, but beginning the trill with the upper auxiliary on the beat is a pedantic effect.

212   The upper auxiliary is on the trill's first beat.

219   This trill consists of three notes plus termination.

XIV

THE FANTASIES, K.394, 397, 475

1 MOZART'S FANTASIES FOR THE PIANO

As early as the fifteenth century the title "Fantasy" was given to certain musical compositions. Eighteenth-century fantasies were noted for their:

> "Freedom of rhythm and tempo ... unfettered exploration of instrumental virtuosity; adventurousness in harmony and modulations..." [1]

To us a fantasy connotes heady inspiration and spontaneous improvisation, yet the greatest pieces in this genre certainly do not lack ingenuity of structure.

No doubt many of Mozart's improvisations at the piano or the organ could have been described as "fantasies," but he wrote few of them down. The only fantasy for piano solo that can be played on its own is the C minor masterpiece, K.475, discussed in the last four sections of this chapter.

The Fantasy (Prelude) and Fugue in C major, K.394, is something of a hybrid in Mozart's output. More an introductory prelude than an independent piece, it would make a strange effect played without its companion *fugue*. However, the prelude is generally known as a fantasy. Therefore, both parts of K.394 are discussed in the two subsequent sections.

Another C minor Fantasy, K.396/385-f, is an interesting fragment. After 22 measures, Mozart became dissatisfied with the piece and abandoned further work on it. This is not surprising as the material is diffuse and only spasmodically inspired. The fiery middle section excites some pianists, but ironically, it and the recapitulation were added after Mozart's death, most probably by Maximilian Stadler.[2] Though the middle section has undeniable panache, it evokes a *Sturm und Drang* atmosphere that is not Mozartian. Worse, the recapitulatory section is academic and atypical in its total lack of variation. Opinions about the completion of this fantasy vary. The editors of the Henle edition of the Assorted Pieces, for example, state that "no edition can omit this work, in spite of Stadler's share in it."[3] To others, including myself, K.396 in this form is merely of interest as an intriguing though dissatisfying study of styles.

Most pianists are still unaware that the much played D minor Fantasy, K.397/385-g, was left unfinished by Mozart. Its date of composition is a total mystery. The manuscript has vanished. Indeed I am not totally convinced that the fragment is by Mozart. Though many historians assume that the piece dates from the period of K.394 and K.475, the D minor Fantasy could also be from the composer's last years, like another unfinished, shorter Fantasy in F minor, K.383-c/Anh. 32, which Alan Tyson[4] convincingly attributes to 1790. Because the D minor Fantasy is known to virtually everyone who can play the piano, and also because to date there has been no proof that the piece is not Mozart's, the fourth and fifth sections of this chapter are devoted to this composition.

The improvisation, variously titled Fantasy or Capriccio, K.395/300-g, seems to be an early work. Because numerous scholars assume that the piece was intended for the organ, K.395 falls beyond the scope of the present study. Readers who are curious about this heady bit of youthful folly are referred to Dennerlein's[5] vivid analysis of the piece.

Though it is regrettable that Mozart took so little time to write down his flights of fancy at the keyboard, this small group of fantasies gives us intriguing insights into the composer's experimentation beyond the standard forms of the time. Because each composition is so individual, the layout in this chapter is somewhat different from other chapters.

2 THE FANTASY (PRELUDE) IN C MAJOR, K.394

OTHER K. LISTING	K.383-a
DATE OF COMPOSITION	April, 1782
TOTAL DURATION	9-10 minutes (with the Fugue)

This pairing is almost schizophrenically strange. Whereas the fantasy (or prelude) does not resemble any other finished composition by Mozart, the fugue is his most ambitious contrapuntal work for solo piano.

In the last decades of the eighteenth century, this type of prelude was already out of fashion. This may explain why the piece was labeled a fantasy when it was published after the composer's death. The

prelude's initial eight measures are grandly baroque; the organ fantasies and toccatas of J.S. Bach come readily to mind. During the solemn opening, the voicing between the hands must be sensitively
judged: the *forti* and *piani* should not be hysterical contrasts but seem
like shifts in orchestral scoring or organ registration. At m.5 it becomes obvious that this *Adagio* progresses with two impulses in each
measure, not four. The RH chords in the following measure could be
arpeggiated.

Andante may seem a peculiar tempo indication for the following
section, but it is a suitable warning against taking a precipitate pace.
Whereas the opening section could be played at an approximate
tempo of ♪ = 84, the *Andante* surges at ♪ = 100. Throughout the
entire piece there is considerable rhythmic freedom.

In the initial stormy sequence, the first-beat bass notes should be
pedaled to the subsequent eighth-note beats. The wedges on the LH
ascending eighth notes surely indicate accents more than *staccati*.
These notes may be pedaled, but never overwhelmed by the RH
ostinato chords. The LH's seething thirty-second notes in mm.10, 12,
14 gain tension if played as written, not as triplet sixteenth notes, a
fine example of the polyrhythmic interpretation that Türk thought
relevant in "compositions of a vehement character."[6] Arguably the
initial paragraph ending in m.15 sounds splendid on a modern piano,
whereas the subsequent six measures, a febrile recitative, are more
suited to the slender tone of a forte piano. The dynamic shaping here
is very subjective. First beat chords could be arpeggiated.

At mm.21-22 the music surges with an energy that seems to evoke
both the baroque and romantic periods. The pedal should be changed
on each eighth-note beat in this and the following dramatic sequence,
the rushing triplets pulling against the inexorable force of the thudding octaves. The frequently heard hesitations before or on the first
beats are artificial. The octaves must be played with a sense of inner
tension, not brute force. Some pianists attack this section as if it were
an *ostinato* by Prokofiev. However, a dainty approach would be even
more inappropriate.

The following sequence, mm.28-30, assumes the breadth of a
tragic opera. Presumably the LH's high-lying phrases are as *legato* as
those in the bass. Often in Mozart's manuscripts there are no slurs
when the music goes this high, simply because there was not enough
space between the staves to notate slurs clearly. From m.31 onwards
there is considerable repetition; the player must have much imagination and energy if some of the material is not to seem redundant. In

the octave doubling at m.42 the organ is evoked, but the following *più adagio* is unmistakably pianistic. The chords could be double-dotted, if the player wishes. The succession of diminished seventh *arpeggi* at m.45 reminds us of J.S. Bach's Chromatic Fantasy. As in Bach's masterpiece, much rhythmic freedom is granted to the player, but wandering too far afield has dangers.

Perhaps the following *primo tempo* and canonic sections sound a bit too "learned" for this stormy landscape. The four cadential measures, with their somewhat mechanical use of diminished seventh harmonies, seem curiously un-Mozartian but suit the generally wild tone of the piece.

3 MOZART AND POLYPHONY: THE FUGUE IN C MAJOR, K.394

Historians and musicologists are rightly fascinated by the role polyphony plays in Mozart's development. During his childhood, Mozart had been trained by his father in counterpoint, but that aspect of the young composer's musical resources apparently had some limitations. When the fourteen-year-old was tested for entrance to the prestigious Accademia Filarmonica in Bologna, he had to write a work in the "ancient strict style." Despite Leopold Mozart's account, often repeated in history books, Wolfgang's offering would apparently not have been accepted without the assistance of Father Giambattista Martini, a leading scholar of counterpoint.[7] Though Mozart had little interest in the counterpoint of the previous centuries, during his last years in Salzburg he studied much contemporary church music to gain more insight into contrapuntal procedures. The polyphony in Mozart's earlier church music was in the *galant* style of the time, considerably different from the counterpoint of J.S. Bach. Yet even the *Orphanage Mass*, K.139/47-a, apparently written when the composer was 12 years old, eloquently displays Mozart's progress in counterpoint.

When Mozart moved definitively to Vienna he soon made the acquaintance of Baron Gottfried van Swieten, director of the Imperial Court Library. Van Swieten had become fascinated by the music of J.S. Bach when he had been the Habsburg ambassador to the Prussian court. He returned to Vienna, bringing with him many of Bach's compositions, some published, some in manuscript. In 1782, Mozart joined a small group of enthusiasts who gathered weekly around van

Swieten to play through works by J.S. Bach and Handel. Alfred Einstein commented:

> "Can it be believed that Mozart was not deeply aware of the superhuman grandeur of this music, as an overpowering quality that was not to be found in the work of any of his contemporaries?" [8]

During the entire final decade of his life, Mozart continued to experiment with contrapuntal techniques. It was assumed by most historians that Mozart's attempts at "learned" polyphony were concentrated in the year 1782, but recent scholarship has revealed that the composer persisted with fugal writing until his death. Alan Tyson[9] maintains that the unfinished Fugue in F for piano, K.383-b (Anh. 33 & 40), presumed to date from 1782, was written on paper the composer never used before December 1787, and continued to use into 1789. There were also several unfinished *Kyries* and a *Gloria* that previously were presumed to date from the Salzburg period.

Though "strict" polyphonic technique seems a less conspicuous aspect of the composer's vocabulary, no one can deny that Mozart's contrapuntal language was unique. In masterpieces like the finales of the mature operas or the *Jupiter* Symphony, it is evident that Mozart's polyphonic skills blended the "learned" and *galant* styles with a command that gladdens the heart and the ear, as well as the intellect. But this mastery was the result of much effort; quite often "Mozart worked out on separate sheets of paper any passage that involved intricate part-writing or polyphonic devices." [10]

About K.394 the composer wrote to his sister on April 20, 1782:

> "I send you herewith a prelude and a three-part fugue. The reason why I did not reply to your letter at once was that on account of the wearisome labour of writing these small notes, I could not finish the composition any sooner ... I hope further that you will like it. Another time I will send you something better for the clavier." [11]

Apparently the evolution of the Fugue, K.394, did not go easily and Mozart's enthusiasm seemed to wane during its composition. Alfred Einstein is one of the scholars who is decidedly negative about the composition:

> "The fugue of K.394 ... though masterly in itself, cannot compete with a Bach fugue ... despite all the art in the handling of augmentation,

diminution, and *stretto*, the theme is too 'learned', too neutral, not Mozartian enough, while Bach's fugues are always Bachian and have, in addition ... a personal character, peculiar to them. " [12]

Einstein's reservations seem relevant, for there is an inhibiting stiffness permeating this C major Fugue, which prevents it from becoming more than a highly competent display of polyphonic skill. Though the theme and counter subject are well contrasted, the listener gradually wearies of both. The winding counter subject in sixteenth notes, first heard in mm.3-4, becomes pianistically awkward later. Though in mm.5, 7-9, 17-19, 24-26 the counter-subject can be divided between the hands, it still often sounds labored. The counterpoint above the augmentation of the bass's theme in mm.29-32 seems rather academic, and some harmonic progressions (mm.19, 47) lack inspiration.

Often the piece sounds better in a church than in a concert hall. The lack of dynamic indications and the addition of the fourth voice in m.61 suggest organ textures. The pompous conclusion, for all its bustling, is less difficult than the rest; here the player can pedal each eighth-note beat without obscuring the lines. Elsewhere pedaling should be minimal.

An approximate tempo of $\rfloor$ = 76 is suitable. The piece becomes livelier if the theme's eighth notes are not played *legato*. Care should be taken to avoid thickness of tone. In mm.20-28, 35-38, 48-58, gentler dynamic levels seem more appropriate than a monotonously robust *forte*. In his fine recording, Walter Klien[13] added an exuberant *arpeggio* rolling up from the bass on the first beat of m.66. His trill on the leading-note before the final chord is also appropriate in such a "baroque" piece. It should be noted that in the NMA edition[14] there are numerous small text changes in the fugue often not found in most other editions.

When played in a church-like acoustic by a performer who believes in the piece's merits, K.394 can be impressive; there is much energy and ingenuity to admire in this fugue. Late in 1783, with the C minor Fugue for two pianos, K.426, Mozart proved that he could produce truly masterly counterpoint for keyboard instruments. All pianists who enjoy playing polyphonic works should look at this splendid creation. Beethoven even made a study copy of the piece. Its resemblance to his *Grosse Fugue*, Opus 133, cannot be denied. About K.426, Mario R. Mercado observed that:

"the skill of its contrapuntal treatment forms part of a total picture in which Mozart's harmonic imagination – in terms of both large-scale design and the use of dissonance for expressive purpose – leads to a work of sublime quality."[15]

Mozart was apparently so proud of the C minor Fugue that in 1788, he arranged it prefaced by a striking *Adagio*, for string quartet (K.546).

FANTASY IN D MINOR, K.397

OTHER K. LISTING   K.385-g
DATE OF COMPOSITION unknown
DURATION   approximately 6 minutes

4 UNIFYING AND DRAMATIZING ELEMENTS IN THE FANTASY, K.397; DIFFERENT COMPLETIONS; MOZART'S USE OF D MINOR

Patrick Gale[16] described this fantasy, together with the C minor Fantasy, K.475, and the Sonata, K.331, as being one of the few Mozart piano pieces that most concertgoers know. Certainly there are few professional or amateur pianists who have not played the D minor Fantasy. But any serious performance of this piece involves confronting major paradoxes.

The background of the fantasy remains obscure; I personally have doubts that the composition is Mozart's at all. There are no references to it in the composer's letters, and the manuscript has disappeared. As the piece remained unfinished, it is not included in the composer's own thematic catalogue. It could be argued that the D minor Fantasy shares certain strengths and weaknesses with the C major Fantasy and Fugue, K.394, but the supposition made by some historians that both pieces derive from 1782 is mere guesswork.

It is astonishing that so few pianists and teachers realize that Mozart never completed this piece. In its first edition of 1804, the fantasy ends at m.97. Two years later when Breitkopf and Härtel were making the first major compilation of Mozart's works, they printed the fantasy with ten measures added after m.97. This anonymous completion, far from ideal, is the version printed by all publishers to date.

Though the fantasy seems to evolve haphazardly, almost somnambulistically, there are subtle threads unifying the piece, and this is perhaps the most Mozartian aspect of the strange composition. If he is unaware of these unifying elements, the player is in danger of losing his way in what can easily become an incoherent maze of unrelated events.

The opening may resemble an improvisatory prelude in baroque style, but there is a significant motif already present. The RH figurations sink from G in m.7 to C-sharp in m.9. This seemingly transitory progression is actually the "key motif" of the entire piece. For the rest, the section consists of triadic figures and suspensions, the final descending RH line in m.10 combining both.

In the *Adagio* theme mournful eighth notes in m.12, coming to rest on the subsequent measure's C-sharp, remind us of the "key motif." The line breaks off in suspensions until two chromatized recurrences of the key motif are heard in mm.17-19. Beginning in m.20, a thudding *ostinato* combines with a chromatic variant of the "key motif" slithering basswards in octaves. The skeleton of the RH line in mm.23-27, is based on the "key motif," now inverted and obscured by suspensions. The melody in mm.50-52 may seem fragmented, but here the "key motif" descends from m.50's B-flat to m.52's E-flat before turning upwards. The tiny recitative of mm.52-53 reverses the same line.

Though the *Allegretto* section sounds utterly different, the D major theme is based on another variant of the "key motif," this time ascending from the A of m.55 to the E's in m.59. This progression is heavily disguised by suspensions, the RH activity pulling against the generally static bass line.

Though its structure seems loose, the D minor Fantasy is based on a single motif battling suspensions and *ostinati*.

DIFFERENT COMPLETIONS of the fantasy are conceivable. Paul Hirsch[17] was the first to offer concrete evidence that Mozart did not complete this piece. Measures 98-107 were probably the work of August Eberhard Müller (1767-1817), an editor of Breitkopf & Härtel's 1806 edition of Mozart. In that edition, a sign indicating a footnote was included after m.97, but no further information was given. Did the publishers have second thoughts about "doctoring" a Mozart piece?

Some maintain that Mozart wrote those last ten measures, but I would agree with Hirsch and the NMA editor[18] that the familiar ending is not by Mozart. However, traditions die hard. Musicians and listeners alike are usually startled if they do not hear the familiar conclusion to the piece. Dennerlein[19] accepted it without question, commenting that in the D major section "life triumphs over death." Paul Badura Skoda maintained that the fantasy "takes its very life from the polarity between minor and major ... of happiness achieved through suffering."[20]

But is the optimism of the major mode conclusion so convincing when the piece has been so overwhelmingly dark? Mozart's final chord in m.97 is identical to the last chord in m.54. This would naturally inspire anyone seeking for a completion to progress in the same manner as in m.55. But if Mozart had wanted such a predictable progression, is it likely he would have broken off at that moment?

Mitsuko Uchida[21] was the one of the first artists to play an alternative conclusion. Apparently inspired by the example of the C minor Fantasy, K.475, her recorded version ends with a recapitulation of the initial section. Unlike Badura Skoda,[22] I find Uchida's version convincing except for her shifting to major mode for the final harmony.

A more objective argument against the traditional ending is that it contains too many un-Mozartian elements. The composer hardly ever transposed soprano-like themes to the "baritonal" register of the piano; the part-writing is awkward and both hands are so close that, even on a forte piano, the texture sounds clogged. Neither the echo effect of the *pianissimo* repetition nor the LH writing in the final six measures are Mozartian. The RH ascending flourish and cadential chords are academic, at most, "Mozart on a bad day," an unusual quantity.

I believe that a return to the opening after m.97 provides the basis for the best conclusion to the piece. After repeating the first four measures, mm.5-6 could be omitted. In mm.7-8, there is a sense of inevitable pull towards a final cadence. After m.8, one could play the tonic harmony in its second inversion, the bass note being the second A below middle C, followed by a measure of the dominant harmony on the same bass, both measures in the same broken triad pattern of the opening. The final tonic chord begins on the D heard at the opening and could ascend in an *arpeggio* to the second A above middle C before descending into the pattern heard in m.10 to the D above middle C.

There has been much commentary on MOZART'S USE OF D MINOR. The key clearly had striking associations for Mozart. In *Idomeneo*

(1781), Elettra's furious aria "Tutte nel cor vi sento" and the terrified choral finale of the second act "Corriamo, fuggiamo" are chilling. In *Don Giovanni*, written six years later, many of the blackest moments are cast in D minor, and in *Die Zauberflöte*, during her tempestuous "Der hölle rache," the Queen of the Night evokes the gods to witness her wrath. Martin Chusid commented that in the operas:

> "Each time Mozart composed in D minor, vengeance is the dominant dramatic element. Furthermore the supernatural is invariably involved." [23]

The turbulence of the D minor Piano Concerto, K.466, is not equaled in any of the other concerti.

It is important to realize that darkness of tone should not be confused with passivity. Unlike the keys of F minor or A minor, D minor is rarely associated with despondency. In Mozart's only solo piano piece in D minor, danger and fury set the tone.

5 INTERPRETATION OF THE D MINOR FANTASY, K.397

Virtually everyone who can pick out a few notes on the piano wants to play this fantasy. With its soulful melodies, nervous modulations, and abrupt shifts of emotion, the piece seems to belong more to the nineteenth century than to the eighteenth. This *avant la lettre* "romanticism" has inspired many inappropriate performing traditions that obscure the essence of the fantasy. As seen in the previous section, the structure is in fact subtle, not at all haphazard.

ANDANTE At the very opening we encounter a dubious tradition; practically all editions have a *piano* marking, but is it likely that on the piano of Mozart's time, music in that register would be so quiet? Given the absence of a manuscript, no dynamic markings have to be unthinkingly accepted. The choice of key (see previous section), the *Andante* and *Alla breve* (approximate tempo ♩ = 88) indications all suggest stormy activity more than murky whispering. During the first six measures, the tension of sound is clearer if as many notes as possible are held longer than marked and the pedal is changed on each quarter-note beat.

Though the lowest note is tied from the first to the second quarter-note beats in virtually all editions, this notation is not to be found in the first edition. Practically all players interpret the two bass notes of the initial six measures as being tied. A baroque notation is suggested here, with the lowest bass note sounding throughout each measure. The editor of the NMA^{24} noted that repeating the bass note on the second beat would be a bizarre effect. The mournful sequence in mm.6-7 is best played with open, vocal tone. Though the bass notes could be held until the next measure, the pedal should not be held through m.9 which, as noted above, is not a misty *arpeggio*, but a highly dramatic line. Only twice in the entire piece does the music rise higher. The two *fermate* in m.11 indicate freedom from the meter, not ponderous prolongations of both the bass note and the rest. Most probably the rest is shorter than the bass note.

ADAGIO   The flow of this striking aria-like theme, apparently still paced *Alla breve*, should feel as if it moves with two, not four impulses to a measure (approximate tempo ♩ = 66). A slower tempo makes nonsense of mm.23-27. Such a quasi-operatic lamentation would never be thin in tone. The melodic eighth notes in m.12 gain rhetorical weight if all are played by the third finger, the pedal changed on each note. Given the inexorability of the accompaniment, the slightest *rubato* in the first four measures would be sentimental, not tragic. The agonized suspensions in mm.13 and 15, often marred by careless prolongation or pedaling, should seem like wailing protests struggling against a remorseless bass. During the entire piece, strict observance of the rests is as important as the shaping of the notes.

Some writers have described the *ostinato* beginning in m.20 as a death knell. This is an appropriate image; such a grim sentence should not be prettified by fussy dynamic effects. A theatrical *crescendo* from *piano* to *forte* would be vulgar. The whole phrase is full-toned and orchestral, suggesting both stringed and low wind instruments. The rest in m.22 should not be swallowed. The following five measures are often played with erratic *accelerandi*, another regrettable tradition even stated in some editions. Observance of the indicated dynamics (for example, no *crescendo* before the middle of m.26) maintains the gruesome tension of these murky lines. In both *crescendi*, pedaling, changed with each LH eighth note, is possible, but the *piano* passages are best played without pedaling, the bass quite *tenuto* and unaccented.

Perhaps the *fermata* in m.28 is more a breath than a prolonged silence; a silence of more than an entire measure would be grotesque here. The ensuing *Presto* is an *Eingang*, a rhythmically free transition passage, not a *cadenza*. This frenzied outburst should not be played so fast that it becomes impossible to hear all the notes. The pedal should be frequently changed, especially in the lower register of modern instruments, if thundering Lisztian effects are to be avoided. The pedal should not be held after the final E-flat has sounded; a brief, deathly silence is appropriate at this rhetorical moment.

The NMA editor[25] maintains that the *fermata* in m.43 does not refer to the final E, but to the preceding F. Because the angular passage work is more difficult for a listener to comprehend than the *Eingang* of m.34, m.44 should not be rushed. However, the ascending chromatic scale in thirty-second notes is quicker than the descending passages marked in sixteenth notes. Surely B-flat, not B-natural,[26] should be played in the bass's written-out turn before the chromatic scale begins.

In mm.50-53 we seem to be back in an opera scene, each suspension expressing a different emotion. How easily words can be imagined to accompany these soulful musings! In mm.50-53, the rests are again as eloquent as the notes. The E-flat sixth chord in m.52 may be marked *forte*, but it is only a fleeting glimpse of hope, which immediately evaporates. The subsequent diminished seventh *arpeggio* is a startling theatrical gesture of fury, a bolt of lightning, which also disappears instantly. The *fermata* rest can be quite long, as it is very unclear what direction the music will take at this suspenseful moment. In m.54 we hear only two utterly exhausted chords, and a strict metric pulse is more eloquent here than a vague slowing down.

ALLEGRETTO This positive turn of events is a total surprise but is perhaps more a memory of past joys than an expression of exuberant cheerfulness. As noted in the previous section, it is based on the "key motif," already heard in various guises. An approximate tempo of ♩ = 108 maintains momentum without haste. The *dolce* character of the theme would be disturbed by any accenting. The frequently heard stressing of second quarter-note beats is unfortunate.

However animated mm.70-82 may seem, the energy remains ensnared in a static D major, the cheerful RH motif repeating itself, a recurring image of hope during a nightmare. With the LH playing in such a high register, the player is advised to lean to the right side of the instrument. One should avoid playing repeated notes mechanically. Some editions have the RH playing the seventh in m.83 only once, but I agree with Badura Skoda,[27] who maintains that this is probably an abbreviation indicating that m.83 is to sound like m.75. As in the finale of the B-flat Sonata, K.333, the graduated note values in the final *cadenza*-like passage at m.86 are not to be interpreted literally, but as a gradual slowing down.

The rest in m.97 could be quite long, forming a rhetorical silence before whichever ending the player chooses. As noted in the previous section, the "traditional ending" printed in all editions is un-Mozartian and seems acceptable only because we are accustomed to it.

6 ORNAMENTATION IN THE D MINOR FANTASY, K.397

m.	
52	The turn can be played in a variety of ways. Most important is the dynamic function, clearly marked *piano* after a *forte* on the third quarter-note beat of m.52. This indication suggests that both turns are more melancholy than energetic, played perhaps with discreet rhythmic freedom. The final E-flat in m.52 and the third G in m.53 are played as sixteenth notes before the subsequent tones.
69	A small but distracting detail is the peculiar *appoggiatura* on the first beat in the "viola line." The NMA editor[28] convincingly asserts that this is a misreading. Unfortunately this error is reprinted in other editions.
86	The trill is perhaps best begun on the lower auxiliary, though some prefer the upper. The first two thirty-second notes after the trill form its termination.

Could the absence of problematic ornaments be another reason for this fantasy's popularity? Some chords, for example, in mm.52,8-5,86,94-96, could be arpeggiated. A telling effect is to play a trill on the penultimate note of m.43, presuming that the *fermata* applies to the dissonance and not to its resolution. A turn on the first beat of m.69 when the melody is repeated is possible.

Teachers must be wary of giving this highly individual piece to students who are too young. The player should be able to comprehend the wide spiritual range of the fantasy. The potent conflicts in this fantasy demand strong presentation.

FANTASY IN C MINOR, K.475

COMPOSITION DATE   May 20, 1785
TOTAL DURATION   11 minutes

7 C MINOR FANTASY, K.475:
BACKGROUND AND ANATOMY

During the years 1784-85, Mozart produced a flood of music for the piano, eight masterly *concerti* as well as the Sonata in C minor. When publishing the sonata in 1785, Mozart decided to preface it with a fantasy in the same key (K.475). According to the composer's own catalogue, the sonata was finished some six months before the fantasy. The thorny issue of whether the two works should be played separately or together is discussed in section 10 of this chapter.

Mozart's *magnum opus* for piano was dedicated to Maria Theresia von Trattner, one of Mozart's first pupils in Vienna. Apparently she had talent. Her husband was an immensely rich publisher, paper manufacturer and bookshop owner. For a short time Mozart and Constanze lived in the von Trattners's newly completed house, the Trattnerhof, "that prestigious house on the Graben that was surely the most famous address in all Vienna."[29] During the spring of 1784, Mozart gave some twenty concerts in the city, including several in the Trattnerhof, and the receipts were so fine that the Mozarts could move from a modest third floor apartment to the grand first floor of the building.

Just after the birth of Karl Thomas, the first of their two surviving children, the young couple moved again, to the house which is now the Mozart Museum. However, they retained contact with the von Trattners, who became godparents to all of the Mozart children. In Mozart's published *oeuvre*, it is rather exceptional that the dedicatee should be female. Inevitably, nineteenth-century writers suggested that wild passions must have inspired such a singular piece, but this is mere speculation.

The reader should note that in the four sections on this fantasy, there will be references to the following sources:

1. MOZ – facsimile of the manuscript printed by the Mozarteum Foundation in 1991.[30]

2. FEB – facsimile of the first edition of a copy in Basel published by Fuzeau.[31]

3. HEN – the Henle edition.[32]

4. NMA – the *Neue Mozart* Ausgabe,[33] which uses a different numbering of measures from m.34 onwards.

The reader must realize that if he is working from an edition other than HEN or NMA, comparisons with these two sources must be made to ascertain which system of bar numbering is used.

This work was unlike most fantasies of the period, as László Somfai points out:

"The presence of figurative and virtuoso passages is minimal; caprice, studied fragmentation or perplexing turns are not major elements in this fantasia-like form. Much more dramatic in effect are the strikingly new keys, and the unexpected characters and themes. One has the feeling of encountering 'scenes', movements that have not been elaborated to their full length..."[34]

The subjective atmosphere of the fantasy attracts some pianists who would otherwise shy from performing Mozart in public. As with the A minor Sonata, an interpretation based only on temperament will probably baffle listeners. An ideal performance of this fantasy certainly requires a theatrical "sense of the moment" but must be supported by an understanding of the structure. The diversity of the piece is apparent to anyone, but the player must be aware of the various threads that hold this colorful fabric together:

1. SUSPENSION FIGURATIONS, sighing semitones, permeate every section. The initial measures are riddled with suspensions; mm.16-17 have chains of suspensions. In the following D major section, suspensions are often camouflaged by changing notes. In the *Allegro* section, however, there are four rhythmic variants in mm.42-56 HEN (36-50 NMA) of suspensions pulling against the inexorable force of the bass. The frightened *piano* responses (mm.48-50 HEN, 42-44 NMA) and the transition in mm.59-61 (53-55 NMA) are entirely based on suspensions. In the restless section that follows, the RH's suspensions are obvious, and during the weighty sequence of mm.79-84 (73-78 NMA), the LH octaves seem to sigh heavily, and the uppermost RH notes suggest suspensions. Some relief from all these stressful figurations seems necessary, and indeed, during the subsequent *Andantino*,

calmer diatonic figurations are more evident. However, suspensions, more gentle than melancholy, are frequently heard at the end of sentences, for example in mm.93-94 (88-89 NMA). Later, at mm.157-165 (152-160 NMA), the climax of the entire work is formed by a chain of suspensions, first in mighty chords, then as weary sighs in the bass line.

2. THE MOTIF OF FOUR DESCENDING, LATER ASCENDING, TONES, is one of the most important motifs recurring throughout the fantasy and is found in the C minor Sonata. Its first occurrence at mm.16-17 of the initial *Adagio* is so inconspicuous that this brooding line in the middle voice of the bass staff can easily be overlooked. At m.22 there is a grandly rhetorical gesture, which is a rhythmic variant of this motif. In the RH of mm.71-78 HEN (65-72 NMA), an ascending version of the motif generates terrible energy. The descending version becomes the predominant motif in the *Andantino*. In the *Più allegro*, this motif in its ascending form propels the first ten measures. Later there are dramatic interjections of this motif played by both hands at mm.149-150 and 153-154 (144-145, 148-149 NMA).

3. CYCLIC FORM is the most obvious contrast to all the harmonic adventurousness, but its unifying force is undermined by the constant modulation in the outer sections. So little of the music is in C minor, that key signature is never used! The relative major key, E-flat, is also conspicuously absent throughout. The *Adagio*'s motifs are so condensed in the final section that the piece seems to end with almost brutal abruptness.

8 INTERPRETATION OF THE C MINOR FANTASY, K.475

Hopefully all readers of this section have studied the two previous sections. This piece can easily become a mere dream sequence of vague emotional associations if the player is unaware of the various factors that hold this fascinating creation together.

It is extremely fortunate that a manuscript of both the Fantasy and Sonata in C minor has been discovered quite recently and printed as a facsimile (MOZ) by the Mozarteum Foundation (see opening of section 7 above). This publication sheds much light on numerous textual puzzles in both pieces. Previously all modern editions had to base their texts on the first editions and a somewhat confusing copy Mozart made for Maria Theresia von Trattner. References to the first edition will be abbreviated as FEB. As in the previous section, divergent numbering of measures will be indicated by HEN (for Henle and other editions with that numbering) and NMA (for the NMA and editions that share that system).

ADAGIO The opening motif has a spaciousness that has inspired other composers. Richard Rosenberg[35] pointed out that it bears striking resemblances to themes from Bach's *Musikalisches Opfer* and Beethoven's String Quartet, Opus 131.

There is a considerable textual puzzle in the opening measures. In MOZ, the second statement of the initial motif in m.3 is articulated very differently than in mm.1 and 5. In m.3 only the first two notes and the last quarter-note beat in the upper staff, as well as the bass's fourth quarter-note beat, are slurred. The third statement of m.5 is the same as the first, but in the bass line there are separate slurs over each half of the measure, creating an even more ominous instability. When these six measures are compressed to four in the final *Adagio*, MOZ still has two clearly separated slurs above each half of the RH line of m.168 HEN (163 NMA). If played with these differing inflections, each repetition undeniably gains even more rhetorical weight; in its splintered articulation, the second statement is even more fatalistic and chilling. The FEB generally respected the original articulations, but in the course of the nineteenth century, the desire for uniform notation inspired editors to adorn all the appearances of this initial motif with a single slur extending over the entire measure. This dulls the opening measures and spoils the motif's transformation at m.6, where it takes on an utterly different character.

The initial *unisono* should evoke a resonant orchestral *tutti* sound. On his marvelous recording, Malcolm Bilson's[36] *forti* in this theme are terrifying, as if his forte piano were about to explode. The atmosphere is so threatening that the player can become physically tense, and a myopic posture does not suit the epic scale of this music. The pianist should be able to breathe deeply, with the arms, the shoulders, hips and knees relaxed. Each statement of the opening motif becomes an inexorable *diminuendo*. The pedal should be changed clearly with each eighth note and not used during the turns.

Another dubious FEB addition is the *pianissimo* in the third beat of mm.2 and 4, found in virtually all editions. The performer should let the music take its natural course, the change of scoring suggesting a *diminuendo*, not whispering. The suspenseful rests must not be shortened by careless pedaling or inaccurate note values. Tempo is very subjective here, but a pace slower than ♪= 76 becomes turgid. The respite felt in mm.6-7 is brief, the pacific D-flat major phrases in the same tempo as the opening. The first beats of mm.6-7 are muffled, very different from the fatalistic thuds on the first beats of the next two measures. In mm.8-9 the *piano* indication in the second quarter-note beat of the bass may seem unlikely, but it can be found in MOZ. Certainly on larger modern instruments, it is advisable to play the first beat bass note not too strongly and to hold it for not longer than an eighth-note beat, with a clean change of pedal. On a forte piano the LH can play the entire first quarter-note beat strongly.

What did Frau von Trattner make of the sequence beginning at m.10, one of the most astonishing passages in all classical music? For us, Beethoven's late quartets come to mind. There are many ways to shape this sequence. Some editions have the first eighth note in mm.11-15 unslurred, but in MOZ each of these notes is clearly joined to the subsequent four eighth notes. Though most pianists pedal this ominous sequence, Maria J. Pires[37] shuns any pedaling, creating an interestingly grim atmosphere, though the effect is somewhat unnatural. Lili Kraus[38] sustains the tension wonderfully, with no relaxation of the inner tension in mm.16-17, where many pianists go adrift. Given the enormous motivic significance (see previous section) of the middle LH line, the bass's upper F-sharps on the main beats of these measures can best be played by the RH thumb. To avoid rushing in m.18, the player must have nerves of steel. This is another suspenseful moment of total stasis, except for the throbbing of a nervous pulse.

Measures 19-21 present a serious textual problem. About the *fortepiani* in m.19 the Badura Skodas commented:

"On grounds both of musical logic and of comparison with countless similar passages in Mozart's slow movements, one is led to the conclusion that short expressive accents should NOT come on the strong beats ... it is a remarkable fact that all modern editions have reproduced this passage incorrectly."[39]

Later some editions did adjust the placing of these dynamic signs. However, in MOZ these indications are very clear and the *forti* do fall on the quarter-note beats! The Badura Skodas are correct in finding this an unusual effect, but shifting the accents to the beginning of each group of thirty-second notes weakens the dramatic tension. Neither the editors of the FEB[40] nor the NMA[41] agree with that interpretation. Mozart probably wanted nervous *crescendi* to the *forte* quarter-note beats, but the actual strength of the *forti* remains subjective.

In MOZ there is no *crescendo* indicated in m.20 and no *forte* in m.21, but these peculiar dynamic indications are in FEB and unfortunately repeated in all the standard editions. It seems unlikely that Mozart himself added such touches to this phrase. Surely the icy polyphony of m.21 is more eloquent when played softly? In mm.22-25, the pianist must direct the music like a fine conductor, giving the rests their full value. The energy of the long sequences disintegrates into gasping recitative, the rests becoming more important than the notes. In the MOZ and FEB the eighth note on the third quarter-note beat of m.23 is not wedged; therefore it should not be shortened, but whispered. The *calando* in m.24, indicating only a tapering of sound, not of momentum,[42] as well as the *pianissimo* and *crescendo* of the following measure may be in FEB but are not in MOZ. As throughout the entire section, razor-sharp timing is more important than the spinning of beautiful tones. The last quarter-note beat of m.23 and all of m.24 are best played *portato* and without pedaling, like woodwind instruments sounding in a funeral procession. The listener and the music seem exhausted, for, as R.D. Levin eloquently remarked:

> "There is scarcely another solo work by Mozart that gazes so unflinchingly into the abyss as does the opening section of the fantasy ... the languages of Schubert and Wagner are suddenly at hand."[43]

The last three eighth notes of m.25 actually belong to the subsequent D major section, where an idyllic theme introduces a totally different world, full of gentle vulnerability. Sensitive phrasing and warm tone make the frequently heard *rubati* as superfluous as they are unstylistic. The rather illogical stresses in mm.26 and 28, like so many fussy dynamic FEB indications are lacking in MOZ and should perhaps be ignored. However, they do suggest that the third beats in these measures are stronger than the first.

Though the section is very lyrical, there are no slurs over the last two RH notes of m.26, or the second quarter-note beat of m.27. Obviously these phrases are still to be conceived vocally (a mezzo soprano in mm.26-27, a soprano in mm.28-29?), but it is arguable that *portato* with pedaling is more expressive here than the usual *legato*. Lili Kraus succeeds in giving different emotions to the two statements of the "woodwind" chords in mm.30-31. Both repeats of this section must be observed.

The tranquillity evident during this interlude is welcome, given the tensions throughout the rest of the fantasy. The final rest of m.35 should not be too long but experienced as a powerful *crescendo* to the eruption in the next section.

ALLEGRO   This is not for those who maintain that Mozart's music is never wild. The fury of this agitation (approximate tempo: ♩ = 80) should not slacken until the *Andantino*. Many players, even major recording artists, shy away from the elemental violence of this music, letting the tension slacken regrettably at mm.48-50 and 62 HEN (42-44 and 56 NMA). During mm.62-78 (56-72 NMA), the only dynamic indication in MOZ is the initial *piano*. Presumably the FEB's *crescendo* and *forte* in mm.66-67 (60-61 NMA) are moderate. These restless sentences heave with barely suppressed violence. Pedaling must not swallow up any rests.

At m.79 (73 NMA), the music begins a nightmarishly slow slide into swirling darkness. The subsequent ten measures are best played with the pedal changed on each quarter-note beat. The inexorable descent to the lowest note of Mozart's keyboard at mm.86-87 (80-81 NMA) calls for a vehemently *non legato* touch. During this *Eingang* the music must surge forward. Some pianists choose to divide the ascending *arpeggio* between the hands, which is certainly technically easier, but may cause less tension in the line. Dawdling on the half-note E-flats of mm.88-89 (83-84 NMA: the numbering of measures becomes more complicated as the NMA adds a bar-line here) should be avoided; no *fermate* are indicated. Most pianists play the lower line of the octaves in m.89 (84 NMA) with the LH. An exception is Malcolm Bilson, whose octaves sound heavy and furious, as if played by one hand. The eighth notes in m.90 (85 NMA) are quick. Romantic pathos is misplaced in this explosion of energy.

ANDANTINO   Again the sun appears, pale but clear. The writing is orchestral and delicate; the pianist must be able to imagine which instruments would be most suitable in this interlude full of subtle nuances. An approximate tempo of ♪ = 108 is suitable. Very supple hands and wrists are needed to shape these lines well. The phrasing is not complicated; here the first notes of slurred groups are the strongest, the last notes slightly shortened. The rests are sometimes like deep breaths, at other moments, like little gasps. The dynamic contrasts throughout this section are moderate, the changes being more in "orchestration" than in emotion.

The MOZ does not have slurs above the ascending sixteenth notes in mm.94, 102 HEN (89, 97 NMA). But the FEB has a slur in m.102 (97 NMA), and many editions reproduce this sleepy articulation in both instances. Is not light detaching of these tones more expressive than a sticky *legato*?

The section is a miniature ternary form, with a serene middle section at mm.107-118 (102-113 NMA). Many players take these measures faster, but such an unconvincing shift of gears is not necessary when the initial tempo is not sluggish. During these delicate woodwind lines, probably the most innocuous measures of the entire fantasy, the pedal should be changed on each eighth-note beat.

The third part of the section is a fragmented recapitulation of the opening material, breaking off in m.123 HEN (118 NMA) to expire into another astonishingly modern sequence. The music seems to be tentatively seeking its way, like a blind person walking in an unfamiliar place. The dynamic progression from each two-measure motif to the next can be conceived in various ways, but again the imagined "orchestration" is more important than fancy "piano dynamics." Here too the rests certainly have as much rhetorical tension as the notes.

PIÙ ALLEGRO As in the *Allegro*, excess is preferable to caution. This outburst (approximate tempo: $\downarrow$ = 69) is as merciless as it is stormy and should not be undermined by compromising *diminuendi*. Technically the section is challenging; the RH thumb must feel as if it were playing *staccato* as loosely as possible, throwing the hand's energy to the uppermost notes. The four-note motif thundering in the bass should be emphasized by the lower line and not by the LH thumb, which should remain as relaxed as possible. The rests are razor-sharp, the pedal in the first nine measures best changed on each eighth-note beat. When the bass motif appears quadrupled in speed (mm.136-138 HEN, 131-133 NMA), many pianists choose to play *misterioso*, which is totally illogical.

It is impossible to be explicit about the interpretation of the last 23 measures of this section, the most improvisatory segment of the whole composition. The player can best ignore the bar-lines and concentrate on the significance of the harmonies and the instrumentation. The *decrescendo* in m.145 (140 NMA) derives from FEB, not MOZ, and is questionable, especially if the pedal has been frequently changed in the ascending passage.

After decades of trying to make sense of the alternating *p* and *f* indications in mm.146-154 (141-149 NMA) found in most reputable editions, I was delighted to discover that MOZ and FEB have none of these indications! It seems clear that the general atmosphere is more energetic than introspective. Whatever the sound levels may be, the pianist must change the pedal frequently: during the sixteenth-note figurations with each eighth-note beat.

The accenting and *rallentando* (a most un-Mozartian indication) in mm.158-161 (153-156 NMA) are lacking in the MOZ but found in the FEB, as are the *pianissimi* in the last two measures of the section. Do the first four steps of this aching sequence increase or decrease in tone? Do they maintain the same fatalistic sound level? These are subjective matters without conclusive answers. It is probably wise not to exaggerate the long *rallentando*, as this can reduce these grim chords to shallow pathos. The *dénouement*, a total collapse, mm.162-165 HEN (157-160 NMA), is even more upsetting. The motif of three repeated notes followed by a longer note a minor third higher is an eerie premonition of Beethoven's *Appassionata* Sonata, Opus 57 (first movement, mm.12-13), composed only twenty years later.

TEMPO PRIMO How chilling is the reappearance of the initial heaviness of spirit. Mozart accentuates this by omitting the second step of the sequence; the third droops wearily rather than turning upwards. There is a strong sense that there will be no more relief from disaster.

The remainder of this terse recapitulation throbs with bitter hopelessness. In m.172 HEN (167 NMA) a terrifying rhythmic inflexibility is required, with the pedal changed on each eighth-note beat. It is better to surge ahead in the second half of m.174 (169 NMA) than to play a Brahmsian *allargando*. But this moment of defiant energy is very different from the second half of m.177 (172 NMA), where most editions reproduce the FEB's four-note RH chords. The MOZ has only the two upper voices of these chords. This seems a more logical version, as this and the following measure are more like an anguished woodwind duet than massive orchestration. Certainly on a modern instrument, a player with good tone does not need the FEB additional notes.

In m.178 HEN (173 NMA), the *forte* found in many editions under the bass line at the third quarter-note beat should be disregarded; in MOZ and FEB, *crescendo*, a very different effect, is clearly indicated. One measure later there is indeed a hollow *forte* thud on the bass A-flat indicated in MOZ and FEB, more suggestive perhaps of total frustration than the uncertain melancholy of the previous measure.

In MOZ and FEB the penultimate RH third in m.180 (175 NMA) is clearly E-flat and G, not C and E-flat. The final ascending scale is terrifying, like a dying person's last futile surge of energy. This should sound laborious, not like a *diminuendo*. It is advisable to play the last two RH notes with the thumb and third finger. A grinding arpeggiation of the final bass chord seems relevant. Though both hands should play this last terrible harmony *tenuto*, it should not sound for longer than one quarter-note beat.

By the end of this piece the player or listener has experienced a lot. Indeed it is arguable that after the wide range of powerful emotions, proceeding to the C minor Sonata is too much. This quandary is discussed in the final section of this chapter.

9 ORNAMENTATION IN THE C MINOR FANTASY, K.475

HEN numbering:

3   If it is not to sound too active the turn should begin as soon as possible, the final principal note becoming a sixteenth note on the sixth eighth-note beat.

29   The *appoggiature* seem frivolous, even cynical, if played before the beat. As the upper line of the thirds forms the melody, it is best to play the onbeat ornamental notes as lightly and swiftly as possible.

32   The onbeat *appoggiatura* seems misplaced if it is too long or too strong.

48   (42 NMA) The usual rendition is to play this *appoggiatura* as a triplet sixteenth note on the second eighth-note beat. This is technically convenient but less correct and effective than playing it before the beat. This is not too difficult if the RH leaves the preceding third quickly and the wrist is not stiff.

64   (58 NMA) The turn begins immediately after the third quarter-note beat.

67   (61 NMA) The compound *appoggiatura* can begin before the first beat but does not have to end on it. Such a slight *rubato* effect in the melody should be accompanied by an absolutely stable bass line.

78   (72 NMA) Given the tempo of this turbulent passage, the ornaments become three-note trills before the terminations.

104   (99 NMA) In such a low register and with the principal note preceding it, this light turn should probably begin on the upper

auxiliary.

112 (107 NMA) At the beginning of a *legato* phrase, the turn should begin on the principal note, played as soon as possible after the second quarter-note beat.

ADDITIONAL ORNAMENTATION seems unthinkable in a piece which Mozart so carefully marked. Some chords gain power if energetically arpeggiated; for example, the RH chords at m.61 HEN (NMA 55), the bass chords in mm.88-90 (83-85 NMA), the second RH chords in mm.93 and 101 (88 and 96 NMA), perhaps all the RH chords written in quarter notes during mm.150-154 (145-149 NMA) and the bass chord of the final measure.

10 RELATIONSHIP OF K.475 AND THE SONATA, K.457

In my opinion, this particular instance of Mozart combining pieces that were not composed chronologically is considerably different from the case of K.533 and K.494 (see Chapters XVI and XVII). Even when played in isolation, the C minor Fantasy or Sonata certainly retain eloquence. When played together, some would say they can gain even more in stature, but there is considerable debate about this. Siegbert Rampe is convinced that there is much structural evidence that the pieces should be played together.[44] Alfred Brendel, for example, was so convinced that this fantasy and sonata should not be combined, that during his 1991 Mozart recitals he played the B minor Adagio, K.540, between the two C minor pieces! Dennerlein[45] maintained that the sonata was conceived considerably earlier than 1784 and was only finished in that period. There are, however, significant and unde-niable thematic threads that seem to bind the Fantasy, K.475, to the Sonata, K.457.

Many writers have commented on the resemblance of the opening themes of the fantasy and the first movement of the sonata.

Suspensions, already seen in section 6 as being significant throughout the fantasy, function rhetorically during the sonata: in the first movement at mm.13-14, 15-16, 98-99. Obviously in such a vo-cally inspired movement as the sonata's *Adagio*, suspensions are conspicuous, especially at the climax of mm.34-37. It is in the finale of the sonata, however, that suspensions assume their most dramatic function. Not only can its initial theme be seen as a conflict between suspension and triadic figurations (reminiscent of the fantasy's opening motif), but the second thematic group is also rich in suspensions. During the extended recitative, mm.228-243, suspensions arguably become the most prominent element of this sonata-drama.

Another unifying element in both fantasy and sonata is the four-note motif discussed in section 6 of this chapter. In the sonata's first movement this is evident in the upper RH line of mm.9-11. In the *Adagio* of the sonata this motif appears in a cunning guise in m.24, where the "second oboe" line played by the RH thumb during the first half of the measure is continued by the LH thumb in the second half. In the sequence leading to the climax of this movement at mm.34-37, the pivotal notes repeat the motif in its ascending form. In the finale, the sequence mm.74-77 echoes the sequence heard in the first movement's mm.59-61, and from mm.91-92 this motif, in its ascending form, really comes into its own.

The cadential formula of the fantasy's mm.173-174 (168-169 NMA) are evoked at the end of the sonata at mm.310-317.

Having performed the C minor Fantasy and Sonata many times, separately or combined, I came to the conclusion that both works have more impact if played together. However, there is no need to be dogmatic about this issue. The apparent danger of the fantasy over-whelming the sonata, mentioned by many commentators, is due, largely, to the apparent terseness of the sonata's first movement. If the performer follows Mozart's indications and plays both repeats in that movement, the problem of imbalance between the fantasy and sonata is largely resolved.

XV

SONATA IN C MINOR, K.457

COMPOSITION DATE   October 14, 1784
TOTAL DURATION   about 23 minutes (with both repeats in i)

1 THE CONFUSION WITH BEETHOVEN; MOZART'S USE OF C MINOR; THE DIFFERENT MANUSCRIPTS AND EDITIONS

For the historical background of this sonata, the reader is referred to Chapter XIV, section 7; for the relationship of the Fantasy, K.475, and this sonata, to Chapter XIV, section 11.

There can be no doubt that the C minor Sonata is one of the most important in the entire piano repertoire. Even those misguided souls who denigrate Mozart's works for piano solo admit that K.457 is an absolute masterpiece. Who can remain unmoved by the symphonic strife of the first movement, the depth of emotion in the *Adagio* and the catastrophic thrust of the finale?

Leopold Mozart wrote to his daughter on March 12, 1785, that Wolfgang had:

"... a large forte piano pedal made, which stands under the instrument and is about two feet longer and extremely heavy." [1]

The C minor Sonata has many robust passages that utilize the lowest register of that period's instruments. Of all Mozart's solo sonatas, K.457 is arguably the best suited to modern pianos, a factor that contributes to the piece's popularity with students and performers everywhere.

However, the sonata's individuality has inspired much wayward thinking. The forebodings of Beethoven detected in the piece have led to regrettable performance traditions. Einstein aptly remarked:

"It has rightly been said that this work contains a *Beethovenisme d'avant la lettre*. Indeed it must be stated that this very sonata contributed a great deal towards making *Beethovenisme* possible." [2]

There have been many comparisons of K.457 with Beethoven's Sonata Opus 13, the *Pathétique*. Actually the opening theme of K.457 is to be found not in Beethoven's Opus 13, but in his D minor Sonata, Opus 31 no.2 (first movement, mm.21-37). Confusion of the two composers' styles began in the nineteenth century, when Beethoven's masterpieces had so much influence on musical taste. In that period Mozart's more "Beethovenian" works, stormy and in minor keys, were popular, whereas most of his less dramatic compositions were not performed. During the last two centuries, dubious performing traditions, partly due to the confusion with Beethoven, have evolved to obscure our perception of masterpieces like K.457. Too often this sonata is played with unsuitable rhythmic license, peculiar dynamics, excessive pedaling, and an astonishingly cavalier attitude towards the text. Of course such attitudes are not relevant to good Beethoven interpretation either, but derive from the Lisztian view, which prevailed into the twentieth century, of how Beethoven should be performed.

After the completion of K.457, Mozart wrote several other piano masterpieces in C minor. The Fantasy, K.475, was finished in May, 1785, the Piano Concerto, K.482, with its magnificent slow movement in C minor in December, and the C minor Concerto three months later. The sixteen-measure gem, the *Kleiner Trauermarsch*, K.453-a, is also presumed to be from this period.

Throughout his operas, from *Bastien und Bastienne* to *Die Zauberflöte*, striking dark scenes are in C minor. It appears that for Mozart, C minor was more fatalistic than the keys of G minor or D minor, which generally were more active, abrasive. Robert D. Levin noted:

"... that the key of C minor represents for Mozart ... anger, brooding, and solemn severity ... not the demonic spirit of D minor or the despair and tirades of G minor." [3]

Previously editors and performers of K.457 were hindered by the absence of an original manuscript. A copy [4] of the sonata, which Mozart made for the dedicatee, had none of the variants in the second movement that appeared in the first edition. It soon became obvious that the composition underwent several revisions.

The recent rediscovery of the original manuscripts of both K.457 and K.475 clarifies numerous textual puzzles. Fortunately the foundation of the Salzburg Mozarteum was able to purchase the document in 1990 and a year later published a facsimile of K.475-457. As in the previous chapter this publication will be referred to as MOZ. Studying MOZ, one quickly realizes that Mozart took much trouble with the interpretive details of the sonata. With its major revisions of both the *Adagio* and the finale, this is one of the few major "working manuscripts" of Mozart to have survived. As in the previous chapter there will also be references to the first edition, here termed FEB.

FIRST MOVEMENT	*Allegro / Molto allegro*
FORM	sonata
APPROXIMATE TEMPO	♩ = M.M. 89-92
DURATION	9 minutes, with both repeats
SUGGESTED LISTENING	String Quintet, K.406/516-b i
	Piano Quartet, K.478 i
	Piano Concerto, K.491 i
	Serenade for Winds, K.388/384-a i
	Symphony, K.550 i

2 INTERPRETATION OF THE FIRST MOVEMENT, K.457

After the adventurousness of the fantasy, the energy of this movement is rigorous, even ruthless. The form is so potent, it seems a perfect model of sonata form. The recurrences of the defiant opening motif are so conspicuous that the resulting tautness of material becomes quite terrifying. Each theme tries to pull against gravity, strives for hope. But the negative forces are always stronger and, at the end, the struggle fades in exhausted bass whimperings. The impact of this movement is greatly increased if the player observes both repeats. This also lends the sonata more weight to counteract the scale of the fantasy. But even when the sonata is played without the fantasy, observing the second repeat makes the final collapse in the *Coda* more eloquent.

The tempo indications for this movement and the finale create considerable confusion. In MOZ, the "dedicatee's copy"[5] and in Mozart's own thematic catalogue (begun eight months before the completion of K.457) *Allegro* is indicated. It is not clear if the composer or an editor changed the indication to *Molto allegro* for the first edition. Had the dedicatee, Frau von Trattner, already played the sonata for Mozart and taken the outer movements at too comfortable a pace? In any case the composer apparently wanted the outer movements to be stormy.

One impulse in each measure, not two, should generate this emotionally fraught first movement.
The initial half notes of the opening motif can be pedaled but not the subsequent quarter notes, which should be clearly separated, like hammer blows. Throughout the movement, care must be taken with the motif's final quarter note; if it is too strong a peculiar syncopation is suggested, but played too gently, the thrust of the theme can be interrupted. Worst of all, if it sounds longer than the preceding quarter notes, the basic meter will be disturbed. If the LH thumb plays too heavily in this motif the sound may be coarse. In the mournful *piano* response, the rhythm must not slacken. No sensitive woodwind players would play a sentimental *ritenuto* in m.4 or shorten the rest.

In the bitter sentence beginning at m.9, the pedal can be changed on each quarter-note beat. Too often the baleful thud of the initial *forte* is regrettably understated. The next *forte* indication at m.11 is an even stronger *forte subito* effect; if preceded by a *crescendo*, its force is weakened. In mm.13-16 the music drives on with almost brutal fury. Inexplicably, some players let the tension slacken here and introduce debilitating echo effects. Note that the RH notes in the second half of mm.14, 16 are *non legato* and that the chords on the second quarter notes must not be shortened. The *piano* in m.17 should startle but not be too weak-toned. The return of the initial motif in mm.19-20, "scored" for higher woodwind instruments, is less full than in the beginning. When the motif recurs in bass octaves a measure later, the tone is suddenly more positive than threatening.

The E-flat theme too strives futilely upwards. More questions than resolutions are suggested here. Despite the bass slurs, excessive pedaling or finger-pedaling on modern instruments confuse this sentence. The turn in m.23 is too quick to be comprehensible and may begin somewhat earlier than written, just after the third bass eighth note has sounded. From m.27 onwards, rests contribute as much to the tension as the notes. The abrupt transition in m.30 is difficult, but if the player does not hunch over the keys, but leans slightly to the right side of the keyboard, this sudden contrast is easier to achieve. For six measures the energy seems stalled, the nervousness internalized. These suspenseful measures should not be "enlivened" by any fussy agogic or dynamic effects.

At m.36 begins the most positive theme of the movement. Too many pianists seem to find this theme such a welcome relief that they reduce the tempo considerably, but a melting tone is very different from a melting tempo! In both MOZ and FEB Mozart's slurring of the

RH figuration first heard at m.36 varies during its numerous recurrences. Some editions extend the slurs to include the final quarter
note, others end the slur on the third quarter-note beat. Either articulation is possible, but in this case consistency seems relevant. Pedaling must not swallow up the rests, the dark elements in this theme.
Here, the frequently heard habit of sentimental lingering before first
beats is another dreadful nineteenth-century tradition. A *diminuendo*
at the slurred octaves of m.45 sounds effete.

The brief respite of major mode is brutally smashed in m.49. The
arms should be very active and relaxed to make this eruption sound
powerful, not primitive. The *forte* in m.51 introduces the strongest
outburst in the entire exposition. Arpeggiating the LH sixth chord
makes for a suitably snarling effect. The bass of m.52 is not entirely
legible in MOZ, but a repetition of the sixth chord (not an octave, as in
many editions) is indicated clearly enough. Why do so many pianists
play a *diminuendo* in mm.55-56, thereby dissipating the terror of the
thrashing F minor figurations? The *piano* in m.57 is surely a sudden
drop in sound. Though the subsequent theme is in E-flat major, it is
so riddled with suspensions and rests that it does not sound positive.
Pedaling should be avoided here and in the even more ruthless *forte*
repetition with its obsessive repeated notes.

In most editions there are differing notations of the final LH chords
in mm.68, 70; should one choose consistency or contrast? The versions (also MOZ) with E-flat as the lowest note seem preferable, giving
the bass a fatalistic quality. This is less evident in a conventional
dominant-tonic bass progression found at the parallel moment in the
recapitulation. It does not seem likely that the difference in notation
was due to haste, but because the expositional statement is made to
conform with that of the recapitulation in FEB, most subsequent editions have, perhaps unwisely, followed that reading.

There should be no diminution of tension or tone until m.72, where
the LH is not too loud nor the RH too soft. Any trace of a *ritenuto* in the
final measure of the exposition reduces tragedy to salon music. A
rhetorical prolongation of the rest can be effective, especially when
progressing back to the opening. The exposition is so terse that, for
emotional as well as structural reasons, it must be repeated.

C major has rarely sounded as ominous as at the beginning of the
development section! The churning diminished seventh outburst that
follows could be accompanied by pedal strokes, but *legato* pedaling
would obscure the eerie return of the RH figuration heard in m.21.
This is cast against the opening motif, both themes locked in furious

combat during the operatic sequence beginning in m.83. Some pianists try to prettify this frightening scene by playing softly in mm.87-90, a ridiculous effect. The section breaks off in two-note gasps, trying to rise, then collapsing in the deathly suspension at mm.98-99. The ensuing *fermata* over the rest can be found in MOZ and FEB but is lacking in some editions. As in some of the *fermate* of the preceding fantasy the rest is more like a *crescendo* thrust to the next theme than a comfortable pause.

The first surprise of the recapitulation is the canonic treatment of the opening motif in mm.118-120, where the quarter notes must not sound slurred by *legato* pedaling. The four subsequent measures are an astonishing moment, wistful but hopeless. To play the grinding interruption of the diminished seventh bass chord in m.125 softly is another awful "romantic tradition;" in MOZ (but not in FEB) there is a *fp* clearly indicated. The nervous RH sequences in mm.140-148 are interpolated between the corresponding themes from the exposition, as if trying to escape catastrophe. But again F minor erupts in a writhing triadic explosion that seems to devour the instrument, descending to what was the lowest bass note of the keyboard in Mozart's time. The violence of this passage should not be moderated by any *diminuendo* before the last quarter-note beat of m.152.

At m.167 C minor sounds like a descent to hell. When it hurls the player back to the beginning of the development (m.75), the ensuing C major sounds even more nightmarish than it did on its first occurrence. During the repetition of the development and recapitulation sections, the tension of the music is so unrelenting that sensitive musicians often do not breathe well and begin to lose the considerable energy necessary to finish the movement.

In the *Coda*, beginning at m.168, the opening motif, reappearing in a raw-boned canon, sounds more threatening than ever. When one hand plays quarter notes against a half note in the other hand, the quarter notes must not become slurred by careless pedaling. The rush to C minor at mm.172-175 cannot be too strong. The player should keep his arms free, to avoid tone that becomes hard rather than massive. A slight rush here is more appropriate than a Brahmsian *allargando*, for these writhing figurations evoke the flickering of infernal fires. The fourth quarter-note beat accents in mm.176-180 do not have to be conspicuous if the subsequent first beats are soft. In mm.182-183 there should be no pedaling or binding of bass notes. Like ghastly twitches of *rigor mortis*, the last muffled chords are to be played without a trace of retardation.

3 ORNAMENTATION IN THE FIRST MOVEMENT, K.457

m.

2   Some pianists begin the trill on the upper auxiliary. If the tempo is sufficiently spirited, it is not easy to play four notes before the termination. If the ornament becomes a four-note turn it loses all tension. I agree with the Badura Skodas[6] that the best choice is a three-note trill, beginning on the principal note, before the indicated termination. This type of nervous figuration is found throughout Mozart's oeuvre, for example, at the opening of the last movement of the *Sinfonia Concertante*, K.364/320-d.

15   This is a difficult ornament, which in MOZ the composer indicated as a *mordant*. The FEB changed this to a trill, which does seem more logical. One often hears a mere *appoggiatura* F played here, but a three-note trill is best. It could begin before the first beat, with the subsequent sixteenth notes somewhat shortened.

63   Before each termination comes an onbeat three-note trill. These are not difficult if the thumb is relaxed and, wherever possible, the repeated notes are played by the second finger.

175 The energetic trill is best begun on the upper auxiliary. More important is the vigor with which the trill is played. There should be no *diminuendo* before the termination, which must be very clear, as the final note is displaced by the rest.

IMPROVISED ORNAMENTATION is not relevant in a movement that is so rigorously constructed. The chords in mm.51-52 and 66 can be arpeggiated. I have in the past improvised exuberant outbursts at the repetition of the m.98's *fermata* but eventually concluded that the grimness of the moment must not be confused by added notes. The important chord in m.125 and the bass chord on the second quarter-note beat of m.146 could be arpeggiated. Occasionally players add turns after the second beat RH C's in mm.155,159, but these effects are too graceful for such weary phrases. The furious dominant seventh chord in the bass of m.167 can be brusquely arpeggiated.

SECOND MOVEMENT	*Adagio*
FORM	Blend of ternary, sonata, rondo elements
APPROXIMATE TEMPO	♪ = M.M. 69, sometimes slower
DURATION	7½ minutes
SUGGESTED LISTENING	*Nozze di Figaro*: Countess's aria "Porgi amor"
	Così fan tutte: Fiordiligi's aria "Per pietà"
	Concert aria, *Misera, dove son*, K.369
	String Quintet, K.406/516-b ii
	Serenade for Winds, K.388/384-a ii

4 INTERPRETATION OF THE SECOND MOVEMENT, K.457

After the enervating strife of the first movement we are suddenly in a calm landscape; love and hope replace conflict and pain. Only in the middle section does darkness return. This *Adagio*, experienced between two enormous struggles, seems to remind us that life's wonders, real as they are, remain fleeting. Pianists will recognize the same spiritual polarity as in the A minor Sonata, K.310. Maturity is essential for comprehending and projecting this music.

The initial theme seems to baffle many players, who resort to inappropriate lingerings and quickenings, which undermine the simplicity of these calm musings. Each musical impulse must flow to the fourth quarter-note beat and not seem to stop on the third. Rests should not be lost in pedaling. As frequently observed in other chapters, there are many discrepancies between manuscripts and first editions. The manuscript (MOZ) of this movement has two additional pages with variants for the theme's repetitions (mm.17-23 and 41-47). Only the second of these has dynamic indications. In both the original MOZ version and the copy made for the dedicatee, before the *sforzandi* of m.16 there are no ornaments or dynamic indications. Even Lili Kraus,[7] who paces these elusive measures with quiet wisdom, unfortunately makes too much of the dynamic markings.

Apparently when the first edition was being prepared, someone (more likely an editor, not the composer) was troubled by the absence of dynamic indications in the initial statement of the theme. It remains uncertain whether the composer added these dynamic markings to the first 16 measures even if he did add some dynamic markings to the theme's repeats in the second MOZ variant.

The initial *sotto voce* can be seriously misleading if interpreted too literally. Other composers have used the same indication to conjure

up an atmosphere; Chopin, for example, at the opening of his Second
Ballade, where, as in this *Adagio*, a calm, almost static sensibility is
desirable, not muffled tone. Frederick Neumann maintains that, for
Mozart, *sotto voce* denoted *mezzoforte*, not *più piano*.[8] The *forte* in the
second measure, if one accepts that reading, surely implies more
sound, not a conspicuous contrast. The thirty-second notes in m.2 are
best played *leggiero*, not too *legato*, whereas those in the last eighth-
note beat of m.4 are *portato*, not *staccato*. Such subtle adaptations of
touch and pedaling contribute to the eloquence of this extremely
poised theme.

Throughout the entire movement the player should avoid bending
too much over the keys, which can result in a myopic interpretation
and insufficient projection of lines. To achieve vocal intensity in the
melody, the arms must remain free and the fingers not too curved.
The lowest bass notes should be finger-pedaled.

On some large modern instruments it may be desirable to use the
UC pedal until the generous sentence that begins in the upbeat to
m.10, but the RH tone in such vocal lines must never become thin or
opaque. It is not only correct but more expressive if the fingers do not
bind the RH thirty-second notes to the subsequent notes in mm.9-10.
Judicious finger-pedaling in the bass and subtle footwork will guarantee that there will be no breaks in LH sound as the RH's imaginary
soprano sings of her joys and apprehensions. The FEB *forte* in m.12 is
more relevant later in that measure. The second half of m.12 and the
first half of m.13 provide a fine example of Mozartian *rubato*, with the
RH playing freely and the LH absolutely steady. If the series of turns,
not included in MOZ and the dedicatee's copy, is not begun softly, the
effect can seem hysterical.

During m.15 the pianist should lean to the right side of the keyboard. In the FEB, the dialogue between the hands in mm.13-15 has
some peculiar dynamic indications. If one chooses to observe these at
all, surely the activity in second half of m.14 suggests nervous impulses more than increased volume. The *mancando* in m.15 seems
best played as a *diminuendo*, not as a long *ritenuto*. However, in
1789, two piano methods appeared, which gave contradictory defini-
tions of this term: D.G. Türk[9] included *mancando* among other terms
indicating a slackening only of tone, but in the same year, G.F. Wolf
defined *mancando* as "decreasing in respect to tempo."[10] In any case,
I would suggest that a slight prolongation of the last rest in m.15 is
more eloquent than slowing throughout the measure.

Certainly mm.15-16 can be seen as improvisatory and nonmetrical.

In some editions the text is incorrect: the RH triad in m.16, marked *sforzando*, is clearly indicated in both MOZ and FEB on the third eighth-note beat, not simultaneously with the first bass octave. How long the low B-flats should sound is a subjective issue. Malcolm Bilson[11] makes a long pedal effect here, whereas another forte pianist, Alexey Lubimov,[12] does not sustain the bass and makes the ascending *arpeggio* vaporize into silence. Another possibility would be to add a simple *Eingang* between the high A-flat and the return of the theme at m.17.

In the first version of MOZ the theme was repeated without any alterations, but later the composer added some beautiful ornamentation. Again, the dynamic indications can seem wilful if they are too conspicuous; slight variations of tone are preferable here to stormy contrasts. The syncopation between the hands in m.19 must not sound jazzy, but like *rubato* effects, the RH wandering slightly from the LH's strict metric pulse. On a modern instrument, the sound will thicken when the LH thumb is not light. If the accents on the *non legato* thirty-second notes in m.21 are rough, they will seem more comical than charming.

In m.24 Mozart seems to speak in minimalistic polyphony. We sense both novelty and familiarity here. Is this the "C" section (mm.8-16 viewed as a "B" section) of a rondo form, or is it the central section of a ternary structure? To complicate our associations, this theme strongly resembles the opening of the slow movement of Beethoven's Opus 13. However, in K.457 the melodic life takes a subtle path. The E-flat heard in the uppermost voice on the third quarter-note beat is the beginning of a new decorative flourish. The much more significant line is formed by the four descending quarter notes, in parallel sixths, the motif first heard in m.16 of the Fantasy, K.475, which became such a powerful unifying force in that piece (see Chapter XIV, sections 7 and 11). In the sonata *Adagio*, this motif seems to recall the deceptive tranquillity of the motif's first appearance in the fantasy.

At m.27 this somewhat austere polyphony, on modern instruments best played with a change of pedal on each sixteenth-note beat, gives way to a song of celestial grace, the most peaceful moment in the entire sonata. Here the lowest bass notes can be finger-pedaled and the short slurs of the melody linked to each other by pedaling but not by the hand.

Many pianists lose the pulse in mm.29-30. If the rapid RH scale passages begin immediately after the second and fourth quarter-note beats, there is enough time to fit in all these notes without slowing. Mozart's notation of thirty-second and sixty-fourth notes implies acceleration in each passage. It is a matter of taste how many LH notes are finger-pedaled here, but the bass rests should be observed. There is a sudden shift to an unearthly G-flat major. The recitative-like transition (second half of m.30 to m.32) is more poignant if played without hysterical *rubato* and with clear separation of the slurs, each sounding unmistakably like a sob. At m.32 we are astonished to hear the four-note motif of m.24 in this very unusual key. Two measures later the atmosphere darkens. A long, very sorrowful sequence begins with exhausted suspensions trying to rise (the four-note motif inverted), only to fall basswards in heavy diatonic figurations. *Rubato* trivializes the overwrought tragedy of this sentence; the dynamic contrasts, taut dotted rhythms and gasping rests, provide more than enough tension. The bass can be finger-pedaled.

The climax of this suffering is reached in the first beat of m.38, which takes flight in a brief improvisation. In the second half of m.38 there is an abrupt *piano subito*, first found in FEB, an un-Mozartian echo effect. Is it not more likely that the *piano* should coincide with the first note of this measure? The *crescendo* to m.40 seems logical, though it should not approach the strength of the preceding climax. The isolated D in the bass on the first beat of m.40 is strange, where a sixth chord would be expected. The ensuing *calando* should not begin too soon; and as has been noted in other chapters, a *calando* in Mozart's works does not presume any reduction of tempo.[13]

To the final statement of the theme Mozart added elaborate ornamentation. Careful pedaling and a minimum of *rubato* will prevent these decorations from seeming too ornate. Quite often the pedal must be changed on each sixteenth-note beat, and some figures are best played without any pedaling. The FEB's turns in m.49 are not found in MOZ or in the dedicatee's copy and are probably best reserved for m.53, where the variant in MOZ includes them; surely such a purely ornamental effect is spoiled when heard twice? Rushing should be avoided in the first quarter-note beat of m.51, where the defiant descending scale can best begin after the first bass note. To play a "mysterious" *diminuendo* in mm.51-52 is another decadent tradition. In such a low register, mysterious muttering deforms this proud, affirmative statement. The MOZ and FEB have no reduction of sound until the last five notes of m.52.

The rest of the movement makes a prolonged farewell to the safe world of E-flat major. Pedaling must not obscure any rests. None of the *forti* should be emphatic. On a modern instrument the LH repeated B-flats are best played with the right pedal changed on each sixteenth-note beat. Without any sentimental dawdling, the music fades away, like a boat gradually disappearing over the horizon.

5 ORNAMENTATION IN THE SECOND MOVEMENT, K.457

m.

2   The turn will not sound supple if the RH thumb on the quarter-note E-flat is tense. The subsequent thirty-second notes are not slurred and should become very light.

4   This calm turn can best begin just after the LH's tenth or eleventh sixteenth note. The numerous recurrences of this turn do not have to be played with identical timing.

9   This turn is better begun just after the bass E-flat.

12 These turns, though absent in both MOZ and the dedicatee's copy, do intensify the line. They can be played with considerable rhythmic freedom as long as the bass remains absolutely metrical.

23 This turn sounds less hurried if begun just after the fourth eighth-note beat.

27 This turn and that in the following measure begin on the sixth sixteenth-note beat.

34 This soulful turn is most expressive begun on the second sixteenth-note beat.

47 The timing of the turn in the final quarter-note beat is very subjective, but there is an unpleasant drawling effect when the initial principal note is too long.

48 The *appoggiatura* sounds on the second quarter-note beat. The resolution of the ornament may sound after the sixth bass note. Glenn Gould[14] interpolates a charming second C before playing the turn.

49 As stated in the previous section, these four-note turns can best be saved for the repetition at m.53.

53 The trill in the last quarter-note beat would sound pedantic if begun on the upper auxiliary. In MOZ that note sounds just before the trill. It is interesting to note that the dedicatee's copy has no syncopation or chromaticism in the RH line, but a simple diatonic descent from B-flat to E-flat. If the player chooses to play this version, the trill can begin with the lower auxiliary.

In a piece where Mozart included so many ornaments, to add more seems impertinent. An *Eingang* in m.16 is possible. The RH chord on the first beat of m.29 sounds more dramatic if vigorously arpeggiated.

THIRD MOVEMENT	*Allegro assai*
FORM	sonata-rondo
APPROXIMATE TEMPO	$\downarrow$ = M.M. 69-72
DURATION	5 minutes
SUGGESTED LISTENING	*Don Giovanni*: Act I, Scenes 3 and 13
	Symphony, K.550 iv
	String Quintet, K.406/516-b iv
	Serenade for Winds, K.388/384-a iv

6 INTERPRETATION OF THE THIRD MOVEMENT, K.457

This is arguably Mozart's most stormy composition for piano solo. Everything is painted in primary colors, but the colors change with breathless rapidity. It is clear that Mozart wanted a driving tempo here. In MOZ and the dedicatee's copy, *Molto allegro* was indicated, and in the latter, *agitato* added. In the first edition, Mozart changed the indication yet again to *Allegro assai*. Leopold Mozart stated in his violin treatise[15] that the term indicated a tempo slightly quicker than *Allegro molto*. As noted earlier, the adverb *assai* denotes "very," not "rather" in Mozart's scores.[16] Certainly this finale should sound as if the pianist is being pursued by a pack of devils. This frenzied quality – *"agitato"* here seems an understatement – creates considerable technical demands.

The first theme swings from anguish to rage at m.16, to exhaustion (m.26), only to explode again in rage (m.30). Some editions have a notation in the initial measures that confuses ties and slurs. In any case, the RH must not make too many floppy vertical hand movements, which could result in a dance like cadence hardly appropriate in such a grim context. If the hand leaves the keys too quickly, the last notes of slurred groups can become grotesquely accented. Throughout the theme there is terrific energy, but the energy is captive, without a trace of a *crescendo*.

Measure 16 explodes in wrath, the RH fourth finger digging into the initial *appoggiatura*. The LH thirds are difficult when the thumb is tense. The arpeggiated chords erupting at mm.21-24 can also be troublesome. In Mozart's time such arpeggiation would have seemed dramatic, but the effect of so many arpeggiated chords in quick succession can sound more diffuse than dramatic if the *arpeggi* are not played extremely rapidly. One could consider ignoring the arpeggiation except for the final triad on the first beat of m.24, a splendid snarling effect. Glenn Gould perversely arpeggiates in all directions, transforming Mozart's angry gesture into a jolly baroque *corrente*.

Throughout the entire movement, rests must not disappear in careless pedaling. The mournful recitative of mm.26-30 is a desolate *diminuendo* from the first note to the last. At m.45 there is a sudden lurch to positive harmonies, the *forte* designation for the dominant seventh chord surely indicating a warm sound, not an abrupt one. However long the player waits during this *fermata*, he must sense this chord as an upbeat to the hyperactive second theme group.

Despite the major mode, the new theme provides only brief respite before it splinters into chromaticism. Some editions have C as the first bass note in m.56, but this passage is not necessarily a transposition of mm.176-179, and C-flat is clearly indicated in MOZ. Finger-pedaling of the lower bass notes throughout this theme is subjective; on some instruments the sound may thicken. Too many pianists ignore the *forte* in mm.56-57, a jolting effect from MOZ. Exact rests contribute much to the eloquence of the vivid scoring of mm.58-65. If all the B-flat bass notes are not to intrude, the pianist's LH must be quick and supple. Some may think that the *forte* accompanying the *staccato* bass notes beginning in m.66 is rough, but in MOZ, Mozart wrote the *forte* indication with an exuberant scrawl, as if very excited while writing these measures, which were quite revolutionary for the time.

Weighty but free arm movement will keep the tone full enough in the sparse scoring of mm.69-71. The *legato* here is enhanced if the LH takes some notes in the lower line of m.70-71. In the shuddering sequence that follows, it is important to play the LH eighth notes with dogmatic exactness. The *forte piano* accents occur in a *piano* context and are more like nervous pin-pricks than heavy blows. The repeated notes in mm.78-81 are difficult if the wrist or thumb are tense. Too many pianists distract themselves here by nervously looking at the bass instead of concentrating on the RH's exact, very quick movements, where, on most instruments, the fingering 4-3-3-3 is better than the old-fashioned changing of finger with each repeated note. Despite all the agitation here, the sound level remains a suspenseful *piano*, with very exact rests in the bass and no theatrical *crescendi*. In MOZ there are no dynamics indicated between m.87 and m.102.

Most editions give two versions of mm.92-101. In MOZ and the dedicatee's copy, Mozart lets the eighth-note line descend to the lowest notes on the instruments of his time. It is unusual that the music remains so long in that sinister register. For the first edition he wrote an "easier" version, which avoids the lowest octave of the bass register and thrusts the RH voice higher; musically this does not seem a desirable compromise. The difficult crossing of hands in the preferable version, necessitated by the descent to the low bass register, can be remedied by inverting the indicated hand distribution starting at the second eighth note in m.92 until m.96. The *forte* at m.96 is missing in MOZ but appeared in the dedicatee's copy as well as in the first edition, so it can be presumed to be authentic. In such a frenzied tempo, this passage could not have been gentle, but many pianists play a ludicrous *diminuendo* in the ascending measures. *"Vibrato"* pedaling is advisable in mm.98-101.

After a repetition of the initial theme group, at the *fermata* of m.142 there is a frightening lurch to F minor, a key that usually expresses deep despair in Mozart's works. During the ensuing sobbing recitatives, the rests are as pained as the tones. The RH's upbeat C's in mm.149,151 are not slurred but wearily *non legato*. The recitative is broken by more rests and another *fermata*. When repeated a tone higher, the anguish is even more intolerable. Although the *fermate* may be quite long in mm.142, 145,156, each of these silences has its own emotional connotation and rhythmic impulse. In m.165, a supremely gruesome moment, the strength of the *forte piano* is subjective, but the *pianissimo* frequently heard here is effete.

Startling contrasts like the furious *forte* beginning with the eighth notes in m.186, the plaintive *piano* in the last quarter-note beat of m.194 and the slight *forte piano* thud on the first beat of m.197 are too often ignored. In MOZ, mm.189-190 are not marked *staccato* but merely lack slurs. Certainly weight is more relevant here than shortness of tone. The FEB dynamic indications in the phrase preceding the final return of the first theme (*forte* at m.211, *piano* at m.213, and *crescendo* at m.215) do not appear in MOZ but enhance the dramatic thrust of this crucial phrase.

At m.221, the initial theme returns for the last time, still cast in a bleak *piano*. The theme suddenly disintegrates into sobbing recitative. Playing the *fermate* indicated on the suspension notes of each fragment as continuous *ritenuti* would be regrettable. This grotesquely prolongs the rests, resolution notes or both, bringing Brucknerian massivity to mind. Perhaps the rests are freer here than the notes. The rhythmic and dynamic shape of all these mournful phrases should not be identical.

The upbeat to m.245 is an inexorable lurch back to C minor. The rhythm must be relentlessly strict here. In the ensuing *Coda*, the crossing of hands can be uncomfortable, but that is no reason for playing the duller FEB version. As earlier in this movement, a redistribution of hands is the most efficient solution; for example, the LH can play the eighth notes beginning on the second eighth-note beat of m.289 while the RH plays the subsequent quarter notes. The sound must be held in, the initial measures of this long push to the tonic key more claustrophobic than dramatic. Only when *forte* is indicated at m.293 does the tone begin to grow. In mm.290-308, the FEB gives a much tamer version, which can be ignored (most modern editions print both versions). At m.301 the hands can reverse, the RH playing the long notes, the LH the eighth notes. The more dramatic MOZ version, with the lower bass notes, certainly sounds stronger on a forte piano or on most modern upright pianos. The effect on many modern "grand" pianos, however, can sound elephantine. It is important to note that in the manuscript, Mozart even crossed out the more conventional version for mm.304-308, written an octave higher.

It takes courage to play the quarter note C in m.309 as short as marked, but such abruptness is appropriate, as this arrival in the tonic key evokes catastrophe, not resolution. The cadential figure in thirty-second notes in the Fantasy, K.475 (first heard there at m.19), makes a nightmarish, deformed appearance to conclude the sonata. Was this figuration brooding in Mozart's imagination when he wrote the fantasy half a year later?

Some artists choose to play mm.314-317 *piano*. This effect has a certain theatrical appeal but seems unlikely, considering the depth of the bass line and the grimness of this final scene. The final rests should be absolutely metrical, with only the last chord in m.319 briefly elongated, perhaps by two quarter-note beats, a suitable conclusion to so much strife. Ultimately black futility wins out.

7 ORNAMENTATION IN THE THIRD MOVEMENT, K.457
m.

16   The onbeat *appoggiatura* is not only strongly accented but preferably ever so slightly prolonged, with the three successive notes played quicker than written, a rhetorical effect described by Nikolaus Harnoncourt[17] among others.

21   As discussed in the previous section, the arpeggiation is problematic. In any case, each *arpeggio* does not begin, but ends, on the beat.

29   The onbeat *appoggiatura* should not be accented. It sounds more ominous if played more like a sixteenth note than as an

eighth note. Tonal control over the RH thirds is better when the hand is turned toward a relaxed thumb.

48 Given the rapidity of tempo, this turn must begin as soon as possible. As part of the ornament, the subsequent eighth note C may be shortened.

243 If played with too much tone, this *appoggiatura* will sound more sentimental than exhausted.

245 The *appoggiatura* is played as a very fast grace note before the first beat.

286 The trill should be played as energetically as possible. It is advisable to begin with the downbeat upper auxiliary slightly elongated and vigorously accented. The auxiliary must not be played as a grace note before the beat, as this would too much resemble the nervous eighth-note upbeats found in the previous eight measures.

ADDITIONAL ORNAMENTATION is hardly imaginable in a piece as tersely action-packed as this. The RH chord in m.45 and the LH chords in m.102, 165 can be arpeggiated. The *forte piano* LH triads of mm.229-234 could also be arpeggiated, but preferably not with identical timing. One could conceivably add some simple decorations to the recitative, but there must be no distraction from the tragic tone of these broken phrases. Arpeggiating either of the final two chords is possible, but arpeggiating both makes for a sleepy effect.

XVI

THE RONDI, K.485, 494, 511

1 MOZART DURING THE YEARS 1786-87

On January 10, 1786, Mozart finished the Rondo in D for piano solo, K.485 (sections 2-4 of this chapter), a cheerful beginning to what was to be the happiest year of his life, a period when he enjoyed recognition, good health, happiness with Constanze and few financial worries. The next months saw the completion of the Piano Concerti in A and C minor, K.488 and 491, as well as *Le Nozze di Figaro*. The revolutionary aspects of that opera created something of a stir, but there was less social dissatisfaction in Vienna than in many other European capitals. Soon after finishing the sunny Quartet for Piano and Strings, K.493, Mozart entered in his thematic catalogue on June 10, a Rondo in F for piano solo, K.494 (sections 5 and 6 of this chapter). Other renowned works for piano from this fertile year are the C major Concerto, K.503, the Trios, K.496 and 502, the four-hand Sonata, K.497, and the *Kegelstatt* Trio, K.498.

The Mozarts were in Prague at the beginning of 1787, where the composer could revel in the overwhelming success of *Nozze*. Not only was he acclaimed in the theater and in salons, but even in less refined surroundings, where waltzes and quadrilles set to Mozart's opera melodies were danced. Not since his *Wunderkind* days, had Mozart been so showered with appreciation. He returned to Vienna with a commission for another opera. There the couple spent their last weeks in their attractive home, now a museum familiarly known as the Figaro House.

The first significant composition of 1787 was a Rondo in A minor for piano solo, K.511 (sections 7 and 8 of this chapter), apparently inspired by the unexpected death of a friend, Count von Hatzfeld. After this unusually emotional piece came three marvelous string quintets, two of which, K.516 and 406/516-b, are noticeably somber. Indeed, throughout 1787, the composer's music gravitated to darker feelings with a frequency that was new and significant.

The Mozarts moved to less expensive lodgings. About this time the composer fell ill and, from a poem written in Mozart's album by his physician,[1] it would seem that the affliction was serious. Among Mozart's prospective pupils that spring was one Ludwig van Beethoven, aged 16, who was soon recalled from Vienna because of his mother's failing health.

Even in his letters Mozart seemed less cheerful than usual. In a famous letter to Leopold, dated April 4, Mozart expressed himself in terms puzzling for a young man who was enjoying success and a happy marriage:

"... I have now made a habit of being prepared in all affairs of life for the worst. As death, when we come to consider it closely, is the true goal of our existence, I have formed during the last few years such close relations with this best and truest friend of mankind, that his image is not only no longer terrifying to me, but is indeed very soothing and consoling![2]

Later in the same letter Mozart referred again to the death of Count von Hatzfeld and reiterated his hope that Leopold had recovered from an illness.

Only weeks later Leopold died. Some historians maintained that Mozart's immediate reaction was to compose the overtly comic quintet *Ein musikalischer Spass*, K.522, the first piece listed in Mozart's catalogue after his father's death. This interpretation of events has been disproved by the research of Alan Tyson,[3] which shows that much of K.522 had been written long before Leopold's death. On September 3, Mozart's physician, Barisani, died. The young man had been a close friend and his death, so soon after Leopold's and Count von Hatzfeld's, was deeply distressing to Mozart.[4]

Don Giovanni had its premiere in Prague. The year ended with the emperor displaying his good will towards Mozart by appointing him *Kammerkomponist* to the court. The primary duty of the *Kammerkomponist* was to provide music for the annual Carnival festivities, hardly the coveted position enjoyed by the imperial court opera composer. But Mozart's new title brought some honor; the previous bearer had been Gluck, and even if the older composer had been paid more than twice as much as Mozart, some steady income was welcome. The emperor had declared a costly, unsuccessful war on the Turks. The economy was depressed. It was becoming increasingly difficult for a free-lance musician with expensive tastes to enjoy a comfortable life style. Mozart had fewer opportunities for concerts and perhaps less patience for teaching.

THE D MAJOR RONDO, K.485

COMPOSITION DATE	January 1786
APPROXIMATE TEMPO	♩ = M.M. 142
DURATION	6 minutes (with repeat)
SUGGESTED LISTENING	Piano Quartet, K.478 iii
	Divertimento for Strings, K.136/125a
	Rondi for Piano & Orchestra, K.382 & K.386
	String Quartet, K.575 i

2 THE UNIQUE FORM OF THE D MAJOR RONDO, K.485

During 1786-87, Mozart apparently wrote nothing in sonata form for piano solo, but the composer made fascinating formal experiments in the three rondi and numerous songs from this period. The D major Rondo is one of Mozart's wittiest creations, but its tone is so carefree that the composer himself seemed to underestimate the piece; it is one of the few completed works from the Viennese years that Mozart did not list in his own catalogue. The style and form of the piece suggest that he wrote it down with lightning speed, and it is also possible that he simply forgot to enter such an inspiration of the moment in his catalogue. The lack of interpretive signs, compared with the previous piano solo piece, the C minor Fantasy, K.475, is conspicuous. The rondo was intended for a "Mlle. W.," who was probably studying with Mozart at the time. Wanda Landowska observed that the theme has an interesting history:

> "It is of little importance that this theme is not really Mozart's, but Johann Christian Bach's, the eleventh and youngest son of Johann Sebastian. Plagiarism? Irreverence? No! On the contrary, it is an homage to an admired master. In the first movement of Johann Christian's Quintet, Opus 11, No.6, the pastoral and joyful oboe plays the theme..."[5]

Mozart was obviously fascinated by this delightful tune. Not only did he use it in the last movement of the Quartet for Piano and Strings, K.478, but also in a composition as early as the String Quartet, K.169.

In 1786, the Viennese publisher Hoffmeister advertised the piece as "Rondo très facile," but there is nothing "simple" about its enigmatic structure, and the pianistic demands of the rondo are far from modest. Being monothematic, it is not really a rondo at all! Sandra P. Rosenblum perceptively remarked:

> "What, then, is the reason for the title? The repetitions of the theme leave some rondo flavor, especially in the recapitulation. But contemporary musicians would have understood that Mozart was calling attention to a type of theme and character – in other words, to certain musical, rather than formal qualities of Classic rondos that give this piece its spirit. Typically rondos display a cheerful lyricism, with a tuneful theme cast in clearly delineated phrases." [6]

The player should understand the unique structure of K.485. The cheeky theme heard in the first four measures has two motifs descending over the interval of a fifth. The first, Motif A, is diatonic; the second, Motif B, triadic. These are answered in m.5 by a turn-like Motif C, while the LH plays a bass line that rarely ventures away from the tonic. Such note repetitions recur so often throughout the entire piece that they assume a structural function (Motif D).

At m.16 a new sentence begins, but very little is truly new. The RH's amiable figure descending from D to G is a disguised version of Motif A. The flute-like repeated A's in m.17 do not belong to the theme but derive from Motif D. The bass line reminds us of Motifs C and D. At the bar-line of mm.17-18 we hear a three-note figure in the uppermost line, Motif E, two repeated notes with the upper auxiliary tone between. This is the only recurring element in the piece that is not heard in the opening measures.

In the following phrase, mm.20-24, the upper line is based on Motif A. The two recitative-like measures, mm.25-26, lead to a theme that seems to evoke the second theme of a sonata form, or the first episode of a rondo form. But however exotic the A minor tonality may sound, the thematic material is not new. The upper line blends Motifs A and E; Motif D is in the bass.

At m.36, a chromatic scale leads to an abridged statement of the opening theme, now in the dominant key. This is repeated in mm.43-46, with the material comically inverted, the LH playing Motifs A and B, the RH, Motif D. The tender *Codetta* theme beginning in m.53 is based on variants of Motifs A and B. If the first 59 measures are repeated, as indicated, the section seems even more like the exposition section in sonata form, increasing the humor of the piece by adding to the listener's disorientation.

The opening of the next section is certainly very like a development section, Motifs A and B stated assertively by both hands. After a transitional phrase we hear the initial theme in m.71 in G major. This is a capricious "false recapitulation," with mm.9-18 being repeated virtually unchanged but in the "wrong" key. Measures 16-18 are recalled at mm.78-80 in G major, but then we still seem to be in a development section, with several modulations leading to the dominant seventh of D major in m.90. This harmony remains for five measures, granting the listener some respite from all the harmonic restlessness.

At m.95, D major returns, but the theme is stated only once before it lurches at m.103 into D minor, erasing any illusions of being in a predictable recapitulation. The theme is interrupted by questioning seventh chords until it reappears at m.112 in a startling F major. After four measures, this too dissolves into nine measures of modulatory passages. At m.125 the first theme returns in the tonic key, in the bass this time, modulating to a very unexpected B-flat major at m.136. The theme is heard in this unlikely key but breaks off at m.142 for some pianistic display which, we sense, must lead to the tonic key. Indeed, at m.148 we hear the *Codetta* theme, the upper line derived from Motif A, with Motif D in the bass. At m.156 the piece could end, but Mozart has not finished teasing our ears. The initial theme returns at m.158, with Motif A repeated three times. The rest of the theme has vanished, an effect reminiscent of the exhaustion after an uproarious comedy; almost all the characters have departed, leaving a single dazed figure on stage.

There has been much attention given here to Mozart's wildly improvisatory fantasy in this piece because the structure can be so confusing. The piece does not conform to neat concepts of standard rondo, sonata, or ternary form.

3 INTERPRETATION OF THE D MAJOR RONDO, K.485

However ingenious the form may be, the interpretation of this capricious piece is fairly straightforward, though many decisions need to be made regarding dynamics, pedaling and articulation. Humor, a constant delight in surprise, and fluent pianism are needed to project this original miniature masterpiece. Dynamic indications exist only in mm.60-66 and the *Coda*, both moments with an overtly operatic character. Elsewhere the player is on his own. The sentences beginning in mm.16, 20 and 26, for example, surely do not have the same sound level. It seems more logical to play the theme's recurrence at m.43 energetically rather than daintily, with less volume in the *Codetta* theme (m.53). A quasi-orchestral sound suits mm.43-52, 109-111, 120-135 and 142-147.

The quicksilver wit of the piece is not easy to capture on a large modern piano. On any modern instrument, pedaling should be avoided except at a few rhetorical moments like mm.25-26,60-67, 109,142-43. Finger-pedaling of the bass line is more relevant in m.42 than in mm.27-33. If the dynamics indicated by the composer are respected, the bass in the *Coda* is best played without any pedaling or finger-pedaling even when it is slurred.

Imagination, articulation and timing are essential to the humor of this delightful piece. If the suspensions of Motif A (see previous section) are joined to each other by the fingers, the theme sounds droopy. Motif B, first heard in m.2, is best played with a tiny separation between the second and third note. The upbeat A's before mm.6-7 are not *legato* and the ascending figurations in mm.20 and 34-35, as well as the bass lines in mm.86-87 and 120-121, can be played *non legato*. Joining the slurs of the nervous upbeat figures in mm.136-137 makes for a peculiar yodeling effect.

The *Eingang* at mm.68-70 may be played freely, as if without barlines. Even more rhythmic freedom is applicable in mm.90-94. Elsewhere *rubato* should be minimal, as the freshness of the piece can degenerate into coyness if the player underlines each surprise in the piece with *caesurae* and *fermate*. The *calando* at the end should not be confused with the later connotation of the term;[7] it indicates a *diminuendo* to *pianissimo* but with no slowing down.

Balance between the hands requires careful judgment throughout, and this is much easier when pedaling is avoided. The mercurial quality of the piece cannot be projected by a player whose technique is stiff or heavy; if the pianist's wrists are not relaxed, charm will be in short supply. Unfortunately, the opportunities for display encourage some players to rush through this rondo as if it were a hurdle race.

4 ORNAMENTATION IN THE RONDO, K.485

1   Usually the *appoggiature* are played on the beat, preferably as approximate sixteenth notes, definitely not as dull eighth notes. Such jaunty onbeat ornaments (often termed "Scotch snaps" or

as being "in Lombard rhythm") are preferred here by many commentators (among them the Badura Skodas[8] and the editor of the Schott-Universal Edition).[9] Conversely Frederick Neumann[10] and Konrad Wolff[11] advocate playing the ornaments before the beat, making for a more graceful, less comical character. Either interpretation is valid.

5   This quick *appoggiatura* usually sounds on the second eighth-note beat, but this can give the *appoggiatura* note an inappropriate emphasis. It is more correct, though admittedly much more difficult, to play the *appoggiatura* before the beat. This is possible if the fingers are close to the keys and the wrist relaxed.

29   A five-note turn sounds muddled here. A four note turn beginning on the upper auxiliary is frequently heard but spoils the clarity of the upbeat. A three-note trill *(Schneller)* is preferred here and in m.31,32.

52   The compound *appoggiatura* begins on the first beat and the trill's termination is on the final eighth-note beat.

67   The prebeat *appoggiatura* can be played quite languidly at this flirtatious moment.

146 *Schneller*, three-note trills, suffice.

147 The cadential trill is best begun on the upper auxiliary, which may be slightly elongated, but not roughly accented.

155 In the manuscript, Mozart clearly writes this *appoggiatura*, which recurs in the *Coda*, differently from the *appoggiature* in m.1. Presumably he wanted a more vocal inflection here. A slight *rubato* effect is possible here, the onbeat *appoggiatura* longer than its resolution note.

ADDITIONAL ORNAMENTATION should be avoided during the theme's multiple appearances. Much of the humor in the piece has to do with the theme appearing in so many unlikely modulations. Some ornamentation is conceivable during the rhetoric of mm.60-66. An *appoggiatura* C-sharp before the first beat of m.62, and an *arpeggio* in m.67 seem apt.

THE F MAJOR RONDO, K.494

COMPOSITION DATE	June 1786
FORM	rondo
APPROXIMATE TEMPO	♩ = M.M. 66
DURATION	6½ minutes
SUGGESTED LISTENING	Lied "Das Veilchen," K.476
	Quartet for Piano and Strings, K.493 ii and iii

5 INTERPRETATION OF THE RONDO IN F MAJOR, K.494

This piece has had a somewhat tortuous history and presents the pianist with special challenges. On June 10, 1786, Mozart listed a "small rondo for piano solo" in his thematic catalogue. Soon after, the D major and A minor Rondi were published by the prestigious Viennese house of Hoffmeister. A much less eminent publisher presented the F major Rondo. In the first days of 1788, Mozart completed two sonata movements for piano solo, the *Allegro* and *Andante*, K.533, which Hoffmeister published later in that year, with a second, longer version of the F major Rondo as finale. Does this hasty compromise result in a truly satisfying sonata? Referring to the first two movements, Einstein wrote:

> "These movements composed later have a grandeur of harmonic and polyphonic conception, a depth of feeling, and a harmonic daring such as we find only in his last works; indeed they are conceived for an entirely different and more powerful instrument than the innocent rondo, which is written mostly for the middle register."[12]

Yet Einstein, like most scholars, concluded that K.533-494 has a certain unity and should be regarded as a sonata. I have reservations about the second version of the rondo.

The NMA editors have done pianists a great service by including, as an appendix[13] to the second book of the sonatas, the original version of the rondo. This version has a sense of proportion that, in my opinion, Mozart's later version lacks. When combining K.494 with K.533, Mozart added to the rondo a long *cadenza*-like sequence of basically ornamental passages (mm.147-169). This is not only in a different style from the rest of the piece but hardly seems an improvement. The repetition of mm.143-144 at mm.147-149 is curiously redundant and un-Mozartian. The polyphonic style of mm.152-160 creates an atmosphere that seems more academic than impressive. There is little substance in mm.163-168. That this beautiful piece is not enhanced but diminished by the *cadenza* remains an opinion. Many think otherwise.

Pianists should consider the option of playing the two movements of K.533 without the rondo. The *Andante* of K.533 is so rich that a subsequent movement seems totally superfluous. Perhaps even Mozart sensed this? Because I believe that the first version of K.494 is a fine composition, which should be heard on its own, I will treat the rondo in this chapter and not in the following chapter on K.533.

In the revised version, Mozart changed the tempo indication to *Allegretto*. Of course it would have seemed bizarre to have two consecutive movements marked *Andante*, but perhaps this shows that in Mozart's time, there was less difference than later between the indications *Andante* and *Allegretto*. In any case, an excessively leisurely tempo sounds ludicrous in the dramatic first episode, beginning at m.51, and ponderous in the second, at m.95. Conversely a hasty tempo can make many of the charming ornaments sound garbled and indistinct. On a fortepiano the tempo may be somewhat swifter than on modern instruments.

The long rondo theme is harmonically quite straightforward, its wistful charm dependent on very sensitive phrasing. The initial six-measure phrase, marked *piano*[14] in Mozart's catalogue, has the simplicity of a folk song. The first beats of mm.2-4 should not be stressed. In the first version (hereafter abbreviated as FV) of the rondo there is no slurring of the RH in m.5. This seems preferable to the slur over the entire measure seen in the later, expanded Hoffmeister version (hereafter termed H). The differences in slurring may cause the player "to not see the forest for the trees." Fragmentation is a danger whenever this theme recurs.

The second note of each two-note slur should not be *staccato*, but also not joined by the fingers to the following note. Occasionally Mozart changed the articulation to suit the tempo; the RH *staccati* in the second half of m.11 seem more suitable in H's *Allegretto* than in FV's *Andante*. During the following phrase, mm.13-18, the rests should be audible without breaking the sense of a longer line. Unslurred upbeat notes, as before the bar-lines of mm.15-16, are better played slightly detached, but not *staccato*.

Thereafter the theme takes the more usual form of two- or four-measure phrases. In mm.23-24 and 27-28, the RH sixteenth notes have more humor if not joined to the subsequent half notes, and in the bass, the notes on the second quarter-note beat should not be pedaled.

In the ornamented repeat of the initial sentence beginning at m.41, the slurs indicate the phrasing: in m.41, for example, the RH should leave the keys after the E has sounded, and the subsequent G – not the longer F – is slightly emphasized. In m.43 the melody's single slur in FV seems clearer than the later version's fussy detaching (or accenting?) of the first note.

Throughout the entire first section of this rondo the hands play closely together, necessitating alert balancing of the tone. Most players will be more comfortable here if they lean slightly toward the right side. The limited spatial scale can be enlivened by imagining some instrumentation: the melody played by a violin and the lower parts taken by other stringed instruments.

D minor is always an assertive key in Mozart. In this first episode (mm.51-82), *piano* can be fuller than during the main theme, the *forti* energetic and orchestral. During the entire section, pedaling is necessary only on the initial arpeggiated chords, which are further discussed in the next section. There are glimpses of the initial theme at mm.55-57 and 63-65, but at m.68 an unexpected theme in B-flat appears, a radiantly optimistic interlude, which should not be hurried. On a modern instrument the bass line here is probably better played quite lightly; *staccato* would sound cynical, but finger-pedaling creates a sticky texture.

The theme's first twelve measures are then repeated, ornamented primarily by syncopations, which must always be vocally shaped and should not sound choppy. There are several differences between the two versions in articulation. The pianist should compare both FV and H texts and try out all the possibilities before he makes any quick decisions.

The second episode, mm.95-116, is unmistakably scored for an imaginary band of woodwind instruments; at the opening, a bassoon plays the bass line, a clarinet and an oboe the upper voices. Throughout the entire section, the coloration of different wind instruments is more relevant than overt contrasts of dynamics. It is interesting that H, but not FV, slurs the RH eighth notes in mm.96-98, 104, etc. Only in FV are the LH eighth notes of mm.104, 106 and 108 slurred. If played with careful pedaling, I find the prevalence of *non legato* in FV more expressive than the generalized *legato* of H. The FV evokes distance and gravity, like many of Mozart's "Masonic" pieces, whereas H seems more accessible and more conventional. If the first repetition is not observed, this episode loses its equilibrium, but respecting the second repetition is a more subjective matter. F minor was a very grim key for Mozart, as we have noticed in the slow movements of the sonatas K.280 and 333. There is much inner tension in these lines, and the contemplative atmosphere should not result in sagging of tempo. Some of the RH's lower eighth notes in mm.110-111 can be played by the LH. The transitional passage in mm.117-119, a playful *Eingang*, calls for some rhythmic freedom but no sentimentality, the triplet eighth notes played with a crisp *leggiero* touch.

The third statement of the theme is longer than the previous one, but not as complete as the opening statement. There are many changes of line and ornamentation. This section is a superb example of Mozart's ability to extensively decorate a melody without smothering it.

In H, the music is interrupted at m.143 by the laborious *cadenza* discussed in the opening paragraphs of this section. If one chooses to include this *cadenza*, mm.143-151 must be shaped with considerable imagination if the repetitions are not to seem redundant. Exaggerated seriousness at the beginning of the canon at m.152 can sound like parody. Pedaling may be used there on each quarter-note beat. A supple RH must allow the uppermost line to sing out, with the difficult alto line subdued. The organistic writing is clearer and more manageable if the half notes are not played *legato*.

In m.170 of H (m.143 in FV), the return to the tonic key is cheerful, not too delicate. It is probably advisable to save the UC pedal for the final four measures. The ornament in H at m.184 (missing at m.157 in FV) is best omitted. If the pianist carefully observes the rests in the last measures and keeps his fingers, especially the thumb, close to the keys, he will be able to play the difficult *diminuendo* to *pianissimo*, an unexpected ending to a unique piece.

6 ORNAMENTATION IN THE RONDO, K.494

m.

29   The onbeat *appoggiatura* could become a slightly prolonged sixteenth note, "robbing time" from the three subsequent notes.

45   This onbeat *appoggiatura* can be played very lightly and quickly.

51   Here we have a fascinating example of rhetorical ornamentation, with two types of arpeggiation being indicated. Though some pianists will be inclined to put the pedal down and simply

enjoy the drama of these fateful chords, the notation, incorrect in some editions, gives us much to contemplate. In the LH, both D's should be written as half notes, the two middle notes as quarter notes. In Mozart's time this was a clear indication that the chord had to be arpeggiated, with all the notes held. The notation in the upper staff indicates a very different effect, with only the uppermost note sounding at the end of the *arpeggio*. Both *arpeggi* can begin simultaneously and are very quick.

98   It is not easy to fit this *appoggiatura* into the solemn line. It should be played very lightly before the sixth eighth-note beat.

112 Though in a different context, this *appoggiatura* is like that in m.98.

115 The *appoggiatura* should sound on the second quarter-note beat but is not stressed.

125 This *appoggiatura* and that in m.127 form suspensions, which become more eloquent if slightly separated from the following unslurred tones.

138 The turn consists of five, not four notes, and ends on the first beat.

145 (in the H version) A five-note turn is possible only if the pianist has very quick fingers and a relaxed arm. The ornament begins before the second eighth-note beat. A three-note trill would seem banal here.

178 (m.151 in FV) This turn adds little character to the line and spoils the charm of the turn in m.180.

184 (only in H) Given the register and the gentle dynamics, this turn is best omitted.

Additional ornamentation in this piece seems redundant.

THE A MINOR RONDO, K.511

COMPOSITION DATE	March 1787
FORM	rondo
APPROXIMATE TEMPO	♪= M.M. 112
DURATION	10 minutes
SUGGESTED LISTENING	Piano Sonata, K.310 ii
	Die Zauberflöte: Pamina's aria "Ach ich fühl's"
	Piano Concerto, K.488 ii

7 INTERPRETATION OF THE A MINOR RONDO, K.511

When Mozart returned from Prague early in 1787, he was shocked to hear that Count August von Hatzfeld had died. Von Hatzfeld was one of Mozart's closest friends and an accomplished violinist who often played for the composer. A commentator writing in a Hamburg music journal wrote that von Hatzfeld:

"became so intimate with the composer's spirit that the latter became almost disinclined to hear his [quartets] from anyone else. Some two months before his death I heard him deliver them with an accuracy and fervor which excited the admiration of every connoisseur and enchanted the hearts of all..." [15]

The death of this friend, the same age as himself, affected Mozart deeply. Several months later, he referred to this loss in a famous letter to Leopold.[16] The A minor Rondo is a rare instance of a personal event in Mozart's life motivating a composition. A possible model for the piece may have been the Rondo in A minor composed by C.P.E. Bach "in his initial grief at the death of his son." [17]

Mozart rarely included as much interpretive detail as in this rondo. Each reappearance of the theme is treated differently, yet a subtle web of motivic relationships unifies the entire work. As in the A minor Sonata, K.310, Mozart's expression seems to anticipate the nineteenth century, but if the player of the rondo takes an overly "romantic" approach he will violate the depth and range of the piece. Stylistically and emotionally this is one of the most challenging Mozart compositions for the piano.

In the theme the tension between the hands is almost schizophrenic, the bass monotonous, more a ghostly waltz than a serious *siciliano*. Above it a melody heavy with morbid chromaticism strives wearily upwards only to slide basswards, exhausted, at the end of each phrase. The rhythm sounding under all this pain seems merciless, remote. William Kinderman observed that this theme:

"whose fervent character is later intensified through elaborate melodic variations, is enclosed within an absolutely objective framework on which it is wholly dependent and from which it cannot escape." [18]

When choosing a tempo it is helpful to imagine one, not two impulses in each measure. This prevents the tempo from dragging and also reduces any excessive emphasis of dance rhythm. Frequently the second main beats are played too heavily. Rushing during *crescendi* and dawdling in *dimuendi* trivializes the tragic vulnerability of the theme. Too much lingering at the end of a phrase can result in "automatic pilot" expressivity, which becomes almost comical.

Similarly, generalized *legato* and pedaling reduce this tragic theme to mere melancholy. The very first RH note may be pedaled, but preferably not slurred to the subsequent ornament. Nor should the upbeat eighth notes before mm.2,4,6,8 and 9 be bound by the fingers to the subsequent first beats. Mozart indicates slurs over the bar-lines only at moments of increased energy or tension (mm.10-11,11-12,14-15). The pedaling is subtle, changing with each gasping rest and with each melodic eighth note. Discretion is also required in interpreting the abundant dynamic indications. The *piano* of mm.3-4 is somewhat fuller than that in mm.7-8, and the *forte* in mm.10-11 should not sound rough. The *crescendo* in mm.17-18 is surely stronger than that in mm.13-14.

Despite its troubled message, the theme has a curiously symmetrical form. There is somewhat less pain in the central C major sentence, but little relief, with the aching repeated notes, persistent rests and dogmatic bass maintaining the tension. The theme's final eight measures are a variant of the first sentence, intensified by even more dissonance.

The first episode, the "B" section, begins at m.30 with the same motif that opened the main theme. The polyphonic writing here is suggestive of string quartet textures, difficult for the pianist whose wrists are not supple. The melody continues in m.32 with a wistful descending line that seems both new and familiar. Beginning on a long C this theme comes to rest on the first beat of m.33; it is an inverted, less chromatic variant of the main theme's second motif, the ascending chromatic figuration of mm.1-3, which also spans a fifth. As in the theme, the dynamic indications need careful gradation. Obviously the *crescendo* in m.31 is less strong than that in m.35. The LH has expressive "cello" lines, very different from the main theme's haunted bass. Pedaling is possible on each eighth-note beat where the "second violin" line moves triadically, but during diatonic figurations, as in m.31, there should be a minimum of pedaling. The tone can be quite powerful during the tortured sentence in minor mode that begins with the upbeat to m.42, the pedal changed with each eighth-note beat.

The startling lurch to D-flat major at m.46 must not be anticipated during the previous measure. Here too a very relaxed hand and wrist are needed to play the "second violin" line with enough discretion. It is much easier when the LH thumb plays the final sixteenth note of each group. There is little respite in this placid key, as the music begins creeping chromatically upwards, reminding us of the initial theme. At m.49 there is another surprise. The first violin line has a slithering chromatic figure of six tones heard against the suspensions played by lower instruments. Chromaticism and suspensions were the main ingredients of the principal theme, and it is chilling to encounter them here too. These subtle string quartet textures are blurred if the pianist is careless about the rests or pedaling. The entire episode is easier to shape if the player does not sit too close to the keyboard, as the arms must be able to move freely to recreate this active "orchestration."

If the climax at m.59 is full-toned, that in m.63 is even stronger. During the subsequent sequence, the pedal should be changed on each eighth-note beat. On modern instruments, the pianist must avoid pounding the bass octaves, but the RH should be played with much energy. The frequently heard lingering before the first beats during this dramatic outburst at mm.64-68 is a mannered effect, not at all "expressive." The long chromatic notes of mm.69-75 remind us again of the chromaticism at the beginning of the piece. The bass slurs are eloquent, creating jagged sobbing figures. In mm.74-80 the music seems to become paralyzed in a dominant preparation for the theme, which finally returns in m.81.

This second appearance of the principal theme sounds even more decimated. It is now stripped of its C major sentence and repetition. The sobbing syncopations of mm.86-87 evoke the world of *opera seria*. This is a type of written *rubato* that needs no underlining by rushing or slowing down in the bass line. However, the rest in m.88 can be considerably lengthened to prepare the listener for the following surprise.

Some musicologists suggest that the idyllic A major theme beginning at m.89 resembles a melody in Gluck's *Orfeo e Euridice*. Gluck's theme occurs in an aria marked *lento e grazioso*, a description equally applicable to this section of the rondo. In that aria, Amor exhorts Orfeo to find strength for his coming trials. It is not known if Mozart was making a conscious quotation here, but recalling Mozart's reflections in the letter to Leopold (see section 1, p.263), Calzabigi's text in this aria is certainly in the same spirit as Mozart's letter:

"to perform with joy what the gods wish,
to bow deeply before them,
and to suffer in silence.
That is what makes a man happy."[19]

The Elysian calm of this music should not be disturbed by wedged tones played too *staccato*. Similarly the *piano* and *forte* contrasts should not be violent.

This brief respite fades into chromaticism and restless figures that express both hope and frustration. In all the swirling triplets of mm.93-96, the RH wrist should remain supple, the fingers as close to the keys as possible. At m.98 the music suddenly sinks into an exhausted B minor. This grim key is barely established when there is a fleetingly hopeful shift to D major in m.101. None of the rests in this astonishing passage must be swallowed up by pedaling. The Gluckian theme returns at m.104, with poignant ornamentation. At m.112 the nervous figuration first heard in m.94 reappears in an obsessive nightmarish sequence churning in the bass. The LH *staccati* are not technically comfortable on a heavy instrument; the player's thumb and wrist must be as relaxed as possible. Exaggerating the shortness of these notes will bring Verdi's martial trombone barrages to mind. A tense sequence passes from A major through F-sharp minor and D major before erupting in a wild chromatic scale.

The listener seems to lose any sense of harmonic focus at the astonishingly modern *piano subito* of m.116. The bass figure of four descending notes reminds us of the ascending chromatic figure from mm.1-2. This leads to another sequence consisting mainly of grinding diminished seventh harmonies. The dominant of A minor is reached at m.122, but this is blasted by angry chromatic surges in the bass and wailing suspensions in the RH. The stress elements of the main theme have triumphed. All this harmonic and thematic conflict can be supported by pedaling, if the pedal is changed on each eighth-note beat. All the activity of mm.116-126 needs a full sound excepting two shuddering *piani subiti*.

At m.124, the dominant harmony is reaffirmed. Pedaling is relevant, again with clear changes on every eighth-note beat. In the figure that heaves laboriously upward in mm.125-126, the slurs indicate that the first note of each eighth-note beat should be slightly accented, whereas from the second half of m.126 until m.129, a chilling *legato* line, there is no accentuation. If the *diminuendo* in m.127 is begun too soon, the ebbing of energy that leads to the third "A" section sounds unmotivated.

Beginning at m.129 the initial theme returns in its original form, but with elaborate ornamentation that sounds more tortured than decorative. Measure 155, for example, should be played with a sense of fatality, without a trace of a *crescendo*. The repeated A's and chromaticism of mm.155-157 evoke the lamentations of someone almost crazed by grief. The theme cadences in m.158, but during the four subsequent measures tries fitfully to reach upwards. The harmonies and the polyphony here could have been written by an Expressionist a century later.

Some authorities maintain that the second LH third in m.161 should be F-sharp and A, creating a logical parallel movement with the melody, but in the manuscript,[20] A and C are clearly indicated. Surely this version is more pained than the smoother parallel movement of voices? The separations between the exhausted slurs of these measures may be pedaled, but the fingers should leave the keys at the end of each slur of this harrowing recitative.

The *Coda* is a heartbreaking recapitulation of the divergent emotions we have experienced throughout this drama; all the motifs return in a grim setting, rather like a family at a funeral. The first six measures heave with angry frustration, collapsing at m.169 into despondency. In such a highly emotional atmosphere it is easy to become careless about details, but the music retains its tragic tone only when the articulation remains accurate, the pedal changed on each eighth-note beat, the unslurred eighth notes not sounding *legato*.

The tonic harmony reached at m.173 seems doomed. In the final sentence at mm.177-181 we hear a premonition of Don Giovanni's demise. Yet again Mozart's structural cunning astonishes; the LH tolling B-flats, and G-sharps trying to pull away from the tonic remind us of the motif we noticed previously at mm.69-70 and 159-160.

Some pianists prefer to play the B-flats with the RH. After all this anguish, only a whispered formal cadence is possible. Artists like Artur Schnabel and Rudolf Serkin found the bass chord on the first beat of m.181 too bare and added a C between the two LH A's, a poignant, aesthetic effect. But by 1787, Mozart certainly did not shun austere sounds. Catastrophe does not sound aesthetic; those three hollow A's are suitably eerie. The final dominant chord must not last longer than an eighth-note beat, the tonic not longer than a quarter-note beat. R.D. Levin eloquently expressed the special atmosphere of this masterpiece:

> "More than any other work it seems forlorn, dejected; its fundamental bleakness drags against the articulateness of the ornamentation, which struggles with increasing intensity against a manifestly hopeless fate."[21]

8 ORNAMENTATION IN THE RONDO, K.511

m.

1   Let us describe the initial ornament, more a compound *appoggiatura* than a turn, as a turn, for the sake of brevity. This is one of the most debated ornaments in the entire piano repertoire. As it has such an important motivic function in the piece, serious thought must be given to its interpretation. One usually hears the ornament ending on the first beat. Even the perceptive Neumann observed that:

"a characteristic design like the *siciliano* rhythm of the A minor Rondo ... will be unreceptive to the intrusion of an onbeat turn. The exact metrical placement of the ornament, which is repeated many times, might occasionally be varied slightly, but basically it ought to have prebeat character and always be unaccented." [22]

Conversely it could be argued that when the ornament ends on the beat, the dance cadence becomes more pronounced, and this could undermine the deeply emotional theme. It is also possible to start the turn before the first beat and complete it after the beat. Context is more important than theory. Certainly the ornament does not have to be played in the same way at each reappearance. As an upbeat to the more cheerful m.9, a prebeat interpretation seems more appropriate. When the turn reappears twice in the emotionally ambivalent context of mm.22-23, the issue is less clear. As an upbeat to m.22, the thrust of the diatonic line is most important and a light prebeat reading seems desirable, whereas a measure later, the ornament could be played in the same manner as it was at the opening of the piece, around the barline. Another disadvantage of the prebeat reading is that most pianists delay the first beat, a type of *rubato* more associated with romantic composers than with Mozart. How this ornament is used when it takes on other functions later in the piece, will be discussed below.

7   The principal note of the slow, melancholy turn is obviously strongest.

10   It is best to play this turn as soon as possible after the second eighth-note beat. According to most authorities, the trill in the second half of this measure should begin on the upper auxiliary, but this sounds academic if not played before the beat.

Because the trill itself creates more tone, the indicated *forte* is perhaps more applicable to the first half of m.11.

13   This nostalgic turn could begin on or after the fifth eighth-note beat and is not included in a *crescendo*. The *crescendo* indication in some editions is premature; in the manuscript it is placed just before the bar-line of mm.13-14.

14   The turn sounds most expressive if the upper auxiliary is played as soon as possible after the fourth eighth-note beat, with no exaggeration of the *crescendo*.

17   Like all the turns in this theme, this has to be played with a loose arm and very sensitive fingertips. It is best begun as soon as possible.

20   Such a cadential trill is usually begun with the upper auxiliary, but here it is also possible to begin with the lower auxiliary, unaccented but slightly elongated.

27   These rapid turns are practically always begun on the upper auxiliary note. Five-note turns beginning on the principal note sound too active in this soulful context.

31   As noted above, this compound *appoggiatura* may resemble the ornament at the opening of the piece but has a totally different thematic and harmonic direction. Here a slight prolongation of the upbeat seems relevant, with the ornament ending on the first beat of m.31.

42   If the player prefers to emphasize tautness of rhythm here, it is best to play the ornaments ending on the beat. I prefer to begin them on the beat and very quickly, thus accentuating the dissonant tensions pulling against the bass line.

54   Mozart did indicate *crescendo* in the "viola" line and a "cello" *forte* in m.53, but the *Urtext* editions place the *piano* in m.54, not in the upbeat to that measure. In the manuscript, the upper line's *piano* is clearly marked before the ornament. The *piano* in the upper line and the *diminuendo* implied in the bass line call for slight slowing down in m.53, the ornament ending on the first beat of m.54.

81   See m.54.

89   This turn begins on the principal note and must be played with a very smooth *legato*. The rather archaic elegance of this motif will be lost if the lower notes of the chords are not sensitively balanced and the upper voice's sixteenth note detached.

92   The turn should be leisurely.

98   Here we have a fascinating dilemma! As Neumann observed,

"Had Mozart wanted this turn started on the beat, surely he would have doubled the turn in thirds."[23] The Badura Skodas[24] also found an onbeat rendition too academic. Yet I am convinced that a prebeat rendition is too cheerful and dance like for this context. The dissonances arising from an onbeat rendition seem highly appropriate at this agonized moment.

134 The *Kettentriller* should not be rattled off with mechanical evenness. Each trill begins with the principal note, onbeat but never accented. Some editions suggest that the trills begin on the upper auxiliary, but this would seriously confuse the line.

148 This trill is best begun on the upper auxiliary. The *crescendo* should not be too vigorous.

150 The duration of this mournful onbeat *appoggiatura* is very subjective, but it certainly should not be too short.

152 These turns are like those in m.27.

156 The turns here and in the next measure are also usually played beginning on the upper auxiliary, but this convenient rendition nullifies the weary repetitions that make the chromatic melodic line so tragic. Five-note turns have a much stronger effect in this rhetorical context and are not difficult if the thumb is relaxed. A slight broadening of tempo here is appropriate, given the recitative-like character of the next six measures.

168 In the manuscript the notation of this high line is unclear. It is surprising that none of the *Urtext* editions have included the *portato* wedges above the A and B after the trill, which give the line a terrible wailing quality. The trill itself should not have more than three notes.

169 In the bass line, beginning the theme's initial ornament on the beat would sound lopsided. But elsewhere in the *Coda* the first two notes of the turn could be played before the beat.

It is hardly necessary to observe that with so much detailed ornamentation by the composer, adding more would be tasteless. None of the ornaments here are mere decorations; all function to heighten or vary the emotion of that phrase. In such a subjective masterwork not every reader will agree with every opinion stated above, but I am convinced that confusions regarding ornamentation have contributed to the rondo's reputation of being "difficult" and "elusive." Yet this stirring and subtle piece always casts a spell when played by a pianist who has studied it with patience and imagination.

XVII

SONATAS IN F, K.533, AND C, 545

SONATA IN F MAJOR, K.533

COMPOSITION DATE	January 1788
TOTAL DURATION	18 min. (i & ii with exposition repeats) iii (Rondo) is discussed in Chapter XVI.
FIRST MOVEMENT	*Allegro*
FORM	sonata
APPROXIMATE TEMPO	♩ = M.M. 82
DURATION	9 minutes (with first repeat),
SUGGESTED LISTENING	Symphony, K.551, "Jupiter" iv
	Piano Concerto, K.459 i
	Piano Concerto, K.537 i
	Piano Trio, K.542 iii
	Die Zauberflöte: Overture

1 INTERPRETATION OF THE FIRST MOVEMENT, K.533

In 1788, the first piece Mozart listed in his thematic catalogue was this *Allegro* and *Andante* for piano. Since the C minor Sonata of 1784, he had not written in sonata form for piano solo. Both movements rank among Mozart's finest creations for the piano, and it is baffling that so many pianists shy away from this astonishing music.

What intimidates them? Is it the quandary of the finale, the Rondo, K.494, which seems to be in a different style from the first two movements? It was written earlier, then revised and added by Mozart in 1788 to the *Allegro and Andante*, as a three movement sonata was more suitable for publication. The pianist can choose to play K.533 with the Rondo, K.494, or, as I prefer, to play K.533 without the Rondo. The latter piece can perhaps best be played on its own in its original form. This important, subjective issue is discussed in Chapter XVI, section 5. The Rondo itself is also discussed in that chapter.

That K.533 is rarely performed may be largely due to its subtlety, for Mozart seems to exult here in ingenious motivic games and cunning polyphony, which present considerable challenges to the player. The piece is impossible for any pianist with a stiff technique. Aside from formal and technical challenges, the lack of dynamic indications troubles many. László Somfai rightly commented that Mozart:

> "saw the dynamics of these two movements as of secondary importance, since they call mainly for merely natural nuances of performance."[1]

However, not all pianists find it easy to discover "natural nuances" in music that is both mercurial and complex.

The opening theme may sound innocuous, but it creates manifold possibilities for polyphonic development later. The first ten notes cling together within the tight range of a sixth. This figuration (Motif A) is promptly answered by an octave leap (Motif B). The theme then turns in on itself with a repetition of A. In mm.5-8 the music seems to take wing with thrusting scale-like patterns (Motif C), but the activity soon reaches a cadence in mm.7-8. The little three-note groups (Motif D) heard in both hands at mm.16-18 delight in temporary freedom from the tautness of the first theme.

The texture at the opening unmistakably evokes a violin, viola and cello. The first wedged note is the violin's upbeat, light and detached. Similarly the wedge above the half note in m.2, not found in all editions, indicates slight separation from the subsequent eighth notes, not a thudding accent. During the entire first thematic group, no pedaling is necessary. A sentimental *ritenuto* at the cadence in m.18 would be regrettable, though the final rest could be slightly prolonged.

Mozart introduces numerous versions of Motif C, in mm.24-26 combined with Motif D. The ensuing polyphony is easier to play if the LH thumb takes the B-flats in mm.28 and 30. There is a sense of suspended animation until a canon based on the opening theme begins in the last quarter-note beat of m.32. In mm.37-39 the contrapuntal acrobatics give way to assertive repetitions, which are more intense if the RH makes clear separations before each half measure. The rhetorical measures, 39-40, are surely full toned, though the final chord in m.41 should not be heavy.

At m.42 the bubbly descending triplets at the beginning of the second thematic group recall both the RH figure at m.19 and the bass line heard at mm.37-39. The RH replies with an ascending series of capricious turns, breaking off in a leap that resembles m.2. These gamboling patterns presumably remain quite light in tone, without overt changes in sound levels. The accents on some half notes presumably indicate that these notes are stronger than the upbeat quarter notes. In mm.53-65 the lines become more expansive, with a witty duality of major and minor modes. Where the first beat has quarter notes in both hands, it could be pedaled to the second beat, but for the rest, pedaling during this theme confuses the bustling scene, which builds to a humorous climax at m.65.

The rather tongue-in-cheek "cello" solo beginning in m.66 seems familiar because it is derived from the RH line of mm.43-44. It too folds into another cadence at m.70 (pianistically a particularly difficult moment, discussed in the next section). It must be presumed that both upper voices in mm.70-71 and in mm.74-75 are to be played with a light *staccato*; Mozart very rarely indicates different touches between two parallel voices or parts. Starting at m.72, our imaginary violinist and violist play a canonic duet, which ends most unexpectedly at m.78. This ambiguous D minor seems questioning.

In mm.79-81 we hear nervous chromaticized variants of Motif A, which predict late romanticism. During the subsequent concerto-like passages, harmonic stability is achieved only in m.89 where the dominant key finally triumphs. Throughout all this activity the RH is so prominent that there is a danger that the bass will not be shaped with enough harmonic alertness.

The concluding scale passages of the second theme group are more playful than dramatic. A lively *non legato* is desirable and, even on dry instruments, pedaling would thicken the texture both here and in the RH triadic figures of the *Codetta* beginning at m.89.

Surely the exposition of what may be the most intricate of all Mozart's piano sonata first movements must be repeated before one proceeds to the development?

The relentless activity of the development section is almost feverish. In the first four measures, Motif A in the RH is cunningly combined with the *Codetta*'s triadic pattern in the LH. The figure of three quarter notes (upbeat and suspension) seems new but was anticipated by the cadences at mm.17-18 and 25-26. This figuration becomes the weighty element in a whirl of activity provided by the *Codetta*'s triadic figures, which predominate until m.125. C minor passes through fatalistic G minor to dangerous D minor before stabilizing in ten measures of dominant seventh harmony.

Throughout the entire section pedaling is unnecessary. Despite all the formal and technical challenges, the player must remain aware of the harmonic shapes and have a clear conception of the "orchestration." From m.125 accents in both staffs indicate that the first beats are often the lightest, but as the dynamic level is not high, any emphases should not be coarse. From m.133 the tone is positive and sunny, not loud.

In the recapitulation, beginning at m.145, Mozart gives the first theme group a considerably more serious character, with a shift at mm.154-168 to the somber key of F minor, where the player must shape the LH figurations with care. During the quarter notes (*legato* or *non legato?*) of mm.161-163, the motivic impulses begin on the fourth, not the first quarter-note beat. From m.156 full tone prevails, and sudden changes of sound levels before the second theme's return at m.168 would create an atmosphere of false theatricality.

A major surprise in the recapitulation is the blossoming of the sequence first heard at mm.78-81 in mm.211-218, a fascinating blend of baroque polyphony with quasi-Wagnerian harmony. The LH line gives a clear profile to this sequence, with slight breaths before m.215 and the third quarter-note beat of m.217. In the rest of the movement there are no more surprises. The conclusion, extending to the highest note on the keyboards of Mozart's time, is even more festive than the exposition.

Though this life-affirming *Allegro* should not sound complicated, the musical and technical demands require immense concentration and imagination. When approaching this music, the player will need some time to distinguish the forest from the trees, but when he achieves a clear view of the landscape the sight is magnificent.

2 ORNAMENTATION IN THE FIRST MOVEMENT, K.533

m.

7 The *appoggiatura* becomes a light and quick grace note. Playing it on the beat creates a heavy effect.

21 The turn will sound most expressive if begun with the upper auxiliary on or just after the third quarter-note beat. The hand must be very relaxed here, otherwise the result will sound like typing. The E in the "second violin part," a touch added on the fourth quarter-note beat in the first complete edition and suggested in some contemporary editions, can be omitted.

43 In such a spirited tempo, three notes before the termination are sufficient.

47 These trills are to be played like those in m.43, for the line would become obscured by beginning the trills on the upper auxiliary.

MOZART AND THE PIANIST

69 Often causing fumbles or delays, this trill is not difficult if played as three notes plus the termination. Beginning with the second finger helps, but the ornament sounds more supple if the RH plays both lines of detached quarter notes until the second beat of m.71. This gives the LH enough time to change on its "pedal note" from the thumb to the fifth finger.

76 The turn begins immediately after the initial F, with the notated eighth note G somewhat shortened.

88 Such an energetic cadential trill can begin with the upper onbeat auxiliary note and terminates on the last eighth-note beat.

113 The trill is usually played with three notes before the termination. An energetic grace note B-flat before the trill arguably gives it more thrust and reduces the octave formation with the bass.

Obviously such exactly conceived music needs no more ornamentation. It is possible to arpeggiate certain bass chords, in mm.22, 40, 86-87, 167, 223-224.

SECOND MOVEMENT	*Andante*
FORM	sonata
APPROXIMATE TEMPO	♩ = M.M. 63
DURATION	9 minutes, with exposition repeat
SUGGESTED LISTENING	Clarinet Quintet, K.581 ii
	Rondo for Piano, K.511
	Symphony, K.550 ii

3 INTERPRETATION OF THE SECOND MOVEMENT, K.533

After the heady delights of the *Allegro*, the pianist must immediately adjust to a totally different sphere. In some respects, this may be the most challenging slow movement of all the piano sonatas. On first hearing, it is difficult to believe that some of these sounds were created in the eighteenth century. How did the ears of Mozart's contemporaries perceive this strange music? Not only are the harmonies daring; the emotional range is extraordinarily broad and volatile, changing in an instant from purest optimism to deepest despair.

The basic tempo is relative; at certain moments, a swifter or slower pulse may be desirable. Anyone capable of playing the entire movement with a single metronomic beat must have a heart of stone! The *Andante* needs an open sound, though communicative tone should not be confused with a muddy texture in which the shorter notes get smothered in a thick sauce of pedaling.

The opening sentence should evoke two violinists and a violist, playing at their best. The middle voice in m.2 is also *legato*. Some editions have a *sforzando* on the first beat of the second measure; this is spurious and does not appear in the NMA.[2] Measures 2 and 3 require more tone than mm.1 or 4, but overt accents disturb the contemplative character of the theme.

The continuing sentence is more expansive. To shape the ascending sixths and thirds, the RH movements should be more horizontal than vertical, especially in mm.8-9, where pumping motions splinter the line. The lack of dynamic indications in the theme offers interesting choices; are mm.8-9 stronger or more subdued than the variant in mm.18-19?

At m.23 the opening theme returns in the bass, heard against ominous, snake-like chromatic RH lines. This sequence builds in tension until m.28, which could be played as a climax or as a depleted *piano subito*. Throughout the sequence of mm.28-30 it is best, certainly on modern instruments, if the pedal is only half depressed and changed on each quarter- or eighth-note beat. Holding the pedal through the entire measure here sounds inappropriately Lisztian.

All the harmonic turbulence disappears in m.33, where a new, wistful F major theme is heard. However, it is soon caught in a series of chromaticized repetitions, which cannot escape the fatalistic pull of the first beat suspensions. The tempo must remain utterly stable, with no romantic *rubato*, and the sound clear, with the pedal changed on each eighth-note beat. Detaching of the LH eighth notes here would create a curious hobby-horse effect. After the climax in mm.39-40 the remaining measures should not sound hectic; the constant swinging between major and minor modes generates enough inner tension. Gasping *Weltschmerz* is irrelevant. Given the exceptional diversity of themes, repetition of the exposition is essential.

Edward Lowinsky astutely observed of this movement that:

"each consequent phrase within each group exceeds the preceding one, while the phrase groupings grow in length ... but with the instinct of a sleepwalker Mozart restores the balance by matching assymetrical phrases in a symmetrical manner. The development is shaped in two groups of 13 measures."[3]

Repetition makes the lurch to the development even stronger. The optimism has been obliterated by D minor, the most striking key of *Don Giovanni*, which was written in the same year as this piece. The initial four-note motif reappears, now in grim bass octaves. The RH's tense, wriggling line may be derived from m.34 but is barely recognizable here. Each series of writhing triplets is crushed by the other hand's remorseless octaves. This is a glimpse into an abyss. Conventional aesthetics are far away.

Obviously not all stages of the sequence ending in m.59 require the same tone, but anything less than a *mezzo forte* in this grim conflict seems misplaced. The triplets must not rush in their descent but seem to pull against the grave weight of the octaves, which are to be played as *tenuto* as possible. The power of this strife ends abruptly in m.59, which should on no account be preceded by a debilitating *diminuendo*. During the triplets of these terrible measures, the pedal, if used, must be very clearly changed on each eighth-note beat.

After what is arguably the most emotionally fraught sentence in all of Mozart's piano music, the response may be the most enigmatic statement to be found in any of these works. The grinding dissonances and slithering chromatic figures of the long sequence beginning in m.59 bring Schönberg's early compositions to mind. Yet the material is not entirely new. The LH pattern of a descending third followed by four ascending diatonic notes was first heard in the sixths of mm.4-5. In the last quarter-note beat of m.62, Mozart ingeniously and abruptly inverts the sequence between the hands. Any relief provided by the RH doubling in thirds is erased by the sour LH minor third stretching up to a minor seventh. As there seems to be more foreboding here than activity, it is probably advisable to play this unearthly passage, mm.59-64, without overt *crescendi*. The tension beginning in m.68 becomes inexorable, but the actual quantity of sound remains a totally subjective issue. Certainly not all these laborious ascending progressions should be shaped with the same intensity of tone.

The sequences of mm.59-72 are more interrogatory than declamatory. Though Dennerlein referred to the entire section as "a passage of enormous violence,"[4] surely the violence is more evident in the first half of the development section than in the second. It is almost with disbelief that we come to rest at the dominant seventh of B-flat in m.71. The unusually wide *arpeggio*, extending over virtually the whole keyboard of Mozart's time, is an expansive line, not a mere harmonic element. It is best played without pedaling and not too gently. But even the conclusion of this extraordinary section leaves room for differing interpretations.

In the recapitulation, the initial ten measures are not changed. In m.83 there is an eerie lurch to minor mode. On a modern instrument, the spaghetti-junction of ornaments at m.85 (see following section) sounds horribly confused if played too assertively. In m.116 the turns begin with an almost grotesque cheerfulness and should be played lightly, though not with the frequently heard halving of tempo. Echoes of the writhing triplets of m.36 and the solemn line of m.39 lead us back to the tonic key. On virtually all instruments the *una corda* pedal is welcome during the final measures. The wedged triplets require unpedaled *portato*, not an assertive *staccato*.

At the end of this movement we sense we have been taken to far reaches of human experience. We are wiser for the voyage. Perhaps the composer too felt that nothing could follow this movement, as he entered the *Allegro and Andante*, K.533 into his own catalogue as a completed work. As stated elsewhere, the Rondo, K.494, was added as a finale only when the pieces were published as a three movement sonata. I am convinced that the Rondo is best played on its own, in its original version. Discussion of that piece is to be found in Chapter XVI.

4 ORNAMENTATION IN THE SECOND MOVEMENT, K.533

m.

3   The repetition of the main melodic note on the first beat seems most important, therefore the compound *appoggiatura* ends on the first beat. It is arguable that, as in the opening to the A minor Rondo, K.511 (see Chapter XVI, section 8), the ornament could "float" over the bar-line, with the bass played with the second or third *appoggiatura* notes.

4   The first editions give confusing notations of the ornament on the second eighth-note beat. The Badura Skodas[5] recommend that this trill be played without a termination. Given the line and close counterpoint, this seems advisable.

40   With such rapid notes surrounding it, the turn can best begin on the upper auxiliary immediately after the third quarter-note beat.

42   Playing this *appoggiatura* simultaneously with the LH on the first beat would create a ludicrous yodeling effect.

56   Some editions have trills indicated on the second quarter-note beats of mm.56 and 58. The NMA editors[6] rejected these as spurious.

85   The compound *appoggiatura* in the bass is a repetition of m.3, but in this busy context it is better that the ornament ends on

the first beat. If the LH thumb takes the middle-voice E-flat, the polyphony is easier to shape. The RH turn on the second eighth-note beat is clearer if begun on the principal note but played extremely lightly. The subsequent *appoggiatura* falls on the second quarter-note beat and is more expressive as a dotted sixteenth note than as a very quick changing note.

91 This *appoggiatura* must sound before the first beat.

116 There is little time to perform the first two turns gracefully, but that is no reason to begin them on the upper auxiliary, a practice that obscures the line. They must be played very lightly, which is easier if each turn begins with the second finger. The third turn, as noted in the previous section, is part of a *crescendo* and can be played quite slowly with vocal breadth.

119 The turn is like the last ornament in m.116.

This movement is not only highly original, but also rich in ornamentation. Any additional decorating seems utterly irrelevant. The bass chords in mm.28-30, 96-98 gain character if arpeggiated energetically; a leisurely arpeggiation would prettify what is surely meant to terrify.

SONATA IN C MAJOR, K.545

COMPOSITION DATE	June 1788
TOTAL DURATION	10 minutes (with first repeats in i, iii)

FIRST MOVEMENT	*Allegro*
FORM	sonata
APPROXIMATE TEMPO	$\downarrow$ = M.M. 66
DURATION	+4 minutes with both repeats
SUGGESTED LISTENING	Piano Trio, K.548 i
	Piano Concerto, K.415 i
	Ein musikalischer Spass, K.522 i
	Four-hand Sonata, K.521 i

5 INTERPRETATION OF THE FIRST MOVEMENT, K.545

For Mozart, the year 1788 was fraught with problems, beginning with the bad reception of *Don Giovanni* at its premiere in May. But on

June 16, Mozart entered in his thematic catalogue the joyous E-flat Symphony, K.543, and his best known piece for piano solo, the *Little Piano Sonata for Beginners* (a title given by the publisher in 1805), K.545.

The following day the Mozarts moved yet again, this time to a modest suburb. The composer's financial worries were becoming serious, the debts to his fellow Freemason, Michael Puchberg, steadily increasing. On June 27, Mozart wrote his creditor a heart rending letter:

> "If you, my most worthy brother, do not help me in this predicament, I shall lose my honour and my credit, which of all things I wish to preserve ... Do come and see me. I am always at home. During the ten days since I came to live here I have done more work than in two months in my former quarters, and if such black thoughts did not come to me so often, thoughts which I banish by a tremendous effort, things would be even better..." [7]

Despite these problems Mozart completed two more of his most famous symphonies, K.550 and 551, during this troubled summer. The motivation for the C major Piano Sonata, K.545, remains unclear. The piece may seem to be obvious teaching material, but it is unlikely Mozart had any piano students at the time of its composition. The harmonic simplicity and lack of polyphony certainly suggest that the sonata may have been intended for a young child. When the piece was first published in 1805, it was labeled *sonata facile*, and this misleading description "easy" has misled many a student or teacher. Though it is technically the most straightforward of Mozart's piano sonatas, K.545 is easier to sight-read than to play well. The sonatinas of Clementi and Kuhlau, which seem more complicated, are generally easier to present with conviction.

Mozart did not make one dynamic marking in the entire sonata; many of the clumsy effects often heard in performance are based on dubious inspirations added by editors and performers during the past two centuries. The dynamic, articulation, fingering, and pedaling indications in so-called pedagogical editions usually obscure the charm of the piece. The student must have the courage and curiosity to study the sonata from an *Urtext* edition.

A fine example of the traditional textual confusions is to be found in the first measure, where the RH's first three tones are not slurred and the quarter notes are best slightly detached and not played with -

equal weight. Excepting the RH slurs in the first half of mm.2,4, the entire first theme is to be played with a bright *non legato* touch, though each note requires a different weight from the note before or after it.

The initial phrase sounds more spirited without finger-pedaling of the bass. Playing the theme with "luscious *legato*" or pedaling robs it of its vitality. Richard Rosenberg[8] observed that the opening theme has a strong resemblance to a sonata in the same key by Johann Gottfried Eckart (1734-1809). Eckart's music was frequently heard in Paris during Mozart's 1778 stay in the French capital.

In the following sequence of scale passages, mechanical blandness or accenting should be absent. The harmonies indicate light first beats. Surely mm.9-12 are playful, not noisy and determined? The RH eighth notes of m.11 can be energetically detached. The cadence creates a comical effect with its "crooked" strong second beat.

At m.13 the second theme is introduced by a bustling second violin or viola figuration often heard in Mozart's quartets or symphonies. The jolly RH theme is an ingenious inversion of the initial four measures. The RH slurring here would suggest that the first two eighth notes are slightly detached from the dotted quarter note, which should not be played too lightly, as it is placed at the beginning of another slur.

The sequence of triadic figures beginning at m.18 is like a coquettish duet between two wind instruments; this effect would be ruined by any trace of pedaling. The delicacy of this writing, with its volatile range of emotional/harmonic changes, is often marred by inattention to note values. If the quarter notes are not played exactly, breathless confusion results.

The climax of the exposition is reached at mm.22-25, which may be full-toned, festive, but not noisy. Again pedaling must be shunned. The vivacity of m.23 is spoiled if the three RH slurred groups are joined to each other. For many fledgling pianists the cadential trill is their first encounter with a "long" trill. Inexplicably some artists, even on recordings, celebrate the end of the trill with a clumsy and illogical bang, perhaps a subconscious memory of childhood wonder at completing the trill with the hands synchronized?

The *Codetta* lasts only three measures. Its violinistic figurations are surely more humorous than vigorous. Pedal strokes, not *legato* pedaling, can enhance the last two chords. The final rest must not be shortened, as it functions as an upbeat to the beginning, or, after the repetition, to the development section. Omitting the repetition suggests an indifferent approach.

The development begins with the *Codetta* figure, now in minor mode. As in the exposition, care must be taken that all the quarter notes following sixteenth notes are not shortened or accented. This sentence has certain resemblances to the development sections in the first movements of two earlier C major Sonatas, K.279 and 309. In Mozart's works, G minor is usually a wild tonality, but here it is not necessary to play roughly. The D minor in m.33 is perhaps stronger. The next sequence of scale-like passages must not seem like an etude but should suggest lively orchestral scoring. There are many possible interpretations of the numerous modulations. The pianist should be encouraged to experiment with various dynamic conceptions. However, overt echo effects should be avoided; they rarely feature in Mozart's music. A *ritenuto* in m.41, though often heard, is a totally artificial effect.

At m.42 it is surprising to hear the opening theme in F major. At first we think this is a "false recapitulation" as in some earlier works, but it soon becomes apparent that this is indeed the beginning of the recapitulation. This structural prank is particularly striking in such a straightforward piece.

With all the changes of register throughout the movement, the pianist's spine must be sufficiently flexible. Sitting fixedly in one position not only blocks free movement of the left arm at certain moments but is hardly suitable body language for such a sparkling piece.

With the childhood Minuets, this movement is among Mozart's most played piano pieces. Though the elementary structure and lack of polyphonic complications make it accessible to young players, the technical demands are not slight. Considerable imagination and vivacity are needed to express the sunny *joie de vivre* of the piece.

6 ORNAMENTATION IN THE FIRST MOVEMENT, K.545

m.

4   The trill may be preceded by the upper auxiliary played as a light grace note. Three notes suffice before the termination, with no accenting of the final note on the third quarter-note beat.

15   To begin the trill on the upper auxiliary sounds fussy. Five notes suffice, as the F-sharp functions as a termination.

22   These *appoggiature* can be played very briskly before the beat but, especially on a fortepiano, it can be an amusing effect to place them on the beat. Playing them as *acciaccature*, simultaneously with the main note, is more a baroque practice. The

duration of the *appoggiature* is subjective, but as eighth notes, they sound soporific.

25   Given the *non legato* context, this cadential trill is best played with the upper auxiliary sounding on the first beat. The trill itself should be as rapid as possible, certainly quicker than the bass notes, with a clear ring in the upper notes. The termination is clearest when played as two sixteenth notes. As already noted, the trill's culmination in the first beat of the next measure, must not be accented.

67   These *appoggiature* arguably sound more comical played on the beat rather than before it.

In a movement of such modest proportions there seem few opportunities for additional ornamentation. The RH chords in mm.57 and 73 will sound fresher if rapidly arpeggiated. Malcolm Bilson[9] and Alexey Lubimov[10] add variants when repeating mm.3-4.

FORM	Rondo
APPROXIMATE TEMPO	♩ = M.M. 63
DURATION	4 minutes (without the repeats)
SUGGESTED LISTENING	*Don Giovanni*: Ottavio's aria "Dalla sua pace"
	Piano Trio, K.542 ii
	Piano Trio, K.548 ii
	String Quartet, K.575 ii

7 INTERPRETATION OF THE SECOND MOVEMENT, K.545

For all its apparent simplicity, this *Andante* presents particular challenges. Like the first movement, it has frequently been savaged by editors adding a wild variety of misleading "improvements." It is absolutely necessary to have an *Urtext* edition of this vulnerable piece, which can easily seem cloying or monotonous.

The atmosphere is quiet, as if someone were calmly recalling the past. The few emotional contrasts should not be exaggerated; any impressions of theatricality break the spell of this wistful monologue. It is essential to maintain a flowing tempo, usually with one, not three, impulses to a measure. However, an impatient approach, like Glenn Gould's,[11] sounds grotesque, his timing of 2 minutes, 19 seconds presumably set the world speed record for this movement!

The LH is restricted to Alberti bass figures, which can easily seem repetitive if played inattentively. Russell Sherman wrote eloquently of Mozart's accompaniments:

> "Yet reason as well as experience dictate that these figures, however impersonal on the surface, are no less part of the discourse, and of an inspiration worthy of that discourse ... deft constructions that support, imitate, or complement the line..."[12]

The RH has shapely lines that bring a violin, sometimes a soprano, to mind. The piano tone is warmer if the fingers are not curled up.

An example of textual confusion can be seen in many old editions, where the first two measures of the RH theme are joined under one slur. Mozart indicated two slurs here, with the last note unslurred. If the fingers gently leave the keys, without any accenting, just before the first and second quarter-note beats of m.2, the result is a phrase that has much more inner life than a single *legato* line. In the subsequent 12 measures, it becomes apparent that the first note of each measure is the fullest in tone, but obviously not always with the same emphasis.

How much pedaling is desirable depends largely on the type of instrument. Certainly on a large modern piano it is best to use as little pedal as possible, with the LH finger-pedaling the lower notes of the bass line, especially when they take on more importance as in mm.14, 38-39, 41-42. That the bass is unslurred throughout does not mean that it is to be played *non legato*; Gould's harpsichordal pluckings of the bass sound sarcastic. Indeed the greatest challenge of the piece is to project the constantly changing relationship of the bass to the melody, for as Anton Ehrenzweig noted:

> "already in the first bar ... the accompaniment grates harshly with the melody by moving with it in three parallel sevenths, which would have been unacceptable in a more flexibly moving accompaniment. Harshness turns into extreme sweetness of sound ... Elsewhere the melody acquires the rhythmical character of the Alberti bass ... or else the bass suddenly frees itself and blossoms into true melody, as happens in the sixth bar..."[13]

On a modern instrument the *staccato* eighth notes in m.5 are better played *portato*. The RH sixteenth notes of m.7 are not easy to shape expressively, but no two consecutive notes should have the same intensity. Slowing down at the quiet cadence in m.8 sounds sentimental.

The following sentence is a variant of the first theme. The RH *staccato* sixteenth notes need not sound stiff if the wrist remains mobile and the palm of the hand sensitive, never far from the keys. The wedge in the second beat of m.13 does not indicate an accent, but that the F-sharp is not joined to the subsequent chromatic notes, creating a welcome, slight syncopation in the melody. The slurs of mm.14-16 clearly indicate which notes are most important and, as in the opening, that the fingers should not join the end of one slur to the beginning of another.

Should the player observe the repetitions of this and the following section? One can hear the purists crying, "Of course! And decorate the repeats as well!" Some pianists and forte pianists cope with this problem by using the *una corda* pedal when playing the repetitions. "Echo effects" of entire themes are rarely appropriate in Mozart. Recordings, even by famous performers, with such effects do not convince me that the practice is justifiable. If both repeats are ignored, a straightforward rondo structure emerges:

Section		
	A	Theme plus variant
	B	mm.17-24 contrasting theme
	A	mm.25-32 repeat of theme variant
	C	mm.33-48 another contrasting theme
	A	mm.49-64 theme plus variant
	Coda	mm.64-74

If the repeats are made one gets a structure that is not only repetitious but also unbalanced. Perhaps the repeat signs indicate demarcations of sections more than actual repetitions. It is interesting to note that such exceptional Mozart players as Lili Kraus[14] and Malcolm Bilson chose to omit both repetitions in their recordings of the sonata. R. Rosenberg[15] also recommends the omission of these repeats.

The "C" section at mm.33-47 is cast in G minor which, for Mozart, usually denotes drama and strife. Excessive *rubato* or too much *una corda* sound can conjure up an inappropriately dreamy atmosphere here. Lili Kraus expresses the melancholy tension of this G minor section beautifully because she does not try to prettify it.

As in the slow movement of K.332, the player could imagine different characters (perhaps two or three sopranos) singing different sentences. Although at moments like mm.29 or 43-47, the RH line can be shaped more freely, the bass must continue flowing metrically. Romantic *rubati*, especially with both hands pausing before first beats or high melodic notes, sound mannered in this piece.

8 ADDITIONAL ORNAMENTATION IN THE SECOND MOVEMENT, K.545

The absence of ornamentation is conspicuous here. It seems unlikely that Mozart intended the movement to be played with unvaried lines throughout. The character and especially the textures of this *Andante* recall the slow movement of the F major Sonata, K.332, to which Mozart added many ornaments before its publication. However, this sonata, K.545, was not published during Mozart's lifetime, so we can only guess at what the composer might have added here.

Ironically enough, these sparse melodic lines do not easily lend themselves to ornamentation. Generally, recording artists have been reluctant to add more than a few innocuous ornaments in this movement. Of course there is a considerable difference between an ornament being added spontaneously during a concert and one that is "immortalized" on a recording. What may seem refreshing in a live performance may become tiresome on repetition. If the player chooses to omit both indicated repeats, there is little necessity to decorate during the first half of the movement. Turns may be welcome in the first quarter-note beats of mm.20 and 36. The line in mm.27-31 seems to call out for some alteration; here Malcolm Bilson is very creative. An octave *appoggiatura* or a triadic arpeggiation before the first beat G in m.51 seems desirable. Alexey Lubimov adds ornaments that are diverting if somewhat unlikely to mm.58-59, 61-62. In m.70 a turn or *appoggiatura* could be added after the second and third quarter-note beats, with a descending figuration before the first beat of m.71.

FORM	Rondo
APPROXIMATE TEMPO	♩ = M.M. 96
DURATION	1¾ minutes
SUGGESTED LISTENING	Four-hand Sonata, K.521 iii
	Rondo, K.382, for piano & orchestra

9 INTERPRETATION OF THE THIRD MOVEMENT, K.545

In this short finale, Mozart apparently forgot that the sonata was to be "for beginners." The LH writing is much more varied than in the previous movements, and the delightful polyphonic touches suggest string quartet textures. Alertness and a supple technique are requisites in this buoyant piece, which is not conspicuously "easy." One of the first editions suggested *Allegretto*[16] at the beginning. This seems appropriate, as a rushed pace spoils the humor of the movement. The other early editions had no tempo indication.

In the theme, the RH repeated thirds are wedged, while those on first beats are not. This does not necessarily indicate that the latter are somewhat longer than the upbeat thirds but rather that the first beats should not be accented. Heavy downbeats spoil the humor of the initial theme. The RH slurs in mm.2-12 indicate the phrasing, the first note of each slurred group slightly emphasized. The sixteenth notes are much livelier if there are audible separations between the slurs.

Pedaling is unnecessary in the entire piece and finger-pedaling of the lower bass notes must be discreet; at mm.8-11, for example, finger-pedaling would sound sticky, but in mm.36-39 it could enhance the sonority of an energetic phrase.

As in any fine quartet playing, all the rests must breathe. There is no need to slow down in m.19 or before the *fermata* in m.52. This abrupt break in the line is a little joke and surely does not imply the interpolation of an *Eingang*. From m.60 onwards, the second beats are harmonically stronger. The first LH note of each quarter-note beat could be finger-pedaled but not accented.

Many budding virtuosi come to grief in the *Codetta*, which is not difficult if m.68 is played absolutely rhythmically and *non legato*. During mm.68-71 only the RH thirds on the second quarter-note beats of mm.69,71 are *legato*.

There is a version of this piece in F major, listed in the Köchel Catalogue as K.547-a. This is often published together with the Allegro in F, K.547-a, and the Variations, K.547-b, to form a very unlikely sonata. It is now presumed that neither the Allegro, K.547-a, which contains distinctly un-Mozartian elements, nor the F major variant of this finale, K.547-a, are by Mozart.

There are no ornaments in the finale. To add any in such a perfectly textured piece would seem inconceivable, though that ever inventive forte pianist Malcolm Bilson does include some delightful touches when repeating mm.4 and 7.

XVIII

1789:
SONATAS IN B-FLAT,
K.570, AND D, K.576

1 MOZART IN 1789

1789 was not one of Mozart's most productive years, but he did finish most of the opera, *Così fan tutte*, and two of the most beautiful sonatas written for the piano: in February the B-flat major, K.570, and in July, the D major, K.576. The composer's income[1] had been dropping for some time and Mozart's financial situation was becoming increasingly serious. Frequent loans from his fellow Freemasons, Michael Puchberg and Franz Hofdemel, were necessary.

In April, a patron and friend of Mozart, Prince Karl Lichnowsky, invited the composer to accompany him on a visit to the Prussian court at Potsdam, just outside of Berlin. Hoping for a commission from the Prussian king, Friedrich Wilhelm II, Mozart set out on what was to be his longest trip without Constanze. The men were gone for two months, visiting Leipzig, Potsdam, Dresden and Prague. Mozart's letters to his wife are uncharacteristically full of anxieties and insecurities. During this tour Mozart wrote virtually nothing but a few smaller piano works like the *Duport* Variations, K.573 (see Chapter XIX, sections 2 and 3), and the Little Gigue, K.574. Mozart did not earn much on this tiring expedition, but he did return with two commissions from the Prussian king, one for six string quartets, and another for six "easy" sonatas for piano, intended for the king's daughter. Eventually he was to complete only three quartets and one piano sonata, the D major, K.576.

Constanze's bad health in the summer caused more stress and financial burdens. Mozart's letters to Puchberg during these weeks are heart rending; on July 12, he wrote:

"Instead of paying my debts I am asking for more money ... in spite of my wretched condition I decided to give subscription concerts at home in order to be able to meet at least my present great and frequent expenses ... but even this has failed ... Do not be offended by my confiding in you and remember that unless you help me, the honour, the peace of mind, and perhaps the very life of your friend and brother Mason will be ruined." [2]

Not only for Mozart was this a summer fraught with tension; in Paris the French Revolution erupted, changing forever the course of Western history. But Mozart's urge to compose overwhelmed personal worries and socio-political currents. Both the String Quartet, K.575, and his final piano sonata, K.576, display a masterly blend of the "learned" and *galant* styles; "works," Einstein wrote, "that originated under the most dreadful spiritual oppression, and yet they rise to heights of pure felicity." [3]

SONATA IN B-FLAT MAJOR, K.570

COMPOSITION DATE   February, 1789
TOTAL DURATION   19 minutes, with first repeat in i and all repeats in ii and iii

2 THE PECULIAR REPUTATION OF K.570

By 1796, when the sonata was published, a violin part had been added. Due to the clear listing in the composer's catalogue as "a sonata for piano solo" and the irrelevance of the violin part, it is now assumed [4] that the version with violin is not by Mozart. Apparently the piece was well received, for during the next decades, further transcriptions of K.570 for various combinations of instruments appeared in Vienna. Perhaps because this sonata was not initially recognized as a work for solo piano, it has remained one of the less frequently performed of Mozart's piano compositions. It is ironic that even some twentieth-century editions of the sonatas omitted K.570, for the piece can be ranked among the finest of these works.

Alfred Einstein maintained that K.570 is "perhaps the most completely rounded ... Mozart's ideal of the piano sonata," [5] and Arthur Hutchings observed that "the piece is decidedly not for beginners. On the contrary, it may serve as a test of connoisseurs." [6]

In both conservatories and concert venues, K.570 is rarely heard. Given the wide range of emotions and structural genius evident in the piece, such neglect is puzzling. But there are undeniable problems confronting the interpreter of this sonata. The length of the *Adagio* is a particularly awesome challenge for many players. As the structure would become unbalanced if the repeats in the slow movement are not observed, the repeated sections confront the pianist with the quandary of improvising ornamentation, a challenge that unfortunately makes many players more apprehensive than creative.

The texture of the writing in K.570 can be inhibiting; virtually nothing in the entire sonata is pianistically conceived. Stringed and wind instruments are evoked in virtually every note. The player must be able to revel in this imaginary scoring. There is also the textual challenge of dynamics. Only the first movement, from m.65 onwards, has survived in manuscript. Throughout the entire sonata, the dynamic indications suggested in older editions are frequently unsuitable, whereas the lack of indications in recent *Urtext* editions makes literal-minded pianists feel insecure.

FIRST MOVEMENT	*Allegro*
FORM	sonata
APPROXIMATE TEMPO	♩ = M.M. 136-138
DURATION	6½ minutes, with expositional repeat
SUGGESTED LISTENING	String Quartet, K.589 i
	Piano trio, K.542 i
	Sonata for Piano & Violin, K.547 ii
	Piano Concerto, K.413/387-a i

3 INTERPRETATION OF THE FIRST MOVEMENT, K.570

Though the music should flow with one impulse, not three, to a measure, a hasty tempo can easily result in muddles whenever sixteenth notes appear. The subtle counterpoint of the movement wears its erudition lightly. The initial motif returns with a counter subject to open the second theme-group at m.41, and, in the development section, the same combination of motifs (mm.101-116), with different articulation and the shift to minor mode, seems like a new theme. At mm.117-123, Mozart deftly combines the nervous eighth notes of the counter subject with the opening of the *Codetta* theme, first heard at m.70. All these thematic transformations create a structure of phenomenal unity.

The articulation of the first theme is a tricky matter. In her *Performance Practices in Classic Piano Music*, S.P. Rosenblum[7] devotes

more than two pages to this enigma. At the beginning of the movement, one-measure slurs are to be found in all *Urtext* editions, though
some suggest alternative articulations. At mm.41-44 contradictory
readings are found; the Henle editor,[8] for example, suggests three-
measure slurs, whereas the NMA[9] has single-measure slurs, with
three-measure slurs as an alternative. In the development section,
most *Urtext* editions have the three-measure slurs indicated in the
manuscript fragment. During the recapitulation the slurring is not
consistent.

In his own thematic catalogue Mozart joined the first two measures
of this theme with a single slur. This shaping of the opening, so rarely
heard, gives a fine swing and direction to the dance-like theme. This
articulation is also appropriate at the beginning of the exposition and
recapitulation, where one-measure slurring can seem limp and pedantic. During the other recurrences of the theme, when it is combined
with a counter subject, the longer three-measure articulation of the
development section, indicated in the manuscript, is logical.

Distracting as this quandary remains, the gentle surge of the initial
theme to the fourth measure is more important than its articulation. If
the music seems to linger on the first beats of the second or third
measures, this flow is lost. Audible separations between the slurs
sound fussy and inelegant. When the fingers leave the keys in the
final beats of mm.2-4, for example, pedaling can prevent actual
breaks in the line. Measures 5-6 and 9-10 have less character if
joined by *legato* phrasing. The wedge on the first RH note of m.7 is
surely a *staccato* indication, not an accent.

Timed and articulated precisely, the humor of mm.12-20 becomes
irresistible. The second-beat RH B-flats must be clearly separated
from the other sixteenth notes, the C's gently emphasized and each
group of sixteenth notes slightly separated from the subsequent first-
beat quarter notes.

At m.21 G minor intrudes on this graceful scene. In the manuscript, Mozart indicated *forte* at m.153, the parallel moment in the
recapitulation. Yet it is surprising how many players play softly here,
nullifying the drama of this startling modulation. Separated pedal
strokes and active arm movements give body to these strong chords,
which are important in establishing the dynamic range of the sonata.

The theme beginning at m.23 is coy and sensual. If the pedal is
used, it should be changed on each quarter-note beat. A dry sound is
troubling here; the modern copy of a Walter fortepiano played by
Alexey Lubimov[10] on his recording sounds much more agreeable than

the original Walter instrument played by Gustav Leonhardt.[11] The melody must be vocally shaped, with all the repeated quarter notes *diminuendo*. Richard Rosenberg[12] noted that the motif at mm.23-24, first heard in mm.12-13, was used by Wagner in no less than three of his operas.

Obviously the first-beat bass third of m.35 belong to the previous theme and should never be accented. The *forte* indicated in most editions cannot be found at the parallel passage (m.165) in the manuscript and therefore can be regarded with some scepticism. For this exuberant moment, a vital touch and absolutely no pedaling are needed. There should not be too much sound, as the climax at mm.61-68 is considerably stronger.

At m.41, the second theme surprises us by beginning with the initial motif. Certainly on modern instruments, the repeated notes of the RH counter subject will sound less choppy if played by the same finger. Pedaling is unnecessary in these contrapuntal sentences. In mm.49-63, each four-note figure takes on a different character, easy to achieve when the pianist actually breathes with the rests. Dry acoustics may necessitate half-pedaling at mm.63-64 and 67-68, but otherwise, throughout this theme pedaling sounds clumsy. Lili Kraus[13] relaxes somewhat in mm.65-66, but a longer *diminuendo* in mm.65-69 like Mitsuko Uchida's[14] seems unnatural. The marvelous *Codetta* theme, beginning in m.69, is both poignant and graceful and should not be disturbed by the accenting of first beats. The *forte* in mm.77-79 does not derive from the manuscript; surely this cadential motif is more playful than forceful?

The wide-ranging counterpoint of the development section is breathtaking, the harmonic and polyphonic tension palpable. All the important motifs of the exposition are recalled here. Even the bass of mm.70-71 makes unexpected appearances in mm.118-123. Leonhardt is masterly in shaping the dialogue in mm.101-117, where Mozart's writing evokes not only the baroque period but also anticipates the stark lines of the late quartets of Beethoven. Playing too gently in m.125 makes the diminution of energy in mm.129-131 difficult to sustain. The transition to the recapitulation in mm.129-132 is like an *Eingang* and can be paced with some freedom but no sentimentality.

The recapitulation presents some variants on the expositional material, but the structure is virtually the same. Given the range of the development section, repetition of the exposition is an absolute must, but I was pleased to read that even the NMA editors[15] do not find the second repeat desirable in this movement.

4 ORNAMENTATION IN THE FIRST MOVEMENT, K.570

m.

7   Given the rapidity of the *appoggiatura*, it is most clearly played on the second eighth-note beat and slightly accented. The preceding wedged note ends the first phrase, and its wedge indicates a separation from this ornament, not an accent.

45   As the trill is indicated on a note that functions as a suspension, a three-note trill *(Schneller)* suffices. The subsequent E's must be very gentle.

56   Given the spritely tempo, a three-note trill plus termination is sufficient here, though a five-note trill has perhaps more character. Many artists play the upper auxiliary as a grace note before the trill, but playing the upper auxiliary on the beat sounds wooden.

68   The energetic trill has the upper auxiliary, either on the first beat or as a lively grace note before it.

The two chords of mm.21-22 can be vigorously arpeggiated, but adding ornamentation elsewhere in these perfectly crafted lines seems irrelevant, even decadent.

SECOND MOVEMENT	*Adagio*
FORM	rondo
APPROXIMATE TEMPO	♩ = M.M. 48-50
DURATION	8 minutes, with all repeats
SUGGESTED LISTENING	*Entführung aus dem Serail*: Belmonte's aria "Welch ein Geschick"
	Die Zauberflöte: Sarastro's aria "In diesen..." Finale, Act II
	Lied *Der Frühling*, K.597
	Piano Concerto, K.491 ii

5 INTERPRETATION OF THE SECOND MOVEMENT, K.570

In Mozart's time it was unusual to have an *Adagio* in rondo form at the center of a piano sonata. The drama of the C minor Sonata's *Adagio* or the tortured harmonies of the K.533 *Andante* are absent here. This is music of contemplation; considerable feeling and maturity are needed to project this unique work. A supple technique and much taste are needed to shape these intense but introspective sentences.

I listened to ten recordings of this movement and was surprised by the immense variety of tempi. Timings ranged from less than 7 minutes to 9½ minutes. As in the slow movement of the F major Sonata, K.332, the tempo indication does not denote a funereal tread but suggests that the content is more serious than graceful. Such pieces, played with a flowing *Andante* approach, lose their ruminative quality and diminish into mere lyricism. Conversely, if the tempo is sluggish, the message becomes more ponderous than profound.

Mozart's numerous articulation indications give a clear shaping to the principal theme. The RH slurs over the bar-lines at mm.1-2, 5-6, 9-10 give the theme its strongest impulses, whereas any accenting on the third quarter-note beats of mm.1, 3, or on the first beats of mm.2, 4, paralyzes the calm motion of the initial phrase. The appealing *cantabile* sentence, mm.5-8, heard only here, is less problematical, perhaps because the scoring, suggesting stringed instruments, is more immediately recognizable than the unusual blend of wind and string textures in the first sentence. The *staccati* in m.3 need no pedal if not too detached. Conversely, on a modern instrument, the *portati* in m.6 may seem rather pedantic without pedaling.

The first episode in C minor is more resigned than dramatic. Thundering dynamic contrasts would be misplaced, but these mournful motifs can be shaped with an *opera seria* intensity. The lowest bass notes in mm.13, 17-18 sound much more ominous if not prolonged by pedaling or finger-pedaling. Exact rests lend these solemn lines a doomed quality, rather like the *Adagio*, K.540. In such a grim context, *rubato* should be minimal. It is not easy to play the "woodwind" sixteenth notes in the first half of mm.16 and 24 rhythmically. Leonhardt double-dots the RH motifs in mm.13, a baroque practice that sounds surprisingly natural here.

Ignoring any of the repetitions may upset the finely balanced structure of the piece, but perhaps the first repetition in each episode is more essential than the second. The transitional phrase, mm.24-27, has an improvisational character and could be played with some rhythmic freedom.

After the truncated reappearance of the principal theme at mm.28-31, comes another episode, utterly different from the first. The clinical atmosphere of the recording studio seems to inhibit inspired expression; it is surprising to hear how many artists seem defeated by the "simplicity" of this tender music. Artur Schnabel,[16] however, plays this episode and the initial theme with a magical blend of wisdom and feeling. The violinistic phrases should have a good focus of tone in the longer notes and subtle *legato* intensity in the shorter ones. Some *rubato* is conceivable here, but of the specifically Mozartian variety, with only the RH line straying from the beat. If the bass line is pulled about, the effect is sentimental. The deeply melancholy RH eighth notes of mm.36-37 seem banal if played *legato*. The NMA[17] gives the lowest note on the first beat of m.41 as C-flat, more expressive than the C stated in most other editions. Despite what may look like thin textures, the tone in this major-minor conflict can be quite full.

After the final appearance of the shortened main theme, the *Coda* at m.48 is in operatic style, very like the end of the *Adagio* of the following sonata, K.576, completed only months later. The repeated RH E-flats in mm.48-49 must not sound *staccato*, with the fingers close to the keys. The lower notes of the bass line may be finger-pedaled in mm.48-49 and 52. During the bass's repeated notes at mm.53-54, the thumb should also stay close to the keys if a noise like mechanical drilling is to be avoided.

It takes involvement and taste to avoid sentimentality or pedantry in this *Adagio*, where a minimum of notes expresses a wide range of human experience.

6 ADDITIONAL ORNAMENTATION IN THE SECOND MOVEMENT, K.570

Throughout the entire movement, all the ornaments have been written out. Therefore the player would be ill-advised to add ornaments that seem merely decorative. A turn added to the upper line in the third quarter-note beat of m.2, for example, may seem an interesting variant in later occurrences of the theme, but the effect is fussy and obscures the little surge of the subsequent sixteenth notes. Just because they are frequently repeated, certain motifs like those in mm.15 and 23 do not require ornamentation. If played with enough response to the emotional color of the harmonies, they will never sound merely repetitious. Again we must remember that repetition is in itself a major aspect of structure and expression. Varying repetitions of the principal theme at mm.9, 28, or 44, is a very subjective choice. Siegbert Rampe gives a convincing variant of the first three measures for those who prefer some variation. [18]

One could differentiate between sentences that are somewhat austere and those that are vocal. When repeated, the phrase, mm.5-8,

certainly lends itself to ornamentation, but the player must not make
elaborate effects, drawing too much attention to a phrase which, after
all, is only heard at the beginning of the movement. Malcolm Bilson[19]
adds delightful syncopations to the first half of m.6 and very beautiful
appoggiature in the following measure. His improvisations in m.8 may
not appeal to everyone but are certainly inventive. His variants in
mm.15 and 23 are perhaps more delightful in live performance than
on a recording. When repeated, mm.32-39 seem to invite some variation, but this should not efface the serenity of that episode. The editors of the NMA[20] suggest that a short *Eingang* may be added before
the final appearance of the principal theme at m.44. A simple series
of ascending *appoggiature* beginning on the F below the first B-flat of
the melody is more appropriate than any "passage work." Nothing
should be altered in the serene perfection of the *Coda*.

THIRD MOVEMENT	*Allegretto*
FORM	rondo
APPROXIMATE TEMPO	$\downarrow$ = M.M. 66
DURATION	4 minutes (with all repeats)
SUGGESTED LISTENING	*Die Zauberflöte*: Overture, Papageno's aria "Ein Mädchen oder Weibchen" Clarinet Quintet, K.581 iv String Quartet, K.589 iv

7 INTERPRETATION OF THE THIRD MOVEMENT, K.570

After the sophisticated *Allegro* and the contemplative *Adagio*, the
finale is earthy. We seem to be in Vienna at Carnival time. The first
beats are more like dance lifts than downbeats. In the principal theme
only a few suspensions are *legato*, but vertical hand movements should
not result in accents, for example, at the third quarter-note beats of the
first two measures. The bass line sounds sluggish if finger-pedaled.
Lubimov even plays the bass *staccato*, a delightful effect on his fortepiano, though this can sound artificial on modern instruments. Each of
the initial four-measure phrases should be shaped in one breath. The
LH slurs in mm.9 and 11 do not extend to the last eighth note, an amusing burping effect. Throughout mm.9-14 the slurring, particularly of the
sixteenth notes, indicates phrasing that is more playful than *legato*. It is
possible to play a *subito piano* at m.12, but baroque "echo" effects in

the following measures should be avoided.

The "B" theme, beginning at m.22, is not only rhythmically related to the "A" theme but is, most unusually, also in the tonic key. A divertimento for wind instruments is clearly evoked here, two horns in the RH, a bassoon in the LH. If the player's right arm is not free of tension, the slurs and *staccati* will sound lumpy. As in the first theme, pedaling should be shunned. The lowest bass notes at moments like m.23 sound better played *staccato* than finger-pedaled.

A cheeky *Eingang* at mm.43-44 introduces the "C" theme. Spluttering repeated notes offer a poker-faced counterpoint to various figurations, very like the overture to *Die Zauberflöte*, written two years later. Older editions frequently recommend change of finger on the repeated notes, but on modern instruments this is unnecessary and can sound stiff. The NMA[21] extends the RH slurs in mm.49-52 over the bar-lines, which seems more expressive than the half-measure slurs found in many other editions. The contrasts of *legato* and *staccato* in the RH lines are so delightful that the bass's articulation and rests can easily be slighted.

The "A" theme's return at m.63 suggests a recapitulation in sonata form, but it lasts only eight measures. After an abridged version of the "B" theme at mm.71-74, Mozart lurches to the "C" theme in mm.75-84. All this swirling activity conjures up the finale of an *opera buffa*, a crowd of people milling about the stage. The LH leaps in mm.75-79 must be visually prepared and not cause any accidental accents. The RH thumb can take the first bass G in m.78.

The bass line of mm.83-84 is livelier if played *non legato*. It is curious that in the first edition the only dynamic indications in the entire movement were in the final eight measures. Obviously m.81 is an orchestral *crescendo* leading to a full sound in the following measure. The *piano* at m.85 is like a delightful smile. Inexplicably, too many players choose to ignore the *forte* in the final measure, surely a clear indication that Mozart did not want a delicate fade-out here but a sudden surge in the upbeat to the final measure, a joyous ending to the eventful journey experienced in this wonderful sonata.

8 ORNAMENTATION IN THE THIRD MOVEMENT, K.570

m.

2   The *appoggiatura* is a light grace note sounding before the beat.

8   The trill is best played as a three-note trill *(Schneller)* before the

beat, the third note becoming the first of the indicated sixteenth notes. This ornament must be fitted into the line with lightning speed, difficult if the thumb playing the previous B-flats is tense.

84   The upper notes of the cadential trill should ring out. The trill may begin with either the upper or lower auxiliary on the first beat.

The bustling activity of this movement calls for little additional ornamentation; a few alterations to the "B" and "C" themes are certainly conceivable when they are repeated. Lubimov adds some cheeky decorations in mm.31-32 and 35-36. Bilson plays an amusing flourish in m.52 and completely transforms mm.69-70. It is possible to insert a short diatonic descent from B-flat to E in the RH of m.34 and to vary the melody at m.40.

SONATA IN D MAJOR, K.576

| COMPOSITION DATE | July 1789 |
| TOTAL DURATION | approximately 15½ minutes (with repeat in i) |

FIRST MOVEMENT	*Allegro*
FORM	sonata
APPROXIMATE TEMPO	♩. = M.M. 86
DURATION	5 minutes (with repeat)
SUGGESTED LISTENING	String Quartet, K.575 i
	String Quartet, K.499 i
	Clarinet Concerto, K.622 i

9 INTERPRETATION OF THE FIRST MOVEMENT, K.576

Was it possible that Mozart's exhausting trip through Germany in the spring of 1789 reminded him of the long tours he had made as a child prodigy? The only music he wrote during those weeks were two pieces for piano solo, the Variations on a Minuet by Duport, K.573, and the Little Gigue, K.574. Once back in Vienna Mozart immediately began to work on the Prussian king's commissions for six string quartets and six "easy" piano sonatas. He did complete a string quartet in June and a piano sonata a month later, but thereafter his motivation to write piano sonatas seems to have vanished. During the last years of his life Mozart made numerous sketches of piano pieces, but these rarely last more than a few measures.

The Sonata in D major, K.576, is presumably the sole product of the commission for six "easy" sonatas. It is such an appealing masterpiece that pianists can only lament Mozart's general lack of interest in writing for their instrument during his final years. The English used to label this work the *Trumpet* Sonata because of its opening bugle-call motif. Unfortunately most students experience this sonata more as a *Tränensonate*, a "Sonata of Tears;" anyone who finds this sonata "easy" would be a prodigious musician. Technically and interpretatively, K.576 remains one of the most challenging sonatas in the entire piano repertoire. All too often the difficulties tend to obscure the delights of this wondrous piece, so full of life's joys, doubts and evaluations.

It is evident that the opening theme has a dance-like character. Landowska[22] heard here "a hunt motif in the rhythm of a gigue," whereas Rosenberg[23] pointed out the similarity to the D major Prelude in the second book of Bach's *Wohltemperiertes Klavier*. The ascending "bugle" motif should not be played too lightly, but a Prokofievian *martellato* would be equally undesirable. The texture sounds brighter if the RH plays stronger than the LH, with a *crescendo* surge to the first beat of m.2. Though the answering trills suggest a change of scoring, whispering them is an artificial touch. Unfortunately, the manuscript of the sonata has disappeared so that all modern editions can refer only to the first edition (hereafter FE). The FE dynamic indications are very sparse, suggesting that this source is true to the manuscript and contains no additions by anonymous editors.

Practically all players rush the repeated A's in m.2 and unintentionally prolong the eighth notes in mm.3-4. This is unmistakably "orchestral" music, and were an orchestra playing, such carelessness would be unthinkable. An accurate rhythm here is easier to maintain if the hands do not make large aerial gestures during rests. There are two important motifs heard just after the initial bugle motif: "A," the four main ascending notes of the trills, and "B," the four descending notes of the answering figuration.

The bass line of the perky canon beginning in m.8 must be played sensitively and without LH accents on the first and fourth eighth-note beats of mm.11 and 15.

All the half-measure slurs in the first phrase of the transitional theme, mm.16-19, suggest a graceful *leggiero* more than a true *legato*, certainly not the artificial *crescendi* frequently heard here. The lowest bass notes could be finger-pedaled, but pedaling should be avoided throughout the entire exposition. The subsequent *non legato* phrase often sounds like a typing exercise but is an ingenious development of motifs we have already heard. The bustling sixteenth notes of mm.20-21 are a delightful variant of the four-note Motif "A" of mm.2-3. The descending form of Motif "B" at mm.3-4 is echoed in the bass at mm.24-25. A sparkling *non legato* touch seems appropriate during the cadential festivity of mm.24-27.

At m.28 we would expect a lyrical opening to the second theme group, but instead we are surprised by another canonic statement of the opening motif. Often this is played too daintily, whereas at m.138, in the recapitulation, the parallel passage in FE is appropriately marked *forte*. If the theme from mm.28-41 is not meant to sound exuberant, the FE *dolce* indication at the upbeat to m.42 would be redundant. The descending lines of sixteenth notes in mm.29 and 31 should not sound like "passage work" but like two figures of sixteenth notes, the first consisting of six notes, the second, six notes with a final eighth note. The bass of mm.35,37 suggests a bassoon playing *non legato*, with two imaginary oboes playing a lovely *legato* version of Motif B in mm.38-39.

The same motif opens the subsequent theme at m.41. The *dolce* indication makes this tender, introspective moment very different from the surrounding bustle. A string quartet would have no trouble with this beautiful phrase, but it is not easy for the pianist. Accents must be avoided and the *non legato* in m.44 should not be too short or heavy.

The humor of mm.50-51 is underlined by a chromaticized version of Motif A in the LH. The *forte* indicated in m.53 is from FE but surely suggests bright character more than loudness. Skittish "echo" effects should be avoided in mm.55-58. The dramatic surprise of the FE *piano* in m.59 would be nullified if the exposition ends too softly. Given the brevity of the exposition and the breadth of the coming development section, the repeat must be observed.

The development section is not only one of the most ingenious that Mozart wrote for the piano, its beauty takes the breath away. The *piano* and *forte* contrasts of the first measures can be theatrically presented. Why do so many pianists choose to play the canonic sequence beginning at m.63 delicately, thereby emasculating the tension of this frenetic polyphony? It is astonishing to realize how cleverly Mozart ornaments the repetitions of Motif B in mm.72-77. The rests, which must never be shortened, lend a gasping excitement to the drama. From m.61 until m.83, the music is angry, driven. Caution is out of place here, but the performer must consider how much tonal weight is suitable for each phrase in this explosive atmosphere. A slight increase in tempo during mm.76-81 is natural, but any noticeable slowing in the rest of the development is debilitating.

The interpretation of the sequences in mm.81-96 remains more subjective. Hopefully no two pianists would experience the unearthly polyphony, serene yet pained, in exactly the same way. Sentimental lingering will weaken the tension here. Pedaling can be used but must be carefully changed with each half-measure. One often hears a *crescendo* in mm.93-96, but a sense of perplexity, even of anxiety, seems more suitable here than an increase of energy.

It is fascinating to realize that the final suspenseful sequences of the development, so unworldly and timeless, are based on motifs A and B. We hear A in the RH at mm.83-86, in the LH of mm.86-89, and in the RH at mm.89-92, where it functions as a counterpoint to the B motif in the LH. During mm.93-96 Motif A is heard twice in the RH's "second violin" line. It wins over the chromatic unease of the bass and leads into the enthusiastic *Eingang* introducing the recapitulation, an abrupt lurch back to gaiety, where the *forte* given in many editions can perhaps be best viewed as a *crescendo*.

In the recapitulation, Mozart changed the sequence of themes with immense cunning. During the extended canon, mm.107-117, the rests should be absolutely precise. The mannerism of raising the hands too far from the keys during these rests can cause annoying rhythmic instability. If the player does not delight in the busy conversation of various orchestral instruments here, this sentence will sound academic. Note that the last eighth note of m.117 and the first sixteenth note of m.118 form a suspension, best played *legato*, and clearly separated from the subsequent triadic figure. How many tears and curses have been provoked by the awkward LH leap in m.141! If the player shapes the six-note figurations clearly, without rushing, this perilous moment is not so traumatic.

There is no *forte* indicated at the beginning of the *Codetta* theme at m.155, which does seem more introspective than at the end of the exposition. A considerable *diminuendo* during the final measures seems justified, but slowing down here brings fading batteries to mind.

Among Mozart's piano sonatas, this is the first movement in sonata form that does not end with an indication that the development and recapitulation sections are to be repeated. Curiously enough, Haydn followed the same practice in his last piano sonata (in E-flat, Hob.XVI, no.52) written five years after K.576. It remains a quandary whether one can cite these two examples to justify omission of final repetitions in other sonata form movements by either composer. What is clear is that Mozart here achieved an astonishing blending of his musical high spirits and "learned" counterpoint.

10 ORNAMENTATION IN THE FIRST MOVEMENT, K.576

m.

2   The trill is almost always played with three notes and the termination. On heavy instruments this is not easy, but if the fingers stay close to the keys, and the thumb does not tense, the trill will sound clear and supple. Occasionally one hears the trill begun on the upper auxiliary, reducing the ornament to a rather banal sounding four-note turn. This also obliterates the outline of Motif A, noted above. Frederick Neumann maintains that beginning on the upper auxiliary "might well be the most elegant of the available options,"[23] but I do not agree.

40   This cadential trill is very energetic and is best begun with an onbeat upper auxiliary note.

52   The *appoggiatura* should be played as a light grace note. Playing it on the second dotted quarter-note beat would disturb both the upper line and the polyphony.

Nowhere in the movement does additional ornamentation seem justified. For example, the *dolce* phrase of 122-125 is restated three times, yet Mozart's changes in the harmonies and lines of each repetition provide a superb example of his subtle mastery of variation technique. Which pianist would dare to tinker with such perfection?

SECOND MOVEMENT	*Adagio*
FORM	ternary
APPROXIMATE TEMPO	♪= M.M. 86
DURATION	5 minutes
SUGGESTED LISTENING	*La Clemenza da Tito*: Sesto's aria "Parto, parto"
	Clarinet Concerto, K.622 ii
	Piano Concerto, K.595 ii

11 INTERPRETATION OF THE SECOND MOVEMENT, K.576

After the ingenious hyperactivity of the *Allegro* we find ourselves in a still place where there is time to contemplate the marvels of existence. Dennerlein wrote:

"This jewel of Mozart's *cantilena* style points to Beethoven's *Adagios*. But even he created nothing finer." [25]

This is certainly a piece to convert anyone who has misguided notions of Mozart's music being cold or remote. Yet a mature experience of life is necessary to project the range of emotion evident in this movement.

As in the previous sonata, Mozart's *Adagio* indication connotes seriousness of content more than an overtly deliberate pace. The initial eight measures sound convincing at virtually any tempo, but if the player has begun too slowly, calmer moments like mm.9-12 or 24-25 become ponderous.

The first section's steady pace of four-measure phrases creates the tranquil atmosphere in this great aria for piano. The player should strive to shape these *legato* lines as a fine singer would, with no two notes having the same color or weight. This is especially challenging when, as in the third measure, the melody moves in notes of the same rhythmic value. If the player's hand is more active horizontally than vertically, a vocal *legato* can be more easily suggested. *Legato* intensity here is more the responsibility of the pianist's hands and soul, not of his feet.

Therefore the first melodic tone must truly sing and the subsequent sixty-fourth notes be played *leggiero*. With too much weight they sound horribly mechanical. The half note of the second measure should sound throughout its duration; here, a modern instrument is preferable to a fortepiano. The LH *staccati* at that moment should evoke two oboes playing very softly, more *portato* than *staccato*.

The entire theme gains eloquence if the sparse LH lines are shaped with alertness and not played as absent-minded "accompaniment." Given the intense *legato* of the RH melody, the upper note of the LH octave in m.3 must make room for the RH line, but in any case the resolutions of the LH suspensions heard on the second quarter-note beats of mm.3-4 are more poignant if played as dotted eighth notes.

The transitional sentence begins with the last three cello-like notes of m.8, which may be pedaled but become soporific if played *legato*.

The middle voices of mm.9-11 should be played with a relaxed LH, the fingers barely leaving the keys. Shaping the lines as a string quartet helps to keep the pulse stable; it is difficult for a pianist to resist haste in the middle of each measure. The unthinking habit some players have of playing descending lines *diminuendo* and ascending ones *crescendo* is certainly not appropriate here. Each step in this sequence must evoke a slightly different emotion.

A heavily romantic *ritenuto* in the chromatic eighth notes of m.16 is unnecessary; the F-sharp minor key in the following measure is ominous enough. This anguished middle section, in a key rarely found in Mozart's music, reminds us of the slow movement of the A major Concerto, K.488. However, too much agonizing in the form of convulsive *rubato* will deflect the inexorable power of these tragic phrases. The RH is not slurred but can be phrased vocally even when the fingers detach all the sixteenth notes with the pedal changed on each note. Unfortunately most pianists play two-note slurs here, a trivial effect, not at all suitable in such a desolate landscape.

The initial bass note of mm.17-18 should not be prolonged by pedaling but sound like pained cello *pizzicati*. In either staff a generalized *legato* weakens the force of the these black emotions. In m.19 the RH sixteenth notes remain unslurred. Like the previous melodic tones they too could be played *portato* with *legato* pedal. At the parallel moment in m.38 the bass line is slurred, and the tension between the various lines is enhanced if the first three bass notes of m.19 are also slurred. Due to the nervous syncopation and unexpected emotional transition, it is difficult to maintain rhythmic steadiness in m.23. With the sudden shift to major mode, suffering seems to dissolve into suspended animation. In mm.24-25, any agogic effects sound totally artificial.

The strange modulations of mm.26-31 seem like a dream sequence. The idyllic world of the opening is far away. If haste or dragging seems difficult to avoid here, the player, while studying, can imagine remorseless accompanying chords on each quarter-note beat. The tenuous lines struggle upwards for space and light only to fall in black resignation. Certainly the LH lines have more energy than the RH's weary responses. Note that each measure does not consist of one long phrase, but of three, with seven, nine, then seven notes. This motivic shaping can be made without any audible breaks. In mm.30-31, pedaling must be extremely discreet to avoid blurring of the RH's troubled melody.

It is something of a shock to hear at m.32 a return to the F-sharp minor theme, sounding even more threatening than before. The music becomes paralyzed in this key for ten more measures, giving the entire sonata a particular *gravitas*. While most of K.576 is cast in bright colors, there can be no doubt of the dreadful pessimism heard here. Amazingly enough, though this "B" section may sound like an improvisation, all these powerful emotions are cast in a perfectly balanced ternary form within the entire movement's ternary structure.

The *Coda* beginning at m.59 brings the soulful postludes of some famous Mozart soprano arias to mind. The pedaling is the same as in mm.17-18, but with the RH now shaping its resigned lines with a *legatissimo* touch. Some ornamentation certainly seems welcome here and is discussed in the following section. Konrad Wolff observed a fascinating motivic link between this movement and the next:

"shortly before the conclusion ... the end of mm.61 and 64 is repeated identically a few seconds later in m.8 of the Finale." [26]

The *staccati* of the final measures should evoke the gentle detaching of a violinist's bow and, especially on a modern piano, must not sound too emphatic. What a curious mix of aesthetic elegance and a dizzying range of emotions Mozart expresses in these sparse lines!

12 ORNAMENTATION IN THE SECOND MOVEMENT, K.576

The only ornament that Mozart did not write out is the trill heard at m.61 and 64. This is to be played as a three-note trill *(Schneller)*, the final note falling on the third quarter-note beat.

Except in the *Coda*, there is no room for ornaments in these wondrously crafted lines. However, the RH repetition in mm.62-64 does invite variation. Playing this phrase as a mere "echo" is in very dubious stylistic taste; there are many other possibilities here. Excellent examples are the RH embellishments by Eva Badura Skoda, quoted in the introduction to the NMA Edition[27] or the variant proposed by the editors of the Wiener Urtext Ausgabe.[28]

THIRD MOVEMENT	*Allegretto*
FORM	rondo
APPROXIMATE TEMPO	♩ = M.M. 84-86
DURATION	five minutes
SUGGESTED LISTENING	Piano Concerto, K.537 i and iii
	"Jupiter" Symphony, K.551 iv
	Piano Trio, K.564 iii
	String Quintet, K.614 iii
	Clarinet Concerto, K.622 iii

13 INTERPRETATION OF THE THIRD MOVEMENT, K.576

The irrepressible *joie de vivre* of this finale, with its dazzling play of ingenuity and humor, leaves the listener not only dizzy with admiration but also deeply frustrated that Mozart did not complete any of the other five sonatas commissioned by the Prussian king. The balance of introspection and extroversion, of cunning counterpoint and pianistic exuberance found here is truly miraculous. The textures range widely; one theme evokes a string quartet, the next a divertimento for woodwinds, and yet another brings a piano concerto to mind. Like the opening *Allegro*, this movement demands a highly sophisticated technique. It is often played too quickly. Surely Mozart would have indicated an *Allegro* if he had wanted a brash tempo here. Landowska rightly observed that the finale is

"in the same spirit as the Finale of the Coronation Concerto. It is solid, precise, and full of humor. Consequently it should not be hurried." [29]

The principal theme has an earthy cheerfulness that predicts Papageno's popular aria in *Die Zauberflöte*, "Der Vogelfänger bin ich ja," but is cast in the more sophisticated textures of a string quartet. It is easy to imagine the initial phrase played by two violins and a viola, the cello sounding only at the cadence. Too many pianists play the eighth notes on the second quarter-note beats of mm.1 and 3 *staccato*, thereby nullifying the charming contrast with the articulation of the second half of m.5. It is also surprising how often one hears unrhythmic or strangely accented LH shaping in the theme, where accents on the last eighth-note beats, for example, are motoric accidents, which no good string player would make. The *piano* sound should suggest mischief more than delicacy.

At m.9 the bass line explodes with an energy that is unmistakably pianistic. Though the RH obviously needs to sound very full here, ugly accents on the final notes of the RH motifs in mm.9-12 must be avoided. The danger of emphasizing last notes of various motifs is constant throughout this movement. Similarly, in mm.13-14 inattentive players often accent the second bass note of each measure.

At m.16 a violinistic theme appears, forming a diatonic descent over an octave. We have already heard this pattern in a very different guise in the RH of mm.5-8. The sound level remains energetic until the end of the theme at m.25. Nowhere is pedaling necessary, but much technical prowess is! How often are mm.20-25 played without panicky rushing?

At m.26 we expect a new theme, but Mozart repeats his device from the first movement, combining a new counterpoint with the initial motif. Here the writing seems to suggest a small group of stringed or woodwind instruments; therefore exactness of articulation and timing are needed. There is an awkward moment in the "viola" line at the second quarter-note beat of m.35. The F-sharp must be played by the RH thumb; however, the abrupt shift to the index finger on the half-note A, which must continue sounding without pedaling, will only succeed if the player's wrist is very supple. Pianistic writing prevails in mm.40-44, the dynamic levels are a subjective matter. One could play mm.44-45 with lighter sound than the preceding four measures, but the frequently heard "echo" effects in mm.41 or 45 sound artificial.

After all this activity, a melting "string quartet" theme provides contrast in m.50. As in two previous themes, this line descends over an octave; this also strengthens the strong organic unity of this movement. The repetition of this theme in the bass line of mm.54-56 sounds delightful when played *non legato*, especially as the busy RH decorations there sound fresher if the slurred groups are not joined to each other by pedaling. In m.58, polyphonic ingenuity is dispelled by exuberant *arpeggi*, best unpedaled. This joyous sentence is not difficult when the player's spine and arms remain completely free. A short transition in mm.63-64 is based on another descending octave pattern.

At m.65 we realize that we are definitely not in sonata form. Retrospectively it becomes obvious that the entire section from m.26 until m.65 could be described as the "B" section of a rondo structure. The second "A" section anticipates Schubert in m.84 with a sudden shift to minor mode, where high spirits are dismissed in a furious whirlwind of dark tonalities. A tense RH line at mm.88-91, another descent over an octave, now chromatic, is heard against frantic triplets. This dramatic moment is often drowned out by excessive pedaling; the RH line will have more power if played as marked, *non legato*.

At m.95, the motifs of m.26 are inverted. There is confusion about the slurring of the bass in mm.96 and 98, but it is logical to play two short RH slurs in each measure as in mm.27 and 29. Mozart's mastery of counterpoint in this "C" section is awesome if only because it draws so little attention to itself. The jaunty initial motif is combined with three different counterpoints, one suggesting a piano concerto raging in G minor (mm.99-102), the next a string or woodwind trio in major mode (mm.103-107), and finally an explosive concerto-like outburst in minor mode but shifting back to major mode at m.110. This dizzying rush of emotions and textures demands much alertness from the player, who should not confuse sound with fury by adding too much pedaling in the stormier passages. The editors of the NMA[30] make the relevant observation that the first notes of the uppermost part in mm.105, 107 are not tied over from the previous measures and should be sounded again. This is much clearer than the tied-over articulation usually heard here.

The rest of the movement can be seen as a more usual progression in rondo form, with a second "B" section (m.117-149), a final "A" section (mm.163-178), with a *Coda*-like thrust to the final cadence beginning at m.178.

Certainly if the sonata is being played in a fairly large space, some pedaling at the climax in mm.152-161 may be welcome. However, even then the "scoring" will be suffocated if the pedal is not changed on each eighth-note beat.

The repeated notes in mm.178-179 give many players difficulty. Various fingerings are possible here; the coordination of a good tennis player is needed, the wrist making a quick downward motion for the second repeated note of each group. The lack of dynamic indications makes the direction of the *Coda* ambiguous. Did Mozart want a vigorous sound from m.171 to the end? Or is a humorous fade-out more suitable? In any case a *diminuendo* before m.186 sounds more weary than witty. Any trace of a sentimental *ritenuto* would be an inappropriate conclusion to such a life-affirming masterpiece.

ORNAMENTATION

The trill from the initial theme, first heard at m.8, the only ornament not written out by Mozart, would sound charmless if begun on the beat. A perky three-note trill *(Schneller)* ending on the first beat suffices. The bass triads in mm.178-183 sound fresher if briskly arpeggiated, but I find further additions or changes to Mozart's perfectly crafted text inconceivable.

XIX

FOUR ASSORTED PIECES FOR PIANO, 1788-91

1 INTERPRETATION, ADAGIO IN B MINOR, K.540

COMPOSITION DATE	March 19, 1788
FORM	sonata
APPROXIMATE TEMPO	♪= M.M. 72
DURATION	10 minutes, with expositional repeat
SUGGESTED LISTENING	Concert Aria, K.425-b, "Misero..."
	Das Lied der Trennung, K.519
	Die Zauberflöte: Pamina's aria
	Requiem, K.626, *Lacrimosa*
	Piano Concerto, K.488 ii

During the first months of 1788, Mozart's imagination became especially mercurial. Only twelve days before completing the *B minor Adagio*, he wrote the uproarious "Ich möchte wohl der Kaiser sein," a rowdy song for baritone and orchestra, worthy of any burlesque theater. A more divergent emotional range is hard to imagine.

Though this *Adagio* is often labeled "romantic," the potent emotions and severe form of K.540 are closer to the world of Classical Greek tragedy. Only a listener with a heart of stone could fail to perceive the weariness and dread voiced here. The blend of compositional techniques is also astonishing, as noted by Arthur Hutchings, who regarded the *Adagio* as:

> "Mozart's finest single work for piano solo ... for all its magnificent integrity, the B minor Adagio reflects during its course facets of expression and details of technique found in works as diverse as variations, rondos, fantasias, and sonatas."[1]

The *Adagio* bears some resemblances to the Andante in B-flat, K.533, completed only two months earlier. Both pieces exhibit harmonic daring and stark polyphonic textures. But the tone of the *Adagio* is even more uncompromising. Whenever Mozart's music touches the key of B minor, the encounter is fleeting, as if the composer feared the threatening sobriety evoked by this tonality. The only other piece by Mozart in B minor is Pedrillo's Romance "Im Mohrenland

gefangen" from *Die Entführung aus dem Serail*, which does not conclude in the tonic key but fades away in the mediant harmony, a very
startling effect in the eighteenth century. B minor is also evaded at
the end of this *Adagio*, with its Picardian shift to major mode.
Like the A minor Rondo, K.511, this *Adagio* expresses both personal and universal conditions. In such a deeply emotional setting the
player must be wary of making stereotyped responses to the text; how
should he, for example, interpret the many dynamic contrasts marked
during the recurrences of the first theme? Surely the accent in the
first measure, an agonized howl in the night, is stronger than the
accent in the following measure, which has a more exhausted quality?
Indeed it is possible that the first measure's emphasis indicates a
rhetorical prolongation of that beat, an effect described in methods of
the period by, among others, D.G. Türk, J.F. Nagel, and N.J. Huell-
mandel.[2] The accent in m.2 can better dissolve wearily but metrically
to its resolution. All the phrases marked *piano* in this piece should
vary in sound level. Presumably mm.2 and 4 are somewhat softer than
mm.1 and 3.

Throughout most of the *Adagio*, the textures of a quartet of
stringed or wind instruments are suggested. The part writing is at
times quite operatic, as in m.5, where the *mf* indication surely refers
to the groaning "viola" line rather than to the melody. Rhythmic
exactness of rests and of the notes preceding them must not be obscured by inattentive pedaling. Prolongation of the last notes in mm.2,6,-
10 or 14 can reduce stark tragedy to mere pathos. Shortening rests at
these crucial moments diminishes the suspense inherent in such
pained silences, but prolongation of too many rests can sound manne-
ristic.

A particularly fatalistic moment is m.6, where sound ebbs until the
mf (a very rare designation in Mozart's music) chord, which is more
like a sigh than an accent. In mm.7-8 the textures open up, but panting anxiety is generated by the rests and the *non legato* LH eighth
notes. The startling shift to D minor in m.9 soon fades into nostalgic
chromaticism.

Throughout the first theme, tense motifs based on wide intervals
alternate with mournful suspensions. The same dichotomy continues
in the second theme, beginning at m.11, the cellist's assertive *arpeggio* figures answered by the first violinist's moaning suspensions.
Plodding between these two motifs is a grim *ostinato*, the second
violin and viola obsessively repeating the dominant. This seems even
more doom-laden than the first *ostinato* in m.3; any visions of hope

have vanished. In this fatalistic atmosphere, rests must be carefully observed; even the thirty-second-note rests should be audible. Many pianists play a *crescendo* in the latter half of m.14, a romantic effect which would have been highly unlikely on instruments of Mozart's time, with their short tone in that register. In any case, Mozart's *forte* in m.15 hardly suggests that the previous measure is to be strong in tone. This *forte* should startle the listener, the chords arpeggiated with vigorous arm movements and three clearly separated pedal strokes. Prolongation of the rest creates a fine rhetorical pause, but prolongation of the third chord sounds elephantine.

The following theme in D, beginning in the latter half of m.15, seems to offer some relief, but the atmosphere is more resigned than cheerful. Use of the pedal should be avoided here, though finger-pedaling of the lower bass notes under the RH thirty-second notes in mm.17-18 seems desirable. On a modern instrument, the *staccati* in m.20 are preferably played slightly *portato*. In the transition back to the opening, the RH chords in m.21 should be arpeggiated, but they are less weighty than the diminished sevenths of m.15.

Difficult as it may be to maintain inner tension while repeating the exposition, evading the challenge seriously impairs the impact of this bleak masterwork. The conflicts of the development section are even more disturbing when the exposition has been heard twice. If a player is willing to confront the composition's fatalism and shuns prettification, any truly sensitive listener will be listening. That so many pianists ignore both repeats is often due to their assumption of a basic tempo that would be more appropriate to a Brucknerian *Adagio*.

The development section opens with a tender sentence in G major. The accents indicated in this more pacific context are slight. But in m.25 gentleness is banned by a *forte* that screams with yearning. In the second half of this measure the diminution of volume and fine balancing between the hands is difficult if the player's posture at the piano is not flexible. Energy is ebbing here, but the sound should not become prematurely soft. Only in the second half of the following measure do the lines seem to disappear in whispers. Laden with the same pessimism that permeates the slow movement of the Piano Concerto in A, K.488, the following phrase in F-sharp minor (mm.26-29) has *forte* outbursts and *piano* whisperings even more dreadful than in the preceding measures. At m.30 the suspensions and grim *ostinato* collapse into an exhausted dominant seventh of G minor. The shuddering suspensions that follow are reminiscent of a string quartet, but compared to the beginning of the piece, the cello and second violin parts are more active, enhancing the restless tension of the modulations and thematic transformations. At m.33 the same agonized statement is stated in A minor, beginning with more energy than the G minor of m.31 but dropping into a terrifying silence. Why this darker side of Mozart, so evident in some of his late works, affects us so deeply was memorably expressed by P.H. Lang:

> "His progress was not struggle but sorrow, and perhaps it was sorrow because it was not struggle. Every force can be vanquished except one: resignation. At the bottom of this brilliant and playful music there burns the warmth of a great suffering, a doomed love and desire for life that are warmer than life itself." [3]

As if to balance the foregoing harmonic unrest, the recapitulation takes its traditional course. In the second theme group, the only textural change is in m.48, where the RH line erupts in an *arpeggio* figuration. How often does C major sound as anguished as here? The horror of this moment is practically always lost because pianists play the RH line *legato* and with excessive pedaling. Played *non legato* and with the pedal changed on each eighth-note beat, the ascending *arpeggio* expresses devastating futility.

At m.51 the player is confronted by a very thorny dilemma: to repeat the second section or not? Arguably the *Coda* is even more poignant when the second repeat is observed. But it is debatable whether the strife and pain of the development section gain eloquence if heard twice. This remains a subjective issue.

The chords from the second version of m.51 leading into m.52 maintain an intimate dynamic level, and, despite the torment evident here, exaggerated *crescendi* or *rubati* would be misplaced. The pain that has been throbbing throughout the entire piece becomes focused in the first violin line, the lower lines barely stirring. During the LH thirds, the pedal should be changed as often as possible. Presumably each step of this intense sequence gains in tone.

Because a meter of 17/16 was unknown in the eighteenth century, Mozart had to squeeze the broken octaves of m.54 into the 4/4 meter with an awkward acceleration in the seventh eighth-note beat. As this line has an *Eingang*-like character, some rhythmic flexibility is justified. The situation recurs in the slow movement of the B-flat Sonata, K.333 (m.4). Playing all the octaves as thirty-second notes with a slight *ritenuto* seems more natural than interpreting the text literally. The shift to major mode in m.55 is an archaic device from the baroque age but also anticipates the ambivalent modality heard in much nineteenth-century music. The B major seems to express release from all the previous suffering. Dennerlein heard here "the depths of a wondrous piece for Good Friday."[4] And it is interesting to note that the *Liebestod* from Wagner's *Tristan und Isolde* also ends in B major.

Whatever the significance of this *Adagio*'s last three measures, they must surely be played with total simplicity, very serenely but without *rubato*. All the anguished suspensions have vanished. Peace has been found.

ORNAMENTATION   As there are virtually no decorations in this piece, a separate section on ornamentation is unnecessary.

The *appoggiatura* first heard in m.3 occurs between an anticipation and a suspension. As such it is a *Zwischenschlag* and must be played before the fourth quarter-note beat. Neumann[5] and Rosenblum[6] agree with this interpretation. The actual duration of the ornament is, of course, a matter of taste and may vary slightly throughout the piece.

The chords in mm.21 and 51 could be arpeggiated like those in m.15, but any additional decoration during this unique expression of despair and acceptance would be as appropriate as giggling during a funeral.

The manuscript[7] is very legible. Challenges exist not in the text, but in the projecting of the emotional range and depth of this masterpiece without lapsing into maudlin platitudes.

2 INTERPRETATION OF THE VARIATIONS ON A MINUET BY DUPORT, K.573

COMPOSITION DATE	spring 1789
TOTAL DURATION	10 minutes (without repeats)
APPROXIMATE TEMPO	$\quad\downarrow$ = M.M.108
SUGGESTED LISTENING	String Quartet, K.499 ii
	String Quartet, K.575 iii
	Clarinet Quintet, K.581 iii

Mozart wrote six variations on this minuet during his visit to the Prussian court in 1789. The theme is from Duport's Six Cello Sonatas, Opus 4. Jean-Pierre Duport (1741-1818) was a virtuoso cellist and organizer of concerts at the court of Friedrich Wilhelm II.[8] Only seven years later, Beethoven composed his two Sonatas, Opus 5, for performances with Duport. Mozart listed six variations in his thematic catalogue but apparently added three more later, the published version of 1792 consisting of nine variations. Unfortunately the manuscript has been lost, and modern editions are based on several early copies. The *Duport* Variations may not be the most original of Mozart's works in this genre, but they are certainly among the most perfectly formed. As in the other D major piano work of that year, the Sonata, K.576, there is an astonishing synthesis of grace and emotion. Unfortunately one often hears these variations rattled off with misplaced exhibitionism or, perhaps even worse, cloying sentimentality.

The fresh elegance of the theme can be easily upset by carelessness or a hasty tempo. Not all the first beats should receive the same weight, and any emphasis of the third quarter-note beats suggests a minuet for drunkards. Slowing down before first beats is a nineteenth-century effect, which must be shunned. The *non legato* "cello" line in mm.10 and 12 should be played without pedaling.

Yet again the issue of repetitions is debatable. The second section of the theme and each variation, mm.9-24, include an ornamented return of the initial phrase in the final eight measures. Perhaps this makes repetition of these sections irrelevant. I believe that repeating the second section of each variation creates a needlessly academic atmosphere.

As in Mozart's other variation works for piano solo, the first variation presents RH decorations that can too readily become mechanical. The difference in articulation between the first measure, with slurs over each quarter-note beat, and the fourth, where the entire measure has a single slur, may imply a contrast between active, dancing moments and more lyrical ones. A slight emphasis of the first note under each slur is more important than whatever separations between the slurred groups the player may choose. Noticeable separation of slurs would sound pedantic here.

The joyous second variation gives the LH a fine run. On a modern instrument heaviness in the bass sound should be avoided, and the RH tone should remain bright. This variation is a fine *etude*; moments like the third measure are extremely difficult if there is any tension in the LH thumb. Posture is also important here; the player will find this variation easier when he leans slightly towards the right side of the instrument, but not closer to the keyboard.

In the third variation, the violinistic lines will have a suitably playful quality if the pianist's rhythm is stable and his wrists relaxed.

The quick triadic figures and repeated notes frequently distract players who nervously rush longer notes.

In Variation 4 woodwind instruments are evoked. As in the previous variations, if pedaling is avoided, the richly varied articulation sounds more vital. In the patterns of repeated thirds and sixths, dull evenness must be shunned; the upper voice should dominate the lower, and the "weaker" beats must sound as such.

The fifth variation is even more joyous, full of delicious changes in scoring. The initial repeated notes are best played with the same finger; changing fingers in such passages makes for a labored sound on modern instruments. The delightful interchange of *legato, non legato* and *staccato* requires no pedaling.

Best played without any dawdling at final cadences, the first five variations form a group within the piece. A brief pause after Variation 5 seems welcome.

There is no change of tempo indicated in Variation 6, but if the music continues to flow with one impulse to a measure, and not three, a slightly more leisurely tempo will not be conspicuous. The piece can be viewed as melancholy or agitated. Everything played by the RH, also the repeated notes, should be inflected as if sung. The frequently heard rushing in the LH's accompaniment would be a distortion of Mozartian *rubato*, which requires that the bass remain steady even when the RH strays from the meter.

The editor of the NMA edition[9] observed that the brilliant seventh variation and the "fantasy-like Coda" must have been among the original six variations, as both pieces are in Mozart's most exuberant style and would have made a big impression at the Prussian court. The bass octaves of the seventh variation sound more festive on a fortepiano than on a large modern instrument. If the player does not keep his thumb and the middle fingers as relaxed as possible, this variation will sound more like a struggle than a celebration.

The *Adagio* variation is in operatic style, calm but not static. Daniel Barenboim,[10] for example, admirably combines intensity in this "aria for piano" with a minuet-like pulse. One often hears heedless LH rushing at serene moments in mm.3,9,13. In mm.9,11 and 13, *rubato* is possible in the melody, but not in the bass line. The RH's florid decorative gestures in mm.10,14,16 certainly do not have to be played absolutely metrically.

The last variation will sound spirited enough if a quarter-note beat is only slightly faster than in the original theme. The humor is diminished if unslurred eighth notes in mm.5-6,10,14 and in the bass of mm.30-33 are pedaled or played *legato*. Ingrid Haebler[11] omits the tie binding the two F-sharps in mm.5-6, an amusing rhythmic touch found in one of the older copies. The *Coda* is enlivened by crossing of the hands, one of Mozart's favorite pianistic gestures. Any overt *piano* effects in mm.29-50 seem artificial as the music sweeps energetically toward the short *Eingang*. Obviously the *tempo primo* of the final 13 measures refers to the initial minuet tempo, not to the *Allegro* pace of Variation 9.

The *Duport* Variations are Mozart's last composition for piano in the *galant* style, his last piano piece that acknowledged the past more than the future. That future can be briefly glimpsed in two unfinished works, the G minor Allegro and the D major Minuet (Chapter XIX, sections 5 and 7). After the *Duport* Variations, Mozart was to write one more variation set for piano, the curious K.613, arguably more interesting to the historian than to the pianist.[12]

It is curious to reflect that the masterly *Duport* Variations, so evocative of courtly grace, were conceived in the same year as the outbreak of the French Revolution. The world mirrored in this composition was doomed, but Mozart was not to witness its demise.

3 ORNAMENTATION IN THE DUPORT VARIATIONS, K.573

THEME

m.

3   The trill can best be played with three notes, beginning on the principal note, and the termination.

7   With its dotted rhythms, this second phrase is even more light-hearted than the first, and therefore this trill could take a prebeat rendition (as in the theme's reappearance at the end of the entire piece). In that case it consists of three notes, played very quickly, the third on the final quarter-note beat.

16   The *appoggiatura* falls on the first beat. It sounds peculiar if played quickly; a slightly prolonged eighth note is best. A certain rhythmic freedom is welcome here, with a *caesura* before the upbeat notes to the following sentence.

23   A prebeat rendition of the ornament is definitely preferable, with the third note on the third quarter-note beat, the sixteenth notes played as marked.

VARIATION 2

12   Perhaps the best solution is to play the turn as a three-note *Schneller*, beginning on the principal note and without a termi-

nation. A five-note turn beginning on the upper auxiliary, suggested in some editions, obscures the line.

VARIATION 3

1   In this case there can be no doubt that the uppermost note of the *arpeggio*, not the lowest, sounds on the first beat (see also F. Neumann[13]).

VARIATION 5

1   An onbeat beginning is pedantic. The turns sound more cheerful when they end on the third quarter-note beat.

4   The *appoggiature* are amusing if played as light grace notes. Playing them on the eighth-note beats is also possible but makes for a more cynical effect.

VARIATION 6

3   Mozart probably wrote out some of the turns in this variation due to chromatisation of some auxiliary notes. None of the turns should sound too hurried. They are best begun slightly earlier than written.

22   These turns (identical with mm.52-53 of the D minor Fantasy, K.397) are more expressive when the subsequent sixteenth notes are played *non legato*. An affirmative arpeggiation of the bass chord, the uppermost note sounding on the first beat, is welcome.

VARIATION 8

3   If the *appoggiatura* does not sound before the beat, the dotted rhythm of the third quarter-note beat is obscured.

9   The first sixteenth note after the turn becomes the last note of the ornament and is therefore played somewhat quicker than marked.

12   The ascending scale should not be metrical. The last four *non legato* thirty-second notes of this measure sound unmistakably like laughter; if these notes are slurred, the line droops.

18   If the *appoggiatura* is not played very gently before the beat, an effect like the braying of a donkey is evoked.

24   Some editions have a turn marked on the final melodic note, but this seems spurious.[14]

VARIATION 9

7   The *appoggiatura* becomes a perky grace note before the second quarter-note beat.

25   This lively ornament resembles that in m.23 of the theme but is more rapid here. With the fingering 2-3-2 and a relaxed thumb there should be no difficulties. The third note sounds on the second quarter-note beat.

53   In this *Eingang* the dominant seventh chord in the bass sounds
        more functional if arpeggiated. This chord can be held until the
        trills begin. The RH takes the chord's uppermost note. The trills
        should be quite long, the first G-sharp not accented. Normally
        the second trill would have a termination, though some editions
        imply there is none,[15] as the upward swing to the highest note
        can be perceived as a termination.

REPETITION OF THEME

1   If played lightly, the turn sounds most charming begun just
        after the second quarter-note beat.

7   That this ornament is written differently in m.9 and 11 does not
        necessarily mean that the difference is noticeable. One could
        play a lively four-note trill, beginning on the upper auxiliary in
        m.7, a *Schneller* (three-note trill) in m.9, and a slower *Schneller*,
        beginning just after the second quarter-note beat in m.11. All
        three ornaments end on the respective third quarter-note beats.

12   The final RH chords sound more festive if rapidly arpeggiated
        and pedaled.

4 MOZART DURING 1790 AND 1791

1790

January   Successful premiere of *Così fan tutte*; death of Em-
                peror Joseph II.

March   Mozart's hopes for the position of second *Kapellmeis-
                ter* at the court of the new emperor are dashed.

May   In a letter to Puchberg Mozart mentions "I now have
                two pupils and should very much like to raise the
                number to eight. Do your best to spread the news that
                I am willing to give lessons."[16]

June   Among the attempts to write some of the piano sona-
                tas commissioned for the Prussian princess during
                this time is perhaps the G minor Sonata Movement,
                K.312/590-a.

September   During his trip to Frankfurt for the coronation of
                Leopold II, Mozart gives a badly attended concert. He
                moves to an apartment in the Rauhensteingasse, in
                the center of Vienna, his last dwelling.

1791

January/   As in previous years, Mozart writes dances for the

February	ball season at the court.
March	Mozart plays his last piano concerto, in B-flat, K.595, during his final concert. The actor and impresario Schikaneder interests Mozart in the composition of *Die Zauberflöte*. The piano variations "Ein Weib ist das Herrlichste Ding," K.613, are composed on a theme from another piece staged by Schikaneder.
April	Mozart applies to the municipal council of Vienna for the unpaid position of assistant to Leopold Hoffmann, *Kapellmeister* of St. Stephen's Cathedral, gets the appointment, but Hoffmann will outlive him. The String Quintet in E-flat, K.614, is finished, but Mozart seems to have lost interest in fulfilling the Prussian commissions for string quartets and piano sonatas.
July	Mozart receives an anonymous commission for a requiem mass. Franz Xaver Wolfgang is born, the sixth of the Mozarts' children and the second to survive infancy. Constanze later changed his name to Wolfgang Amadeus in the hope of furthering the boy's modest pianistic career.
August	Mozart makes his last trip, to Prague, where Leopold II is being crowned King of Bohemia. The opera *La clemenza di Tito*, commissioned for the occasion, is written so quickly that Mozart had to work on the score traveling in the carriage to Prague.
September	Not only *La clemenza*, but *Don Giovanni* is staged in Prague, where the composer still enjoys much acclaim. In Vienna *Die Zauberflöte* is premiered with great success.
October	The last extant letter from Mozart is to Constanze in Baden, where she is again taking a cure, expressing his concern about the education of their son Karl. Constanze returns to Vienna. The Clarinet Concerto is completed.
November	The composer makes the last entry in his catalogue, the *Freemasons' Cantata*, K.623. After months of overwork and variable health, he becomes bedridden.
December	On December 5, Mozart dies of an affliction resembling rheumatic fever.

5 ALLEGRO (SONATA MOVEMENT) IN G MINOR, K.590-d

OTHER K.NUMBERS	K.312, K.189-i
COMPOSITION DATE	1790-91
FORM	sonata
APPROXIMATE TEMPO	$\downarrow$ = M.M. 132
DURATION	6 minutes (with both repeats)
SUGGESTED LISTENING	Symphony, K.550 iii
	Symphony, K.173-d-B iii
	String Quintet, K.516 i
	String Quartet, K.387 ii

This *Allegro* has had a peculiar history, or rather, lack of history, as few musicians know of its existence. Dennerlein[17] thought that the piece was originally intended for the B-flat sonata, K.281. Hutchings[18] also assumed the movement derived from the period of the Munich Sonatas, K.279-284. Alfred Einstein initially agreed with this view but later concluded that the *Allegro*:

> "... is realized in a fusion of styles, and with a mastery of which Mozart in 1774 was by no means yet capable. The fact that no one knows this movement or plays it and that none of the popular editions of the piano works contains it is no argument against it."[19]

In the 1941 supplement to the Köchel Catalogue, Einstein gave the piece a new numbering, K.590-d. Since then the piece has been included in several editions of the "assorted pieces."[20] More recently, that invaluable Sherlock Holmes of classical music, Alan Tyson, studied the manuscript and observed:

> "Mozart wrote everything up to four measures before the recapitulation, the rest is by an unknown hand ... The watermark of the autograph is almost cut off (the two leaves were trimmed to fit into a volume Mendelssohn gave to his bride), but it is nevertheless possible to identify it. The paper-type was first used by Mozart in the middle of his work on *Così fan tutte*, and was then available to him up to the end of his life. So the fragment dates from 1790 or 1791."[21]

Perhaps this piece was an attempt by Mozart to fulfill the commission for six "easy" piano sonatas for the daughter of the Prussian king.

The *Allegro*'s strong lines and almost parched textures are not unlike the "Masonic" sections in *Die Zauberflöte* or certain movements of the Requiem. Whoever completed this rugged torso for publication in 1805 fulfilled the task with taste, but it is unlikely that Mozart would have written a recapitulation so utterly lacking in surprise elements. This is, however, insufficient justification for the total neglect of a fascinating composition. It is possible that the remote atmosphere of the piece does not attract players. This could be one of those late pieces by Mozart, which seem:

"... veiled, death-chilled, melancholy, or merely sad... The music does not communicate as unselfconsciously as it did, as though the composer, less involved, is beginning to lose interest in his audience." [22]

A string quartet is evoked at the beginning, with the first violinist clearly leading the discourse. The opening theme pulls inexorably toward m.5, the rests not breaking the thrust of the longer line. The rest in m.6 is more rhetorical and may be slightly lengthened. There is no denying the severe beauty of the polyphonic writing in mm.7-19, preferably played without pedaling or *rubato*. During the following sequence the motivic impulses in mm.23-24 start in the second quarter-note beats, not the first.

The second theme group, from m.25, becomes shapeless if not projected with considerable drive. Was the crossing of hands in mm.27-35 for the amusement of the Prussian princess? Alternative distributions between the hands are possible there, but accents resulting from aerial traffic would be unpleasant. This theme certainly sounds better on a fortepiano than on a modern instrument. To avoid unpleasantly thick sound, the pedal should be changed on each quarter-note beat or totally omitted. The RH triplets of mm.37-40 are difficult if the player's thumb is tense. There is another tremendous surge of energy to m.44.

The subsequent *legato* theme may be more wistful, but the tempo should not droop. The three part writing needs careful balancing of tone. In m.52, B-flat major suggests affability, but this is nervous and brief. The RH repeated notes must not be played mechanically and the lower bass notes could be finger-pedaled. Use of the pedal throughout this theme would result in blurring.

In the masterly *Codetta*, beginning in m.64, there is a shift back to a desolate G minor; then Mozart startles us by repeating the same figure in B-flat. The uncertainty concludes with a violent lurch in m.69 to the dominant harmony. Omitting the first repeat belittles the intense emotional strife of the compact exposition. After repeating the section, the shift to the development could be played more gently. As in the first three measures of the piece, the bass octaves of mm.68-71 are pedaled but played *non legato*. The rhetorical writing here is more communicative when the player, particularly on a modern instrument, does not resort to monotonous loudness. Except during the turns, pedaling can add body to the sound. The beatific harmony at m.79 is a sudden ray of sunshine in this dark landscape. During the rest of the development section, the lack of dynamic indications does not imply a continuation of m.76's *piano* sonority; a considerable *crescendo*, seems justified in mm.102-107.

In his sensitive recording of this piece, Alexey Lubimov[23] observes the second repeat, but with the recapitulation ending on the first beat of m.177, and the two last whispered chords forming a minimal *Coda*. Given the brevity of this dense drama, the second repetition certainly seems welcome.

Despite its inherent challenges, it is regrettable that pianists so rarely perform this potent piece. H.C. Robbins Landon aptly remarked:

"The superb quality of this fragment makes us regret once again the untimely death of music's greatest genius."[24]

6 ORNAMENTATION IN THE G MINOR ALLEGRO, K.590-d

m.

1   The trill sounds pedantic if not begun on the principal note. Playing the upper auxiliary as a grace note before the trill would create a most unsuitable light-hearted effect. A three-note trill before the termination is sufficiently gritty to propel the grim theme forward.

43   It seems preferable to begin the trill on the principal note, which could be somewhat elongated so that its function as a suspension becomes clear.

48   The compound *appoggiatura* sounds before the first quarter-note beat. On the beat it would become inappropriately cheerful.

63   The trill is energetic, with the upper auxiliary on the first beat and the termination sounding in the final eighth-note beat.

64   Played before the third quarter-note beat, the *appoggiatura* would seem humorous, hardly a suitable effect in such a melan-

choly phrase. Therefore the ornament sounds on the beat, creating a *rubato* effect, with the two subsequent notes somewhat shortened.

Sparse textures do not necessarily motivate added embellishment. The diverting but baroque-like decorations of the opening theme in the recording by Ton Koopman[25] do not seem particularly Mozartian, though elsewhere he adds some touches that are relevant, like the trills before the second quarter-note beat of m.133 or the first beat of m.134.

7 INTERPRETATION OF THE MINUET IN D MAJOR, K.594-a

OTHER K. LISTINGS	K.355-a, K.576-b
COMPOSITION DATE	probably 1789-91
FORM	ternary
APPROXIMATE TEMPO	♩ = M.M. 82-84
DURATION	1½ minutes (with first repeat)
SUGGESTED LISTENING	String Quartet, K.589 iii
	Piano Trio, K.542 i
	String Quintet, K.516 ii

The divergent Köchel listings given above illustrate the uncertain history of this composition. Alfred Einstein concluded that the Minuet was definitely a late work, even suggesting that it could be a discarded movement of the D major Sonata, K.576.[26] The startling polyphony certainly suggest that the piece is from Mozart's last years. The Minuet is not listed in the composer's own catalogue because it lacks a *Trio* (middle section) and is therefore, technically at least, incomplete. In 1801 the Minuet was published with a *Trio* by the eminent church musician Maximilian Stadler (not to be confused with Anton Stadler, the virtuoso clarinettist for whom Mozart wrote several masterpieces). Maximilian Stadler became the principal musical advisor to Constanze Mozart in 1796. He finished several fragments found among Mozart's manuscripts, such as this Minuet and the C minor Fantasy, K.396. Because the manuscript of the Minuet has vanished, its publication in 1801 was extremely fortunate, for the piece, though not well known, is a miniature masterpiece.

All fine editions of Mozart's piano works include this miniature among the "assorted piano pieces." Stadler's *Trio* evinces craftsmanship but lacks Mozart's inspiration. The attempts of Stadler and several twentieth-century composers can be ignored; even if it is only 44 measures long, the Minuet fragment remains a totally satisfying whole. The modulatory section in mm.17-28 is so adventurous and such a contrast from the first section, itself so rich in surprises, that the listener experiences a perfectly balanced ternary form.

It is not possible to know if it is Mozart's indication, but the *dolce* at the beginning of the Minuet rightly suggests that the expressive aspects are more important than the dance-like elements. This music is obviously more than merely graceful; it sighs, wails, later even giggles. Robert Dumm gave a marvelous image of this piece:

> "Its melting chromaticism and dynamic shocks suggest a composite memory of a thousand distantly heard minuets. It balances a remarkable degree of dynamic tension between sound and movement, as if the brain suffers waves of vertigo even as the feet perform their well-rehearsed mime..." [27]

In the second measure the chromatic double-thirds sound daring, but the observation by the NMA editor[28] that E, not E-sharp, should sound on the second eighth-note beat in the lower RH line seems contradicted by the consistent chromaticism of the following measure. Slurred notes must be played with a very melting *legato*, but the creeping chromatic motif in the viola part in m.6, though it derives from the first three slurred bass notes, could be played with weary *non legato* strokes. Except where turns are sounding, the pedal, changed on each quarter-note beat, can be used until mm.12-16, where grace and levity suddenly, almost schizophrenically, take over. How surreal this bumptious tune sounds after the enigmatic darkness of the preceding sentence!

The writing in the middle section suggests an ensemble of stringed or wind instruments. The section begins with a harmonic jolt that seems modern but which Dumm observed can also be heard in the *Trio* of the *Menuet* of Bach's French Suite in B minor. The chromatic motif heard in the bass line at the beginning of the piece, then extended by a note in mm.5-6, is inverted here and becomes the thread of a mournful sequence that would not be out of place in Beethoven's last quartets. Even the uppermost line of mm.17-20 forms an augmentation of this motif.

In the third quarter-note beat of m.20 Mozart suddenly reverses the direction of the music. Another sequence, tentative but more hopeful, ascends to a few measures of D major. The player must be very careful to let the long upper notes here sound with a sunny tone that can dominate the activity of the lower voices. The cheerfulness is soured by chromatic alterations in m.24. Any deviation from the tempo during mm.25-27 diminishes the seriousness of this fateful descent. In m.28 the tension evaporates in a *mancando* (which, as noted previously, is in Mozart a *diminuendo*, without slowing down).[29] Measures 28-30, suggesting a twelve-tone row, are among the most modern moments in all of Mozart's music. Between the second eighth-note beat of m.28 and the second quarter-note beat of m.30, we hear all but one of the tones in the chromatic scale, a startling prediction of late Liszt, even Schönberg!

The return of the first theme in the upper line at m.29 is barely recognizable heard against the tortured chromaticism in the second violin and cello parts. Perhaps these measures give us an intimation of how Mozart might have progressed had he lived longer.

In m.31 the music returns to "normalcy," the rest of the third section becoming a straightforward affirmation of the tonic key. But the breezy closing sentence seems eerie, like someone whistling in a bomb shelter, far removed from the nonchalant grace of an eighteenth-century minuet.

The only ORNAMENTS are the five-note turns in mm.4 and 11. Arguably the first is best begun on the upper auxiliary, as this accentuates its melancholy character. In m.11 an assertive beginning on the principal note seems more appropriate, but if the piano has a thick tone, beginning on the upper note may be preferable.

EPILOGUE

This last amazing, enigmatic Minuet in D epitomizes the astonishing genius of Mozart, which never ceases to enrich our lives.

Barely 25 years after Mozart's death, Franz Schubert noted in his diary:

"A light, bright, fine day this will remain throughout my whole life. As from afar the magic notes of Mozart's music still gently haunt me ... Thus does our soul retain these fair impressions, which no time, no circumstances can efface, and they lighten our existence ... Immortal Mozart, how many ... comforting perceptions of a brighter and better life hast thou brought to our souls!"[30]

Saul Bellow made some fascinating observations about Mozart in our time:

"We have learned from history that enlightenment, liberation, and doom may go together. For every avenue liberation opens, two are closed. Within Mozart's cheerful daylight secularity there is always an otherworldly darkness. And the freedom he expresses is never without sadness, a deep submission to melancholy. We are endowed — so I interpret him — with comprehension, but what we are required to comprehend is too much for us."[31]

That marvelous pianist and thinker, Russell Sherman, gets to the heart of the Mozart mystery:

"Mozart is the prince of cordiality, the prince of tolerance (who never sneers at but enjoys our foibles), the prince of kindness. His message can be distilled in different ways, but I prefer the simple injunction — listen before you talk. You might learn something which could inform your own thoughts, making them more perceptive, bearable, and winged."[32]

NOTES

INTRODUCTION

1. Schubart, C.F.D., *Ideen zu einer Aesthetik der Tonkunst* (Leipzig, 1977) p.373.
2. Badura Skoda, E. & P., *Interpreting Mozart on the Keyboard* (London, 1962).
3. Rosenblum, S.P., *Performing Practices in Classic Piano Music* (Bloomington, 1988). This is an invaluable reference book for all serious pianists and piano teachers.
4. Neumann, F., *Performance Practices of the Seventeenth and Eighteenth Centuries* (New York, 1993) and *Ornamentation and Improvisation in Mozart* (Princeton, 1986).
5. Rampe, S., *Mozarts Claviermusik: Klangwelt und Aufführungspraxis*, (Kassel, 1995), as yet available only in German, is a serious study, heavily documented, but for the modern pianist often confusing, sometimes irrelevant, because many of his observations derive not only from historical texts and attitudes, but also from a conviction that many of these works are best played on the harpsichord: a curiously unhistorical premise. However, this is a very useful publication for those more interested in eighteenth century performance practices than in the performance of the individual works.
6. Schachter, C., "20th-century analysis and Mozart performance," in *Early Music* (London, November 1991) p.620.
7. Levin, R.D., "Mozart's Solo Keyboard Music," in *Eighteenth Century Keyboard Music*, ed. R.L. Marshall (New York, 1994) p.343.
8. Neumann, *Performance Practices*, p.8.
9. Among the best editions at the time of writing are the *Neue Mozart Ausgabe* (published by Bärenreiter, Kassel), *Henle Urtext Edition* (Henle-Verlag, München) and the *Wiener Urtext Edition* (Schott-Universal, Vienna). The *Henle* and *Wiener Urtext* editions published after the mid-1980's are better than earlier printings of these editions and the otherwise fine *Urtext* Editions of Peters (Frankfurt) and T. Presser (New York), which contain occasional textual inaccuracies. Publications based on the *Breitkopf und Härtel Complete Works* are, despite the impressive sounding title (not to be confused with the modern *Neue Mozart Ausgabe*), so riddled with nineteenth century misconceptions that they should never be used.
10. Schnabel, A., *My Life and Music*, (New York, 1961) p.122.
11. Craft, R., *Current Convictions*, (New York, 1977) pp.8-9.

CHAPTER I

1. Wolff, K., *Schnabel's Interpretation of Piano Music* (London, 1972) pp.116-117.
2. Somfai, L., notes accompanying M. Bilson recording of the Mozart sonatas, Hungaroton HCD 31009-14, 1989-1991, p.7.

3. Neumann, F., *Performance Practices of the Seventeenth and Eighteenth Centuries* (New York, 1993) p.277.
4. Notably Marty, J-P., *The Tempo Indications of Mozart* (New Haven, 1988).
5. Lateiner, J., "An interpreter's approach to Mozart" in *Early Music*, Vol.XX, No. 2 (Oxford, 1992) p.250.
6. Robert, P., ed., *Dictionnaire de la Langue Française*, Vol.IV (Paris, 1959) p.57.
7. Onions, C.T., ed., *Shorter Oxford English Dictionary* (Oxford, 1993) p.1099.
8. Quantz, J.J., *On Playing the Flute* (New York, 1966) p.120 (English translation of *Versuch einer Anweisung die Flöte traversiere zu spielen*).
9. Neumann, p.350.
10. Türk, D.G., *School of Clavier Playing* (English translation of *Klavierschule*) (Lincoln, 1982).
11. Neumann, *Ornamentation and Improvisation in Mozart* (Princeton, 1986) pp.165-174, and *Performance Practices*, pp.293-530.
12. Levin, R.D., "Improvised embellishments in Mozart's keyboard music," in *Early Music*, Vol.XX, No.2 (Oxford, 1992) p.222.
13. Rampe, *Mozarts Claviermusik: Klangwelt und Aufführungspraxis*, (Kassel, 1995) p.205.

CHAPTER II

1. Gounod, C., *Le Don Juan de Mozart* (Paris, 1890, English translation 1895).
2. Glock, W., *Notes in Advance, An Autobiography in Music* (Oxford, 1991) p.86.
3. Anderson, E., ed., *The Letters of Mozart and His Family* (New York, 1989) p.355.
4. Ross, A., "Classical View," in the *New York Times*, August 28, 1994.
5. Neumann, F., *Performance Practices of the Seventeenth and Eighteenth Centuries* (New York, 1993) p.8.
6. Harnoncourt, N., interview with H. Canning, in *The Gramophone* (London, November 1991) pp.72-73.
7. Rosen, C., "The Shock of the Old," in the *New York Review of Books* (July 19, 1990) pp.46-52.
8. Rosen, C., "Should Music be Played 'Wrongly'?" in *High Fidelity*, Vol.XXI, No. 5 (May 1971) p.58.
9. Gruber, G., *Mozart and Posterity* (Boston, 1994); highly recommended reading for those who are interested in the reception and perception of Mozart's music throughout the last two centuries.
10. Barth, G., "Mozart Performance in the Nineteenth Century," in *Early Music* (London, November 1991) p.550.
11. Schulenberg, D., *The Keyboard Music of J.S. Bach* (New York, 1992) p.9.
12. Rosen, C., "The Shock of the Old," p.49.
13. Harnoncourt, N., in an interview with S. Smit, in *Entracte* (Amsterdam, June 1990) p.34 (translation, M. Davidson).
14. Schachter, C., "Twentieth-century Analysis and Mozart Performance," in *Early Music* (London, November 1991) p.620.

CHAPTER III

1. Biographies are included in the bibliography at the end of the guide.
2. Anderson, E., *Letters of Mozart and his Family* (New York, 1989).
3. Hildesheimer, W., *Mozart* (New York, 1983) p.10.
4. Sherman, R., *Piano Pieces* (New York, 1996) p.194.
5. Solomon, M., *Mozart: A Life* (New York, 1995). This superlative biography offers the most information and interpretation of the complicated relationship between Leopold and Wolfgang Mozart.
6. *Köchel Verzeichnis*, various editors (Wiesbaden, 1965) p.3.
7. Little, M.E., in *The New Groves Dictionary of Music & Musicians*, Vol.XII, ed. S. Sadie (London, 1994) pp.353-354.
8. Little, p.354.
9. Marty, J-P., *The Tempo Indications of Mozart* (New Haven, 1988) p.192.
10. Anderson, p.121.
11. Rosenblum, S.P., *The Interpretation of Classic Piano Music* (Bloomington, 1988) p.338.
12. Marty, p.193.
13. Rampe, *Mozarts Claviermusik: Klangwelt und Aufführungspraxis*, (Kassel, 1995) p.234.
14. Rampe, p.255.
15. Tyson, A., *Mozart: Studies of the Autograph Scores* (Cambridge, Mass., 1987) p.29.
16. Anderson, p.329.
17. Einstein, A., *Mozart: His Character, His Work* (London, 1966) p.124.
18. Till, N., *Mozart and the Enlightenment* (London, 1992) p.17.

CHAPTER IV

1. Dennerlein, H., *Der unbekannte Mozart* (Leipzig, 1951) p.31.
2. Plath, W. & Rehm, W., ed., NMA *Klaviersonaten*, Vol.I (Kassel, 1986) p.3.
3. Miller, M., "Leopold Mozart's formative influence on Wolfgang Amadeus Mozart's early piano sonatas," in *Piano Journal* (London, October 1996) pp.14-15.
4. Bilson, M., Hungaroton recording HCD 310013-14, 1991.
5. Neumann, F., *Ornamentation and Improvisation in Mozart* (Princeton, 1986) p.154.
6. Badura Skoda, E. & P., *Interpreting Mozart on the Keyboard* (London, 1962) p.88.
7. Bilson, M., "Do We Really Know How to Read Urtext Editions?" in *Piano & Keyboard* (July-August 1995) pp.24-30.
8. Somfai, L., notes accompanying M. Bilson recording, Hungaroton HCD 31009-10, 1989, p.12.
9. Rosenblum, S.P., *Performance Practices in Classical Piano Music* (Bloomington, 1988) pp.320-21.
10. Sherman, R., *Piano Pieces* (New York, 1996) p.188.

11. Rampe, *Mozarts Claviermusik: Klangwelt und Aufführungspraxis*, (Kassel, 1995) p.231.
12. Neumann, p.73.
13. Einstein, A., *Mozart: His Character, His Work* (London, 1966) p.242.
14. Anderson, E., *Letters of Mozart and his Family* (New York, 1989) p.368.
15. Neumann, pp.131-132
16. Plath, W. & Rehm,W., ed., NMA *Klaviersonaten*, Vol.I (Kassell, 1986) p.32.
17. Plath & Rehm, p.33.
18. Gould, G., CBS-Odyssey recording MB2K 45612, 1989.
19. Neumann, p.52.
20. Einstein, p.242.
21. Cole, M.S., in *The New Grove Dictionary of Music and Musicians*, ed. S. Sadie (London, 1994) Vol.XVI, p.175.
22. Wolff, K., *Masters of the Keyboard* (Bloomington, 1983) p.90.
23. Neumann, p.53.
24. Neumann, F., *Performance Practices of the Seventeenth and Eighteenth Centuries* (New York, 1993) pp.440-442.
25. Bilson, M., Hungaroton recording HCD 31009-10, 1989.
26. Plath & Rehm, p.36.

CHAPTER V

1. Einstein, A., *Mozart: His Character, His Work* (London, 1966) p.241.
2. Till, N., *Mozart and the Enlightenment* (London, 1992) p.31.
3. Denis Matthews, in his edition of the sonatas for the Associated Board of the Royal Schools of Music (London, 1979) p.56, and Malcolm Bilson on his superlative recording of this sonata (Hungaroton HCD 31013-14, 1991) also concur with this opinion.
4. Neumann, F., *Ornamentation and Improvisation in Mozart* (Princeton, 1986) p.16.
5. Plath, W. & Rehm, W., ed., NMA *Klaviersonaten*, Vol.I (Kassel, 1986) p.43.
6. Newman, A., Newport Classic recording NCD 60121, 1990.
7. Landowska, W., *Landowska on Music* (New York, 1964) p.317.
8. Bilson, M., Hungaroton recording HCD 31009-10,1989.
9. Dennerlein, H., *Der unbekannte Mozart* (Leipzig, 1951) p.48.
10. Landowska, p.317.
11. Dennerlein, p.148.
12. Kraus, L., Sony recording SM4K 47222, 1991.
13. Levin, R.D., "Mozart's Solo Keyboard Music," in *Eighteenth-Century Piano Music*, ed. R.L. Todd (New York, 1994) p.315.

CHAPTER VI

1. Anderson, E., *The Letters of Mozart and his Family* (London, 1989) p.340.
2. Anderson, p.399.

3. Abert, H., *Mozart*, Vol.I (Leipzig, 1955) pp.329-330 (translation, M. Davidson).
4. Anderson, pp.328-329.
5. Girdlestone, C., *Mozart and his Piano Concertos* (New York, 1964) pp.462-463.
6. Plath, W. & Rehm, W., ed., NMA *Klaviersonaten*, Vol.I (Kassel, 1986) pp.140-142.
7. Rosenberg, R., *Die Klaviersonaten Mozarten* (Hofheim a/Taunus, 1972) p.56.
8. Latner, L.G., "Topical content in Mozart's keyboard sonatas," in *Early Music* (London, November 1991) p.616.
9. Zacharias, C., CD recording EMI CBC 7 490382, 1986.
10. Sadie, S. & Mathews, D., *Sonatas for Pianoforte*, Vol.I, Associated Board of the Royal Schools of Music (London, 1979) pp.85,89.
11. Kraus, L., Sony recording SM4K 47222, 1991.
12. Neumann, F., *Ornamentation and Improvisation in Mozart* (Princeton, 1986) p.116.
13. Rosenblum, S.P., *Performance Practices in Classic Piano Music* (Bloomington, 1988) p.249.
14. Lubimov, A., CD recording Erato 2290-45618-2.
15. Wolff, K., *Masters of the Keyboard* (Bloomington, 1983) p.98.
16. Uchida, M., Philips CD recording 420 185-2, 1986.
17. Plath & Rehm, NMA *Klaviersonaten*, Vol.I, p.68.
18. Neumann, p.116.
19. Neumann, p.134.
20. Gould, G., CBS Odyssey CD recording MB2K 45612, 1989.
21. Ránki, D., Hungaroton LP recording SLPX 11835-37, 1980.
22. Dennerlein, H., *Der Unbekannte Mozart* (Leipzig, 1951) p.53.
23. Einstein, A., *Mozart: His Character, His Work* (London, 1966) p.243.
24. Bilson, M., Hungaroton recording HCD 31011-12, 1990.
25. Neumann, pp.125-26.
26. Plath & Rehm, p.82.

CHAPTER VII

1. Broder, N., "Mozart and the 'Clavier,'" in *The Creative World of Mozart*, ed. P.H. Lang (New York, 1963) p.78.
2. Anderson, E., *Letters of Mozart and his Family* (New York, 1989) p.340.
3. Anderson, pp.373-74.
4. Anderson, p.414.
5. Kerman, J., "The Miracle Worker," in the *New York Review of Books*, March 23, 2000, p.32.
6. Plath, W. & Rehm, W., ed., NMA *Klaviersonaten*, Vol.I (Kassel, 1986) p.84.
7. Dennerlein, H., *Der unbekannte Mozart: Die Welt seiner Klavierwerke* (Leipzig, 1951) p.77.
8. Anderson, p.374.

9. Lubimov. A., Erato CD 2292-45590-2, 1991.
10. Kocsis, Z., Hungaroton LP SLPX 12219-22, 1980.
11. Plath & Rehm, pp.84 and 88.
12. Bilson, M., Hungaroton HCD 31013-14, 1991.
13. Rosenblum, S.P., *Performance Practices in Classic Piano Music* (Bloomington, 1988) p.314.
14. Rosenberg, R., *Die Klaviersonaten Mozarts* (Hofheim a/ Taunus, 1972) pp.63-64.
15. Plath & Rehm, pp.90-91.
16. Plath & Rehm, p.63.
17. Rosenblum, pp.230-31.
18. Dennerlein, p.78.
19. Rosenblum, p.68.
20. Landowska, W., *Landowska on Music* (New York, 1964) p.319.
21. Wolff, K., *Masters of the Keyboard* (Bloomington, 1983) p.106.
22. Landowska, pp.318-19.
23. Neumann, *Ornamentation and Improvisation in Mozart* (Princeton, 1986) pp.118-19.
24. Rowland, D., *A History of Pianoforte Pedalling* (Cambridge, 1993) p.84.
25. Neumann, p.92.
26. Rosenblum, pp.230-31.
27. Neumann, pp.92-93.
28. Landowska, p.320.
29. Plath & Rehm, p.121.

CHAPTER VIII

1. Anderson, E., *The Letters of Mozart and his Family* (New York, 1989) p.507.
2. Anderson, p.508.
3. Solomon, M., *Mozart: A Life* (New York, 1995) p.149.
4. Notably the famous letter to Leopold dated July 9, concerned mainly with musical matters (Anderson, pp.561-66).
5. Anderson, pp.581-88.
6. Feldman, D.H., "Mozart and the Transformational Imperative," in *On Mozart*, ed. J.M. Morris (Cambridge, Mass., 1994) p.55.
7. Tyson, A., *Mozart: Studies of the Autograph Scores* (Cambridge, Mass., 1987) pp.29-30.
8. Robbins Landon, H.C., notes for A. Lubimov recording of Mozart Sonatas, Erato CD 2292-45590-2, 1991, p.18.
9. Rosenberg, R., *Die Klaviersonaten Mozarts* (Hofheim a/Taunus, 1972) p.73.
10. Wolff, K., *Masters of the Keyboard* (Bloomington, 1983) p.92.
11. Rosenblum, S.P., *Performance Practices in Classic Piano Music* (Bloomington, 1988) pp.74-83.
12. Available as a facsimile accompanying the Schott-Universal Edition of the sonata (Vienna, 1973).

13. Levin, R.D., "Mozart's Solo Keyboard Music," in *Eighteenth-Century Keyboard Music*, ed. R.L. Marshall (New York, 1994) p.318.
14. Lelie, C. & Huizing, J.M., "Het moment waarop de muziek geboren lijkt te worden," een gesprek met Mozart-kenner Marius Flothuis, in *Piano Bulletin* (Delft, 1993) No.3. These measures and mm.43-50 of the slow movement are singled out by Prof. Flothuis as being atypically "unpianistic."
15. Badura Skoda, E. & P., *Interpreting Mozart on the Keyboard* (London, 1962) p.85.
16. Neumann, F., *Ornamentation and Improvisation in Mozart* (Princeton, 1986) p.37.
17. Neumann, p.37.
18. Badura Skoda, E. & P., pp.84-85.
19. Neumann, pp.37-38.
20. Neumann, F., *Ornamentation and Improvisation in Mozart*, pp.118-19; *Performance Practices of the Seventeenth and Eighteenth Centuries* (New York, 1993) pp.440-41.
21. Landowska, W., *Landowska on Music* (New York, 1964) p.321.
22. Girdlestone, C., *Mozart and His Piano Concertos* (New York, 1964) p.111.
23. Levin, pp.319-320.
24. Badura Skoda, E., "Aspects of Performance Practices," in *Eighteenth Century Keyboard Music*, ed. R.D. Marshall (New York, 1994) p.50.
25. Neumann, *Ornamentation and Improvisation in Mozart*, pp.55-56.
26. Neumann, *Ornamentation and Improvisation in Mozart*, pp.77-78.
27. Wolff, p.88.
28. Landowska, p.322.
29. Somfai, L., program-notes accompanying M. Bilson recording of Mozart sonatas, Hungaroton HCD 31011-12, 1990.

CHAPTER IX

1. Anderson, E., *The Letters of Mozart and his Family* (New York, 1989) p.739.
2. Einstein, A., *Mozart: His Character, His Work* (London, 1966).
3. An Alberti bass was a broken chord figuration, suitable for accompaniments, named after Domenico Alberti (1710-40). The device was frequently used by composers of piano music during the latter half of the eighteenth century.
4. Tyson, A., "Proposed New Dates for Many Vienna Works," in *Mozart Studies*, ed. C. Eisen (Oxford, 1991) p.216.
5. von Fischer, Kurt, ed., *Kritische Berichte, Variationen für Klavier*, Bärenreiter (Kassel 1962) pp.82-85.
6. Anderson, pp.879-80.
7. v. Fischer, p.144.
8. v. Fischer, p.58.
9. v. Fischer, p.59.
10. Gale, Patrick, in *The Mozart Compendium*, gen. ed. H.C. Robbins Landon (London, 1990) p.305.

11. Anderson, pp.809-10.
12. The Paisiello score can be found in the Oesterreiches Nationalbibliothek, Vienna. For that library's assistance, I am grateful. The libretto translation is my own.
13. Haebler, I., Philips reissue 426 892-2, 1991.
14. Sidgwick, J., English translation, libretto accompanying the Erato CD recording 2292-45516-2, cond. J.E. Gardiner, 1991.
15. v. Fischer, p.109.
16. v. Fischer, p.110.
17. v. Fischer, p.110.
18. v. Fischer, ed., NMA *Variationen für Klavier*, (Kassel, 1961) Introduction, p.11 and 18.

CHAPTER X

1. Einstein, A., *Mozart: His Character, His Work* (London, 1966) pp.244-245.
2. Tyson, A., *Mozart: Studies of the Autograph Scores* (Cambridge Mass., 1987) p.30.
3. Anderson, E., *Letters of Mozart and his Family* (New York, 1989) p.880.
4. Tyson, pp.73-81.
5. Einstein, p.245.
6. Bilson, M., Hungaroton recording HCD 31009-10, 1989.
7. Haskil, C., Philips recording LP 6588008, 1970.
8. Plath, W. & Rehm, W., NMA *Klaviersonaten*, Vol.II (Kassel, 1986) Introduction, p.IV.
9. Uchida, M., Philips recording LP 412 616-1, 1984.
10. Rosenblum, S.P., *Performance Practices in Classic Piano Music* (Bloomington, 1988) pp.174-75.
11. Neumann, F., *Ornamentation and Improvisation in Mozart* (Princeton, 1986) pp.70-75.
12. Rosenblum, pp.220-24.
13. Neumann, pp.66-67.
14. Rosenblum, p.246.
15. Leonhardt, G., ABC Classics recording AX 67044/2, 1973.
16. Kraus, L., Sony recording SM47222, 1991.
17. Plath & Rehm, Introduction, p.IV.
18. Neumann, F., *Performance Practices of the Seventeenth and Eighteenth Centuries* (New York, 1993) p.171.
19. Levin, R.D., "Mozart's Solo Keyboard Music," in *Eighteenth Century Keyboard Music*, ed. R.L. Marshall (New York, 1994) p.321.

CHAPTER XI

1. Dennerlein, H., *Der unbekannte Mozart* (Leipzig, 1951) pp.102-11.
2. Robbins Landon, H.C., Notes, A. Lubimov recording Erato 2292-45731-2, 1991, p.15.

3. Einstein, A., *Mozart: His Character, His Work* (London, 1966) p.245.
4. Hutchings, A., "The Keyboard Music," in *The Mozart Companion*, ed. H.C. Robbins Landon & D. Mitchell (London, 1956) p.45.
5. Dennerlein, pp.103-11.
6. Plath, W. & Rehm, W., ed., *Klaviersonaten*, Vol.II (Kassel, 1986) p.14.
7. Plath & Rehm, p.18.
8. Neumann, F., *Ornamentation and Improvisation in Mozart* (Princeton, 1986) p.53.
9. Neumann, pp.63-64.
10. Plath & Rehm, p.20.
11. Bilson, M., Hungaroton recording HCD 31009-10, 1989.
12. Kraus, L., Sony recording SM47222, 1991.
13. Neumann, p.166.
14. Badura Skoda, E. & P., *Playing Mozart on the Keyboard* (London, 1962) p.98.
15. Rosenblum, S.P., *Performance Practices in Classic Piano Music* (Bloomington, 1988) p.286.
16. Landowska, W., *Landowska on Music* (New York, 1964) p.33.
17. Marty, *The Tempo Indications of Mozart* (New Haven, 1988) p.107.
18. Dennerlein, p.107.
19. Plath & Rehm, pp.24-24.
20. Plath & Rehm, p.25.
21. Wolff, K., *Masters of the Keyboard* (Bloomington, 1983) p.81.
22. Plath & Rehm, both versions stated, p.27.
23. Neumann, pp.87-88.
24. Plath & Rehm, Introduction, p.v.

CHAPTER XII

1. Tyson, A., *Mozart: Studies of the Autograph Scores* (Cambridge, Mass., 1987) pp.29-30.
2. The two unfinished stage works, *L'oca de Cairo* and *Lo sposo deluso*, previously attributed to 1783, are now presumed to date from a later period. See Tyson, A. "Proposed New Dates for Many Vienna Works" in *Mozart Studies* (Oxford, 1991) p.219.
3. Einstein, A., *Mozart: His Character, His Work* (London, 1966) pp.245-46.
4. Abert, H., *Mozart*, Vol.I (Leipzig, 1955) p.612 (translation, M. Davidson).
5. Bilson, M., Hungaroton CD 31011, 1991.
6. Kraus, L., Sony recording SM4K 47222, 1974/1991.
7. Bilson, M., "Execution and expression in the Sonata in E-flat, K.282," in *Early Music* (Oxford, May 1992) p.243.
8. Wolff, K., *Masters of the Keyboard* (Bloomington, 1983) p.82.
9. I am especially grateful to William Scheide for providing access to both the manuscript and a copy of the FE in the Special Collections of Princeton University Library.
10. Plath, W. & Rehm, W., NMA *Klaviersonaten*, Vol.II (Kassel, 1986) p.28.

11. Lohmann, L., *Die Artikulation auf den Tasteninstrumenten des 16.-18. Jahrhunderts* (Regensburg, 1990) pp.45-46.
12. Rosenberg, R., *Die Klaviersonaten Mozarts* (Hofheim a/Taunus, 1972) p.90.
13. Sherman, R., *Piano Pieces* (New York, 1996) p.202.
14. Neumann, F., *Ornamentation and Improvisation in Mozart* (Princeton, 1986) p.172.
15. Neumann, pp.66-67.
16. Landowska, W., Biddulph recording LHW 013, 1993.
17. Lubimov, A., Erato recording CD 2292-45619-2, 1991.
18. Ránki, D., Hungaroton recording SLPX 11837-B, 1980.
19. Uchida, M., Philips recording 412 123-1, 1984.
20. Rosenblum, S.P., *Performance Practices in Classic Piano Music* (Bloomington, 1988) p.379.
21. Robbins Landon, H.C., notes accompanying A. Lubimov recording of the Mozart sonatas, 1991, p.16.
22. Rosenblum, pp.320-21.
23. Rosenblum, pp.320-21.

CHAPTER XIII

1. Einstein, A., *Köchel Verzeichnis*, seventh edition (Wiesbaden, revised 1965) p.329.
2. Tyson, A., *Mozart: Studies of the Autograph Scores* (Cambridge, Mass., 1989) p.73.
3. Tyson, p.81.
4. Harnoncourt, N., *The Musical Dialogue* (Portland, Oregon, 1989) p.115.
5. Lohmann, L., *Die Artikulation auf den Tasteninstrumenten des 16.-18. Jahrhunderts* (Regensburg, 1990) pp.228-29.
6. Plath, W. & Rehm, W., ed., NMA *Klaviersonaten*, Vol.II (Kassel, 1986) p.48.
7. Levin, R.D., "Mozart's Solo Keyboard Music," in *Eighteenth Century Keyboard Music* (New York, 1994) p.325.
8. Neumann, F., *Ornamentation and Improvisation in Mozart* (Princeton, 1986) p.73.
9. Plath & Rehm, p.vi.
10. Uchida, M., Philips recording CD 412616-2, 1984.
11. Kraus, L., Sony recording SM4K 47222, 1991.
12. Rosenberg, R., *Die Klaviersonaten Mozarts* (Hofheim a/Taunus, 1972) p.100.
13. Hutchings, A., "The Keyboard Music," in *The Mozart Companion*, revised edition (New York, 1969) p.46.
14. Lubimov, A., Erato recording 2292-45622-2, 1991.
15. Bilson, M., Hungaroton recording HCD 31011-12, 1990.

CHAPTER XIV

1. Helm, E., *New Groves Dictionary of Music & Musicians*, Vol.VI, ed. S. Sadie (London, 1980, revised 1994) p.389.
2. Further information concerning M. Stadler is found in Chapter XIX, opening of section 7.
3. Wallner, B., ed., Henle Edition *Ausgewählte Stücke für Klavier*, (Munich, 1955) p.5.
4. Tyson, A., "Proposed New Dates for Many Works and Fragments Written by Mozart from March 1781 to December 1791," in *Mozart Studies*, ed. Cliff Eisen (Oxford, 1991) pp.217-18.
5. Dennerlein, H., *Der unbekannte Mozart* (Leipzig, 1951) pp.92-95.
6. Türk, D.G., *School of Clavier Playing*, English translation (Lincoln, Neb., 1982) pp.101, 116-17.
7. Einstein, A., *Mozart: His Character, His Work*, (London, 1966) pp.147-48.
8. Einstein, p.153.
9. Tyson, p.217.
10. Hertzmann, E., "Mozart's Creative Process," in *The Creative World of Mozart*, ed. P.H. Lang (New York, 1963) p.27.
11. Anderson, E., ed., *Letters of Mozart and his Family* (New York, 1989) pp.800-01.
12. Einstein, p.152.
13. Klien, W., LP recording Turnabout TV 37011 S, 1967.
14. Plath, W., ed., NMA *Einzelstücke für piano* (Kassel, 1982).
15. Mercado, M.R., *The Evolution of Mozart's Pianistic Style* (Carbondale, 1992) p.67.
16. Gale, P., in *The Mozart Compendium*, ed. H.C. Robbins Landon (London, 1990) p.300.
17. Hirsch, P., in *Music and Letters* XXV, No.4, 1944, pp.209-12
18. Plath, footnote p.xvi.
19. Dennerlein, p.211.
20. Badura Skoda, P., ed. *Fantaisie en ré mineur* (Paris, 1987).
21. Uchida, M., recording Philips 412 123-1, 1984.
22. Badura Skoda, Introduction.
23. Chusid, M., "The Significance of D minor in Mozart's Dramatic Music," in *Mozart Jahrbuch 1965-66*, Mozarteum Foundation (Salzburg, 1967).
24. Plath, p.xvi.
25. Plath, p.32.
26. Plath, p.32.
27. Badura Skoda, p.7.
28. Plath, p.33.
29. Braunbehrens, V., *Mozart in Vienna* (London, 1990) p.113.
30. Plath, W. & Rehm, W., ed., facsimile edition of the manuscript of K.475 and 457, (Salzburg: Internationale Stiftung Mozarteum, 1991).
31. Kaltz, N., ed., facsimile edition of K.475 and 457 (Paris, 1991).
32. Lampe, W., ed., Klaviersonaten, Vol.II (Munich: Henle, 1965, later revised).

33. Plath & Rehm, ed., NMA *Klaviersonaten*, Vol.II (Kassel, 1986).
34. Somfai, L., notes accompanying Hungaroton recording by M. Bilson, HCD 31013-14, 1991, p.14.
35. Rosenberg, R., *Die Klaviersonaten Mozarts* (Hofheim a/ Taunus, 1972) p.105.
36. Bilson, M., Hungaroton recording HCD 31013-14, 1991.
37. Pires, M.J., DGG recording 431 275-2, 1990.
38. Kraus, L., Sony SM4K 47222, 1991 (CD reissue).
39. Badura Skoda, E. & P., *Interpreting Mozart on the Keyboard* (London, 1972) p.132.
40. Kaltz, p.18.
41. Plath & Rehm, Introduction, *Klavierstonaten*, p.viii.
42. Rosenblum, S.P., *Performance Practices in Classic Piano Music* (Bloomington, 1988), pp.74-83.
43. Levin, R.D., "Mozart's Solo Keyboard Music," in *Eighteenth-Century Keyboard Music*, ed. R.L. Marshall (New York, 1994) p.326.
44. Rampe, *Mozarts Claviermusik: Klangwelt und Aufführungspraxis*, (Kassel, 1995) pp.270-271.
45. Dennerlein, p.205.

CHAPTER XV

1. Anderson, E., *The Letters of Mozart and his Family* (New York, 1989) p.889.
2. Einstein, A., *Mozart: His Character, His Work* (London, 1966) p.247.
3. Levin, R.D., "Mozart's Solo Keyboard Music," in *Eighteenth-Century Keyboard Music* (New York, 1994) p.326.
4. In the Jewish National and University Library, Jerusalem.
5. Plath, W. & Rehm, W., ed., NMA *Klaviersonaten*, Vol.II (Kassel, 1986) pp.viii and 80.
6. Badura-Skoda, E. & P., *Interpreting Mozart on the Keyboard* (London, 1962) p.114.
7. Kraus, L., Sony recording SM4K 47222, 1991.
8. Neumann, F., *Performance Practices of the Seventeenth and Eighteenth Centuries* (New York, 1993) p.171.
9. Türk, D.G., *School of Clavier Playing* (Lincoln, 1982) p.113.
10. Rosenblum, S.P., *Performance Practices in Classic Piano Music* (Bloomington, 1988) notes p.425.
11. Bilson, M., Hungaroton HCD 31013-14, 1991.
12. Lubimov, A., Erato 2292-45590-2, 1991.
13. Rosenblum, pp.74-83.
14. Gould, G., CBS recording 7464-45612-2/4, 1989.
15. Mozart, L., *A Treatise on the Fundamental Principles of Violin Playing* (Oxford, 1985) p.50.
16. Rosenblum, pp.320-21.
17. Harnoncourt, N., *The Musical Dialogue* (London, 1989) p.115.

CHAPTER XVI

1. Deutsch, O.E., *A Documentary Biography* (Stanford, 1965) p.289.
2. Anderson, E., ed., *The Letters of Mozart and his Family* (New York, 1989) pp.907-08.
3. Tyson, A., *Mozart: Studies of the Autograph Scores* (Cambridge Mass., 1987) pp.234-45.
4. Deutsch, p.296.
5. Landowska, W., *Landowska on Music* (New York, 1964) p.323.
6. Rosenblum, S.P., "Mozart's Masquerade," in *The Music Teacher* (December 1990-January 1991 issue).
7. Rosenblum, S.P., *Performance Practices in Classic Piano Music* (Bloomington, 1988) pp.74-78.
8. Badura Skoda, E.& P., *Interpreting Mozart on the Keyboard* (London, 1962) p.81.
9. Müller, H.C., Urtext-Edition & Facsimile (Vienna: Schott-Universal Edition, 1973) p.1.
10. Neumann, F., *Ornamentation and Improvisation in Mozart* (Princeton, 1986) pp.76-78.
11. Wolff, K., *Masters of the Keyboard* (Bloomington, 1983) p.108.
12. Einstein, A., *Mozart: His Character, His Work* (London, 1966) p.248.
13. Plath, W. & Rehm, W., ed., NMA *Klaviersonaten*, Vol.II (Kassel, 1986) pp.166-172.
14. Plath & Rehm, p.166.
15. Deutsch, p.295.
16. Anderson, pp.706-08.
17. Dennerlein, H., *Der unbekannte Mozart* (Leipzig, 1951) p.322.
18. Kinderman, W., "Subjectivity and Objectivity in Mozart performance," in *Early Music* (London, November 1991) p.597.
19. Gluck, C.W., *Orfeo e Euridice*, No.15 (translation, M. Davidson).
20. Gal, H., facsimile final page.
21. Levin, R.D., "Mozart's Solo Keyboard Music," in *Eighteenth-century Keyboard Music*, ed. R.L. Marshall (New York,1994) p.330.
22. Neumann, pp.156-57.
23. Neumann, p.157.
24. Badura Skoda, E. & P., *L'art de jouer Mozart au piano* (Paris, 1973) pp.345-46. Unfortunately this interesting chapter on the A minor Rondo apparently appeared only in the French edition of *Playing Mozart on the Keyboard*.

CHAPTER XVII

1. Somfai, L., notes, accompanying the M. Bilson recording of the Mozart sonatas, Hungaroton HCD 31013-14, 1991.
2. Plath, W. & Rehm, W., ed., NMA *Klaviersonaten*, Vol.II (Kassel, 1986) p.108.
3. Lowinsky, E.E., "On Mozart's Rhythm," in *The Creative World of Mozart*, ed. P.H. Lang (New York, 1963) p.52.

4. Dennerlein, H., *Der onbekannte Mozart* (Leipzig, 1951) p.245.
5. Badura Skoda. P. & E., *Interpreting Mozart on the Keyboard* (London, 1962) p.122.
6. Plath & Rehm, Introduction, p.9.
7. Anderson, E., *The Letters of Mozart and his Family* (New York, 1989) p.917.
8. Rosenberg, R., *Die Klaviersonaten Mozarts* (Hofheim a/Taunus, 1972) p.125.
9. Bilson, M., Hungaroton HCD 31013-14, 1991.
10. Lubimov, A., Erato 2292-45510-1, 1990.
11. Gould, G., Odyssey reissue MB2K 45613, 1989.
12. Sherman, R., *Piano Pieces* (New York, 1996) p.203.
13. Ehrenzweig, A., *The Hidden Order of Art* (London, 1967) p.129.
14. Kraus, L., Sony recording SM 4K 47222, 1991.
15. Rosenberg, R., p.127.
16. Plath & Rehm, p.ix.

CHAPTER XVIII

1. Solomon, M., *Mozart: A Life* (New York, 1995) p.523.
2. Anderson, E., *The Letters of Mozart and his Family* (New York, 1989) pp.929-31.
3. Einstein, A., *Mozart: His Character, His Work* (London, 1966) p.184.
4. Plath, W. & Rehm, W., ed., NMA *Klaviersonaten*, Vol.II (Kassel, 1986) Introduction, p.x.
5. Einstein, pp.249-50.
6. Hutchings, A., in *The Mozart Companion*, ed. H.C. Robbins Landon and D. Mitchell (New York, 1969) p.49.
7. Rosenblum, S.P., *Performance Practices of Classic Piano Music* (Bloomington, 1988) pp.179-81.
8. Lampe, W., ed., *Mozart Klaviersonaten*, Vol.II (Munich: Henle, 1955) p.277.
9. Plath & Rehm, pp.133-34.
10. Lubimov, A., Erato recording 2292-45731-2, 1991.
11. Leonhardt, G., ABC Classics recording AX-67044/2, 1973.
12. Rosenberg, R., *Die Klaviersonaten Mozarts* (Hofheim a/Taunus, 1972) p.132.
13. Kraus, L., Sony reissue of 1968 recording SM 4K 47222, 1991.
14. Uchida, M., Philips recording 420 185-2, 1986.
15. Plath & Rehm, p.x.
16. Schnabel, A., EMI recording HQM 1142, 1948.
17. Plath & Rehm, p.142.
18. Rampe, *Mozarts Claviermusik: Klangwelt und Aufführungspraxis*, (Kassel, 1995) p.286.
19. Bilson, M., Hungaroton recording HCD 31012, 1990.
20. Plath & Rehm, p.142.
21. Plath & Rehm, p.146.
22. Landowska, W., *Landowska on Music* (New York, 1964) p.324.

23. Rosenberg, p.137.
24. Neumann, F., *Ornamentation and Improvisation in Mozart* (Princeton, 1986) pp.114-15.
25. Dennerlein, H., *Der unbekannte Mozart* (Leipzig, 1951) p.248.
26. Wolff, K., *Masters of the Keyboard* (Bloomington, 1983) p.96.
27. Plath & Rehm, Introduction, p.xi.
28. Füssl, K.H. & Scholz, H., ed., *Wiener Urtext Ausgabe, Klaviersonaten*, Vol.II (Vienna, 1973) Introduction.
29. Landowksa, p.324.
30. Plath & Rehm, Introduction p.xi.

CHAPTER XIX

1. Hutchings, A., in *The Mozart Companion*, ed. H.C. Robbins Landon & D. Mitchell (London, 1956) p.64.
2. Lohmann, L., *Die Artikulation auf den Tasteninstrumenten des 16.-18. Jahrhunderts* (Regensburg, 1990) pp.45-46.
3. Lang, P.H., Introduction to *The Creative World of Mozart* (New York, 1963) p.13.
4. Dennerlein, H., *Der unbekannte Mozart* (Leipzig, 1951) p.260.
5. Neumann, F., *Ornamentation and Improvisation in Mozart* (Princeton, 1986) pp.43-44.
6. Rosenblum. S.P., *Performing Practices in Classic Piano Music* (Bloomington, 1988) pp.229-30.
7. The manuscript is in the Stiftelsen Music Foundation, Stockholm.
8. Cyr, M., *The New Grove Dictionary of Music and Musicians*, ed. S. Sadie, Vol.V (London, 1994) p.732.
9. von Fischer, K., ed., *Variationen für Klavier, Kritische Berichte* (Kassel, 1962) p.125.
10. Barenboim, D., EMI recording CDS 7543622, 1991.
11. Haebler, I., Philips recording 422 728-2, 1990.
12. *The Eight Variations on "Ein Weib ist das herrlichste Ding,"* (1791) form a somewhat distended piece, best suited to domestic consumption. The length of the theme soon obliterates the thin charm of the material. Compared to the *Duport* Variations, K.613 seems a *pièce d'occasion*, written in great haste. The last, extended variation has interesting aspects.
13. Neumann, F., *Performance Practices of the Seventeenth and Eighteenth Centuries* (New York, 1993) pp.490-92, a fine exposition of a much debated issue.
14. v. Fischer, p.130.
15. v. Fischer, p.131.
16. Anderson, E., *The Letters of Mozart and his Family* (New York, 1989) p.939.
17. Dennerlein, p.59.
18. Hutchings, p.41.
19. Einstein, A., *Mozart: His Character, His Work* (London, 1966) p.251.
20. Exceptionally, the NMA, at the time of writing, includes this piece only in Vol.II of the hardbound edition of the Piano Sonatas.

21. Tyson, A., *Mozart: Studies of the Autograph Scores* (Cambridge, Mass., 1987) p.20.
22. Kerman, pp.33.
23. Lubimov, A., Erato recording 2292-45622-2, 1991.
24. Robbins Landon, H.C., notes accompanying recording by A. Lubimov, Erato 2292-45622-2, 1991.
25. Koopman, T., Philips recording 426-892-2, 1991.
26. Einstein, A., chief ed., *Köchel Verzeichnis*, seventh edition (Wiesbaden, 1964) pp.651-52.
27. Dumm, R., "Mozart's Menuet in D, K.355," in *Clavier*, Vol.XXX, No.10 (Northfield, Ill., 1991).
28. Plath, W., NMA *Klavierstücke* (Kassel, 1985) p.xviii.
29. Rosenblum, pp.75-77.
30. Deutsch, O.E., *Schubert; A Documentary Biography*, English translation by E. Blom (London, 1946) p.86.
31. Bellow. S., "Mozart: An Overture," in *It All Adds Up* (New York, 1994) p.11.
32. Sherman, R., *Piano Pieces* (New York, 1996) p.205.

BIBLIOGRAPHY

Abert, H. *Mozart*. 2 vols. Leipzig, 1955.

Anderson, E. *The Letters of Mozart and His Family*. New York, 1989.

Badura Skoda, E. "Aspects of Performance Practices." *Eighteenth Century Keyboard Music*. Ed. R.D. Marshall. New York, 1994.

Badura Skoda, E. & P. *Interpreting Mozart on the Keyboard*. London, 1962.

Barth, G. "Mozart Performances in the Nineteenth Century." *Early Music*. London, November 1991.

Bellow, S. "Mozart: An Overture." *It All Ends Up*. New York, 1994.

Bilson, M. "Do We Really Know How to Read Urtext Editions?" *Piano & Keyboard*. July-August 1995.

Bilson, M. "Execution and Expression in the Sonata in E-flat Major, K.282." *Early Music*. Oxford, May 1992.

Braunbehrens, V. *Mozart in Vienna*. Trans. London, 1990.

Broder, N. "Mozart and the 'Clavier.'" In *The Creative World of Mozart*. Ed. P.H. Lang. New York, 1963.

Chusid, M. "The Significance of D minor in Mozart's Dramatic Music." In *Mozart Jahrbuch 1965-66*. Salzburg, 1967.

Craft, R. *Current Convictions*. New York, 1977.

Dennerlein, H. *Der unbekannte Mozart: Die Welt seiner Klavierwerke*. Leipzig, 1951.

Deutsch, O.E. *Mozart: A Documentary Biography*. Stanford, 1965.

Deutsch, O.E. *Schubert: A Documentary Biography*. London, 1946.

Dumm, R. "Mozart's Menuet in D, K.355." *Clavier*, Vol.X, No. 10. Northfield, 1991.

Ehrenzweig, A. *The Hidden Order of Art*. London, 1967.

Einstein, A. *Mozart: His Character, His Work*. London, 1966.

Einstein, A. and other editors. *Köchel Verzeichnis*. Wiesbaden, 1964.

Feldman, D.H. "Mozart and the Transformational Imperative." *On Mozart*. Ed. J.M. Morris. Cambridge, Mass. 1994.

Fischer, K. von., ed. *Kritische Berichte, Variationen für Klavier*. *Neue Mozart Ausgabe*. Kassel, 1962.

Fischer, K. von., ed. *Variationen für Klavier, Neue Mozart Ausgabe*. Kassel, 1961.

Füssl, K.H. & Scholz, H., ed. Mozart *Klaviersonaten*. 2 vol.*Wiener Urtext Edition*. Vienna, 1973.

Gal, H., ed. Facsimile Rondi K.485, 511. Vienna, 1923.

Girdlestone, C. *Mozart and his Piano Concertos*. New York, 1964.

Glock, W. *Notes in Advance, An Autobiography in Music.* Oxford, 1991.

Gounod, C. *Le Don Juan de Mozart.* Paris, 1890.

Gruber, G. *Mozart and Posterity.* Boston, 1994.

Harnoncourt, N. *The Musical Dialogue.* Portland, 1989.

Harnoncourt, N. Interview by H. Canning. *The Gramophone.* London, November 1991.

Harnoncourt, N. Interview by S. Smit. *Entracte.* Amsterdam, June 1990.

Hertzmann, E. "Mozart's Creative Process." In *The Creative World of Mozart.* Ed. P.H. Lang. New York, 1963.

Hildesheimer, W. *Mozart.* Trans. New York, 1982.

Hirsch, P. *Music and Letters.* Vol.XXV, No. 4. (1944)

Hutchings, A. "The Keyboard Music." *Mozart Companion* (revised). New York, 1969.

Kaltz, N., ed. Facsimile edition K.475-457. Paris, 1991.

Kerman, J., "The Miracle Worker," in the *New York Review of Books*, March 23, 2000, pp.32-35.

Kinderman, W. "Subjectivity and Objectivity in Mozart Performance." *Early Music.* London, November 1991.

Landowska, W. *Landowska on Music.* New York, 1964.

Lang, P.H., ed. *The Creative World of Mozart.* New York, 1963.

Lampe, W., ed. Mozart *Klaviersonaten*, 2 vols. Munich: Henle, 1955, later revised.

Lateiner, J. "An Interpreter's Approach to Mozart." *Early Music*, Vol.XX, No. 2. Oxford, 1992.

Latner, L.G. "Topical Content in Mozart's Keyboard Sonatas." *Early Music.* London, November 1991.

Lelie, C. & Huizing, J.M. "Het moment waarop de Muziek geboren lijkt te worden." Interview with M. Flothuis. *Piano Bulletin*, No.3. Delft, 1993.

Levin, R.D. "Improvised Embellishments in Mozart's Keyboard Music." *Early Music.* Vol.XX, No.2. Oxford, 1992.

Levin, R.D. "Mozart's Solo Keyboard Music." *Eighteenth Century Keyboard Music.* Ed. R.L. Marshall. New York, 1994.

Little, M.E. *The New Groves Dictionary of Music & Musicians.* Vol.XIX. Ed. S. Sadie. London, 1994.

Lohmann, L. *Die Artikulation auf den Tasteninstrumenten des 16.-18.-Jahrhunderts.* Regensburg, 1990.

Lowinsky, E.E. "On Mozart's Rhythm." *The Creative World of Mozart.* Ed. P.H. Lang. New York, 1963.

Marty, J-P. *The Tempo Indications of Mozart.* New Haven, 1988.

Matthews, D., ed. (with S. Sadie) *Mozart Sonatas*. 2 vols. London: Associated Board of the Royal Schools of Music, 1971.

Mercado, M.R. *The Evolution of Mozart's Pianistic Style*. Carbondale, 1992.

Miller, M. "Leopold Mozart's Formative Influence on Wolfgang Amadeus Mozart's Early Piano Sonatas." *Piano Journal*. London, October 1996.

Mitchell, D., ed. (with H.C. Robbins Landon) *The Mozart Companion*. New York, 1969.

Morris, J.M., ed. *On Mozart*. New York, 1994.

Mozart, L. *A Treatise on the Fundamental Principles of Violin Playing*. Trans. Oxford, 1985.

Müller, H.C., ed. *Einzelstücke*. Vienna: Schott-Universal Edition, 1973.

Neumann, F. *Ornamentation and Improvisation in Mozart*. Princeton, 1986.

Neumann, F. *Performance Practices of the Seventeenth and Eighteenth Centuries*. New York, 1993.

Onions, C.T., ed. *Shorter Oxford English Dictionary*. Oxford, 1993.

Plath, W., ed. *Einzelstücke für piano*. *Neue Mozart Ausgabe*. Kassel, 1982.

Plath, W. & Rehm, W., ed. *Klaviersonaten*. 2 vols. *Neue Mozart Ausgabe*. Kassel, 1986.

Plath, W. & Rehm, W., ed. Facsimile edition manuscript K.475-457. Salzburg, 1991.

Quantz, J.J. *On Playing the Flute*. Trans. New York, 1966.

Rampe, S., *Mozarts Claviermusik: Klangwelt und Aufführungspraxis*. Kassel, 1995.

Robbins Landon, H.C., general ed. *The Mozart Compendium*. London, 1990.

Robbins Landon, H.C., ed. (with D. Mitchell) *The Mozart Companion*. New York, 1969.

Robbins Landon, H.C. Notes for A. Lubimov recording, Mozart Sonatas, Erato 2292-45731-2, 1990.

Robert, P., ed. *Dictionnaire de la Langue Française*. Paris, 1959.

Rosen, C. "The Shock of the Old." *New York Review of Books*. July 1990.

Rosen, C. "Should Music be Played 'Wrongly?'" *High Fidelity*, Vol.XXI, No. 5. 1971.

Rosenberg, R. *Die Klaviersonaten Mozarts*. Hofheim a/Taunus, 1972.

Rosenblum, S.P. "Mozart's Masquerade." *The Music Teacher*. December 1990-January 1991.

Rosenblum, S.P. *Performing Practices in Classic Piano Music.* Bloomington, 1993.

Ross, A. "Classical View." *New York Times.* August 28, 1994.

Rowland, D. *A History of Pianoforte Pedalling.* Cambridge, 1993.

Sadie, S., ed. *The New Grove Dictionary of Music and Musicians.* London, 1994.

Sadie, S., ed. (with D. Matthews) *Mozart Sonatas.* 2 vols. London: Associated Board of the Royal Schools of Music, 1971.

Schachter, C. "20th Century Analysis and Mozart Performance." *Early Music.* London, November 1991.

Schnabel, A. *My Life and Music.* New York, 1961.

Schubart, C.F.D. *Ideen zu einer Aesthetik der Tonkunst.* Leipzig, reprint 1977.

Schulenberg, D. *The Keyboard Music of J.S. Bach.* New York, 1992.

Sherman, R. *Piano Pieces.* New York, 1996.

Sidgwick, J., trans. Libretto. *Les Pèlerins de la Mecque.* Erato CD recording 2292-45516-2, 1991.

Solomon, M. *Mozart: A Life.* New York, 1995.

Somfai, L. Notes accompanying M. Bilson recording of Mozart sonatas, Hungaroton HCD 31009-14, 1989-91.

Till, N. *Mozart and the Enlightenment.* London, 1992.

Tyson, A. *Mozart: Studies of the Autograph Scores.* Cambridge, Mass., 1987.

Tyson, A. "Proposed New Dates for Many Works and Fragments Written by Mozart from March 1781 to December 1791." *Mozart Studies.* Ed. C. Eisen. Oxford, 1991.

Türk, D.G. *School of Clavier Playing.* Trans. Lincoln, 1982.

Wolff, K. *Masters of the Keyboard.* Bloomington, 1983.

Zimmermann, E., ed. Mozart *Variationen für Klavier.* Munich: Henle, 1963.

RECORDINGS OF MOZART PIANO MUSIC REFERRED TO IN THE GUIDE

Barenboim, D., Variations, EMI 3-CD CDS 7 54362 2, 1991.

Gould, G., Sonatas CBS 4-CD 7464-45612-2/4, reissue 1989.

Haebler, I., Variations, Philips 3-CD 426 892-2, reissue 1991.

Haskil, C., Assorted Pieces by Mozart, Beethoven, Schubert, Philips LP 6588008, reissue 1970.

Klien, W., Assorted Pieces, Turnabout LP TV 370011 S, 1967.

Kocsis, Z., Sonatas, Hungaroton 4-LP SLPX 12219-22, 1980.

Koopman, T., (harpsichord), Assorted Pieces, Philips CD 422 727-2, 1991.

Landowska, W., Assorted Works, Biddulph CD LHW 013, reissue 1993.

Leonhardt, G., (fortepiano) Sonatas and Pieces, ABC Classics 2-LP, 1973.

Lubimov, A., (fortepiano) Sonatas, Erato 6-CD 2292-45731-2, 1990.

Newman, A., (fortepiano) Sonatas, Newport Classic NCD 60121, 1990.

Pires, M.J., Sonatas, DGG 431 275-2, 1990.

Ránki, D., Sonatas, Hungaroton 3-LP SLPX 11835-37, 1980.

Schnabel, A., 6 Concertos, 2 Sonatas, Rondo K.511 EMI 3-CD CHS 7 63703 2, reissue 1990.

Uchida, M., Sonatas and Assorted Pieces, various Philips LP and CD, 1983-1991.

Zacharias, C., Sonatas, EMI CD CDC 7 49038 2, 1986.

Especially recommended are:

Bilson, M., (fortepiano) Sonatas, Hungaroton 6-CD 31009-14, 1989-91.

Kraus, L., Sonatas, 1968 recordings, Sony SM4K 472222, CD reissue 1991

INDEX